REGIONS OF IDENTITY

Regions of Identity

THE CONSTRUCTION OF AMERICA IN
WOMEN'S FICTION, 1885-1914

Kate McCullough

STANFORD UNIVERSITY PRESS
STANFORD, CALIFORNIA

Stanford University Press
Stanford, California
© 1999 by the Board of Trustees of the
Leland Stanford Junior University

Printed in the United States of America

CIP data appear at the end of the book

*This book is dedicated with all my love
 to the memory of
Louise Papanek McCullough
 (1918–1997)
My first and most enduring example of
 the strength and complexity of
 American Womanhood*

Acknowledgments

Writing acknowledgments for this book has been a pleasure because it has given me a chance to reflect on just how thoroughly feminist community structures and nurtures my life. Many people have helped me over the years, providing support both intellectual and emotional. For financial support, leave time, and widespread institutional support I would like to thank Miami University and especially C. Barry Chabot. For helping me to think through issues at stake here, I thank my English 680 graduate seminar of Spring 1994, especially Nancy Dayton. Many friends and colleagues have read parts of this project over the years and provided me with perceptive and inspiring feedback; many have shared ideas and listened to me endlessly rehash my own. I would like to thank Alice Adams, Elizabeth Ammons, Mary Jean Corbett, Fran Dolan, Catherine Gallagher, Tom Foster, Anne Goldman, John Gruesser, Sandra Gunning, Karen Jacobs, Marcy J. Knopf, David Levin, Michael Moon, Susan Morgan, Fred Moten, Carolyn Porter, Laura Mandell, Nancy Nenno, Judith Rosen, Mary Ryan, Eve Kosofsky Sedgwick, Jacqueline Shea-Murphy, Stephanie Smith, Victoria Smith, Theresa Tensuan, Françoise Verges, and Sandra Zagarell. I would also like to thank Stacey Lynn and Helen Tartar at Stanford University Press, as well as John Brewer for his fine copyediting.

Other friends have contributed to this project in more diffuse ways, feeding me both literally and figuratively, laughing with me, and sharing both pleasures and frustrations over the years. For combining heroic levels of both professional and personal support, I would especially like to thank Eva Cherniavsky, Jane Garrity, Laura Green, and Lori Merish. Thanks to my family, especially my mother, Louise Papanek McCullough, for various kinds of support, and thanks to Katie and Annie McCullough for being the wise and hilarious souls they are. I will always remember and be grateful to Craig Fawcett for being the first to suggest to me that I should write. I was lucky enough to work as an undergraduate with Roger Henkle, who has become my measure of a fine teacher and who provided me with endless encouragement and more than a few drinks over the course of my graduate school career. Thanks also to Marla Kahn for persistence, patience, and insight and to Rena Alex for showing me that true friends appear in all regions. For renewing my faith in women at a crucial time, I would like to thank Leslie Hamanaka.

In Berkeley I have been blessed with the best of families, the core of which is made up of Lisa Fink, Esther Ehrlich, and Mike Weston, friends and kin as we have watched and helped each other grow. For years of fun and love, in addition to his endless help, beginning in our high-school chemistry class and continuing up to the very formatting of this book, I give love and thanks to Mike Weston. Thank you, Esther, for teaching me the importance of process, as well as for many a fine dog walk, and so much more. And Lisa, since the day we discovered we both loved purple, your place in my heart has only continued to grow. I look forward to more adventures with the next generation of this family as well—Sophie and Lena.

Mary Pat Brady's entry into my life has given me a cherished comrade of the heart and mind, as well as a fabulous companion in loitering. Her presence and support—from cooking me dinner to handling computer crises—has been essential to the completion of this project as to so many other things. Finally, for nursing me through a serious illness, I give all my love and thanks to Eva Cherniavsky, Lisa Fink, Jane Garrity, and Margaret A. Tyre, whose faith, love, compassion, and patience gave me a lifelong model of what friendship can be.

K.M.

Contents

REGIONS OF IDENTITY

*The Construction of America in
Women's Fiction, 1885-1914*

Introduction

> The American is only satisfied when all foreign elements are
> thrown into the national turning shop and come out turned
> to his own exact proportions. . . . He of Anglo-Saxon stock
> regards American civilization as the highest in the world . . .
> the turning shop works successfully. The Indians are shaved
> down almost to annihilation; Mexicans of California and
> Texas assume the national shape; Alaskans even are being
> cut down to the required model; and as for the Irish, they are
> hardly landed on the Battery before declarations are filed and
> they are turned out after the approved pattern.
> —Albert Rhodes, "The Louisiana Creoles" (1873)

> It is good for everyone to know how to forget.
> —Ernest Renan, "What Is a Nation?" (1882)

> The idea of the nation is inseparable from its narration: that
> narration attempts, interminably, to constitute identity
> against difference, inside against outside, and in the assumed
> superiority of inside over outside, prepares against invasion
> and for "enlightened" colonialism.
> —Geoffrey Bennington, "Postal Politics and the Institution
>   of the Nation"

In his influential lecture/essay "What Is a Nation?" Ernest Renan argues that, "forgetting, I would even go so far as to say historical error, is a crucial factor in the creation of a nation. . . . Indeed, historical enquiry brings to light deeds of violence which took place at the origin of all political formations. . . . Unity is always effected by means of brutality . . . the essence of a nation is that all individuals have many things in common, and also that they have forgotten many things" (11). This passage suggests two important claims: first, the construction of a national identity requires a misremembering of history involving both disavowal and creation; second, this misremembering produces an enabling national fiction, a narrative process crucial to the formation of the nation and to the multiple narratives out of which it evolves and maintains itself. The imperative both to remember and to forget produces the consequent imperative to narrate: as Homi K. Bhabha puts it, being "obliged to forget becomes the basis for remembering the nation, peopling it anew, imagining the possibility of other contending and liberating forms of cultural identifications" (311). But at whose expense do these originatory "deeds of violence" occur; when and for whom do these other identifications serve as "liberatory"; who is doing the narrating? And what if one were obliged simultaneously to forget and remember not just one national tradition, but several? What if several languages, ethnicities, religions—several cultural traditions—had to be negotiated or obliterated in order to form a national identity? Within "American" cultures and subjects, nation formation was never simply a matter of shifting from one identity to another or from one unified national category to another, particularly in the nineteenth century, given the complicated and multiple vectors of nationality at play during this period of nation-building in North America. Rather, nation formation involved a process of taking a national identity that was already split and multiply constituted and turning that constellation into a fiction of a single entity, into a seemingly unified category masking the amalgamation of other categories that constituted it.

As Albert Rhodes's comment above makes clear, a multitude of "foreign elements" cluttered the American "national turning shop," putting this process of national amalgamation at the center of American narrative production from the postbellum period on into the turn of the twentieth century.[1] A range of texts—legal discourse, historical accounts, personal narratives, published fiction, and other sites of cultural production—attempted to reconcile numerous conflicting narratives of class, race, gender, region, religion, and transnational political and economic relations, all grounded in an ideology of imperial capitalist expansion. The second half of the nineteenth century saw the emergence of the United States as a nation-state in part through the mechanisms of capitalism, through what Barbara Fields calls "an enterprise of bourgeois democracy" grounded in market politics (164). U.S. ideologies of nationalism and capitalism were linked not only to each other but to ideologies of imperialism as well: the United States's struggle to create a unified national identity was constituted in part by its struggle both within Northern America and without—globally—to expand its markets and absorb other nations' territories and peoples. As Lisa Lowe observes, the "contradictions of the 'nation' are never exclusively bounded in the 'local'; rather, local particularisms implicate and are implicated in global movements and forces" (34). Moreover, deeply imbricated in geographical and regional politics and articulated in the concept of Manifest Destiny, this imperialist project was also linked to—indeed, grounded in—a racial discourse, a use of "race" as what Toni Morrison in *Playing in the Dark: Whiteness and the Literary Imagination* calls "a way of referring to and disguising forces, events, classes, and expressions of social decay and economic division far more threatening to the body politic than biological 'race' ever was" (63).[2] Simultaneously, systems of race and nationalism were inextricably bound up with discourses of gender (which served to naturalize family-state relations) as well as increasingly with discourses of sexuality (which naturalized heterosexuality as the basis of the family and produced homosexuality as a deviant identity category).

By the last quarter of the century, then, the question of just what got to count as "American" was being debated on many grounds. The dominant version received by the twentieth century—the notion that, as Elizabeth Fox-Genovese puts it, "to be an American meant to be, or to aspire to become, white, Protestant, middle class, male, and probably from the Northeast" (7) as well as, I would add, part of a heterosexual family unit—was (then as now) contested by other, competing narratives. Priscilla Wald reminds us that dominant national narratives, or what she calls "official stories," exist in a dialectical tension with counternarratives: "neither static nor monolithic, they change in response to competing narratives of the nation that must be engaged, absorbed, and retold: the fashioning and endless refashioning of 'a people'" (2). Given the racial, regional, ethnic, and sexual divisions produced and exacerbated by the Civil War, Reconstruction, increased immigration, Westward expansion, and the policy of Manifest Destiny, it is clear that by the end of the century any notion of a unified national identity was not simply a hotly contested fantasy but a particularly urgent and necessary fantasy in the cultural imagination of the period. One crucially important site for the production of this national fantasy is, of course, literature, both in terms of literary texts and in terms of the critical interpretations and positionings of these texts. Although literature as a vehicle for national identity construction in the United States is not new in the postbellum period, given the multiply intersecting and shifting discourses of gender, race, ethnicity, region, and sexual orientation in circulation then, the turn-of-the-century period is a particularly rich and compelling moment to assess the cultural work done by fiction.

This cultural-historical moment is one context for my exploration of the role played by turn-of-the-century American women's fiction in the production of a national fantasy of "American" identity. The second context for this study is the literary-historical process of American canon formation. These two contexts are inextricably linked: the twentieth-century literary critical dismissal of women's "regional fiction," for instance, is one manifestation of an American literary enactment of nation building, a means of suggesting that "we" have a single and unified literary tradition. While I am interested in historically situating the texts under discussion here, examining such issues as, for example, Kate Chopin's rejection of the label "regional writer," I am also concerned with locating the criticism of this fiction in a historical context, exploring the ways in which critics have seen and labeled these writers and their work. Recent work by feminist critics has prompted the reevaluation of literary categories such as sentimental fiction, categories once gendered female and consequently dismissed from serious critical consideration, while contemporary work in American Studies has challenged the notion that "regional" denotes the avoidance of "national." This book grows out of both these critical developments: it contributes to the reformulation of American literary canons by exposing the ways that the privileging of a certain gender and of certain genres helps maintain the fiction of a unified national literature while also shaping both the authors' production and our reception of their texts. Differentiating American women's fiction into categories such as "Local Color fiction" or "race fiction," for instance, whether such differentiation is done *by* the author or *to* the author, has a long-lasting effect on how we as readers understand such texts. At best, we have been trained to see the work of various women writers as marginal, as unrelated to each other, and as unrelated to the construction of a national literary tradition, while at worst, we have been trained not to see such texts at all.

In the interests of refocusing this vision of American literature, I relocate these writers' texts in relation to both generic categories and the literary canon. Hence, in addition to situating these texts in broader cultural discourses, I also read them across our received generic lines—lines drawn not only between the novel and the short story but also, and for my purposes more crucially, between Realism and regionalism or Local Color fiction, and between Realism and the sentimental novel. In doing so, my goals are threefold: to call attention to the limitations of the generic boxes these writers usually occupy; to reveal the ways in which each writer's own location on the grid of American identities shapes both the form and content of her attempts to forge a narrative of America; and to interrogate the uses to which genre construction has been put by those critics—both then and now—who have produced a narrative of a unified

American national literary tradition. I pursue these goals unequally in each chapter in response to the fact that the writers under consideration here received differing levels of attention from critics in their day and ours, and in response to the fact that these writers displayed varying degrees of interest and self-consciousness in positioning their own work in relation to broader literary/generic debates.

Regions of Identity focuses on novels and short stories by a handful of women writing at the century's cusp: both canonical and noncanonical fiction by Sarah Orne Jewett, Florence Converse, Pauline Hopkins, María Amparo Ruiz de Burton, Kate Chopin, and Sui Sin Far. I place these authors and their works in the context of nineteenth-century discourses of racial, ethnic, sexual, regional, and national identity in order to show how fictional and nonfictional discourses overlap, bringing together a disparate group of writers—Northerners, Southerners, Californios, African Americans, Chinese Americans, Anglo Americans, heterosexuals, and homosexuals—not traditionally grouped together. I have chosen to focus specifically on these six writers not simply because they explore a variety of American regional, racial, ethnic, and sexual orientation subject positions (and so provide a rich vista of American literary representation), but more crucially because each of them understands American identity as located at the intersection of a number of different axes. Further, I have focused on these authors because in attempting to represent American identity in this way, they were operating largely without narrative models.[3] All six of these writers understand and trouble the link between "True Womanhood" and a long-standing U.S. equation of New England with "America." They also all employ the figure of "woman" as a site for the recasting of both regions and the nation as a whole. Bringing these writers together accomplishes a great deal, for while their initial concerns are often quite disparate and their conclusions vary, they nonetheless produce fiction that repeatedly coalesces around a concern over national identity, women's relation to it, and the importance of region to representations of this identity. Questions of race, ethnicity, region, religion, and sexual orientation are at stake for all of these writers, although these questions are asked in a variety of ways and come in and out of focus according to the specific narrative investments of the text. Various factors are foregrounded and various ones made invisible with diverse narrative effects. The interlocking effects of these various social discourses in turn shape the narratives' productions of "America." Following the shifts in character and proportion of these central issues, the emphasis of my analysis shifts on a chapter-by-chapter basis: my study of Chopin emphasizes issues of ethnicity's relation to race, for instance, more than my analysis of Converse, which focuses on a regional coding of sexual orientation. Grouping these writers together and approaching them with a flexibility of emphasis thus allows me to elucidate both what the texts' shared central questions have in common, and what is particular about their formation in any given text. To return for a moment to Renan's formulation, this approach allows me to examine more closely which particular elements of identity each author "forgets" in order to "remember" a fantasy of "America" that includes her characters.

Eve Kosofsky Sedgwick captures a sense of the constantly intersecting and shifting cultural discourses of identity—both national and individual—that I see at play in these authors' texts when she argues,

The 'other' of *the* nation in a given political or historical setting may be the prenational monarchy, the local ethnicity, the diaspora, the transnational corporate, ideological, religious, or ethnic unit, the sub-national locale or the ex-colonial, often contiguous unit; the colony may become national vis-a-vis the homeland, or the homeland become national vis-a-vis the nationalism of its colonies; the nationalism of the homeland may be coextensive with or oppositional to its imperialism; and so forth. Far beyond the pressure of crisis or exception, it may be that there exists for nations, as for genders, simply no normal way to partake of the categorical definitiveness of the national, no single kind of 'other' of what a nation is to which all can by the same structuration be definitionally opposed. (150)

There is no monolithic, definitive entity identifiable as "the" nation, Sedgwick suggests; neither is there a single Other to that nation. Instead, at various historical moments and from variously embodied positions, both the nation and the Other are configured in response to diverse pressures. What is central for one writer—Ruiz de Burton's argument for the inclusion of the Californio as American, for instance—can thus become unimportant for another—New England's cultural primacy allows Jewett, for instance, to ignore other regions, while Chopin's defense of the South as American leads her to elide all U.S. regions except the North and the South. One way to begin to understand the complications and nuances of discourses of national identity, I suggest, is to consider these discourses from the perspectives of writers variously situated, considering the differing ways in which their representations of region and nation are specifically inflected in relation to specific categories of otherness.

At the same time that these texts demonstrate diverse narrative specificities, however, they also share an investment in gender and region. The region is central both to these texts and to their efforts to imagine a nation. The region, in fact, operates in these texts not as a nostalgic, pastoral refusal of the national but rather as a specific narrative location for these authors' negotiation of it. In some of these texts this translates to a formal reliance on regionalism, a literary category dismissed by critics as "female" and "marginal," while in others it allows for a racing of region. In all cases the authors go about reconfiguring the nation by reconfiguring the relationships among its constituent regions. Consequently, it becomes clear in looking at these writers' works that far from being marginal texts, these texts were deeply involved in the central questions of "American" literature of their day. Just as these "female" texts are central to American letters, gender is central to these writers' representations both of region and nation. Representations of femininity, that is, specifically inflected by various combinations of region, race, ethnicity, and sexuality, serve as vehicles for these authors' constructions of national identity. What the disparate narratives under consideration here share is a reliance on gender as an axis that organizes race, ethnicity, sexuality, region, and nation. Gender's centrality results from its immense representational potential and its ability to cut across other categories of difference. Because of the already naturalized and universalized status ascribed in this period to the category of "the feminine," this category seems to offer a narrative model for imagining a universalized national identity out of regional and other fragments. These authors make femininity—a cultural category defined as tangential or marginal to "serious" issues of national identity—central to the working out of national and regional tensions. Hence, female protagonists become the vehicle for the very national identity that excludes them in the political sphere. At the same time, however, these attempts to mobilize the naturalized "feminine" to stabilize a fractured and exclusionary American identity inevitably reveal the fissures that undermine the universality of *both* categories. Implicit or explicit claims for the female characters' status as sources of "American" values are ultimately always undermined, not only by their inevitable insertion into a particular discourse of gender, but also by their equally inevitable placement within other formative cultural discourses—discourses on race, region, ethnicity, and sexual orientation. In texts that both destabilize and reify—sometimes simultaneously—dominant versions of femininity, "American" thus emerges not as a seamless unity synecdochically represented by any given heroine but rather as the sum of various regions or pieces tenuously bound together by multiple narrative strategies.

The texts under consideration here offer compelling examples of the ways late-nineteenth-century American women's fiction participated in the cultural work of formulating an American identity. They also provide a corrective to the American claim of exceptionalism, a corrective that stood not only as part of the nineteenth-century evolving national discourse but also stands today as a reminder to the late-twentieth-century reader of the ways in which "America," as both a nation and an imaginative category, has always been and continues to be formed in relation both to its many internal parts and to the rest of the world. Ruiz de Burton, for instance, shows us that the seemingly domestic issues emerging from the Civil War are imbricated in the claims and demands made in the name of Manifest Destiny. These writers thus prefigure Amy Kaplan's important argument that

Not only about foreign diplomacy or international relations, imperialism is also about consolidating domestic cultures and negotiating intranational relations. To foreground cultures is not only to understand how they abet the subjugation of others or foster their resistance, but also to ask how international relations reciprocally shape a dominant imperial culture at home, and how imperial relations are enacted and contested within the nation. (14)

Texts such as *The Squatter and the Don* help us ask Kaplan's questions and enable us to retell the story of nineteenth-century American history and literary representations. Ruiz de Burton's fiction makes it impossible to see the question of slavery in isolation, as not specifically connected to American imperial expansion, while Converse's novel attests to the interwoven nature of discourses of "normal" American sexuality and xenophobia. Carolyn Porter, in her incisive recasting of American studies, "What We Know That We Don't Know," asks,

what if we viewed 1848 not only as a moment in US history but also as a moment in Pan-American history? What if we foregrounded the fact that President Polk tried to buy Cuba from Spain for a million dollars in 1848? What if 'manifest destiny' were provisionally displaced from its traditional role in a national history to its protoimperialist role in a hemispheric history? In that case, the war with Mexico that ended with the treaty Polk signed in 1848 would not so much cast the 'shadow of the Civil War to come' . . . as it would open up the larger geopolitical arena in which the politics of race and slavery were played out. (519)

Porter thus suggests that American history and the literature so deeply imbricated in it must be recontextualized in a larger geopolitical sphere. Additionally, however, as Walter Benn Michaels usefully reminds us, "if the racism of internal oppression and the racism of external conquest were not separable, they were not exactly identical either" (185). My goal here is to see the big picture with all its interrelated parts in all of its complexity. The work of the writers under consideration here—Sui Sin Far's

representation of transnational relations and borders, for instance, or
Hopkins's representation of the international economics of slavery—
demonstrates that just such a broadening of geopolitical arenas, just such
a complexity of vision, was already evident in the fiction of now marginalized, turn-of-the-century women writers.

In pursuit of this complex vision—both literary and cultural—I will be
concerned with a cluster of issues and relationships surrounding the question of who and what gets to count as American: relations between regional and national identity; relations between geographical and generic
notions of "region"; racialization and gendering of regions; slippages between ethnicity and race; blurring lines or borders within and among national, ethnic, and racial categories; presumptions of a stability of heterosexuality as an identity category; and, finally, the naturalizing of femininity as inherently maternal and heterosexual. The book is organized around
these issues, with chapters grouped according to shared thematic emphases. The opening two chapters focus on New England and Boston
marriages, exploring the ways both Jewett and Converse—in distinctly
different ways—naturalize the Boston marriage as at the heart of "America" by associating it with, and hence borrowing from, the cultural capital of New England. Chapter 2 also, like Chapter 3, looks at texts that
script American conflict in terms of a North/South divide articulated
through Boston and New Orleans, interweaving sexual orientation and
race, respectively, into narratives structured around a major nineteenth-
century U.S. sectional divide. The third and fourth chapters share a central concern with the racing of regions resulting from the Civil War, an interest that overlaps with chapters 4, 5, and 6's attention to texts that ethnically mark regions as they simultaneously reveal dominant standards of
womanhood to be regionally and ethnically inflected. The final three chapters contrast to the earlier three, however, in that while the first three explicitly draw on, while also recasting, conventional images of New England, the second half of the book explores texts that leave New England
behind, reacting to it only to the extent of indicting it as inadequately representative of the United States.

Chapter 1, "(Re)Drawing Boundaries: Looking Back at a Boston Marriage in *The Country of the Pointed Firs*," explores the relationship between regional identity, national identity, and Boston marriages through
a reading of the structure and thematics of Sarah Orne Jewett's 1896
novel. Generally, critics have read texts like *The Country of the Pointed
Firs* simply as old-fashioned Local Color stories "about" old-fashioned,
politically conservative female worlds that are structured in terms of

metaphorical mother-daughter relationships and that turn away from the urban, masculine world of the future. More recently, critics such as June Howard, Sandra A. Zagarell, and Richard Brodhead have situated Jewett's work in relation to national cultural discourses as well as literary ones. Starting from this point I argue that Jewett offers a coded version of the Boston marriage and then makes it the basis of a paradoxically gender-inclusive but nativist female community that stands as representative of regional identity and, finally, becomes a model of a clan or a sort of national family. The Boston marriage thus becomes a way of delineating who "belongs" to the "American" family through Jewett's construction of a synecdochical genealogy of the Boston marriage from individual couple to female community to family clan to the nation itself.

In contrast to Chapter 1's focus on Jewett's use of the Boston marriage, Chapter 2, "'But Some Times . . . I Don't Marry,—Even in Books': Boston Marriages, Creoles, and the Future of the Nation," centers on Florence Converse's recasting of this relationship in *Diana Victrix* (1897). Here I examine how discourses of inversion and homosexuality intersect with American race and class debates via degeneration theory. This intersection of cultural narratives helped establish the parameters of "American" identity within turn-of-the-century U.S. culture. Against this backdrop Converse's representation of the Boston marriage speaks in conversation with competing cultural narratives of female "inversion." In providing a rhetorical counterattack to the contemporary sexological representations of deviant inverts, the novel draws particularly on the vocabulary of evolution and degeneration as an organizing principle. It connects racial, regional, and sexological discourses to produce a vision of America that includes the middle-class women of the Boston marriage. Revealing sexuality as implicitly formative in and formed by the construction and maintenance of a pure or undiluted national identity, the novel displaces a rhetoric of degeneration from the women of the Boston marriage onto the Creoles of New Orleans. *Diana Victrix* ultimately posits modern sexual identity as constructed from within regional and national identities, refiguring a North-South reunification plot as the story of two Northern "spinsters" who embody the promise of the nation's future, the natural outgrowth of dominant American ideologies of independence, productivity, and self-reliance.

"Slavery, Sexuality, and Genre: Pauline E. Hopkins's Negotiations of (African) American Womanhood," Chapter 3, situates Pauline E. Hopkins's reworking of sentimental narrative form within a racial discourse of the 1890s, arguing that in her 1900 novel, *Contending Forces*, the racialized and sexed body of the mulatto becomes the founding term for and emblematic of African-American community. Further, the mulatta figure establishes that community as central to American identity: national identity here foregrounds the "race question" as played out against regional divides of North and South. The chapter examines the function of Sappho, the mulatto heroine, exploring Hopkins's many simultaneous uses of her: Sappho is the heroine of the domestic plot; she is a symbol of homoerotic female community; she is a figure of the reunification of the black community in post-Reconstruction America; she is a figure of the reconciliation of black and white America; and, finally, she is a figure of national reunification through the discourse of North and South, in which her character is steeped.

Chapter 4, "María Amparo Ruiz de Burton's Geographies of Race, Regions of Religion," focuses on Ruiz de Burton's recently republished historical romances, *Who Would Have Thought It?* (1872) and *The Squatter and the Don* (1885). The chapter examines the ways Ruiz de Burton draws on an evolving discourse of regional identity and imperial expansion to critique U.S. expansionism and relocate "America" in relation to both competing internal groups and external forces. In her first novel Ruiz de Burton introduces a Mexican protagonist into Civil War New England in order, I argue, to dismantle the myth of New England as representative of national culture and as the source of universal "American" values. She accomplishes this by using both the geographic division of North/South and the racial division of the color line to expose "America" as an always regionally and racially multiple nation in which the relationships of internal parts to the nation are intimately linked to the relations of the nation to the world. In *The Squatter and the Don*, in contrast, by shifting the locus of "America" from New England to Southern California, and by shifting the salient geographic distinction from North/South to East/West, Ruiz de Burton recasts America. In confronting both the American history of colonial expansion and the Californio Dons' position as colonized, but also, historically, as colonizers, the novel uses gender to locate the Californios as part of the U.S. white elite, representing the Californio women as "American," for instance, by revealing the model of American True Womanhood as regionally inflected and by disturbingly displacing outsider status onto the California Indians.

Chapter 5, "Kate Chopin and (Stretching) the Limits of Local Color Fiction," turns to the short fiction of a writer often viewed as a "regional" or "Local Color" writer of the South. I locate Chopin's work at the center of turn-of-the-century debates over regionalism both as an American literary form and as a part of the broader cultural discourse on national identity. Chopin's self-conscious participation in these debates through both her essays and her short stories (published throughout the 1890s) helps us to see the ways that regionalism as a literary form became a gendered category while at the same time contributed to ongoing discourses of national identity. Her self-positioning as vehemently (not) a Local Color writer reveals the complexities of her relation to regionalism, a literary category she exploited even while insisting, on the level of plot, on an American culture made up of internally fractured and marked regions. Simultaneously, Chopin uses regionalism to subvert the terms of middle-class models of womanhood. She dismantles a monolithic image of "America" and American True Womanhood by representing women whose identities are marked by a variety of ethnic, racial, regional, religious, and class identifications internal to the South, particularly Creole, Cajun, and African American women. However, she also succeeds in opening up new representational terrain for her white heroines only by replicating the racist convention that displaced erotic desire onto the Othered woman. Ultimately, Chopin uses Local Color to write about female identity and sexuality while also using female identity and sexuality to write about regional identity and, implicitly, national identity. In both cases her work demonstrates the limits of a strategy that employs, even if it reworks, racist conventions of Local Color fiction.

Finally, Chapter 6, "Transnational Geographies of Race: 'Eurasian' Communities and the Nation in *Mrs. Spring Fragrance*," focuses on Sui Sin Far's journalism and her 1912 collection of short stories, *Mrs. Spring Fragrance*, and their attention to the key role that borders and border-crossings play in the production and cloaking of geographic and ethnic regions within American culture. This chapter shows that Sui Sin Far's representations of community—specifically Chinese, Chinese-American, and Chinese-Canadian communities—challenge a cultural discourse of blood as the basis of identity while also recognizing and protesting the real and material effects of this discourse. Debiologizing race, she stresses instead the cultural, juridical, and economic terms in which it has been constructed in U.S. society. In so doing she uses gender roles to both signal and help produce racial location and identity. As a result, Sui Sin Far locates Chinese-American community as intimately and complexly connected to "American" national identity rather than as marginal or Other to it: a gender-shaped sense of cultural identity locates Chinese-American borderlands (both literal, national borderlands and figurative, racial borderlands) as simultaneously marginal and central to "American" life.

Also of interest to me here and throughout the book is the critical reception of these texts and the ways that reception has not simply located
them as specific, literary genres or types but also naturalized those very
political locations within literary history and consequently obscured the
determining influence that such categorical placements entail. Finally, the
critical reception has elided other possible approaches to the texts. Thus,
I analyze the ramifications of the fact that Hopkins has been read as writing "race" fiction but not as contributing to discourses of region, while
Chopin, held up as a regionalist par excellence, has only recently begun to
receive attention for her use of racial discourse. Like my attention on the
textual level to the various issues at play in the narratives, my attention to
critical commentary and its effects is uneven from chapter to chapter, according both to the amount of critical attention the author garnered and
to the author's own engagement with the critics. Thus, I spend consider-
able energy delineating the ways critics marginalized and then reclaimed
Jewett but in both cases elided the homosocial from both her life and her
writing. On the other hand, in my reading of Converse, whose work was
ignored by virtually all the major critics, I focus primarily on the text itself and its relation to sexological discourses of the day.

As part of several larger and ongoing conversations within feminist
literary criticism and genre criticism—the reevaluation of nineteenth-
century women writers, the critique of the politics of genre construction,
and the uses and limits of identity politics—I want thus to suggest both
new understandings of the literary texts discussed here and, more broadly,
new understandings of the ways in which literary categorizations shape
our expectations and interpretive approaches to fiction. Challenging the
nation-building of the canonical representation of a unified national literary tradition, I focus instead on the nineteenth-century's ongoing worrying of the issue of nationality, its attempt to articulate—both in the sense
of expressing and in the sense of fitting together the pieces of—"America." Stuart Hall argues that cultural identity

is not a fixed origin to which we can make some final and absolute Return. Of
course, it is not a mere phantasm either. . . . It has its histories—and histories have
their real, material and symbolic effects. The past continues to speak to us. But it
no longer addresses us as a simple, factual 'past'. . . . It is always constructed
through memory, fantasy, narrative and myth. Cultural identities are the points of
identification, the unstable points of identification or suture, which are made,
within the discourses of history and culture. Not an essence but a *positioning*. (226)

In this book I hope to illuminate some of the "memor[ies], fantas[ies],
narrative[s] and myth[s]" through which the late-nineteenth-century U.S.

produced its points of identification, points that linger today with ramifications as powerful and powerfully violent now as they were then.

In an illustrative moment of self-reflection, Toni Morrison observes, "My work requires me to think about how free I can be as an African-American woman writer in my genderized, sexualized, wholly racialized world" (4). Part of my own interest—both in the multiple representations of American identity offered by the writers I survey here and in the multiple and shifting locations of their work in the American canon—reflects a more personal interest in the question of freedom Morrison poses. Attempting to become and remain aware of, as well as to negotiate my own various positions of both privilege and oppression in this "genderized, sexualized, wholly racialized" as well as heterosexist and classist world has led me to endlessly reconfigure my understanding not simply of myself but also of "American" culture and literature. To return to the terms with which I opened, I have been led to explore just what sorts of forgetting and remembering have enabled my understanding of my "self" and my "America." This book is the product of that process. It seems to me that as contemporary feminists theorizing and working toward justice, we would do well to inform our efforts by looking to the late nineteenth and early twentieth centuries, a historical period analogous to our own. In this transitional, turn-of-the-century era American women of various sorts attempted, through focusing on the physical and imaginative space of regions, to claim a rhetorical space for themselves within the discursive realm known as "America." They confronted a range of identities and issues similar to those we confront today and they, like us, imagined solutions from within the terms of the discourses of their culture. They foundered, some of them, on the issues that divisively and often violently separate us now, and they made mistakes—ranking oppressions, maintaining willful blind spots about privilege, and empowering themselves at the cost of disempowering others—that are far from obsolete today. Perhaps by analyzing these writers' attempts we can also become more aware of the limits of our own theories and praxis, more aware of how dominant discourse constrains our formulations both of capitulation and resistance, and as a result, more aware of the need to challenge the limits of our own understanding.

1 *(Re)Drawing Boundaries*

LOOKING BACK AT A BOSTON MARRIAGE
IN 'THE COUNTRY OF THE POINTED FIRS'

At its most compelling, American local-color realism thus points toward an imaginative sociology that is at once objective and visionary. The images it yields up compose the fragments of a book of the people, an essential history of their lives' common conditioning. Paradoxically, at this level of realization the particular local circumstances begin to appear incidental. The same stories are told, in more or less detail, on all sides. Indeed, it is in the nature of American life, heterogeneous and disorderly and yet oppressively uniform, that any sector of it, honestly examined, is likely to reveal a logic of occurrence (or nonoccurrence) that holds true for the whole national experience. Yet at different times, different particular sectors seem to lie nearer the center.
—Warner Berthoff, *The Ferment of Realism*

Like a web, which consists of strands radiating from a common nucleus, *The Country of the Pointed Firs* at its largest level begins with, constantly returns to, and ends in the relationship between the narrator and Mrs. Todd.
—Elizabeth Ammons, *Conflicting Stories*

As in all of Miss Jewett's writing, the touches are delicate rather than striking, and the tone is subdued and quiet. . . . But the work is very fine and very true. *The Country of the Pointed Firs* is a story of wholesome, simple, rural life, with the breath of the sea for tonic and the sunshine of summer for warmth.
—Anonymous, *The Bookman* (1897)

Reading Critical Readings of Jewett

To open this study with Sarah Orne Jewett (1849–1909) is both to open with a focus on the region of America most often read as representative of America itself—New England—and to begin with perhaps the most canonical writer under consideration here, a writer who, as Michael Davitt Bell has so aptly put it, "has been accorded a fairly consistent place in the American literary canon, although even her most enthusiastic partisans have felt compelled to insist that this place is very small" (61). That Jewett's "particular sector" was New England and that she herself was a privileged, white Maine writer transplanted into Boston literary circles of the century's end helps, of course, to explain why her work has never fully disappeared from the canon. But to understand the shifting critical approaches to, and evaluations of, Jewett's work is to track not simply the vagaries of American literary history but also the degree to which regionalism as a literary form contributed to national identity formation, as well as (through its marginalization) to national literary canon formation. While Jewett's specific choice of an already culturally privileged "sector" helped guarantee her a page in Berthoff's allegedly but never really democratic "book of the people," her representation of what *The Bookman*'s reviewer calls "simple rural life" and its gendering as female—both on the content level in her stories' focus on women and on the generic level as a "female" genre (as critics defined regionalism)—helped guarantee her works' marginal status therein. It is this doubled status, as both canonical yet marginal, both read but patronized, that concerns me here and that can, I will argue, be explained by a more careful look at Jewett's representation of the relationship between the two heroines of *The Country of the Pointed Firs* (1896)—her coded representation of love between women. In this chapter I will read Jewett's work both in the context of her day and our own in order to explore this relationship. I will argue that in *The Country of the Pointed Firs* Jewett offers a coded representation of a Boston marriage, a representation that stands as a kind of rhetorical "both/and." The Boston marriage relationship can help us to understand and indeed bring together the various critical issues historically at stake in Jewett criticism. As I will show, *The Country of the Pointed Firs*'s Boston marriage serves as a figure for both region and nation, both male and female cultural spheres, and both preindustrial matrifocality and imperial expansion. As the structural center of the text, the Boston marriage can be read—in a ripple effect—as a figurative model for the family, the community, the region, and the nation, offering a model both grounded in women's community and reflecting Jewett's own race and class privilege.

When Jewett began publishing in the 1870s, American literature was being molded largely from Boston in a literary circle increasingly centered around the *Atlantic Monthly* and its editors James T. Fields and, later, William Dean Howells, Thomas Bailey Aldrich, and Horace Scudder.[1] Regional fiction was in vogue, providing an available and immediately deployed category for Jewett's work. The *Bookman* headnote above offers a typical view of Jewett's fiction: from the publication in 1877 of her first novel, *Deephaven*, onward, critics read her as a regional writer and described her with diminutives that were both gender and class coded. Howells himself reviewed *Deephaven* in the *Atlantic Monthly*, for instance, calling it "a pretty little book" and a "simple treatment of the near-at-hand quaint and picturesque" (25). Using descriptions such as "charmingly" (25) and "delicious" (26), Howells offers as praise his assessment of Jewett's work as "so refined, so simple" (26). Similarly, the *Continent*'s anonymous reviewer of Jewett's 1884 novel *A Country Doctor* describes it as holding "charm in every page . . . quaint characters . . . gentle thought" (33) while *The Bookman* reviewer quoted above goes on to attribute "charm" to the book due to its "quaint wisdom," but he notes that the "little volume"'s "quiet ending" makes it clear that it is too "delicate" to make a "deep impression" (80, 81). As in reviews of Kate Chopin, Sui Sin Far, and, indeed, nearly all writers considered regionalists (as well as many other women writers of the period), descriptions such as these—particularly "quaint," "charming," and variants of "little"—appear over and over in reviews of Jewett's work. These terms rhetorically locate her as a part of a marginalized literary form focused on the representation of a specific local and rural past, a reading replicated by critics until very recently.

This vision of Jewett's work and often of her life is filtered through a lens not only of region but also concurrently and conflatedly of gender. In a 1915 retrospective on what he calls "a golden age" of American publishing and literature, Henry James, for instance, describes Jewett as "mistress of an art of fiction all her own, even though of a minor compass" (23, 30) This tone of patronizing praise continues as he identifies "her beautiful little quantum of achievement" as being of "subdued character, a sort of elegance of humility or fine flame of modesty" (30). More recent critics have continued this linking of diminutive status, femininity, and regionalism, although the valence of this link has shifted over time. Ann Douglas Wood, for instance, in a 1972 article, sees women regionalists as writing a literature of impoverishment, "an exercise in nostalgia or a release for despair" (13) and even goes so far as to claim that the "same note of attenuation, even impoverishment, characteristic of the life and career patterns of the women Local Colorists, is sustained also in their actual work . . . the Local Colorists' imaginary territory is dominated by the laws of scarcity" (16).[2] More constructively, Josephine Donovan, leading the feminist literary critical reassessment of regionalism and Local Color, argues in "A Woman's Vision of Transcendence" that a "central concern in Jewett's work issues . . . from her intimate awareness of the limited emotional and social condition of women; most of her stories deal with women's efforts to transcend their condition" (366). Elsewhere Donovan articulates what was to become representative of a certain kind of liberal humanist argument launched by early (and mainly white, middle-class) feminist literary critics who took up and simply inverted the terms set by a largely male American literary critical establishment. In her ground-breaking book, *New England Local Color: A Woman's Tradition*, Dono-van argues that women Local Color writers "created a counter world of their own, a rural realm that existed on the margins of patriarchal soci-ety, a world that nourished strong, free women. The culmination of this tradition is to be found in Jewett's master-work *Country of the Pointed Firs*" (3). Donovan goes on to argue specifically about *Pointed Firs* that "while the work is marked by a tone of elegy, a sense that the rural world is irretrievably passing as an historical entity, there is nevertheless a sense of joy and of faith that such a world must also remain as a timeless way of being. . . . The community is an enduring world sustained by Jewett's great matriarch, Mrs. Todd, and her mother, Mrs. Blackett" (113). Here Donovan retains the conflation of a rural, nostalgic village life with a fe-male world but views this as a positive rather than a negative literary value, a representation of a kind of transcendent women's culture.

More recently the very terms of this discussion have come under de-bate. The ideological underpinnings of the generic distinction between re-gionalism and realism, for instance, have been made more explicit, re-vealing a hierarchy of literary value based on criteria far removed from the "literary." Eric J. Sundquist points out in "Realism and Regionalism," for instance, that "economic or political power can itself be seen to be de-finitive of a realist aesthetic, in that those in power (say, white urban males) have more often been judged 'realists,' while those removed from the seats of power (say, Midwesterners, blacks, immigrants, or women) have been categorized as regionalists" (503). Relatedly, the vision of re-gionalism as provincial and unrelated to the nation has also been chal-lenged. Amy Kaplan, for instance, has noted the extent to which the generic container "regionalism" contributed to the cultural work of na-tional reunification in the second half of the nineteenth century. She ar-gues in "Nation, Region, and Empire" that

On the one hand, regionalist fiction expands the boundaries of the imagined com-munity and democratizes access to literary representation, which can be heard in the multivocal introduction of the vernacular through the dialect of different regions. On the other hand, regionalism contained the threatening conflicts of social difference. . . . By rendering social difference in terms of region, anchored and bound by separate spaces, more explosive social conflicts of class, race, and gender made contiguous by urban life could be effaced. (251)

Richard Brodhead's important work on regionalism has further clarified the cultural work done by this genre: he suggests that "regionalism's representation of vernacular cultures as enclaves of tradition insulated from larger cultural contact is palpably a fiction . . . its public function was not just to mourn lost cultures but to purvey a certain story of contemporary cultures and of the relations among them: to tell local cultures into a history of their supersession by a modern order now risen to national dominance" (121). According to these critics, then, regional fiction is not simply the more backward and female cousin of realism but is, on the contrary, deeply imbricated in a national cultural project, part of what June Howard calls "the movement to invent traditions that pervades Europe and the United States from about 1870 to the First World War" ("Unraveling" 368).

Current work on Jewett locates her and her work in this context, at long last recasting the image of the isolated, genteel, country spinster writing stories of the rural past.[3] Perhaps the most important location of this revision is in the 1994 edition of *New Essays on The Country of the Pointed Firs*. June Howard, the editor of this consistently insightful collection, points out in her introduction that the "received view of regionalism in American literary history has emphasized its effort to render the local and conserve the traditional, rather than the way in which the impulse to do so is dependent on and part of a drive toward national unification" (23). Susan Gillman, in her essay in this collection, similarly notes that "in most American literary histories, the late-nineteenth-century turn in fiction toward region is assumed to signal a rejection of nation and national issues. Regionalism is envisioned as a limited form, just as 'local color' is seen, sometimes pejoratively, more recently affirmatively, as minor literature associated with local places, 'little' forms, and women" (101). These critics, along with others, work against this view of regionalism, showing how it is indeed part of a larger national literary effort of imagining America. More specifically, they locate Jewett as involved in this process, as what Howard calls "a participant in the culture industry, a highly successful writer negotiating a nexus of gendered institutions for producing literary meanings and commodities" (4).

This reevaluation of regionalism's status and role in American literary history has been accompanied by a revisioning of its relation to gender. In Jewett's work, as in the work of many women regionalists, this has taken place on several fronts simultaneously. As exemplified in Josephine Donovan's work as well as more recent work such as Judith Fetterley and Marjorie Pryse's Norton Anthology *American Women Regionalists* 1850–1910 (1992), regionalism's emphasis on communities of women has been revisioned as a strength rather than a weakness. This liberal feminist strategy, while urgently needed as a corrective to a male literary dismissal of women regionalists, has tended toward a certain form of essentialism, a naturalized gendering of terms such as "nurturing" and "community" as female. As a result, as Brodhead argues, "the feminist reconception of regionalism has tended to repeat the autonomy fantasies of the nineteenth-century ideology of separate spheres" (144).[4]

Relatedly, the formal elements of the genre have come under scrutiny, its tendency to the short story now viewed less as indicative of an author's inability to "master" the privileged novel form and more as signaling the need for an alternate form to express alternate contents. This is certainly true of Jewett criticism, particularly that on *The Country of the Pointed Firs*. Formally, this text has been viewed as either a series of very tightly connected short stories or a rather plotless novel. The focus of the text is character; plot is slight. What little action there is centers on a nameless narrator's summer stay in the home of Almira Todd, a widowed herbalist who lives in the Maine fishing village of Dunnet Landing. The narrator meets village people and learns their stories, is taken by Mrs. Todd on a series of visits, the most important of which is to Mrs. Todd's mother and brother—Mrs. Blackett and William—on nearby Green Island, and attends with Mrs. Todd and Mrs. Blackett their family reunion. Much of the narrative concentrates on local people and retrospective accounts of their lives but through the eyes or words of Mrs. Todd or the narrator. The two women interpret these accounts either for each other or together, so that the real focus of the book is the narrator's relationship with Mrs. Todd. This is obviously not a realist novel, but only recently have critics begun to ask what it might be instead.

In writing a narrative without a forward-moving action and in focusing her tale on life in the fishing village in an age when the great fishing and whaling industry of New England is dead, Jewett is clearly writing against the tradition of the canonical American male Romance. Indeed, we can read Jewett as specifically resisting the hierarchies of literary value expressed in reviews of her work, refusing to dismiss, as James would go on to do, her own subject matter as "minor" in comparison to a presumably larger scope of "real" literature. She makes this point explicitly in the novel through the figure of one of the old local sea captains, Captain Littlepage. The very name "Littlepage" signals Jewett's evaluation of the man's tale: it is reduced from heroic quest to slightly tedious and self-indulgent story. The Captain represents a male version of the tale-teller and his tale. His is the plot of life at sea, an adventurous male life that, he observes, "made men of those who followed it" (20).[5] It is the conventional nineteenth-century American male plot, a plot that Jewett parodies: Littlepage's tale is, the narrator notes, "a little dull" (19). Against Littlepage's story, then, Jewett's non-linear narrative can be read not as a failed novel but rather as a refusal of the American Romance: Jewett mocks the narrative of the male quest out from female, domestic, culture into the wilds of Nature and offers in its place a story located within a community made up of women where no one travels far or conquers much.[6]

Recent critics have explored other links between the narrative structure and gender as well. As the headnote of this chapter suggests, Elizabeth Ammons has identified the structure of *The Country of the Pointed Firs* as "vortic, centric, weblike" (*Conflicting Stories* 46). Drawing on the work of Carol Gilligan, Ammons, in her early work on Jewett, genders this structure female, describing it as "a pattern of development and experience based on retaining and maintaining relationships and connectedness, as opposed to achieving radical individuation, as the most important adult challenge and human need, a process traditionally associated with 'feminine' values and perspectives in the west and embodied in Jewett's narrative in an encompassing structure that is webbed, networked" (52).[7] Joseph Boone similarly reads Jewett's form—what he calls "the logic of incremental repetition" (21)—as linked to gender, arguing that the "centric structures" of texts such as Jewett's "pivot upon and centralize the very stasis that appears to hold the single female protagonist 'captive' within her environment, only to reveal that her stationary confinement is a cache of freedom, integrity, and power invisible in the external world of love and marriage" (286). Ammons and, to a lesser extent, Boone exemplify recent feminist critics' tendency to replicate, this time on the level of form, the terms of the established critical discourse on Jewett while inverting the valences of its gendering. To pose the critical problem more explicitly, how might we redress the critical marginalization of Jewett's work on the basis of its investment in regionalism and women without simply repeating the received terms of this evaluation and inverting their valences?

Telling Jewett's Life: Historical Revisionism and the Boston Marriage

To answer this question I will first look at yet another shift in critical readings of Jewett, both biographical and literary. Joseph Boone asserts that "experimentations with centric narrative structures have accompanied the articulation of the story of women's relationships with each other rather than with men" (322). While Boone is not referring specifically to Jewett's work, I would suggest that we can use his observation as a way into answering the critical question I pose above. One way of understanding the centric, nonlinear plot of *The Country of the Pointed Firs* is to read it as the formal articulation of a Boston marriage, both in its circling around the relationship of the two heroines and in its refusal of the conventional comic plot's building to the climax of the heterosexual marriage. Understood in these terms, the Boston marriage also allows us to see Jewett's representation of community as one in which regional, national, and international spheres connect and overlap. In order to explore this, I will turn to the Boston marriage, both as a biographical element in the situating of its author, and, more importantly, as a structuring device in the text itself.

As a historical phenomenon, the Boston marriage must be contextualized within the broader and long-established nineteenth-century convention of female friendships. This convention emerged from what Carroll Smith-Rosenberg has characterized as a "female world of love and ritual," a world in which, partly in response to the gender segregation of nineteenth-century middle-class social life, a wide spectrum of emotional, social, and physical bonds between women developed, ranging from "the supportive love of sisters, through the enthusiasms of adolescent girls, to sensual avowals of love by mature women" (53). Smith-Rosenberg's work reveals both the broad range of these relationships and the extent to which passionate and sensuous relationships were included among commonly accepted—indeed, even valorized—forms of female interaction. Not explicitly sexually eroticized, not pathologized, and actively socially sanctioned, many of these relationships were clearly both physically and emotionally intimate and often continued well beyond the marriage of either or both of the women involved.[8]

The "Boston marriage" grew out of this late-nineteenth-century, white, middle-class female sphere and was used to describe long-term monogamous relationships between two women, relationships often described by the women themselves as a kind of spiritual marriage.[9] Such "marriages" were originally culturally sanctioned as part of the larger female sphere: the women were viewed, as Martha Vicinus notes, as "highly respectable couples" ("They Wonder" 442). Linked to the increase of class-privileged, white women in higher education and the work force, the Boston marriage in part resulted from the increased economic and social autonomy of many middle-class and upper-class white women by the last quarter of the century, women who for the first time had the possibility of remaining financially independent, pursuing careers on their own, and, consequently, living outside the birth or marriage family unit. While the level of physical intimacy in such relationships is unclear, historical sources indicate that the women involved considered the Boston marriage their central relationship and a source of sustenance and support for both their personal and their professional lives.

Boston marriages, of course, did not occur only in the United States; they appear to have been more class-specific than nation-specific. Vicinus comments that "in New England the longevity and the erotic undertones of relations between women appear to have been publicly accepted, for so-called 'Boston marriages' were commonplace in literary circles" but also goes on to note that "we have numerous other well-documented examples in every Northern European country where women were making inroads into the professions" ("They Wonder" 442). Given the name, however, it does seem safe to assume that the phenomenon either originated in New England or was at least seen as most prevalent there, and certainly there are many accounts of such relationships in the last quarter of the century throughout New England. Hence, while the relationship as a model of female-female union is class-specific and so generally (although not exclusively) racially specific (that is, white), it is both regional and transnational at the same time.

Although by the 1890s this positive interpretation of female-female relationships was being challenged, for women like Sarah Orne Jewett—a privileged and educated member of Boston's literary elite—it was still possible to understand the Boston marriage in generally positive terms.[10] That she herself, as a member of a Boston marriage, understood it in these terms is hardly surprising but becomes more significant when viewed against the subsequent literary critical erasure of this biographical fact. Jewett's Boston marriage and the female community to which it was linked were central to Jewett's life and work. Of a wealthy New England family, she had both the education and the financial security to pursue her career as a writer. Through this career she entered Boston literary circles and there met Annie Adams Fields, the woman who was to be her partner in a Boston marriage of nearly thirty years. Although they met around 1877, it was not until the death in 1881 of Fields's husband, the editor James T. Fields, that the women's relationship intensified into a union that lasted until Jewett's death in 1909. Letters from Jewett to Fields express Jewett's belief that her work was nurtured by her relationship with Fields, and in a larger sense, by her community of artists, largely women, many of whom were involved in Boston marriages of their own.[11]

Although the two women lived together for nearly three decades, corresponding daily in the periods when they were not together, critics—in what can only be seen as an instance of virulent heteronormative tunnel vision—have until recently either ignored the relationship entirely or characterized it as anything but romantic/erotic. The historical trajectory of representations of the Jewett-Fields relationship can stand as typical of a more general approach to Boston marriages from Jewett's day to ours. That is, a relationship seen by its contemporaries as positive and socially acceptable increasingly came, as the twentieth century unfolded, to be seen as deviant and embarrassing and thus as a "problem" to be either elided or explained away. Helen Howe's memoir of her father Mark De-Wolfe Howe's life contains an account of his friendship and editorial relationship with the couple and articulates, even from well within the twentieth century, a nineteenth-century view:

Mrs. Fields was by no means the only magnet to draw Father to the long drawing room in Charles Street [the Fields home]. There were, in my parents' circle of friends in Boston, several households consisting of two ladies, living sweetly and devotedly together. Such an alliance I was brought up to hear called a "Boston marriage." Such a "marriage" existed between Mrs. Fields and Sarah Orne Jewett. Father wrote of it as a "union—there is no truer word for it." (83)

Henry James describes Jewett in the period after James T. Fields's death as the "young friend of great talent whose prevailing presence in her [Annie Fields's] life had come little by little to give it something like a new centre" (30).[12] But James's representation offers us one of the first examples of a simultaneous recognition of the strength of this relationship and an attempt to recode it into what was becoming a more recognizable and culturally acceptable form. Despite the fact that James's own sister was part of a Boston marriage and the fact that, as Judith Fryer has argued, his depiction of such a relationship in *The Bostonians* was probably based not only on his sister's relationship but also on the Jewett-Fields relationship (615), James codes this relationship specifically in terms of a mother/daughter model, asserting that Jewett had come to Mrs. Fields as an adoptive daughter, both a sharer and a sustainer, and nothing could more have warmed the ancient faith of their confessingly a bit disoriented countryman than the association of the elder and the younger lady in such an emphasized susceptibility. Their reach together was of the firmest and easiest, and I verily remember being struck with the stretch of wing that the spirit of Charles Street could bring off." (30)

We might perhaps read James's somewhat coy confession of disorientation here as symptomatic of the transitional moment in which he wrote this memoir, for by 1915 a mother-daughter model of female friendship would have seemed more culturally acceptable than a Boston marriage. So that while Donovan has documented in "The Unpublished Love Poems of Sarah Orne Jewett" that Jewett wrote at least thirty love poems to women (and none to men), and while her letters to Annie Fields are full of passion and play, including the use of pet names (so much so that according to Fields's biographer Judith Roman "nearly all of Jewett's letters to Annie could be called love letters" (117)), after Jewett's death in 1909 DeWolfe Howe convinced Fields to cut these elements from the collection of Jewett's letters that she edited, lest, as Helen Howe recounts, they "have all sorts of people reading them wrong" (84).[13] James's and DeWolfe Howe's discomfort here points not simply to the shift in models of and attitudes toward female sexuality underway during this period, but also to the dual nature of the problem that this shift has caused critics. One aspect of the problem might be simply put as the question of what to call the Jewett-Fields relationship; the other aspect is the question of the critical investment in calling it anything at all.

By now the biographical details are clear: as biographer Paula Blanchard notes, Jewett's "diaries show that by her late teens Sarah had developed a pattern of intense, though often temporary, attachments to other women. Beginning with a series of adolescent crushes, these attachments became more powerful and enduring as she grew older, culminating in her lifelong attachment to Annie Fields" (50). Blanchard then contextualizes these attachments by noting that Jewett's letters and journals all show "the same sexual indifference [to men]. There is no sign that she was ever strongly moved by the friendship of a man, or that she ever languished for the sight of a male friend or tormented herself with fear of his defection. She was so moved, and she did languish and torment herself over a succession of girls and women" (51). While Donovan's work on Jewett's unpublished love poems has more or less put to rest, at least among informed contemporary critics, the notion of Jewett as what Donovan terms a "passionless 'spinster'" ("Unpublished Love Poems"

26), critics still feel compelled to categorize at least Jewett's relationship with Fields, if not her sexual orientation itself. Donovan, for instance, argues in her analysis of the love poetry that "Jewett's emotional orientation was lesbian" (26), while Judith Fetterley, in "Reading *Deephaven* as a Lesbian Text" bases her reading of Jewett's first novel in part on Jewett's "lifelong relationship with another woman" (165), a relationship Fetterley clearly considers, if she does not explicitly name it, lesbian. Blanchard, on the other hand, simply concludes—apparently on the basis of the fact that Jewett's papers indicate no erotic attraction to men—that Jewett was celibate and locates her within a romantic friendship, defending against the idea that such a friendship might contain an erotic element. Roman similarly acknowledges the Fields-Jewett relationship as a Boston marriage or romantic friendship but refuses to call it lesbian, in part because the term is anachronistic in the period (106).[14]

I delineate these critical reactions not in order to side with one or another of them but to call attention to the degree to which our twentieth-century mindframe has made Jewett's sexual orientation an issue demanding contemporary critics' attention (regardless of the opinion that attention produces). This is partly due, of course, to the naturalized status of heterosexuality in our culture and of the resulting cultural imperative either to "explain" or to erase anything not clearly heterosexual. But it also speaks to critics' desire to categorize experience clearly. This desire might be read not simply as an arguably homophobic desire to not put Jewett into the category of "lesbian" but also as the desire to find any category into which we can put her, given that there is no adequate available twentieth-century discursive category or name to account for Jewett's relationship/orientation.[15] Several critics, for example, presumably for lack of a better option, have described the Fields-Jewett relationship as a mother-daughter bond, a description growing, in part, out of the fact that Fields was fifteen years older than Jewett. Although this model seems perfectly reasonable, I would suggest that it need not be exclusive. Consider, for instance, the fact that while Fields was fifteen years older than Jewett, she was also seventeen years younger than her husband. Yet a father-daughter model is not prevalent in descriptions of their relationship, and even when it is mentioned, in keeping with broader cultural models of heterosexual marriage, it certainly has not precluded anyone's seeing James and Annie Fields as husband and wife.[16]

Similarly, I would suggest that the Boston marriage might be seen as allowing for a range of relationships between its members. Judith Roman, in "A Closer Look at the Jewett-Fields Relationship," argues that the "secret of the success of this relationship for both their personal and their professional lives lay in its complete reciprocity and in their ability to create for themselves a form of marriage in which all roles were interchangeable and neither partner was limited by the relationship" (127). This multiplicity of forms of relationship, as Roman here implies, also links the personal to the professional and helps clarify how and why this discussion of biographical interpretation is linked to Jewett's work. Sarah Way Sherman frames the issue most clearly:

Although Annie Fields remained the central figure in Jewett's life, theirs was not an exclusive relationship. There was room for several other intensely affectionate, loving friendships. The women with whom Jewett formed bonds in her maturity are impressive. They reveal not only Jewett's charm but also the emergence of a network of professional women whose lives centered not on their families and domestic duties but on their cultural, public contributions, whether paid or voluntary. (74)[17]

The Boston marriage thus both contained multiple roles for Jewett and functioned for her not only as the core of her personal "family" but also as the core of her professional circle, her literary world. Analogously, in *The Country of the Pointed Firs*, what I will read as a figurative Boston marriage between the narrator and Mrs. Todd both contains multiple possibilities for their relation and serves as the core of the text's representation of a community of women.[18] As a structural model the Boston marriage—in its less utopian aspects—will also come to figure the larger Bowden clan and ultimately a national "family" with transnational ties.

Let me return for a moment to the headnote with which this chapter opens, Warner Berthoff's claim that "it is in the nature of American life, heterogeneous and disorderly and yet oppressively uniform, that any sector of it, honestly examined, is likely to reveal a logic of occurrence (or nonoccurrence) that holds true for the whole national experience. Yet at different times, different particular sectors seem to lie nearer the center" (100). Here the fragment becomes representative of the whole; the region synecdochically stands in for the nation. But at the same time, however disingenuously Berthoff puts it, a hierarchy of regions also operates to privilege some while marginalizing others. Jewett benefited from this hierarchy, coming from and writing of a region long associated with Americanness and carrying a good deal of cultural capital. Her fiction, grounded in the regional and local (and assisted by its author's class and race privilege), gained Jewett entrée into the cultural elite, giving her access to both rural and urban life, to both local and national circles. As Richard Brodhead puts it, Jewett "grew up as a member of the sort of local gentry class characteristic of a village order of social organization. Her connection with Annie Fields might be said to have given her a bridge into the more modernized version of the American social elite—less place centered, more citified, more leisure-oriented, and more *culture*-oriented— that emerged with a postvillage world in the mid-nineteenth century" (154, emphasis in original). One might argue that Jewett hence had access to, in Berthoff's terms, both the sector and the center and that New England functions literally as the former and synecdochically as the latter.

This access might simultaneously be read in terms of gender: the class-privileged, white female regionalist writer Jewett gained access to both sides of the gendered separate spheres; she gained access to both the male, public, professional world of publishing and the private female worlds (as well as, more broadly, the feminized rural region and the "masculine" urban center). As Brodhead notes, she won "the backing of the high-cultural literary establishment and of the women's artistic community nested *in* that establishment for her literary self-assertion" (156, emphasis in original). Both these sets of access—to regional and national as well as to male and female cultural spheres—can be explained by Jewett's Boston marriage with Fields. Further, Jewett's Boston marriage not only gave her access to several spheres, it also enabled a relation among spheres in her life, reconfiguring as overlapping or interconnected spheres that were generally posited as oppositional. For as what Donovan calls "the emotional center of an extended circle of women writers, including those of the local color school" (39), Fields organized a number of different worlds for Jewett, and their relationship embodies the multiple positionings of both women.[19]

In the same way that the Boston marriage allows us to understand areas of Jewett's life as connected and overlapping rather than separate, it can also allow us to resolve a critical debate similarly structured in separate and oppositional terms. Judith Fetterley accuses Richard Brodhead of casting Jewett, along with other nineteenth-century women writers, as "simply complicit in a variety of cultural projects designed to consolidate their own race and class privilege," claiming that his "use of class and race as categories of analysis" functions to "cancel rather than complicate attention to gender" ("Commentary" 607, 608). Meanwhile, June Howard understands Brodhead as challenging "the claim that Jewett should be located in a woman's culture" on the grounds that her class privilege and consequent access to Boston literary circles distanced her from the women she represented in her fiction ("Unraveling" 370). My interest here is not in Fetterley's and to a lesser extent Howard's rightful concern over Brodhead's both insightful and problematic reading of Jewett, but rather in the symptomatic binary oppositions both his and their analyses assume. The oppositions—attention to class and race versus attention to gender; membership in "women's culture" versus membership in high culture—point toward a sort of scholarship that does a disservice to *The Country of the Pointed Firs*. The implication of the first binary is that Jewett's attention to gender issues is rendered invalid by the classism and racism resulting from her own privilege, while the implication of the second binary is that Jewett must have belonged to one or the other cultural group. I would suggest, rather, that both Jewett's cultural location and her literary text can more fruitfully be read in terms of a "both/and" formulation than in terms of an "either/or" one. As the history of feminism makes so painfully clear, both Jewett's life and her work can quite easily be, and indeed are, both radical in their gender politics and conservative in their racial and class politics. Similarly, rather than being a member of one or the other, Jewett was, in fact, both a member of "women's culture" and a member of the literary elite.[20] As Fetterley points out, writers such as Jewett "emerge from and represent in their works complex combinations of privilege and disadvantage, of acceptance and critique" ("Commentary" 608). The most productive approach to both her biography and her texts, then, would be neither to dismiss her altogether for being classist and racist (which she was), nor to celebrate her for focusing on women (which she did), but rather to recognize and analyze the complexity of these intertwined and sometimes contradictory positions. Reading her through the lens of the Boston marriage allows us to move beyond a critical practice grounded in binary opposition. It resolves the seeming contradiction of her simultaneous membership in women's and high culture and it helps explain the structure of *The Country of the Pointed Firs*. Both as a biographical element that allowed her to negotiate the various spheres of her life and as the literary trope functioning as the central organizing figure of Jewett's text, the Boston marriage offers a model both radical and conservative on which Jewett bases her representation of community, region, and nation.

The resulting figurative representation of a Boston marriage within *The Country of the Pointed Firs* offers Jewett a narrative space of multiplicity and of polyvalent meaning within clearly defined limits. Elizabeth Ammons rightly points out in "Material Culture, Empire, and Jewett's *Country of the Pointed Firs*" the Dunnet Landing houses "do articulate a vision of preindustrial matrifocal harmony, health, and happiness. But they also stand for white colonial settlement and dominance" (97). We can thus use the figure of the Boston marriage between the narrator and Mrs. Todd to understand the connection between these two important and seemingly unrelated meanings of the New England houses. If we read the relationship between the narrator and Mrs. Todd as a coded version of a Boston marriage, and if we work from the assumption that the Boston marriage in this text follows the Boston marriage in Jewett's life in its ability to contain a variety of forms of relationships between its members, then the two critical interpretations suggested by Ammons can be brought together. The Boston marriage—as a model of white, class-privileged female-female union—figures both supportive female space and white colonialism, inclusion based on gender sameness, and exclusion based on class and racial hierarchies. Additionally, and perhaps more importantly, this reading also allows us to see this complicated and contradictory set of relationships as a figure for Jewett's concept of both region and nation. Rather than viewing *The Country of the Pointed Firs* as offering the nuclear family (as represented at the Bowden family reunion) as the model of the national family, we can view the Boston marriage as both replacing and figuring the nuclear family, reconstituting community by providing simultaneous access to both region and nation. A model that conflates and mixes various kinds of relations among women (mother-daughter, teacher-student, lovers, friends, etc.) but grounds this polyvalent relationship in the erasure or incorporation and diffusion of difference, the Boston marriage becomes the vehicle for Jewett's simultaneously radical and conservative vision of both a regional and a national community. Offering an implicit critique of the model of nation grounded in the heterosexual family, Jewett's use of the Boston marriage, like Florence Converse's, locates the homosocial at the heart of the nation. But while this model offers increased options for inclusiveness, it ultimately depends upon the same structure of exclusion that the family-as-nation model uses: the homosocial is written in, but other Others remain necessarily outside, guaranteeing the limits of the nation.

Figuring the Boston Marriage

> The road was new to me, as roads always are, going back.
> —*The Country of the Pointed Firs*

The relationship between the unnamed narrator and Mrs. Todd has long—particularly since the advent of feminist literary criticism—claimed the attention of critics of *The Country of the Pointed Firs*, who have read that relationship as a friendship, a figurative mother-daughter relationship, and/or a tenant/landlady relationship, readings I would agree with but augment.[21] Marjorie Pryse, in her introduction to the Norton edition of *The Country of the Pointed Firs*, describes the book as portraying "a world in which women are alone but not tragic" (xviii), a description that is a fundamental misreading of the text, for these women are not alone; they are merely without men, a distinction that is crucial. This is not a text about lack: it is a text about plenitude, about friends who furnish a spectrum of relationships for each other. What seems to me to be the salient term of Jewett's representation of the relationship between the narrator and Mrs. Todd is its multiplicity. The narrative repeatedly represents this relationship as several different relations simultaneously, often reworking other, more conventional relationships such as mother/daughter or husband/wife. As Elizabeth Ammons puts it, the text "is a love story, though unconventional. The standard man/woman/ marriage plot is replaced with a narrative about a passionate bond between two people whose relationship falls outside that narrow frame" (*Conflicting Stories* 55). *The Country of the Pointed Firs* circles around the relationship of the two women, defining them in terms of their relationship to each other rather than in terms of their relationship to a man or even to a child. It locates them in what is nearly entirely a female world, a metaphorized, separate sphere in which the women look to each other for both knowledge and emotional intimacy. It is both this narrative location and structure that I link to the Boston marriage and hence it is on a figurative level that I perform a "queering" of this text.[22]

A number of recent critics have observed but not analyzed an extra dimension to the relationship between the narrator and Mrs. Todd. As long ago as 1972 Ann Douglas Wood comments of the narrator that "in a strange way she has fallen in love with the older woman" (29), but she does not expand upon this comment even to explain her use of the modifier "strange." Similarly, Donovan compares *The Country of the Pointed Firs* to Willa Cather's *My Antonia*, asserting that "both deal with a strong female protagonist and both stories are told by an emotional, nostalgic narrator who was once in love with the central character" ("Unpublished Love Poems" 28), while Ammons refers simply to "the writer-narrator's love affair with Mrs. Todd" (*Conflicting Stories* 44). I would like to begin my discussion of this relationship by looking at this extra dimension, an erotic charge that the narrative structures as a cyclical series of returns with retrospective longing standing in for explicit erotic desire.

For the nameless female narrator of *The Country of the Pointed Firs*, the literal "road" of the headquote above is a road leading back from the Bowden family reunion to her friend and hostess Mrs. Todd's home in Dunnet Landing. But this is only one of several instances in the narrative when the narrator, a city woman, returns to Mrs. Todd's home and experiences her journey as both a new adventure and a reunion with a long familiar object of desire. That object of desire turns out to be not only the village but also the woman for whom it stands. The doubleness of this representation is typical of Jewett's narrative strategy: the Boston marriage in this text is figurative rather than explicit and is always multivalenced, a status, as I will argue, that allows it to figure regional and national relations in addition to personal ones. A central element of this narrative strategy is Jewett's use of a first-person female narrator who employs a curiously removed rhetoric, a rhetoric that includes passive voice and third-person narration along with first person narration. As a result, the text takes on a doubleness in which external and objective description seems to stand in for and mirror first person internal experience.

The text's opening chapter, for instance, titled "The Return," depicts the narrator's approach to Dunnet Landing. Rather than directly describe the narrator's feelings at this return, the language of the passage focuses on the village and the feelings that the village produces, without ever specifying in whom those feelings are produced. The village presents itself for attention like a person, becoming "more attractive than other maritime villages of eastern Maine," partly, the narrator suggests, because of "the simple fact of acquaintance with that neighborhood," an acquaintance that makes it "so attaching," and gives it "such interest" (1). With houses that "make the most" of themselves and whose windows watch the harbor like "eyes," the village is personified as human; collective or community identity is figured as individual identity, and friendship overlaps with love. The narrator notes that "when one really knows a village like this and its surroundings, it is like becoming acquainted with a single person. The process of falling in love at first sight is as final as it is swift in such a case, but the growth of true friendship may be a lifelong affair. After a first brief visit made two or three summers before in the course of a yachting cruise, a lover of Dunnet Landing returned" (1–2). What this unspecified "lover," the narrator, returns to is both the village and, as the title of Chapter Two proclaims, "Mrs. Todd" (3).[23] Sarah Way Sherman comments of this passage that "it is, in a curious sense, the opening of a love story, a courtship. . . . Her subject is the place and her relationship to that place. We will come to know *her* only through her relation to this other, a place that is also a person" (202). This use of "a place that is also a person" recurs throughout *The Country of the Pointed Firs* and is one of the central means by which the narrator's relation to Mrs. Todd is articulated, the love for the woman conflated with and representative of the love for both the village and the region, this country of the pointed firs.

While the village itself stands in for Mrs. Todd in the passage above, more frequently it is Mrs. Todd's house that Jewett uses to symbolize her. Willa Cather, in her preface to Jewett's stories, recounts a conversation with Jewett that highlights the importance of houses to Jewett: "she once laughingly told me that her head was full of dear old houses and dear old women, and that when an old house and an old woman came together in her brain with a click, she knew that a story was underway" (xvi). Jewett repeatedly associates houses with personal boundaries and identities, noting that "a man's house is really but his larger body, and expresses in a way his nature and character" (119), whereas the narrator in "William's Wedding" notes that on her return to the island and Mrs. Todd, she feels strange in the house, "like a hermit crab in a cold new shell" (216). This shell imagery occurs elsewhere, for while living with Mrs. Todd, the narrator finds the prospect of a visiting guest unnerving:

> I had been living in the quaint little house with as much comfort and unconsciousness as if it were a larger body, or a double shell, in whose simple convolutions Mrs. Todd and I had secreted ourselves, until some wandering hermit crab of a visitor marked the little spare bedroom for her own. Perhaps now and then a castaway on a lonely desert island dreads the thought of being rescued. I heard of Mrs. Fosdick for the first time with a selfish sense of objection; but after all, I was still vacation-tenant of the schoolhouse, where I could always be alone. . . . (55)

This image of a "double shell," a shared body, might be read (in a typically Jewett multivalenced fashion) as the image of a child occupying the body of the mother, or the image of a lover occupying the body of the beloved, or both. Although her reference to the solitude of the schoolhouse suggests that what the narrator objects to in Mrs. Fosdick's visit is a loss of privacy, her objection might also be read as stemming from the disruption of union with Mrs. Todd. Further, that it is the loss of Mrs. Todd's attention that disturbs the narrator is suggested once the guest has arrived and disappeared into the kitchen with Mrs. Todd. The narrator confesses that she waits "impatiently" to be introduced to Mrs. Fosdick, commenting, "I sat in my high-backed rocking-chair by the window in the front room with an unreasonable feeling of being left out, like the child who stood at the gate in Hans Andersen's story" (57). Purposely ambiguous, the narrator's comparison aligns her with a child yet also differentiates her from one, both because of her ability to use the rhetorical language of a simile and because a simile by definition presumes both a similarity and a distance or difference between its terms.

On one level, here and throughout the text, Jewett figures the narrator's and Mrs. Todd's as a metaphoric mother-daughter relationship; the narrator, a city woman who has come to Dunnet Landing, inhabits Mrs. Todd's house/space as a child inhabits the maternal body. Mrs. Todd feeds and nurtures the narrator in what can be read as a maternal fashion: the narrator notes that in terms of lunch, Mrs. Todd "was always peculiarly bountiful in her supplies when she left me to fare for myself, as if she made a sort of peace-offering or affectionate apology" for what might be read as a mother's abandonment (191). The narrator's "homesick heart" returns to Mrs. Todd (215), and the act of leaving the metaphorical womb of a house, becomes a kind of death for the narrator. Looking at her empty room on the day of her departure, she states, "I and all my belongings had died out of it. . . . So we die before our own eyes" (130–31).[24]

At the same time, however, this is not a literal mother-daughter relationship, and the narrative always locates the maternal metaphor as only one of a number of possible readings, layering other possible readings on top of this one. In the quotation above, for instance, one might interpret Mrs. Todd's generous offerings of provisions as the offering of lover to her beloved or as a maternal gesture or as some combination of both, while the narrator's metaphorical homesickness could be for a parental home or a home made with a spouse/partner or some overlap of the two. This structure of multiple readings operates throughout the text, although one of the possible narrative locations allowed Mrs. Todd is nearly always that of mentor and friend to the narrator. Mrs. Todd, whom even the country doctor acknowledges as an authority on herbal healing, comments on the narrator's abilities in the herbal healing business, for instance, by noting, "I have never had nobody I could so trust. All you lack is a few qualities, but with time you'd gain judgment an' experience, an' be very able in the business. I'd stand right here an' say it to anybody" (7), a statement that locates her as both teacher and potential business partner. The narrator herself replicates this notion of the older woman as experienced teacher of the younger by stating, "She was a great soul, was Mrs. Todd, and I her humble follower" (199).

A curious passage near the opening of *The Country of the Pointed Firs* establishes the text's insistence on multiple readings. After explaining how "my hostess and I had made our shrewd business agreement" in terms of meals, a description that establishes theirs as a financial rela-

tionship but that also suggests the less formal friendliness implied in the
term "hostess," the narrator goes on to say,

The spruce-beer customers were pretty steady in hot weather, and there were
many demands for different soothing syrups and elixirs with which the unwise curiosity of *my* early residence had made *me* acquainted. Knowing Mrs. Todd to be
a widow, who had little beside this slender business and the income from one hungry *lodger* to maintain her, *one's* energies and even interest were quickly be-
stowed, until it became a matter of course that she should go afield every pleasant
day, and that the *lodger* should answer all preemptory knocks at the side door.
  In taking the occasional wisdom-giving stroll in Mrs. Todd's company, and in
acting as business partner during her frequent absences, *I* found the July days fly
fast. . . . (6, emphasis added)

The move from first to third person is striking here, and, given that Jewett demonstrates elsewhere a perfect capability for consistency of narrative voice, I would suggest that this shifting takes place in order to call
our attention to the variety of relations between the narrator and Mrs.
Todd and to the variety of emotional investments implied therein. Subject
and object at once, the lodger becomes the servant, perhaps peeved, perhaps with an appreciation of the irony of the shift. The discussion of the
lodger also establishes the narrator as well aware of the economic dispar-
ity in her relation to Mrs. Todd; this is not a naïve denial of her tourist
privilege. Moreover, in using "lodger" in place of the first person, the passage emphasizes the structural position of the narrator—the temporary
slot she fills as the payer of rent—and so calls attention to role-playing as
an aspect of the relationship between the narrator and Mrs. Todd. As ten-
ant, concerned friend, student, and business partner, the narrator moves
among overlapping personal and structural positions; even a change in
their business relations provokes a response in Mrs. Todd that can be read
as located in the register of romance rather than simply in economics.
When the narrator "withdraw[s]" from minding Mrs. Todd's business,
Mrs. Todd becomes "more wistfully affectionate than ever in her expressions" (7), and the narrator comments,

Mrs. Todd and I were not separated or estranged by the change in our business relations; on the contrary, a deeper intimacy seemed to begin. I do not know what
herb of the night it was that used sometimes to send out a penetrating odor late
in the evening, after the dew had fallen, and the moon was high, and the cool air
came up from the sea. Then Mrs. Todd would feel that she must talk to somebody, and I was only too glad to listen. We both fell under the spell, and she . . .
told . . . all that lay deepest in her heart. It was in this way that I came to know
that she had loved one who was far above her. (7)

Here changes in their "business relations" lead to increased emotional intimacy, represented in language that draws on codes of romance—evening dew, moonlight, sea air, and, arguably, a romantic spell.[25] Taken together, these passages offer examples of the way the narrative positions the narrator as both an insider and outsider at once, both a tourist representative of high culture and an intimate member of a community of women.

The multiplicity of terms in the narrator's and Mrs. Todd's intimacy are foregrounded repeatedly in the text, particularly in a series of moments of increasing intimacy between the two women. In the first the above notion of a spell shared between the two women recurs when Mrs. Todd shares her homemade beer doctored with herbs with the narrator and tells her, "I don't give that to everybody" (31), a comment the narrator glosses by admitting, "I felt for a moment as if it were part of a spell and incantation, and as if my enchantress would now begin to look like the cobweb shapes" (31). In the second moment of this sort Mrs. Todd takes the narrator to the pennyroyal field where she and her husband courted, admitting, "there, dear, I never showed nobody else but mother where to find this place; 'tis kind of sainted to me" (48). It is sainted, the narrative implies, as much because it is the location of the best pennyroyal in the state as because it was the scene of Mrs. Todd's courting of the husband she married but never, according to her, really loved. Mrs. Todd's pronouncement that the pennyroyal in this field is "the right pattern of the plant, and all the rest I ever see is but an imitation" (48) calls attention to this herb which, as Elizabeth Ammons points out, is traditionally associated with women, either as a facilitator of birth or as an abortifacient (*Conflicting Stories* 56) and so links the place with female tradition and ritual. More crucially for my purposes, Mrs. Todd's comment also explicitly puts the narrator into the structural position of both mother and lover, narrative locations that overlap here and throughout the text.[26] Moreover, these two locations are immediately linked to that of the friend, both in the narrator's comment, "I felt that we were friends now since she had brought me to this place" and in Mrs. Todd's admission that Nathan, her husband, occupied the place of friend rather than lover in her heart (49).

Marjorie Pryse, in her discussion of an unpublished Jewett holograph called "Outgrown Friends," quotes Jewett as asserting there that in genuine friendships "we take the friend for better for worse as the man and woman when they marry" ("Archives" 54), a comment that puts friendship on the same level of intensity and commitment as (heterosexual) marriage. But in *The Country of the Pointed Firs* friendship is not simply a friendship, and the representations of heterosexual marriage lack an erotic charge. Using the passage above as an example, we can see two important and related ways that *The Country of the Pointed Firs* maps the terrain of the narrator's relationship to Mrs. Todd. First, it reconfigures the possible relations between the two women by blurring and overlapping the boundaries of the categories they occupy, locating them in various and shifting roles. Second, it rewrites heterosexual relations in a way that deeroticizes them and transforms them, to all intents and purposes, into friendship. Consequently and very importantly, this transformation strips heterosexuality of its privileged position of ownership of the erotic and opens instead a wider space for the erotic's circulation. Hence, the narrator, conventionally defined as friend within a system that presumes all lovers to be heterosexual, is located as lover as well as many other things, while the husband Nathan, who would conventionally occupy the place of lover, is figured as a friend. Michael Davitt Bell, noting the text's emphasis on Mrs. Todd's desire to leave Green Island for a wider world, suggests that her hopeless love for the "one who was far above her" (7) "may matter less as a love story than as another example of Mrs. Todd's restlessness, of her desire for scope, for 'the world'" (74). Carrying Bell's point further, one might conclude that in Almira Todd's story Jewett turns the heterosexual love plot into a plot motivated not by erotic desire but rather by the desire fueling any number of women's plots: the desire to escape the constrictions and restrictions of a "woman's place."

Blanchard notes that the "marriages in these late stories are hardly distinguishable from friendship, based as they are on affection lit by only the mildest of sexual afterglow" (330) then comments specifically of the relationship between William and Esther represented in "William's Wedding" that "it lacks the intensity that characterizes, for example, the love between Kate and Helen in *Deephaven* or between the *Pointed Firs* narrator and Mrs. Todd. Heterosexuality in the old was as bewildering to Jewett as it was in the young. . . . For Jewett's ideal of passionate friendship, the kind that can powerfully influence the course of a life, we must turn to her stories about women" (331). Although Blanchard turns here to a discussion of Jewett's "Martha's Lady," a story taken by her and others as exemplifying what Glenda Hobbs calls "passionate" female friendships that combine "amorousness" with "spirituality" (27, 25), her comment also applies to *The Country of the Pointed Firs*.[27] As in the passage above, the multiple valences of friendship are suggested in Jewett's text when the visitor who has disturbed the narrator in her crab shell of Mrs. Todd's house claims that old friends are the best kind. In response, "Mrs. Todd gave a funny little laugh. 'Yes'm, old friends is always best, 'less you can catch a new one that's fit to make an old one out of,' she said, and we gave an affectionate glance at each other which Mrs. Fosdick could not have understood, being the latest comer to the house" (62).

This moment of ambiguous intimacy takes on a further resonance when read against the narrator's arrivals and departures, which are imaged as lovers' reunions or separations.[28] She arrives in the village— an arrival, recall, described as a "process of falling in love at first sight" with the place (1), Mrs. Todd's place—as "a lover of Dunnet Landing," whereas on her later return in "William's Wedding," the narrator describes her heart "beating like a lover's . . . on the way to the door of Mrs. Todd's house" (214). Much later, at the narrator's departure, the depth of the two women's bond is depicted in a typically multileveled fashion. The narrator sits "with regret for company," the two seem "on the edge of a quarrel," and, the narrator notes, "it seemed impossible to take my departure with anything like composure" (130). Finally, the narrator relates, "I glanced at my friend's face, and saw a look that touched me to the heart. I had been sorry enough before to go away" (130). The look she sees is never named; her relationship to this friend never fixed; the discourse surrounding it is always shifting.

However, the heart that beats like a lover's opens up a reading of this friendship as a figurative romance, a reading supported by the depiction of the narrator's relationship to William, Mrs. Todd's double. There is a displacement of the narrative's romantic energy from the relationship between the narrator and Mrs. Todd to the relationship between the narrator and William. This displacement is suggested under the cover of William's courting of Esther in "A Dunnet Shepherdess," when William appears at Mrs. Todd's home ostensibly on his way up country to go fishing. There is an unmistakable sense of disappointment in the narrator when she is left behind: "the truth was," she confesses, "that my heart had gone trouting with William." When he reappears with "a small expectant smile upon his face" and two fishing lines, she states, "words seemed but vain to me at that bright moment. I stepped back from the school house window with a beating heart" (139).[29] In the narrative proper this displacement appears in passages such as the one in which William takes the narrator up to see the view from Green Island: "he asked politely if I would like to go up to the great ledge while dinner was getting ready; so, not without a deep sense of pleasure, and a delighted look of surprise from the two hostesses, we started, William and I, as if both of us felt much younger than we looked. Such was the innocence and simplicity of the moment that when I heard Mrs. Todd laughing behind us in the kitchen I laughed too, but William did not even blush" (44–45). Mrs. Todd—the lover, the one with the gift of vision—sees the moment as one in excess of sheer innocence and simplicity, and the narrator shares with her the laughter that William does not notice. As a whole the Green Island section of the text records Mrs. Todd's sharing of her life—her childhood home, her family, and her romantic history—with the narrator. Thus, when, at the end of the visit, Mrs. Blackett tells the narrator "I want you to come again. It has been so pleasant for William," William functions once again as a narrative marker for Mrs. Todd.

Similarly, in the story "William's Wedding," William's plot is only the ostensible focus of the narrative; in fact, the story focuses more on the relationship between the narrator and Mrs. Todd than on William and his bride, and William's marriage ends with William and Esther's sailing to Green Island and the two women walking home silently joined. The narrator states, "we held each other's hands all the way" (226). Sherman notes of this wedding that it "is the closure of a love story, of a romance. . . . But there are always two stories in these sketches, and this conclusion gives us two images of integration: "that of the bride and groom, and that of the narrator and Mrs. Todd" (265).

The juxtapositioning of the two pairs can be linked to a comment made by the narrator at the end of the narrative proper: watching Mrs. Todd disappear from sight, the narrator describes her as "mateless and appealing" (131). Jewett's choice of the word *mate* here returns us to the multiple valences of the narrator and Mrs. Todd's relationship, as well as to the narrow ways in which most critics have read it. Barbara Johns, for instance, interprets *mateless* in terms of the category of spinster, then reclaims *spinsterhood* as a positive, albeit somewhat compensatory, term; working within the terms of compulsory heterosexuality, she argues that the narrator and Mrs. Todd "know that in their matelessness they must appeal to each other to heal the private pain and to celebrate the secret joy. Yet, in another sense, these two mateless women are appealing to each other and to other women precisely because they know that . . . they mysteriously and powerfully possess themselves" (162). Johns's comment implicitly defines the two women as simply friends and, moreover, rules out the possibility that their turning to each other in pain and joy constitutes its own form of mating. Marjorie Pryse, meanwhile, understands *mate* here in the sense of "a fisherman's word for trustworthy friend" ("Archives" 64), a meaning that is certainly applicable but not fully adequate to Jewett's usage. Sherman offers the fullest gloss of the term, pointing out that the word *mate* "suggests friendship but also a kind of twinship: one shoe in a pair is mate to the other. It also suggests marriage: a spouse is one's mate. Finally, it suggests the companionship of those who share the same labor: mates on the same voyage. The term is rich and genderless, suggesting commonalities of work and love, marriage and friendship" (265).[30] It is in this textured and multiple sense that I understand the narrator and Mrs. Todd as mates. The narrator, when she leaves, might well be said to leave Mrs. Todd "mateless," "appealing" to her departing mate both in the sense of being desirable and in the sense of wordlessly beseeching her to stay.[31]

Broadening Narrative Circles: The Marriage, the Family, and the Community

The multiplicity of roles suggested by the term "mate" bespeaks Jewett's representation of layered and shifting relations between the two women and marks this representation as a figurative Boston marriage. But while a Boston marriage describes the specific relationship between the narrator and Mrs. Todd, it also stands, within *The Country of the Pointed Firs* as a whole, as a model of flexible roles available more generally to characters, structuring the roles and relations not only between the narrator and Mrs. Todd but also between them and other characters in the text. The role of the child, for instance, occurs as one possible role within the Boston marriage (both in *The Country of the Pointed Firs* and in Jewett's own Boston marriage), but it is reworked and made available on a broader level in the narrative. The caretaker role is consistently valorized and represented as deeply gratifying in the novel, but the narrative also consistently associates a metaphoric state of childishness with pleasure and joy, allowing the characters a certain symbolic interchangeability of roles, a shifting of positions that is always associated with pleasure. Although Mrs. Todd herself represents mother-child relations as fixed, claiming that "you never get over bein' a child long's you have a mother to go to" (35), the narrative suggests otherwise, offering the position of child to anyone with an appreciation of joy. Coming to greet the narrator and Mrs. Todd on their visit to Green Island, Mrs. Blackett had the "affectionate air of expectation like a child on a holiday" (36), and, pleased with her company, takes on "a sudden look of youth" (40). Arriving unexpectedly in order to go to the family reunion, Mrs. Blackett looks "pleased and triumphant as a child" and is greeted by her daughter with "there, mother, what a girl you be!" whereas later Mrs. Todd's enthusiasm and joy cause her mother to speak to her "as if she were a child," and Mrs. Todd becomes "alert and gay as a child" (86, 95, 105). To occupy the structural position marked "child," then, is to have access to pleasure and joy, as well as to the protective caretaking of a mother, an access open to all the women in this narrative. This flexibility of roles repeats the structure of the Boston marriage, where historically the members perceived their shared gender as enabling each to be both nurturer and nurtured. Paula Blanchard notes the correlation specifically between Jewett's text and biography here by noting that the "interchangeable mother-daughter aspect of the relationship between Mrs. Todd and Mrs. Blackett, wherein each is sometimes the 'child' and sometimes the 'mother,' mirrors the same flexibility between Jewett and Annie Fields, or for that matter between Jewett and any of her women friends"(293).[32]

The usefulness of reading the Boston marriage as a narrative structure designed to create flexibility of roles extends beyond a reading of the narrator and Mrs. Todd in several related ways. First, as in Jewett's reworking of the category of the child, the flexibility afforded to the narrator and Mrs. Todd's relationship becomes available to other characters, such as William or Mrs. Blackett. At the same time, other relationships—sibling, maternal—are figuratively drawn into, made a part of, the Boston marriage of the narrator and Mrs. Todd. A series of doublings and displacements in the relationships among Mrs. Todd, her brother William, and her mother Mrs. Blackett provide the first level of overlap between figurative Boston marriage and nuclear family roles. This occurs in a narrative structure that insists on shuffling and reworking these relationships throughout the book. As a result, Mrs. Todd and the narrator always stand in more than one relation to each other, while other characters have a variety of narrative spaces open to them as well.[33]

Mrs. Todd and William, for instance, are mirror images of each other, both in the sense that they are oppositional and identical. The oppositional relation functions at least partly in terms of their social relations: Mrs. Todd describes the difference between herself and her brother by saying, "he was always odd about seein' folks, just's he is now. I run to meet 'em from a child, an' William, he'd take an' run away" (41). Mrs. Todd appears throughout the narrative as constantly in social contact with her community, whereas William is almost always figured as solitary and silent. The analogue of this in terms of physical space, of course, is the fact that William stays on Green Island, their childhood home, while the adult Mrs. Todd moves to the mainland. This geography suggests that the island might be read as a region of the mainland community figured by Mrs. Todd, but the narrative also represents Green Island as its own country/nation, as when the narrator comments, "one could not help wishing to be a citizen of such a complete and tiny continent and home of fisherfolk" (39). The island region is simultaneously a nation, giving a region/nation model the sort of flexibility and interchangeability that William and Mrs. Todd have with each other. Moreover, while William and his mother are figured as doubles, living together and imaged as thinking in tandem, unable to separate one's opinion from the other's (51, 54), William is also a double for his sister, Mrs. Todd, a mirror image in the "identical" sense of the term, a condition that the narrative represents as locating him as mediator of the relationship between his mother and his sister. "I take after father, large and heavy, an' William is like mother's folks, short and thin," Mrs. Todd comments, constructing herself in opposition to her mother/brother. She goes on, however, to acknowledge the reverse of this: her identification with her mother, which William does not share; "he never had mother's snap an' power o' seeing things," she observes (47), describing the vision that she and her mother share—a vision that the narrative attributes to mythic female figures such as the sibyl (8).[34]

That Mrs. Todd and Mrs. Blackett are figured as doubles in *The Country of the Pointed Firs* is suggested most simply by the fact of their shared title. But, in fact, the "Mrs." here signifies not wife but widow, and it is the other central relation associated with the wife—that of mother—that dominates Jewett's representation of the two. Interestingly, *The Country of the Pointed Firs* offers only one literal mother and, significantly, she is not Mrs. Todd but Mrs. Todd's own mother, Mrs. Blackett. Mrs. Blackett embodies the power of literal mothers: everyone loves her, and she is queen of the Bowden Family Reunion (98), "the mistress by simple fitness of this great day" (105). Mrs. Todd's position as heir to this primacy of her mother is noted by the narrator, who comments, "I had often noticed how warmly Mrs. Todd was greeted by her friends, but it was hardly to be compared with the feeling now shown toward Mrs. Blackett" (90). The narrative explicitly identifies Mrs. Blackett as the main source of both Mrs. Todd's goodness and her power. Elijah Tilley makes the direct link between Mrs. Todd's being "the best o' women" and her mother, saying of Mrs. Todd, "there ain't a better hearted woman in the State o' Maine. I've known her from a girl. She's had the best o' mothers" (127).

But if Mrs. Todd's big heart is inherited from her mother, Jewett is quite emphatic in representing Mrs. Todd's maternal skills as figurative rather than literal: Almira Todd is a widow who is literally childless but who nurtures the narrator and the community through both her conversation and her role as herbalist. Hence, her status as double of Mrs. Blackett operates through her incorporation of the maternal role in purely figurative terms. Jewett goes to great lengths to identify Mrs. Todd's power and emotional empathy as inherited from a variety of women, deriving from the larger community as well as from Mrs. Blackett. Listening to Mrs. Todd talk to "two stout, hard-worked women from the farm" who are her customers (8), for instance, the narrator observes that the two "seemed to give much from their own store of therapeutic learning. I became aware of the school in which my landlady had strengthened her natural gift" (9). Similarly, in comforting the lonely French woman who is the title character of "The Foreigner," Mrs. Todd extends to the woman a sense of community; in return the French woman shares with Mrs. Todd her knowledge of herbs, one source of Mrs. Todd's power, and teaches her the more prosaic arts of cookery and mushroom-gathering as well. By using motherhood as a discursive space rather than a biological limit, then, Jewett can give Mrs. Todd the positive values associated with the maternal without having to reduce her to a single female location. The maternal thus becomes only one of several narrative spaces occupied by Mrs. Todd rather than, as with Mrs. Blackett, her sole identity.[35]

One means by which Jewett formulates this relationship between Mrs. Todd and the maternal is a quite self-conscious emphasis on narrative representation in her depiction of Mrs. Todd, whom the narrator both describes as an individual woman and represents as a symbol, an archetype of strong, independent, and artistically stylized women. Mrs. Todd is not merely maternal in terms of her caretaking of the community, she is also both linked to the power of mothers and simultaneously distanced from the category of literal mother by the aesthetic terms in which the narrator describes her. The narrator transforms Mrs. Todd into a mythic woman, making her hugely powerful and detaching her from local time and history, constructing her as a powerful monument, and then standing in awe of her as a result. Physically, Mrs. Todd is imaged over and over as a large woman; strong and stately, she is "grand and architectural, like a *caryatide*" (30). Aligned here with cultural artifacts and spaces, she is also aligned with timeless forces of nature and through them to supernatural powers. As an herbalist, she summons the scent of herbs by her very footsteps: treading upon an herb in her garden, she makes "its fragrant presence known with all the rest. Being a very large person, her full skirts brushed and bent almost every slender stalk that her feet missed" (3). Similarly, she has special powers over the weather: we are told that before any great excursion Mrs. Todd "first came to an understanding with the primal forces of nature" (83). The narrative goes so far as to give her force enough to create her own weather. At one point the narrator notes, "our large hostess returned to the little room with a mist about her from standing long in the wet doorway, and the sudden draught of her coming beat out the smoke and flame from the Franklin stove" (73). At another point, sailing impatiently to reach Green Island and her mother, Mrs. Todd, we are told, "gave an impatient look up at the gaff and the leech of the little sail, and twitched the sheet as if she urged the wind like a horse. There came at once a fresh gust, and we seemed to have doubled our speed" (35). Elsewhere her herbal practices rouse "a dim sense and remembrance of something in the forgotten past . . . mystic rites . . . some occult knowledge" (3–4). The narrative describes Mrs. Todd brewing compounds in a "simmering caldron" (4, 62), and the narrator suspects that Mrs. Todd's herb garden may hold magical cures to "love and hate and jealousy and adverse winds at sea" (4) as well as the more mundane physical ills.[36]

Mrs. Todd is linked by the narrator not merely to natural and fairy-tale sorts of powers. She is also imaged more specifically in terms of historical, mythological figures of powerful women, a metaphorization that both increases her power and her distance from the merely human. A "huge sibyl" (8), Mrs. Todd speaks "like the oracle that she was" (85). In the course of the book she is compared to both Medea (220) and to "a large figure of Victory" (40). Lest all this metaphoric transformation render Mrs. Todd frighteningly monumental, however, the narrator also figures her friend as the embodiment of a distinctly human spirit of human emotions. After telling the narrator the story of her marriage to one man and her love for another, both now gone, Mrs. Todd comes to stand for a common soul of humanity:

She looked away from me, and presently rose and went off by herself. There was something lonely and solitary about her great determined shape. She might have been Antigone alone on the Theban plain. It is not often given us in a noisy world to come to the places of great grief and silence. An absolute archaic grief possessed this country-woman; she seemed like a renewal of some historic soul, with her sorrows and the remoteness of a daily life busied with rustic simplicities and the scents of primeval herbs. (49)

Mrs. Todd thus occupies a universalized and a particularized position of power, emotion, and desire at once, detached from the category of human mother and imaged by the narrator as both a figure of mythic power and her friend the country herbalist. That she is imaged as intensely alone may be the price to be paid by a woman at this historical moment for standing as an individualized figure of power.

Nevertheless, if she registers as alone in the terms of dominant culture, she is not alone here if read in terms of a Boston marriage, for while this mythic status elevates Mrs. Todd above the limitations of the mortal maternal, it also serves as a rhetorical device allowing the narrator a means of connection with Mrs. Todd. At one point, when she consults the coals of the fire for "some augury," Mrs. Todd is described by the narrator as looking "like an old prophetess as she sat there with the firelight shining on her strong face; she was posed for some great painter. The woman with the cat was as unconscious and as mysterious as any sibyl of the Sistine Chapel" (183). Passages like this one metaphorize Mrs. Todd into a woman with mythical and magical powers, linking her to larger forces of insight and vision, natural and supernatural powers of healing and knowledge, but at the same time they grant the narrator a certain artistic or narrative power of her own and through that power, a connection to Mrs. Todd. For if Mrs. Todd is "posed" waiting to be represented, surely the metaphoric painter of the scene is the narrator, whose representation might be read as one more articulation of her desire for Mrs. Todd. Echoing Florence Converse's depiction of writing's role in the relationship of her two heroines, such a tableau suggests the complicated interplay of power and desire between the narrator and Mrs. Todd, as the power and status of one woman furnishes the subject matter of the other's artistic production, a production that is itself a source of power and pleasure.

Artistic production in the form of writing in this text serves both as a source of difference between the narrator and Mrs. Todd and as a link between them, a bond in the Boston marriage as well as a means by which the narrator as outsider is enabled to join the Dunnet Landing community embodied by Mrs. Todd. On the one hand, the narrator's status as writer thematizes her status as outsider. This happens literally on the level of plot: recalling a long piece of writing she must do, for instance, the narrator says "unkind words of withdrawal to Mrs. Todd" and fleeing the "further temptation" of a "friendly gossip," escapes Mrs. Todd's house and rents herself the vacant schoolhouse in which to work. This is a move that, she notes, "had now made myself and my friends remember that I did not really belong to Dunnet Landing" (7, 9, 8, 15). More figuratively, writing differentiates the narrator from a community that is built in part on an oral tradition of storytelling. The narrator twice notes that talk is woman's province: neither the four fishermen friends nor William talk (114, 144), while Elijah Tilley, who has given up the wandering seaman role for that of a domestic watcher (a role here gendered female), speaks only of his dead wife.[37] The women, in contrast, build their community through tales told of friends and kin, with stories serving as a positive force, a comfort to distract one from fears of a storm (as in the framing of Joanna's tale or "The Foreigner") and a means of connection.[38]

Writing becomes the structural means not only of differentiating the narrator from Mrs. Todd but also, on the other hand, of linking the two women. Figuratively, while the narrator leaves Mrs. Todd in order to write, she produces the narrative of *The Country of the Pointed Firs*, thus becoming a storyteller of sorts herself. This link also happens spatially: the narrator is forced to leave Mrs. Todd's house in order to write about her—leaving either for the day (to go to the schoolhouse) or for the season (to return to the city). But although she leaves, she also returns to Mrs. Todd to gather more subject matter. The use of writing here, like the tableau above, might be seen to emblematize the historical Boston marriage's ability to serve as a source of power and encouragement (particularly in the professional careers) for its members. It also replicates that structure's presumption of the privilege that allows the mobility of the narrator/writer.[39]

The image of the Boston marriage at the heart of female community—both literally, in Jewett's life, and figuratively, in *The Country of the Pointed Firs'* structure—is a rosy one when viewed from a perspective that privileges the happy inclusion of such a community's members, a perspective arising from the notion of a "women's culture" that is constituted by a transcendent unity based on gender. Although it does radically challenge patriarchal power by giving over power to women, this perspective contains a serious blind spot. The notion of a women's community based on a universalized understanding of gender violently erases or suppresses real and salient differences among women. Ultimately, then, it is not being a "woman" that is the real criteria for inclusion but rather being a very particular kind of woman. Viewed from this perspective, this notion of female community remains deeply conservative, premised on exclusion as much as inclusion. Turning specifically to the Boston marriage, we can see this question of inclusion/exclusion at issue, both historically and consequently within *The Country of the Pointed Firs*.

Historically, the Boston marriage was the province of middle-class to upper-class, usually white women who were economically and racially privileged, generally educated, and cultured. As a structure it is thus based on sameness—both within the relationship, where the partners were of the same sex, and within the broader terms of dominant culture, where the partners, in general, belonged to the cultural elite, sharing its privilege and conforming in many ways to its norms. While other variables of difference—generational, geographical—existed, they were subsumed within this general rubric of sameness, a sameness that produced the Boston marriage's simultaneous location within high culture and "women's culture." Hence, as a structural model the Boston marriage offers only a limited space for difference. In this section I have traced the narrative benefits offered to members of a community based on the model of the Boston marriage: a flexibility and multiplicity of roles providing a kind of freedom, play, and pleasure. In the next section I will turn from these benefits to the limits of the model, limits that become clear in Jewett's application of this model not to the realm of the purely private or familial in *The Country of the Pointed Firs*—where it offers the characters' flexibility and multiple locations—but rather in her application of it to the connected and overlapping realm of the regional and national. Here Jewett's negotiation of difference in community reveals the intrinsic, problematic exclusivity of the Boston marriage model. Where the model allows for innovation and play on the individual level, it turns conservative when applied to the more abstract level of region and nation, as Jewett draws careful lines, both breaking and establishing boundaries in a narrow delineation of just how much difference is too much for her community/family clan/region/nation to accept.

Writing Difference

Susan Gillman observes that conventional readings of regionalism assume that "regionalists respond to national conflict—whether over old sectional and racial divisions or new ethnic and economic tensions—by turning their backs on it" (101), an assumption she and other recent critics have contested in terms of Jewett. Indeed, while Jewett's narrative as a whole celebrates community based on sameness, it also selectively engages the broader national conflicts arising in Jewett's day out of issues of difference. These issues are particularly at stake in the text's representation of Dunnet Landing's place in an international shipping industry, as well as in the narrative emphasis on race and "blood" present in the depiction of the Bowden family reunion and elsewhere. The region emerges here—as in the other texts under consideration in this study—not as an insulated pastoral island of the past but rather as an area deeply imbricated in larger national questions.

Jewett represents region consistently located in relation to transnational and imperial interests, both in commercial and leisure arenas. As June Howard puts it, "Jewett is deeply and systematically concerned with circuits of communication and transportation. . . . She describes a shift from a system of global interconnections through shipping to one in which the relationship between the village and other parts of the world is mediated by the metropolis" ("Introduction" 26). This shift has ramifications on a number of levels in the narrative. It accounts, firstly, for the text's representation of Dunnet Landing as suffering a loss of prestige, a loss that critics have read as evidence of a regionalist celebration of the past. Jewett represents the shipping industry—gone by Jewett's day and by the narrative present of *The Country of the Pointed Firs*—as having had a positive impact on the world of Dunnet Landing, both because it prevented a provincialism in the inhabitants and because it afforded everyone, even women, more freedom and mobility. Jewett makes this point repeatedly in the course of the text and from a variety of characters' points of view. Captain Littlepage articulates the position most fully, telling the narrator,

a community narrows down and grows dreadful ignorant when it is shut up to its own affairs, and gets no knowledge of the outside world except from a cheap, unprincipled newspaper. In the old days, a good part o' the best men here knew a hundred ports and something of the way folks lived in them. They saw the world for themselves, and like's not their wives and children saw it with them . . . they were some acquainted with foreign lands an' their laws, and could see outside the battle for town clerk here in Dunnet; they got some sense o' proportion. . . . Shipping's a terrible loss to this part o' New England from a social point o' view, ma'am. (20)

He goes on to contend that "there's nothing to take the place of shipping in a place like ours. . . . No, when folks left home in the old days they left it to some purpose, and when they got home they stayed there and had some pride in it" (21).[40] Littlepage's comments exemplify the intertwining of commercial and cultural privilege that results from shipping. Here shipping provides the opportunity for travel and a broader world view, a sense of "proportion";[41] simultaneously, it reinforces a class-privileged perspective by teaching better judgment than the "cheap, unprincipled" newspaper and implicitly by bolstering the "taste" that enables people to take "pride" in the local at the expense of the "foreign." A seafarer's knowledge of the "foreign" is put in relation here to his knowledge of the village or the region, linking the regional to, rather than isolating it from, the national and international.

A related means by which the local region is represented as confronting various Others is through incorporating them: the characters' possession of tea-caddies from Tobago and china from Bordeaux, for instance, signals not simply worldwide commercial interchange but also cultural appropriation (51; 124). This appropriation of the foreign outside by a national inside (the local inhabitants of Dunnet Landing) is paralleled in the narrative on an intranational level by the narrator's appropriation of Dunnet Landing. As a tourist the narrator represents a combination of regional and class difference and privilege: she is, recall, a privileged outsider who has discovered Dunnet Landing "in the course of a yachting cruise" (2). Richard Brodhead has detailed regionalism's link to "an elite need for the primitive made available as leisure outlet" (132) as well as the way regionalist fiction like Jewett's fed the leisure class's "cultural or cross-cultural acquisitiveness" (133). He reads regionalist fiction as a kind of "exclusion mechanism or social eraser, an agency for purging the world of immigrants to restore homogeneous community" so that the region becomes "a *haven* for readers, a space of safety constructed against an excluded threat" (136). Similarly, Sherman links the regional with tourism, but also introduces a link to gendered spheres, arguing that "for tourists escaping the rigors of city life, towns like South Berwick and York functioned as analogues to the domestic sphere, 'havens in a heartless world.' Here, just as in the home, one could find the values of an agrarian past, the continuity of tradition, and perhaps the strategies of a disenfranchised populace eager to 'influence' the monied and powerful out of a dollar" (49). In these terms region becomes the antidote to the "threat" of difference, for insofar as it represents economic or regional difference to the tourist—it is the vacation periphery, not the urban center—it embodies a difference that can be incorporated or possessed, made one's own. It thus becomes a space where difference is erased and privilege—of the mobility and money of the tourist and/or the male inhabitant of the public sphere—is central but naturalized. Here the regional response to difference draws on the Boston marriage model's similar response, in which the privileged status of the members is the elided but utterly necessary precondition of the pleasures and flexibility provided by membership.

While the region itself functions here as homogenized margin for the tourist in general and at least to some extent for the book's reader and its narrator in particular, within the narrative, other forms of difference exist within the region, where they are handled in several ways. If slight, internal regional difference is incorporated into the community; if of greater degree, it is either located safely in the past or attributed outsider status.

Mrs. Fosdick and Mrs. Todd discuss this issue explicitly. Mrs. Fosdick contends, "how times have changed; how few seafarin' families there are left! What a lot o' queer folks there used to be about here, anyway, when we was young, Almiry. Everybody's just like everybody else, now; nobody to laugh about, and nobody to cry about," to which Mrs. Todd responds, "there was more energy then, and in some the energy took a singular turn. In these days the young folks is all copy-cats, 'fraid to death they won't be all just alike" (64). The "queer" one they go on to discuss is Joanna, a recluse whose story occurs in the past time of the narrative, but the narrator thinks of both Captain Littlepage and William, to whom we might add both Elijah Tilley and Santin Bowden, as examples of what Sandra Zagarell calls the "Dunnet eccentrics" (47). Susan Gillman reads William and Elijah Tilley's "gender reversal or duality" as making them unacceptable to the Dunnet Landing community (110), but I would argue that their feminization along with Littlepage and Bowden's emasculation (each a parody of masculinity, of the adventurous or military man, respectively) renders these men's difference nonthreatening in the present. Indeed, in a world modeled on female relations, these men fit in better because of their gender reversal. Their gender "difference" paradoxically brings them closer to the community norm.

Joanna's reclusiveness, in contrast, separates her from a model of female community; hence, her story is assimilable only when located in the past. Similar to this treatment of deviant gender expression, the narrative confronts racial or ethnic difference either by temporally displacing it or by marking it as Other, outside of the community. There are traces of the disappeared Indians, for instance, but only traces: one of Mrs. Todd's herbal potions is called "the Indian remedy," while Shell-heap Island is covered with Indian "stone tools" (4, 63). Moreover, a conventional use of a rhetoric of savagery links these local but now gone Indian Others to an extranational set of Others, further linking this not-at-all isolated region to the broader national undertaking of imperialism (as well as the exoticizing rhetoric of tourism). Mrs. Fosdick, Mrs. Todd's friend, comments of Shell-heap Island,

Twas 'counted a great place in old Indian times; you can pick up their stone tools 'most any time if you hunt about. . . . Yes, I remember when they used to tell queer stories about Shell-heap Island. Some said 'twas a great bangeing-place for the Indians, and a old chief resided there once that ruled the winds; and others said they'd always heard that once the Indians come down from up country an' left a captive there without any bo't, an' 'twas too far to swim across to Black Island, so called, an' he lived there till he perished. (63)

While this description links the Indians to both magic and cruelty, Mrs. Todd offers a slightly different interpretation, producing the following interchange between the two women:

> "there was Indians—you can see their shell-heap that named the island; and I've heard myself that 'twas one o' their cannibal places, but I never could believe it. There never was no cannibals on the coast o' Maine. All the Indians o' these regions are tame-looking folks."
>
> "Sakes alive, yes!" exclaimed Mrs. Fosdick. "Ought to see them painted savages I've seen when I was young out in the South Sea Islands! That was time for folks to travel, 'way back in the old whalin' days!" (64)

Mrs. Fosdick's comment, ranking the "savagery" of local and foreign Others, points to the way that the travel of "old whalin' days" produced a broader world vision, but one here focused through an imperialist lens. It also locates "the Indians o' these regions" as American in comparison to the South Sea Island "Indians," suggesting that the salient difference here is nationality rather than race and implying that local difference is defined in part against transnational difference.

Mrs. Todd's defense of the Indians, along with the narrative's aligning her with them both through her use of "the Indian remedy" and through her ability to control the winds like "the old chief" of Shell-heap Island, complicates her positioning in the narrative and suggests the possibility that Mrs. Todd figures as a source of community in part because she functions as a mediator of difference. Karen Oakes reads Mrs. Todd as "a person whose heritage is (at least metaphorically) mixed-blood, for she possesses the herbal skill not only of her colonial counterparts but of her Indian predecessors" (157), a claim that curiously and seemingly unironically rehearses a discourse of blood current in Jewett's day in order to implicitly align Mrs. Todd with sensitive appreciation of indigenous knowledge (rather than, say, simple appropriation of it). Referring to the eponymous protagonist of "The Foreigner," she goes on to align Mrs. Todd with "a woman who parallels the figure of the Indian outsider, a French woman from Jamaica who significantly can't speak Maine and who horrifies her sober and asexual counterparts by singing and dancing in the meeting-house vestry in a shockingly 'natural' manner" (158). While Oakes's formulation comes close to collapsing all narrative others, she does call attention to Mrs. Todd's support of the "foreign" Mrs. Tolland. But support in what terms?

"The Foreigner," while not part of the narrative proper, is a story that augments our understanding of *The Country of the Pointed Firs* in that it offers an extended discussion of one treatment of difference in Dunnet

Landing. Indeed, its narrative location might be said to enact *The Country of the Pointed Firs*'s treatment of difference in general: the foreigner cannot be made part of the community of the main narrative, but its presence at the edges of the text is utterly necessary to limn that border. The core story revolves around Mrs. Tolland's alienation in the Dunnet Landing community, where she has been brought like a foreign souvenir by a local sea-captain, who marries her after rescuing her from a bar brawl in Jamaica.[42] Mrs. Tolland's "difference"—she is Catholic and French, speaks little English, and observes noticeably non-Puritan gender standards—causes the village, led by Mari' Harris, to reject her. This in turn causes Mrs. Blackett, and through her Mrs. Todd, to come to her defense. The story thematizes mothers as the solution for foreignness: after "a sight o' prejudice arose," Mrs. Blackett reaches out to Mrs. Tolland and then orders her own daughter to do the same, saying, "I want you to neighbor with that poor lonesome creatur'. . . . She's a stranger in a strange land, . . . I want you to make her have a sense that somebody feels kind to her. . . . What consequence is . . . your comfort or mine, beside letting a foreign person an' a stranger feel so desolate. . . . Think if 'twas you in a foreign land!" (169). This moment of maternal power exercised to bring a woman into community is echoed at the story's close, when the dying Mrs. Tolland and Mrs. Todd see the ghost of Mrs. Tolland's mother who watches over her daughter, waiting, with "a kind of expectin' look," for her death (186). When the dying woman asks Mrs. Todd if she has seen the ghost, Mrs. Todd recounts her response: "I says, '*Yes, dear, I did; you ain't never goin' to feel strange an' lonesome no more.*' An' then in a few quiet minutes 'twas all over. I felt they'd gone away together" (186 emphasis in original). The intervention of the mother makes one not strange, not foreign, not isolated; maternal outreach—literally embodied by Mrs. Blackett and Mrs. Tolland's mother and figuratively represented by Mrs. Todd—becomes a model of community formation in an image that echoes conventional uses of a trope of the nation as mother country.

Yet, this model of the maternal, in its own right and as an aspect of the Boston marriage, retains its limits: even as Mrs. Tolland's story remains structurally outside the collection proper, years after the woman's death, Mrs. Todd still views Mrs. Tolland as an outsider, noting, "yes, there was something very strange about her" and stating definitively, "she come a foreigner and she went a foreigner, and never was anything but a stranger among our folks" (171; 170). Ultimately, it is only death that can make her no longer "strange": she must return literally to her own mother/country, for her Frenchness prevents her from ever fully crossing the na-

tional border that limns the local community. Sarah Way Sherman's reading of this story offers another formulation of Jewett's complicated formulation of the lines of inclusion and exclusion. Sherman asserts that "in
Mari' Harris and Mrs. Blackett we have two poles of Dunnet Landing's
culture. The first is ethnocentric. Mari' Harris cannot imagine other roads
to the New Jerusalem besides her own. . . . But in Mrs. Blackett there is a
tolerance born of the seafarer's life" (240). Sherman's comment seems to
me to capture perfectly the limits of Jewett's community: the most open
version of meeting difference here is expressed through a mother's "tolerance." Tolerance, of course, implies the acceptance by the open-minded
and forbearing of a thing that is somehow wrong or inferior, a position
implied, for instance, in Mrs. Todd's comment, "I always thought Mis'
Tolland was good-looking, though she had, as was reasonable, a sort of
foreign cast, and she spoke a very broken English, no better than a child"
(168).[43] Although the story does, as Sherman notes, represent Mari' Harris's position as narrow-minded and exclusionary, *The Country of the
Pointed Firs* as a whole demonstrates precisely that attitude toward Harris herself. Mrs. Todd and others criticize her housekeeping and refer to
her as "that Mari' Harris," while the narrator describes her as "a very
common-place, inelegant person" (14, 17). The narrative treatment of
both Mrs. Tolland and Mari' Harris thus reveals the limits of community
in Jewett's text. As in the Boston marriage model, in Jewett's vision of female community certain forms of difference—in these cases, class and national—disqualify a woman from membership. The Boston marriage
model thus offers an alternate but not a utopian model of community, as
it continues to draw on the structure of exclusion that undergirds the
family model of community/nation.

The narrative most explicitly locates Mari' Harris as an outsider at the
Bowden family reunion, the scene of the text's most definitive drawing of
borders. The reunion, through its discussion of the French Norman
"blood" of Mrs. Todd's extended family, the Bowdens, brings together
family, regional, and national issues of inclusion and exclusion, drawing,
as Susan Gillman points out, on a dominant American discourse of race,
"the popular language blending eugenics and evolution that characterized
a wide range of efforts to conceptualize 'race' and nation . . . in the late
nineteenth century" (111). It is here, amongst a representation of family
as clan, that Jewett most explicitly displays a racist and ethnocentric
ranking of humanity, what Ferman Bishop calls "an aristocratic emphasis
upon the racial inequalities of mankind" (249).[44] It is also here that we
can see most clearly the ways in which the Boston marriage's multiple and

overlapping relations structure Jewett's representation of regional, national, and transnational relations.

At the Bowden reunion the model of Boston marriage as the core of women's community becomes the model for the family as well, in terms of both the Boston marriage's inclusivity and its exclusivity. The power of women's relationships and women's ability to forge relationships that come to constitute first family and then community is thematized at this reunion. Although men are neither feminized nor written out, they are largely ignored, forming a backdrop for the women, who constitute the heart of the family. Mrs. Blackett is here again the agent of community, drawing, for instance, a stranger into the family circle, commenting "I wish we'd asked her name. She's a stranger, and I want to help make it pleasant for all such." Even the old Bowden house is described as a "motherly brown hen waiting for the flock that came straying toward it from every direction" (91, 97). Importantly, it is at the reunion that the narrator is drawn into Mrs. Todd's family, for as a large family gathering the reunion also stands as a sort of symbolic wedding for the narrator and Mrs. Todd. The narrator comments that on her arrival at the reunion, by virtue of accompanying Mrs. Todd and Mrs. Blackett, she immediately "felt like an adopted Bowden in this happy moment" (99) and then repeats herself by saying at the end of the day "I came near to feeling like a true Bowden" (110). Figuratively, then, her Boston marriage provides her membership in this clan. The narrative goes on to universalize this family, as the narrator claims, "we were no more a New England family celebrating its own existence and simple progress; we carried the tokens and inheritance of all such households from which this has descended, and were only the latest of our line" (100). Community comes thus to mean a universalized and ahistorical vision of an inclusive American family, an image descended from the universalized and ahistorical notion of a women's culture that the Boston marriage suggests.

Although this version of the family stresses inclusiveness, this family clan also operates, as Zagarell has detailed, as a model of exclusiveness, through Jewett's use of the language of hereditary theory in her emphasis on the French Norman roots of the family. Mrs. Todd notes that her family "came of very high folks in France" (102), while the narrator takes note of

the curiously French type of face which prevailed in this rustic company. I had said to myself before that Mrs. Blackett was plainly of French descent, in both her appearance and her charming gifts, but this is not surprising when one has learned how large a proportion of the early settlers on this northern coast of New

England were of Huguenot blood, and that it is the Norman Englishman, not the Saxon, who goes adventuring to a new world. (101–2)[45]

This passage is typical in its conflation of physical and cultural traits, as well as the assumption that both are passed through family lines.[46] It is also typical in its implicit celebration of imperialist expansion, a celebration already demonstrated in Jewett's depiction of the seafaring life.[47] But what is most significant here is the intertwining of regional and national. For the region—Maine—occupies the "northern coast" not simply of New England but of the nation as well; that is, Maine as a region is also one of the borderlands of the United States, so that the state border is simultaneously the national border. Further, the fact that Maine borders in part on Quebec means that national difference here intersects with cultural/ethnic/linguistic difference. Unlike authors such as Florence Converse, then, who will use the region as a straightforward synecdoche of the nation, Jewett defines region in complicated and overlapping relation to the national and international arenas, both defining of and defined by them.

Within these shifting borders it becomes clear that just as not every woman can be a member of the community, not everyone can be a member of the family clan and the nation. If some forms of difference, to borrow Sherman's formulation, can only be tolerated in the past—Joanna, the Indians—some forms cannot be tolerated at all: Jewett's family/nation does not have room for at least some racial Others. It is here that the figure of Mari' Harris returns to prominence, as the narrative locates her as one of the unassimilable "foreign" or "strange." Immediately following Mrs. Todd's comment that "strange folks has got to have strange ways," an insider, a "sister," marks Mari' Harris—later referred to as a "sordid creatur'" (103)—as outsider by commenting, "I always did think Mari' Harris resembled a Chinee'" (103)—the figure of the very limit of the American nation, as I will discuss in Chapter Six.[48] Jewett goes on to make explicit this definition of family as dependent on race and nation, as the narrator comments,

Perhaps it is the great national anniversaries which our country has lately kept, and the soldiers' meetings that take place everywhere, which have made reunions of every sort the fashion . . . I fancied that old feuds had been overlooked, and the old saying that blood is thicker than water had again proved itself true. . . . Clannishness is an instinct of the heart,—it is more than a birthright, or a custom; and lesser rights were forgotten in the claim to a common inheritance. (110)

In this passage we slide from family to clan to nation, with the result that, as Zagarell so insightfully notes, "citizenship, by implication, is natural and inborn; it is endowed by an organic quality, 'instinct,' not by 'birth-right or custom.' As the analogies and equations multiply, the Dunnet family becomes the essence of the American nation, and what is truly American seems to be Anglo-Norman" (46). The family thus becomes both universal and limited, inclusive and exclusive.

I would suggest that this cluster of associations can be tracked back not simply to the family but to women as the core of the family and then, more specifically, to the structural model of the Boston marriage, a model of sameness based here in white, upper-class privilege but simultaneously containing multiple and reconfigured relations among its parts. In an early reference to the reunion the narrator comments, "when, at long intervals, the altars to patriotism, to friendship, to the ties of kindred, are reared in our familiar fields, then the fires glow, the flames come up as if from the inexhaustible burning heart of the earth; the primal fires break through the granite dust in which our souls are set. Each heart is warm and every face shines with the ancient light. Such a day as this has transfiguring powers" (96). This statement, with its altars dedicated to friendship, family, and nation, not only links these three but literally grounds them in re-gion: the "earth" and "dust" of New England. Similarly, Jewett's con-temporary Alice Brown, in a review of *The Country of the Pointed Firs*, grounds the text's representation of regional in the national, asserting that the "pointed firs have their roots in the ground of national being" (37) and then goes on to suggest a complicated set of associations that the text sets forth, stating, "the Reunion indeed bears a larger significance than its name. It stirs in us the dormant clan-spirit; we understand ancestor-worship, the continuity of being . . . you throb like them with pride of race, you acquiesce willingly in the sweet, loyal usages of domesticity" (38). This comment, bringing together evolutionary discourse with gen-dered spheres, evokes an image in which proper white ladies serve as the guarantors of American values. Put another way, it suggests, as Elizabeth Ammons has argued, that the reunion celebrates both a "rural matrifocal community in which women . . . have real power and status" and "the triumphant colonization of Indian land by white people of British and Norman ancestry" (92).

In its yoking of these two, Brown's comment brings us back to the Boston marriage and its ability to figure a complex variety of relations—both radical and conservative—in *The Country of the Pointed Firs*. If the rural and urban spheres of the novel can be read as gendered female and male, and if the female rural is a "haven" for the urban vacationer, thus linking this gendering of spheres to the thematization of class privilege, then the narrator, a writer inhabiting both spheres, embodies the flexibility and privilege that the Boston marriage afforded its members, and embodies the access it provided to both region and center, region and nation. In this she resembles Jewett herself, a writer who was, as Richard Brodhead puts it, "a Maine resident since renaturalized as a city person" (154) and who enjoyed through her Boston marriage a new flexibility of roles for women, but a flexibility grounded in her class and racial privilege. Susan Gillman argues that "*Country* creates and then debates conflicting images of the past in order to critique new social and sexual relations emerging in the present. Among these new arrangements would be not only the threats posed by domestic immigration and global expansion, but also the possibilities opened up (and closed) by the New Woman" (115). The figure of the Boston marriage, with its simultaneous challenge to gender roles and rehearsal of established race and class hierarchies, allows Jewett to offer such a critique within the limits of her world. On the level of the plot itself, where a woman's challenge to conventional gendered behavior is tolerable only if contained in the past—consider Mrs. Fosdick's stint in trousers as a child (61) or Joanna's desire to be "free" (65)—there is no overt place for the representation of a Boston marriage. For that we must turn elsewhere, as the next chapter turns to Florence Converse's explicit representation in *Diana Victrix*. But read in more figurative terms, *The Country of the Pointed Firs* does tell a story of a Boston marriage, and the Boston marriage, when used as an interpretive model, explains the story of two women who stand in multiple relation to each other, whose flexible and shifting roles constitute their relationship. It can also explain Jewett's simultaneous radical and conservative reconfiguring and rehearsing of the borders of and relations among community, region, and nation. The Boston marriage stands here as an alternate model of the nation, a model with severe limits but one in which women, through their flexible roles and pursuit of pleasure, can reach out to some small forms of difference, accommodating them slightly, although ultimately unsuccessfully. As a result this model is significant even as it fails, evidence of one writer's effort, from within the limits of her privilege, to recast the terms of national identity by including the homosocial in that identity. Ironically, the critical tradition that has kept Jewett a part of American literature has done so in part by thwarting that effort, by deporting the Boston marriage from the *The Country of the Pointed Firs*.

2 "But Some Times . . . I Don't Marry,—Even in Books"

BOSTON MARRIAGES, CREOLES, AND
THE FUTURE OF THE NATION

> She was a New England woman and a woman's woman.
> —*Diana Victrix*

"A Genuine, Though Not Precisely Sexual, Preference for Women Over Men"

What might it have meant to be a New England woman and a woman's woman in the 1890s? And what intimate relation between the two does the conjunction above suggest? It has become clear that the decades surrounding the turn of the century saw the emergence of the modern identity category of the "lesbian" through a discourse played out everywhere from the pages of scientific journals to those of popular newspapers. But although the embodied version of what Esther Newton so aptly dubbed "the mythic, mannish lesbian" could be found by the 1920s from Berlin to San Francisco, the discourse that produced her was a contested and contradictory one, emerging at varying rates in various places, encountering various counterdiscourses along the way, and taking varying forms that intersected and overlapped with other cultural discourses. Lisa Duggan suggests that identity formation is "a historical process of contested narration, a process in which contrasting 'stories' of the self and others—stories of difference—are told, appropriated, and retold as stories of location in the social work of structured inequalities" (793). This is certainly true of the making of the modern lesbian, whose cultural narration was a product of many and varied voices (voices of individual women as well as voices within the medical system, the legal system, and the press) engaged in a debate that drew both on older models of female friendship and newer sexological and psychological models of "inversion" and "arrested development."

At the same time, this varied and widespread narrative shaped and was shaped by historically specific discourses of race, class, region, and nation. The discourse around inversion and homosexuality intersected with American racial discourse and class debates in the fields of degeneration theory and eugenics, while homosexuality as "abnormal" came more and more to define by opposition not only a sexual norm but also an American norm centered on heterosexual family life.[1] Homosexuality thus became one of the formative cultural narratives of turn-of-the-century America, helping to establish the parameters of "American" identity even as it was being categorized deviant and homosexuals were increasingly being represented as outside the "normal" American family. It is within this context that I situate Florence Converse's *Diana Victrix* (1897) and its representation of a Boston marriage. Written by a woman who was herself a part of a Boston marriage, the novel offers a fictional space for the voicing of the "woman's woman"'s own story. Not surprisingly, this story is in conversation with competing cultural narratives of female "inversion," rejecting, reworking, and even at points replicating them. What *is* surprising is that Converse's representation of the Boston marriage between Enid Spenser and Sylvia Bennett posits modern sexual identity as constructed from within regional and national identities and refigures a North-South reunification plot as the story of two Northern "spinsters" who embody the promise of the nation's future. Class and race specific, Converse's portrait of a marriage limns a "woman's woman" who is not only not deviant, but is in fact utterly and undilutedly "American," the natural outgrowth of dominant American ideologies of independence, productivity, and self-reliance. As the embodiment of these American values, the women of the Boston marriage provide a Yankee narrative that locates white middle-class female-female relationships comfortably within mainstream American culture.

Converse was writing at a particularly significant moment in the history of sexuality, "deviant" and otherwise, a moment when old and new models of sexuality came into conflict. As I discussed in Chapter 1, Boston marriages enjoyed a measure of social approval in middle-class and upper-middle-class contexts of the end of the century, sanctioned by dominant culture and seen as a supportive personal relationship by the women involved in them. Converse's Boston marriage to Wellesley professor Vida Scudder, for instance, allowed figurative room for both their careers while also allowing literal room in their home, as Helen Horowitz notes, for the expanded female community of Scudder, Converse, and both their mothers (188). The Boston marriage, as typified here, was thus

seen as fostering women's entrance into the public sphere, usually in social reform careers, while at the same time reconfiguring her private
sphere by challenging both older models of mother-daughter female relations and the older tendency of "separate spheres" ideology to encourage
a split between domestic and public life.[2]

Concurrently, in the last quarter of the century, the discourses of sexology and psychoanalysis began to compete with these benevolent interpretations of such relationships as female friendships, smashes, and
Boston marriages. In both America and England, in media spectacles as
well as legal battles (the most famous of which was Britain's Oscar Wilde
trial), and their attendant public discourse/scandal, the medical categories
of female inversion and homosexuality vied with the older historical models of (working-class) passing women and (middle-class) female friendships[3] in what George Chauncey has described as "the intellectual confusion and anachronism of the period . . . the inconsistencies and fluctua-
tions in explanations offered for inversion and homosexuality. . . . "
(102–3). Vicinus, Horowitz, and others have pointed out that although
Boston marriages and passing women can be found into the twentieth
century, starting in the 1870s and coming into full force by the 1890s, the
sexologists, most notably Havelock Ellis and Richard von Krafft-Ebing,
were articulating an alternate cultural narrative that would eventually
pathologize the spectrum of erotically charged female-female relationships, resulting in the categories of the invert and the homosexual.[4]

Two features mark the work of both Ellis and Krafft-Ebing as in conflict with earlier conceptualizations of female-female relationships. The
first is precisely the pathologizing of them. Sexological discourse located
female-female desire as outside of dominant heterosexual cultural structures rather than as the logical extension of the ideology of separate
spheres. Here the medical discourse was responding, in the face of widespread challenges by both British and American women to prescribed
gender roles, to the political rather than to the sexual or erotic ramifications of female-female relations. As many critics have noted, the descriptions that the sexologists offered as evidence of their case studies' deviance had more to do with these "patients'" social behavior than with
their alleged innate physiological differences.[5] Ellis, for instance, links a
rise in homosexuality to the influence of the women's emancipation
movement (147) as well as single-sex education systems (192). This pathologizing is thus clearly symptomatic of a larger cultural effort to police female behavior at a moment when it was in a state of threatening
flux.

Sexological (and later psychoanalytic) discourse—as well as the popular discourse it both reflected and helped shape[6]—also explicitly eroticized female-female relations, offering—in opposition to the image of the two genteel, sexless spinsters spiritually bonded—the model of active and passive "inverts." This model was patterned on what Chauncey has labeled the "heterosexual paradigm" (94): an assumption that the only way a woman could erotically love another woman was through a relationship in which one of the women occupied the structural position of the man. Ellis, for instance, in distinguishing between two sorts of inverted women, codes the active or congenital (one might almost say "real") invert male, while coding the passive or pseudo invert female:

A class of women to be first mentioned, a class in which homosexuality, while fairly distinct, is only slightly marked, is formed by the women to whom the actively inverted woman is most attracted. These women differ . . . from the normal, or average woman in that they are not repelled or disgusted by lover-like advances from persons of their own sex. . . . On the whole, they are women who are not very robust and well-developed, physically or nervously, and who are not well adapted for child-bearing, but who still possess many excellent qualities, and they are always womanly. . . . So far as they may be said to constitute a class, they seem to possess a genuine, though not precisely sexual, preference for women over men. . . .

The actively inverted woman differs from the woman of the class just mentioned in one fairly essential character: a more or less distinct trace of masculinity . . . in the inverted woman the masculine traits are part of an organic instinct . . . she makes advances to the woman to whom she is attracted and treats all men in a cool direct manner. . . . Usually the inverted woman feels absolute indifference toward men. . . . (133–34)

In this schema the passive invert, who remains closer to normative models of femininity, may sometimes be recuperated into heterosexuality, but the active invert, masculine at heart, cannot be changed and is, moreover, likely to exhibit her cross-gendering by cross-dressing. Ellis notes that while not all cross-dressing women are congenital inverts, there is "a very pronounced tendency among sexually inverted women to adopt male attire when practicable" not merely because of convenience or a wish to impress other women, "but because the wearer feels more at home in them" (140–41). This view of female-female love thus differs from and pathologizes the female-friendship model of the Boston marriage both in explicitly eroticizing that relationship, and in casting (at least) one of its members as cross-gendered.

Krafft-Ebing, similarly, differentiates among shades of inversion, four in his schema. In his famous *Psychopathia Sexualis* he outlines the "stages" of female homosexuality, noting that in the least developed stage the women do not show masculine sexual characteristics but that many of them have larynxes of "a decidedly masculine formation" (263–64). Even in its most benign form, then, female homosexuality betrays the mark of the anatomically "masculine." Overt cross-dressing marks the other three stages, as does the assumption of male gender roles:

The female homosexual may chiefly be found in the haunts of boys. She is the rival in their play, preferring the rocking-horse, playing at soldiers, etc., to dolls and other girlish occupations. The toilet is neglected, and rough boyish manners are affected. Love of art finds a substitute in the pursuits of the sciences. At times smoking and drinking are cultivated even with passion. . . . The masculine soul, heaving in the female bosom, finds pleasure in the pursuit of manly sports, and in manifestations of courage and bravado. There is a strong desire to imitate the male fashion in dressing the hair and in general attire, under favourable circumstances even to don male attire and impose in it. (264)

In the extreme form, Krafft-Ebing concludes, homosexual women possess "of the feminine qualities only the genital organs; thought, sentiment, action, even external appearance are those of the man" (264). This model thus understands congenital female inversion in terms of both anatomical characteristics or traits *and* transgressive social behavior imitative of the masculine.

What the sexologists helped to name, then, was a parody of the heterosexual system, a system of female love that aped the normative model: a "masculine soul" trapped in a female body, loving a more "normal" female.[7] They created what would in the twentieth century come to be represented as the butch-femme pair: the female homosexual couple in which one woman took on a "male" persona and the other the "female" persona.[8] Desire itself becomes defined as constitutively heterosexual, so to name female-female desire as erotic presupposes recoding it as in imitation of male-female desire.[9] Such a naming also significantly entails locating this desire within a couple, and specifically a couple structured by difference: the congenital invert is defined in relation to the pseudo invert, while the pseudo invert disappears entirely without the congenital invert. As Teresa de Lauretis notes in reference to the twentieth-century butch-femme couple, "it takes two women, not one, to make a lesbian" (92).[10] This definition replicates and thus reinforces the normative heterosexual couple, the dyad legitimized through the institution of marriage and so central to the "normal" family unit.

The turn of the century thus provides particularly rich ground for an examination of the complicated and often contradictory narratives being told as identity categories come into view. Given her historical positioning, by the time Converse published *Diana Victrix*, she was undoubtedly familiar with the various narratives explaining women who chose to live without men and with the national discourses with which these narratives intersected, a familiarity that must have resulted in part from the fact that the sexological narratives increasingly produced attacks on women's colleges and communities like the ones Converse and Scudder inhabited.[11] Not only was Converse herself a member of a Boston marriage, she also had personal experience of American regional difference as well as literary exposure to a broad group of women writers whose work focused on regionalism. Converse (1871–1967), originally from New Orleans, met Scudder (1861–1954) at Wellesley, where Converse went to study shortly after Scudder was hired to teach in the English Department (where she taught from 1887 to 1927). Converse graduated in 1893 and after one year in New Orleans returned to live the rest of her life in New England. She and Scudder were active in settlement houses and Socialist politics throughout their lives together. Hence, one must read *Diana Victrix*'s portrait of a marriage as at least informed by Converse's own life. As the novel's publishing house indicates, Converse must be also read in the context of a generation of New England women writers, many of whom were published by Houghton Mifflin and fostered both by its editor, James T. Fields, and, perhaps even more importantly, his wife, Annie Fields.[12] This cluster of writers, including women such as Alice Brown, Rose Terry Cooke, Mary Wilkins Freeman, and Jewett, were reworking representations of regional and national identity in relation to gender identity. In what follows I will locate *Diana Victrix* against the backdrop of this group, arguing that the novel offers both a contribution to ongoing regional/national discourses and a response to sexological theories of inversion through a rhetorical counterattack on the representation of deviant inverts. Drawing particularly on the vocabulary of evolution and degeneration, the novel connects racial, regional, and sexological discourses to produce a vision of America that includes the middle-class women of the Boston marriage, revealing sexuality as implicitly formative in and formed by the construction and maintenance of a pure national identity.

Stiff Northern Old Maids and French Families

> "I could not make you happy," she began, but he inter-
> rupted her with:—
> "Let me judge of that!"
> "No, no! There is something else you cannot understand.
> I do not need you. It is true I have no man friend whom I
> enjoy as much as I do you, but I have a woman friend who is
> dearer to me."
> "But I told you once before, that is different," insisted
> Jacques.
> "Yes, I know you told me," she answered, "but I know
> my own heart. I share with her thoughts that I have no wish
> to share with you. I give to her a love surpassing any affec-
> tion I could teach myself to have for you. She comes first. She
> is my friend as you can never be, and I could not marry you
> unless you were a nearer friend than she. You would have to
> come first. And you could not, for she is first."
> "And this is all that separates us?" said Jacques, in a tone
> of amazement. "Only a woman?"
>
> —*Diana Victrix*

The conversation above is only one of several in *Diana Victrix* in which Enid tries to explain to her suitor Jacques the nature of her relation to her friend Sylvia and why this friendship renders Jacques's suit hopeless. As it turns out, more than just a woman separates the New England socialist from the French New Orleanian capitalist, but the woman alone is enough to keep them apart. Although Jacques cannot initially bring himself to view Sylvia as competition, Enid herself repeatedly represents her love for Sylvia as analogous to a woman's romantic love for a man, and the novel figures this as one viable option for the modern woman. *Diana Victrix* is very much the portrait of a modern woman—read a New Woman—who lives within the modern heterosexual world and links her love of her "friend" to her lifelong political commitment to social reform. Enid and Sylvia's story follows what is in some ways a conventional heterosexual romance, complete with (male) rivals, quarrels, and reconciliation, but it is not a plot resolved by heterosexual marriage, and it is at the same time the story of a friendship.[13] Unlike later novels that adopt the sexologists' invert model wholesale and merely rewrite conventional heterosexual romances with a congenital invert in the role of the man, *Diana Victrix* presents the story of female-female desire in terms of both romance and friendship. By drawing upon but reworking both the structure and the content of a conventional marriage plot, Converse produces a novel that qualifies as part of what Joseph Boone has identified as "a small but subversive attack upon the evolving hegemony of the marriage tradition in Anglo-American fiction" (2). In the process, by foregrounding the Boston and New Orleans settings, the novel rewrites a North-South unification plot, offering a romantic relationship that stands as a figure for national unity but emerges from a model of sameness rather than difference.

The novel's plot tracks the relationship of Sylvia Bennett and Enid Spenser (whose name recalls her status as "spinster"), two New England New Women, from the winter they spend in New Orleans (for the sake of Sylvia's health) in the home of Jacques Dumarais—which he shares with his stepbrother Jocelin Castaigne and his stepsister Jeanne Castaigne—to a summer visit to New Hampshire, then back to the women's Boston home. In a convoluted love plot the somewhat old-fashioned but basically noble Jacques falls in love with Enid, who rejects him because she already loves Sylvia, who strays in her love for Enid by falling in love with the artistic but immoral and dissolute Jocelin, who is figured as depraved and incapable of loving anyone. Jocelin's dissipation kills him in the end but not before Sylvia's love for him has been replaced by pity, and she has reconciled with Enid. A subplot involves Roma Campion, a New Orleans native who becomes a friend of Enid and Sylvia. Her heterosexual courtship with Curtis Baird, a Northern capitalist who forms a business partnership with Jacques, acts as a foil to Sylvia and Enid's plot while providing narrative space for heterosexual marriages in the future of the nation.

In broad terms, the novel is geographically structured around a North/South divide, synecdochically represented as Boston and New Orleans, cities that both represent their regions and signify, less directly, nations. That is, the Boston/New Orleans opposition not only stands in for North/South but also signals an American/French opposition. Converse draws on New England's claim to cultural primacy and representative American status to establish a chain that slides from Boston to New England to America while also drawing on New Orleans's long-standing reputation as anomalous in the South, more French than American.

The novel opens with a "Prelude," in which the three New Orleans characters appear as children and manifest the character traits that will define their place in the novel. We are also introduced to New Orleans, a city that is granted a role close to that of a character and is repeatedly characterized as specifically French. In the opening pages the narrator, for instance, following a comment by Jocelin, intervenes by noting, "it will be observed that Jocelin was French. The first part of the above remark is a translation, Jocelin's knowledge of English being limited, at that time, to such phrases as: 'Ow do you do?' and 'Mair Kreesmus!'" (6). Similarly, Jacques is introduced by, "'I swam from the big wharf,' said the boy, also in French" (10) and is even given dialogue which reads as a literal translation of French syntax, as when he says, "But you are conceited, yes" (11). Although Jocelin, Jacques, and the other characters speak fluent English by the time we are reintroduced to them as adults, Converse both peppers their dialogue with French phrases and occasionally has the narrator note that she is translating a conversation "really" occurring in French.[14]

The association of New Orleans with France works here to code the city as exotic, romantic, imaginative, and languorous, in contrast to the industrious, commercial, pragmatic, and progressive New England.[15] That this coding of New Orleans also applies to the South in general in this period points first to the fact that the privileged point of view is Northern, and second to the fact of a certain interchangeability in what/who can fill the space of Other for the North. This fairly conventional stereotyping of North and South is rehearsed in varying forms by both the Northern and Southern characters, with the Northern point of view always articulated by Enid and Sylvia. Enid, for example, describes New Orleans in terms of "romance and quaintness" (58), implicitly contrasting this with the seriousness of the North. After speculating on whether two characters are in love, she comments, "Dear me! What is happening to me that I sit up here in broad daylight, and gossip about love and matrimony like a sentimental girl of seventeen, when I ought to be reading Socialism? It is something in the atmosphere of this place" (77). The New Orleans characters articulate a similar regional divide but reverse the valences so that New Orleans becomes a standard of grace and culture against the cold, rushed, industrial North. The Dumarais family, for instance, hesitates to take two Northern women as boarders specifically because they are Northern. Jacques envisions them as "stiff, Northern old maids with cranks" (25) and characterizes them as wholly foreign to the Dumaraises' world:

> "I do not anticipate that they will be gay, these women," said Jacques sarcastically. "Noisy, doubtless, with that disagreeable, hard voice of the North. But as for gayety! these Northerners do not understand how to enjoy themselves; that is an established fact. Ours will be old maids, mournful and cranky, drinking a great deal of tea, and shocked at the sight of the claret on the table."

"Grand Dieu, seigneur!" exclaimed Jocelin, "and are we then to keep the claret off the table?"

. . . "Je dis non! they have come to see a French family. Let them see, let them learn! We live as we have always lived." (26)

Jacques here conflates the stereotypical coldness and Puritanicalness of Northerners with the women's unmarried state as well as their propensity for "cranks,"[16] a conflation that effectively aligns New England/the North with spinsters and New Orleans/the South with heterosexual romance (and, implicitly, the nuclear family it is meant to produce). These regional sexualities structure *Diana Victrix* and, given the North's ultimate status within the novel as representative of America, lead inevitably to the valorizing of the Boston marriage as representatively American.

This structural opposition of North/South is linked to an opposition of American/French by the novel's use of the French and English languages, particularly as played out by Jacques. Unlike Jeanne, Jacques writes and speaks perfect English, a fact the narrator explains by identifying it as the language of commerce: "for he was a man of affairs, this marvelous Jacques, and one must speak much that is not French if one would be successful on the Cotton Exchange, even in New Orleans. And Jacques was successful" (29). Moreover, after he has fallen in love with Enid, Jacques switches from French to English with his stepsister Jeanne ("There seemed to be less intimacy about it" [194]), trying to stave off romance with her. Aligned with business and prosperity, English registers as cold, removed from the (heterosexual) romance and intimacy offered by French.[17] That these alignments are also regionally inflected becomes clear in a passage curiously inserted in the midst of Jocelin's long confession to Sylvia of his failed past:

These occasional quaint lapses in Jocelin's English only enhanced the ordinary precision of his phrases. Sylvia, listening to him, could not but wonder, now and then, where he had learned the language. His enunciation was utterly different from that of Jacques; for while, on the one hand, he had retained distinct *traces of accent* in his voice, and Jacques only betrayed *his French origin* at rare intervals by a misplacement of emphasis upon syllables, on the other hand he gave his words a roundness, an exactness, *an almost Bostonian finish*, which were entirely absent from the speech of his step-brother, who flattened his 'a's' *like a true Southerner*. (110, emphasis added)

A dizzying set of contradictions is established here by the narrator's use of "on the one hand" and "on the other hand." Most immediate is the opposition between Jocelin's foreign/French accent and Jacques's nearly standard American English. Next, a Bostonian accent comes to signify a

Northern accent in opposition to the accent of a "true Southerner." The brothers' language thus speaks to both national and regional divides. Turning to the internal contradictions of each man's accent, language functions to connect region and nation. Since Jocelin's French accent is posited as the opposite of his "Bostonian finish," Boston here stands in for American, native in contrast to the foreign French. An American accent, then, means a Bostonian or Northern accent. Meanwhile, Jacques's nearly standard English is set in opposition to his Southern accent. Because he has a Southern "accent" and his brother has a French one, standard English is again implicitly aligned with the North, so that in both sets of oppositions New England/Northern English comes to signify standard American English.[18]

It is, of course, a small step from Northern English as representative of American English to the North as representative of America. The New Orleans characters reflect this slide, for they most often understand regional divides as national ones, referring to the Northerners as "Americans" and themselves as "French." Jocelin, for instance, explains his language by stating, "I have been in Philadelphia, New York, Boston, Washington, all the large cities of the North. I learned my English in the theatrical companies. Before that, I had known very little of Americans. Jacques went to the American University, but I went to a French school" (115). This comment sets in motion a complicated train of regional associations that will dovetail ultimately with the novel's positioning of the Boston marriage's claim to undiluted and authentic American identity. For Jocelin's explanation of the source of his "Bostonian finish" creates a paradox: although this "finish" would seem to have a positive valence in the novel because it links Jocelin to New England, we learn that it is, in fact, an act, an imitation, an inauthentic voice learned as part of a theatrical career. The character who will bear the burden of the novel's discussion of degeneration and dissolution, then, is also the character whose language is affected, impure, and diluted by a "foreign" accent. His "Bostonian finish," because inauthentic, becomes just another signifier of Jocelin's dissolution.

His brother Jacques, in contrast, presents another paradox, embodied in his attendance of the American University in New Orleans. Jacques's university career, like his use of English, is in the service of his public self—the man of business whose use of English links him to the industrial North. At the same time, his French New Orleans origin suggests another aspect of Jacques: if he is American in the public sphere, he is French in the private sphere of home and culture. His language replicates this public/private split; his French and English are distinct in their sound as well as their arenas of use, neither tainted by nor mixed with the other.

Of course, both Jacques's language and his regional identity are ultimately as complicated, if not as dissolute, as Jocelin's. Jacques's English is inflected, marked by an accent that locates him as regionally Other rather than culturally foreign. While his standard English betrays no sign of his other linguistic identification, it does hint at a regional one: his English carries an occasional Southern (rather than French) accent. This points to the multiple and even contested ways in which Jacques (like the other New Orleans characters) is positioned: he is Southern in relation to the North, but New Orleanian in relation to the South. This construction of New Orleans in part reflects the historical position of New Orleans as anomalous in the South, but it also (here and elsewhere in representations of New Orleans of the period) gives New Orleans a slight advantage in the eyes of the North. New Orleans profits from its association with France in being different from "the South": it is slightly removed from the taint of Civil War loss, and slightly privileged because of the cultural capital that its link to France gives it.[19] Ultimately, the New Orleans identification contributes to the novel's representation of Jacques and the Dumarais family as hybrids: not quite Southern because they are New Orleanians, not quite French because New Orleans is not a part of France, and not quite American because they are both (partly) Southern and (partly) French.

Bloodlines, Creoles, and American New Orleans

Having set up this complex series of alignments, however, the novel further complicates them through its detailed portrait of Creole culture in New Orleans and through noting the presence in the city (in addition to the "French" families like the Dumarais) of "American" families, principally represented by Roma Campion.[20] Converse's representation of French Creole New Orleans provides the ground for a discussion of regional, national, and racial identities and their intersection, through a discourse of "blood" that draws both on theories of individual and cultural inheritance and on the racial discourse of the day. This discussion indirectly puts Converse into conversation with sexological models of inversion, as the narrative displaces the sexological label of "degeneracy" from female-female relations onto the creole Southerner. Because of the contrast it offers to the Boston of Enid and Sylvia, in the end New Orleans stands as the Old—old blood, old models of family and nation—which must adapt to the future or eventually die out.[21] But unlike the sexologists, who understood degeneracy as always destined to die out, Converse (although she does kill off the degenerate Jocelin) is ambivalent about the concept in her portrait of New Orleans.

Her use of a discourse of blood and degeneration locates Converse squarely in the midst of late-nineteenth-century American culture, in conversation with medical, legal, and rhetorical deployments of these concepts. Blood had become a central metaphor in hereditary theory, which, in conjunction with the social determinism of the discourse on degeneracy, fed debates on miscegenation and sexual inversion. George Chauncey has discussed the importance of degeneration theory in turn-of-the-century British and American culture, noting that "in the last years of the nineteenth century degeneration theory had come to dominate explanations of nervous and mental disease in general. The theory drew from those currents in late Victorian thought that postulated an organic relationship between the processes of evolution and civilization" (99). Used to explain dissipated individuals of decaying families like Jocelin's as products of sexual degeneration, degeneration theory located the origins of decay in a family's ancestors, who were seen as transmitting it from one generation to the next, an explanatory model that drew upon the belief in blood as carrier of disease.[22] Ultimately, degeneration theory argued that married, intraracial, heterosexual monogamy was the biological as well as moral basis of civilization. Hence, sexual deviance or debauchery ultimately, as Chauncey puts its, "represented not only a degeneration to an earlier lower state of evolution, but threatened civilization itself" (110).

Informed by degeneration theory, racial discourse and the discourse on miscegenation were explicitly grounded in the metaphor of blood. Eva Saks asserts that miscegenation law "occupied a central position in American family romance" in part because of its implications for inheritance and legitimacy and in part "because it upheld the purity of the body politic through its constitution of a symbolic prohibition against the dangerous mixing of 'white blood' and 'black blood,' casting social practices as biological essences" (40). Blood thus was read as a symbol of race as well as an index of one's cultural, moral, and sexual status and heritage. Virginia Domínguez, tracking the legal and social construction of whiteness in Louisiana, identifies as "widespread assumptions about the properties of blood" the beliefs "that identity is determined by blood; that blood ties, lineally and collaterally, carry social and economic rights and obligations; and that both racial identity and class membership are determined by blood" (89). As this confluence of biology and morality might suggest, the ideological weight of "blood" was enormous and extended into both public and private arenas of American life. Converse's claims take on their full complexity within this broad American use of blood, as well as within the more specific Southern discourse on race and within the New Orleans discourse on Creole blood. In conversation with the sexologists she uses these discourses in two ways. First, she shifts the charge of degeneracy from the Boston marriage onto the Creole. Second, by treating the Creole as a cultural category rather than a racial one, she invokes but simultaneously elides a discussion of race and miscegenation. As a result the individual body comes to figure the national body for Converse as for many of her contemporaries. However, unlike her contemporaries Converse figures the Boston marriage not as degenerate but as advanced, the sameness of Enid and Sylvia's bodies signaling the unadulterated Americanness of the New England New Woman.

Converse's portrait of Creole New Orleans focuses her discussion of American blood, race, sexuality, and degeneracy. By using the terms "French" and "Creole" interchangeably, the narrative collapses an extranational term with a description of a group internal to America: although Converse calls the Dumarais and their like French, as the Creole descendants of the French Louisiana settlers, they are, in fact, ethnically French but nationally American. Converse's treatment of the Creoles operates on several levels, beginning with a literal, plot level on which she depicts distinctively New Orleans Creole customs, delineating their cultural specificity by tracking the tourist/visitor's response through Enid and Sylvia. She devotes several chapters to a representation of the Mardi Gras, for instance, and offers a prolonged description of a dinner banquet composed of Creole specialties, including "raw oysters, and *gumbo filé . . . court-bouillon* of red snapper with any amount of spices in the tomato-sauce. And there was terrapin stew. And there was *jambalaya*, . . . And finally there was the *brûlot*" (170). The food—in addition to underscoring the sensuality and pleasure associated with New Orleans—differentiates New Orleans's Creoles from the French and marks them as specifically, uniquely Creole-*American* through a cuisine that grows out of and borrows from classic French cuisine but reshapes it through a use of American and African food and culinary traditions.

The Creole also functions in the novel on a more figurative level. The opposition of Creole and Puritan, as embodied in Jocelin and Sylvia, articulates a view of regional character that is filtered through the lens of hereditary theory combined with a heavy dose of Puritan cultural determinism. Using the conceit of prolonged roads that finally intersect with Jocelin and Sylvia's meeting, the novel represents their characters—both

as individuals and as regional types—as deriving from family legacy. Jocelin's road is tracked back to

. . . a sound of laughter and revel, a clashing of swords, a clinking of wine-cups,
a rumble of oaths, and a musical flow of words that were poems. And looking,
you saw, behind and beyond on the road, pale, drink-sodden, passionate faces,
and slender white fingers that trembled; and, backward still, beauty, and pride of
bearing, and gay-colored garments. You saw debauch, and chivalry, and brilliant
wit, on that road. Genius and Love-of-Pleasure came down all the length of it,
sinning together, now one, now the other pursuing, polluting, polluted, and lan-
guid with passion. And there at the cross-roads Jocelin lay. (117)

Jocelin is thus read as the natural end product of a long line of dissipated
ancestors, his passionate musical skill and his depravity both legacies
from the past.

Sylvia's "strait and narrow way," in contrast, begins with Puritans,
"Gray-garmented figures" who are "demure" and "staid" (117):

The murmurs of prayers are their poems, the terrible exhortation of preachers is
all the sound of riot along this road. In the dead of night, if you walked, you
stumbled on kneeling figures that knelt the long night through, immovable,
wrestling in the spirit. . . . The men are steeled to contemplate the logic of justice
and judgment their intellect bids them accept as the end of creation. The faces of
mothers are thin and drawn with the terror of bearing children destined, perhaps,
to go down headlong to destruction. . . . Down this road comes Genius, too. . . .
Down this road comes Master Puritan What-is-my-Duty, terrified, shrinking, loving the rainbow Genius. . . . And between is the width of the roadway, all too narrow for terror and indecision. (117–18)

These "roads" draw on the language of determinism, in which both Jocelin's depravity and Sylvia's terror of misstepping are attributed to a conflation of culture and heredity ("blood"), and individual identity is col-
lapsed into regional type. The narrative thus understands the Creole and
Puritan as regional instances of the devolution and progress (respectively)
of humanity, a narrative move that has ramifications on the development
of the nation and one that privileges the North. If the Puritan is imaged
as overwrought, s/he is at least not degenerate like the Creole is, a comparison that suggests that the Creole, and by association, the South, will
fade away as the Puritan North struggles into the future.

Converse works out her theory of "blood" and its regional ramifications most explicitly through the story of Jocelin, contrasting his blood
with Jacques's. When Jocelin says, "Jacques and I were always different"
(115), he is referring not simply to their respective use of English and
French, or even to Jacques's business sense and his own artistic sensitiv-

ity, but to their blood lines and the effects of them. The preoccupation with blood appears first in the very opening pages of the "Prelude," where a portrait of Jocelin's "earliest known ancestor" (5) provides the occasion for the narrator's meditation on familial inheritance. Jocelin's nose, we are told, "was an ancestral nose; from generation to generation it had been handed down" (5); "French also was inherited from the ancestor," as is his "artistic temperament" (6). That this notion of inheritance is grounded in degeneration theory becomes clear when the narrator explains that Jocelin's "ancestor had written poems and fairy tales; this Jocelin could never do. The music in him came, not from his brain, but from his lungs and vocal chords; and every low, sweet note of that strange child-voice was a revealing of the record of those lives, wild, passionate, dissolute, artistically tempered, from which Jocelin's frail, worn-out, young vitality had feebly taken its rise" (7). Jocelin is thus represented as the damaged product of his ancestry, an explanation he echoes in accounting for his failed voice and career: "the failure of my voice was due to faults that were not mine. . . . The doctors said to me, . . . it is an inherited delicacy of constitution" (111). He understands this as stemming from his ancestors, who, he comments bitterly,

had thrown me the rags of their flesh and the dregs of their blood, these ancestors; they had sighed a last gasp of genius into my soul. In the North. . . . I learned that these ideas were well known, were ordinary, but for me they were new . . . must I sit down and let that fellow at the opera house come out and sing Rigoletto's song, and bellow, and be heard and praised,—because he is not so well born as I, and his strength has not been sapped, and the root of his tree is not rotten and dead? (112)

The developing scientific inquiry into genetics (represented here as the product of the scientifically advanced North) and its use within the eugenics movement can be heard in the margins of this passage, whereas the class inflection of Jocelin's statement, evoking images of the sturdy farmer and the enervated aristocrat, reflects a bourgeois American rhetoric of democracy. Jocelin might thus be read as simply the result of his "blood," and so, like the sexologist's version of the invert, not responsible for his own decadence. Indeed, Jocelin functions in *Diana Victrix* as a double for the sexological version of the invert, as opposed to the woman of the Boston marriage. As a figure of born-not-made dissipation, he *is* deviant, but he cannot help being so;[23] therefore, the narrator takes a sympathetic tone toward him, never exactly blaming him but nonetheless writing him into an ending that shows him dying out because he cannot live within society.[24]

While Jocelin serves as the site of the narrative's displacement of the rhetoric of inversion, the comparison of him to Jacques enables another, related narrative displacement—that of a discussion of race. Consider the following words of the narrator:

Energy is not usually considered a creole trait, but Monsieur Dumarais, although a boy when he came to America, was a Parisian of the Parisians; and young Jacques, being, as it were, the first stop-cock from the source of supply, set free a flow of energetic power more than sufficient in force and volume to run three step-families. . . . Fortunate Jacques! to be in at the beginning, where one tingled with the rush and the shock of the tearing stream. Farther away, in the days of the third and fourth generations, perhaps the stream might only percolate. Jocelin, for example, was a third or fourth generation. He felt no rush and tug of energy. (35–36)

This passage at first glance appears simply to be asserting the power of national integrity undiluted across time: Jacques retains his vitality because he is closer to his French origins than Jocelin: he is more Parisian (read French) than creole. But this line of explanation makes sense only if nation is read as an essentially racial construct, a slippage signaled by the non-capitalized use of *creole* above. That is, while the term *Creole* in New Orleans has historically been taken to mean the prominent (European) "first families," the American-born descendants of the French and/or Spanish settlers, the term is also understood by some to mean, as its lower-cased form does, of racially mixed blood.[25] The diluted or mixed nature of Jocelin's "stream" can thus be read as being of both culture and race. Metaphorically, this passage suggests that Jacques's strength comes from his "purity" of blood, whereas Jocelin's weakness is the result of the mixed nature of his. Converse here draws on the racist discourse on miscegenation, using its vocabulary not so much in the service of an explicitly racist call for racial purity but rather to privilege the sameness of terms on which the Boston marriage is based.[26]

This contrast between energy and languor sets up an association between race and region, because the energy/languor dichotomy also functions as part of the North/South opposition. This slide between race and region is established even more specifically in Jocelin. In the logic of the novel Jocelin's "mixed" or diluted blood figures as typically Southern. As a figure of inherited immorality and dissolution, Jocelin here condenses and collapses various of the novel's axes of identity. As a representative of creole New Orleans, he can be read in regional and national terms as collapsing dissipation, racial "impurity," and the South. This set of alignments pervades the novel and plays off of an image of the South/New Orleans as slow, hot, and languorous, an image of nearly tropical beauty and pleasure that can easily slide into one of rot and decay. This fine line is rhetorically suggested when Enid attributes her slip into gossiping about heterosexual courtships to the atmosphere of New Orleans, a city she has come to for Sylvia's sake, and says, "I shall hold you responsible for my degeneration, Sylvia Bennett" (77). The South and New Orleans, like Jocelin, are used here to signify both decadence and racial "impurity." In contrast, while Jacques's energy marks him as undilutedly Parisian, it also links him to the energetic North. This logic equates energy and purity of blood with French (and not creole) as well as Northern (and not Southern). Given that the North functions as a synecdoche of the nation, the concentrated nature of Jacques's Frenchness paradoxically marks him as typically American. As his stepmother puts it, Jacques "becomes more and more American" (39) through his identification with Northern energy and commerce. Ultimately, what is being celebrated as American here is a concentrated, homogeneous energy, undiluted across time (as represented by Jacques) or across ethnicity or race (as negatively represented by Jocelin). This cluster of associations suggests that the nation's progress will entail a fading of the degenerate South and a growth of the vigorous North, just as Jocelin is destined because of his faded and dissipated blood to disappear, while Jacques, the more up-to-date American, adapts and moves energetically into the future (a process which would presumably entail the development of his Northern traits at the expense of his Southern ones).

This figurative use of diluted or mixed blood enacts a narrative displacement: Converse borrows the vocabularies of a national, racial discourse as well as the intersecting nativist discourse but sidesteps a direct discussion of immigration, race or, more particularly, miscegenation, all of which were issues at stake both nationally and in New Orleans in this period. The closest she gets to a direct confrontation of these issues is a curious scene in which she walks a blurred line between race and ethnicity/nationality. In a seemingly gratuitous conversation at dinner Enid and Jacques debate a local murder of Italians by a mob at Congo Square. The use of Congo Square—the former meeting place and celebration/dance location for slaves—suggests that this incident can be read as a metaphor of the racial violence so prevalent in New Orleans at the time, specifically the lynchings of African-American men carried out by white supremacist groups like the White League. At the same time, however, Converse is here drawing on an actual historical event that brought anti-Italian sentiment to a peak in American culture. As Jacques explains, "a band of ruffians has murdered the chief of police" and so have been "righteously executed" by a mob after being acquitted in court (85). The event Converse is depicting here occurred in 1891, when the New Orleans superintendent of police was murdered, "under conditions," notes John Higham, "which pointed to the local Sicilian population. Wholesale arrests followed in an atmosphere of hysteria. . . . But when some of the accused were tried, the jury . . . stunned the city by refusing to convict. While officials stood idly by, a mob proceeded 'to remedy the failure of justice' by lynching eleven Italian suspects. With apparent unanimity local newspapers and business leaders blessed the action" (91). Converse makes Jacques the spokesperson for this local opinion. When Enid objects to the lynchings as murder, Jacques defends them as justifiable, claiming "my dear young lady, there wasn't a man in this town that would have dared to call his soul his own twenty-four hours afterwards if we hadn't done it. The beggars were so elated, they were ready to murder us in our beds without compunction, every mother's son of us. . . . We took them out and shot them and strung them up, and then we went home" (87). Jacques further argues that he is not obligated to obey "rotten" laws (87) or a "bribed and corrupted and intimidated" judiciary (88)—both arguments used by white supremacists of the day.

This scene allows for several readings, suggesting the complex and interrelated production of racial and ethnic categories of American identity in the period. By 1890 the United States saw a rise in a "new" immigrant population from Southern and Eastern Europe, including a large concentration of Italian and Jewish immigrants. These populations were hostilely perceived. As John Higham points out, arriving in a period of increased nativism, Italian immigrants were seen as "degraded . . . as bloodthirsty criminals" associated with "deeds of impassioned violence" (66, 90). This stereotype was used to reinforce both established ethnic and racial hierarchies, for not only were Italians immediately categorized as ethnic Others, their racial identity and allegiances were also at points called into question. Higham points out that particularly in the South, Italian immigrants were seen as potentially endangering "not only the purity of the white race but also its solidarity. In other words, the foreigners, partly because of their low cultural and social status, more largely because they had no background of southern traditions and values, might relax the pattern of white supremacy. Particularly the Italians, who sometimes worked beside the blacks on large plantations, seemed to lack a properly inflexible spirit" (169). Converse draws upon this context, exploiting a local New Orleans incident that became a national scandal in order to further her representation of a backward South.[27]

In Converse's portrait it is certainly as ethnic and possibly as racial Others that the Italians are subjected to the power of the society's white men—in the form both of mob violence and of the white community's support of it. But the fact of their lynching also links this event to innumerable accounts in both fiction and journalism of the time of the lynched bodies of African-American men. Hence, the Italians here stand as specifically Italian immigrant, racial/ethnic Others and simultaneously as doubles for the African American, the South's predominant figure of the racial Other. The lynching of the Italians produces an effect similar to the lynching of African Americans: it terrorizes the community under attack and reinforces the white population's sense of power. According to Jacques, "that afternoon and the next day they [the Italians] were getting out of town like ants pouring out of an ant-hill. When they couldn't afford to go by train, they walked along the railroad tracks. . . . They say that women, ladies even, went down after it was over, to see the place, and, if possible, the men before they were taken down" (93). Both the dominant culture's ongoing fears over the level of immigration at the end of the century and white America's fears about the role of African Americans at the time are thus reflected here, as are contemporary national debates over lynching, racial violence, and "miscegenation."[28] Locating Jacques as the voice of the white Southern man while clearly making Enid the narrative's privileged point of view (opposing mob rule and demanding respect for the American legal system) is as close as Converse gets to intervening directly in the racial or nativist discourses of the day. Instead, she displaces these discourses onto the intersecting discourse of regional identity (as she does by sliding from reading Jocelin as representative of creoles to Jocelin as representative of the South), for on a plot level this scene reinforces a Northern stereotype of Southern whites as racist, barbaric, and lawless. Enid and Jacques debate the finer points of morality in the case until Jacques closes the discussion by asserting, "we did it then, and we'd do it again to-morrow, every man of us, and not turn a hair" (90). Ultimately, "the (white) South" once more turns monolithic in this representation of a backward, violent, racist, and divisive region that hates all racial and ethnic Others, a representation that displaces national racism and nativism onto the South alone and establishes the North as civilized, advanced, and progressive.

The complicated and intersecting regional, racial, and national discourses surrounding Jocelin and Jacques thus disrupt a vision of a monolithic South while simultaneously reinscribing it to the North's advantage. This narrative strategy is seemingly motivated less by a Northern desire to condemn and contain the South (the narrator seems genuinely fond of New Orleans) than by a narrative desire to set up the argument for the New England New Woman of the Boston marriage as America's most advanced citizen.[29] In keeping with her representation of New Orleans as more complex than simply "French," Converse's portrait of Jacques paints him as both a French and Southern man who shares many of the values attributed to the North and who thus, unlike Jocelin, is able to live and prosper into the future. Similarly, the novel's treatment of the other central New Orleans character, Roma Campion, works to the same end. For while young Jeanne's conventionality destines her to an early death, in this view of the progress of the species/nation, Roma Campion represents both a figure of geographical mediation and an intermediate option provided by the narrative for women. Confounding dichotomous oppositions throughout the book, Roma complicates most of the novel's categories before stepping back into a more or less conventional plot.

Roma disrupts Northern stereotypes of New Orleans as solely French by representing the garden district, that is, "the American quarter" (136). Her family is depicted in conventional terms of Southern gentility: they have an "old-fashioned Southern house . . . classic with many pillars . . . a staff of colored retainers . . . and a plantation down the river" (136, 137). Her character thus disrupts the novel's dominant representations both of New Orleans as French as opposed to American and of New Orleans as French as opposed to Southern, for Roma embodies a Southern, American New Orleans, thus linking the city to the South rather than proving its divergence from it. Roma further confounds North/South regional affiliations, for although she is a Southern lady, she hates the South and spends as much time as she can in New York and Paris, being, as the narrator describes her, "that Southern woman, of all others, least Southern in speech and tendencies" (155). The narrator asserts that the "typical, the ordinary New Orleans girl" (137) believes that New Orleans (and by extension the South) is the best place in the country, but she notes that Roma scorns the "self-satisfaction" of her "native city." The narrator reports that Roma "tried to instill this haughty discontent into her little sisters, but without success; they were proving themselves two as placid, self-satisfied, provincial little creatures as ever had been born" (138). Thus, in both her structural positioning in the novel and in the geographical and regional values she articulates, Roma serves as a mediator of national meanings.

The novel links Roma's resistance to regional provincialism to her resistance to conventional prescriptions urging women to marry, a yoking achieved by the novel's locating Roma between two opposing influences: on the one hand, her sisters and Jeanne Dumarais, who embody what the narrator represents as conventional loyalty to both the South and New Orleans while also clinging to conventional notions of marriage; on the other hand, Enid and Sylvia, New Englanders who are "untroubled by lack of suitors, indifferent to matrimony" (140). Roma is described by Jeanne as a woman who "does not marry, but everybody falls in love with her" (78). Like Enid and Sylvia, Roma is bored by the idea of a conventional marriage, turning to the New England women as a possible model of escape. Contrasted to this is young Jeanne's attitude, the attitude of the extremely conventional New Orleans girl who is uninterested in developing her musical talent and hopes only for the life of a society wife. But while Roma respects and admires the Northern women, she is also influenced by social expectation; she herself realizes that at thirty, "to a woman of her education and standard, marriage was the only something to be done at the present crisis" (139), an opinion her sisters reinforce. Roma tells Enid and Sylvia, "I have been educated with the idea that it showed stupidity to be an old maid. My little sisters are already beginning to regard me as a grievance; it is funny to see the superior airs they give themselves when I offer my opinion. I am afraid I should feel as if I hadn't managed my life cleverly, if I did not marry. I should feel ashamed of myself" (142–43). The narrative here sets up the South as a conservative proponent of the heterosexual marriage and family unit; as such it serves as a foil to the representation Converse offers of New England/the North as the home of the Boston marriage. Hence, Roma is most Southern in her eventual capitulation to marriage and most resembles her Northern friends in her earlier resistance to the institution.

Roma does finally marry, which suggests both that not every woman is independent enough to be a New Woman and that Roma's "Southern" blood helps determine her plot's resolution: she ultimately lacks "any desire to change her comfortable habits of life" (150). This identification with the South is salient too in that she marries a New Yorker, Curtis Baird, forming a marriage that provides a comment on the North/South reunification marriage plot, replicating but also complicating it. The marriage does represent a sort of reconciliation of North and South but only after a bitter conflict over where the couple is to live. Roma marries Curtis in large part because she thinks he will take her to live in New York and help her escape her regional affiliation. In fact, however, the marriage forces her to claim her Southern identity and live in New Orleans. Although Roma nearly leaves Curtis when she learns that his business partnership with Jacques will compel them to live in New Orleans, she is constrained from divorce because of the social cost: it is, as her husband puts it, "so horrid vulgar" (252). Interestingly, the descriptions of Roma's change of heart toward her husband are among the most awkward and least convincing in the novel, as if there is a certain narrative resistance to depicting her shift into the conventional role of wife. From the beginning a strong and independent figure, in these scenes Roma is represented for the first time as weak, dependent, and flirtatious. The first indication of her shift is a moment in which the narrator describes Roma thinking, "she liked being taken care of. She liked his being such a gentleman" (263), then goes on to compare Curtis favorably to the other men present (265) and to blush at his complimenting her (266). Her decision to accompany him South is accompanied by tears of contrition and fear of the dark, so that by the time Roma returns home to New Orleans from her trip North, she has been transformed into a sweet and conventional wife. But Converse allows for some ambivalence in this representation. When Roma has a daughter at the novel's close, she names it Enid in what might be read as a gesture toward the future: naming Enid as the godmother, she explains that Enid has "given her her highest ideal of what a woman ought to be" (361). Roma might thus be read as an intermediate step—both in terms of gender roles and regional affiliations—in Converse's notion of the progress of the nation. Stronger and more independent than her sisters, more complicated in her identifications, she is advanced enough to admire Enid and Sylvia but not advanced enough to live like them, and thus ends up mediating both regional divisions and the gap between conventional women like her sisters and New Women like Enid and Sylvia.

Only a Woman? Representation, Invisibility, and Boston Women

Converse's discussion of New Orleans and the complexities she ascribes to it builds toward showcasing her central characters, Enid and Sylvia, and the future they represent. In a representation both inflected by and resistant to the discourse of the sexologists, Converse constructs a chain that links the New Women of the Boston marriage to New England women to the North to the nation. As a result, a relationship soon to be labeled deviant and degenerate provides the site where competing narratives of homosexuality and inversion intersect with narratives of national identity. This produces a vision of the nation in which the women of the Boston marriage stride purposefully and patriotically into the future, bearing the nation along with them.

From the beginning the New Woman is depicted as the logical outgrowth of New England values of independence, progress, and hard work. Converse redirects conventional American ideological platitudes to produce independent, public-minded, college-educated women who find their intellectual and personal community with other women. Conversely,

through Jacques Dumarais, she explicitly marks these women as not embodying Southern values: Jacques displays, the narrator comments, "the
conservative Southern man's prejudice against modern women and higher
education, and always went out of his way to avoid women with views"
(132). But Enid and Sylvia have plenty of views, views that Enid herself
attributes to her independent "Boston" identity. Advising Jacques to give
his talented stepsister professional musical training, despite the girl's wish
to simply become Jacques's wife, Enid says, "forgive me if I seem to med-
dle, but I am fond of her, and we Boston women, who haven't as many
men to depend upon as the girls have down here, learn early the need of
being able to take care of ourselves" (183). Later, when she realizes that
she does not know how to forestall a proposal from Jacques, Enid ascribes this inability to the fact that she is "a New England woman and a
woman's woman" (233). Both comments conflate a New England Yankee
spirit of independence with the New Woman's spirit of independence,
specifically figured as independence from men.

The novel portrays hard work—the Puritan work ethic—as a specifically Northern trait as well. Both Northern and Southern characters rehearse this opposition: Enid compares the South to "reading light literature" which she loves doing "when my conscience allows me to indulge
in it" (58), while Roma describes Enid and Sylvia as "interested. . . . They
care for life; they are not ennuyées," traits she attributes to their being
from Boston (151). The narrator underscores this contrast in her description of Enid and Sylvia's horror when they discover that little Jeanne is
uninterested in developing her innate musical talent: "all the inherent and
trained New Englandism in the two women stood forth amazed, out-
raged. To their two minds, that . . . were used to hoard and husband
every talent jealously,—were used to work their little allotments of ap-
pointed or mistaken vocation with never-flagging conscientiousness, har-
vesting rocks in fortitude and patience year after year,—this light dallying
with a great gift was incomprehensible, this irresponsible laziness seemed
a crime" (69). Jeanne, like Jocelin, wastes her talent, a "crime" the novel
punishes by writing both characters out of the future.[30] Only those who
materially contribute to America—Jacques (productive within the market), Roma (who produces a child), and Enid and Sylvia (who produce
work, social change, and a book)—are allowed to survive.[31]

The combination of independence of thought and the drive to hard
work results in the college woman, a woman who develops her skills to
their highest level and then uses them to work for social good. The college woman then becomes a partner in a Boston marriage, a slide that
works to make the women of the Boston marriage the embodiment of na-

tional values. Converse's portrait of the college woman and her likely involvement in a Boston marriages parallels Smith-Rosenberg's account of
the New Woman who removed herself from the domestic world of her
mother in order to dedicate herself to public service, seeing in higher education "an opportunity for intellectual self-fulfillment and for an autonomous role outside the patriarchal family" (247). Converse's literary
portrait of the college woman and the national future she represents, like
Smith-Rosenberg's historical model, also naturalizes and elides the class
and race privilege on which it depends. This Yankee independence is
available only to middle-class or upper-class, usually white, women. Enid
and Sylvia enact this privileged movement from college to public service:
they meet in college, which Sylvia tells Enid is the part of her life "that belongs to you,—to you and me . . . the happiest time in my life when I look
back" (74). Later they form a partnership in which the sickly but wealthy
Sylvia funds the crèche and reading-room created and run by the poor but
energetic Enid. Like many members of actual Boston marriages, the two
women live together and view their relationship as supporting rather than
interfering with their public careers, as they fear a heterosexual marriage
would. When Enid refuses Jacques for the second time, she tells him, "I
do not love you well enough. . . . Leave my people? My work? Leave
Sylvia? Above all, I could not think of leaving Sylvia now" (339) and later
thinks, "and her work! Oh, the thought of being deprived of that! With
only his love in return, his love and his amiable domestic tyranny!" (340).
In contrast to this, Enid tells Sylvia, "you know you are more to me than
he could ever be. We are congenial, we understand each other" (352) and
goes on to recount her early dreams of life with Sylvia: "How I used to
build air-castles when we were girls! Do you remember? I used to say we
would work together, vindicating our theories of democracy and industrial economy, you by writing, I by living"(353). Enid thus assumes a continuum between Sylvia and her work but locates Jacques in absolute opposition to it.

Jacques proves Enid's point by telling her, "you could still do your
charity work if you married me. . . . The married women in New Orleans
are always busy over that sort of thing" (237). As Jacques so innocently
establishes, a shift from single to married entails the diminution of the
woman's career, the exchanging of a life work for a hobby. The yoking of
region, marriage, and frivolous "charity work" in Jacques's statement not
only indicates that the North here stands for serious social work done by
college-educated women, it also implies that these women cannot constitute part of a traditional family unit, here coded as Southern.

But what sort of unit women in a Boston marriage do constitute is somewhat less clear both in the eyes of the characters and in the terms of the narrative, which articulates various of the competing explanatory narratives of Converse's day. The novel represents Enid and Sylvia's relationship as both friendship and romantic love, coding it for the most part in positive terms but showing the influence of sexological discourse in the structure of the relationship and the language used to describe it. Although Enid and Sylvia, as well as Roma, value their friendship, the men in the novel see it mainly as a preparatory stage for marriage. At one point even the narrator describes it as a sort of inadequate consolation prize for women who cannot marry:

As a woman advances towards thirty unmarried, her women friendships possess more and more a stability, an intensity, which were lacking in the explosively sentimental intimacies of her youth; they are to her instead of many things. And as she passes into the region of the middle-aged . . . she will thank God for her friends. We all want to mean something to somebody, and the friendships of a single woman satisfy to her this desire,—except in certain moods. (76)

Here female friendship is represented within a heterosexual matrix, where it fits only in relation to the heterosexual family unit: it either prepares the woman for marriage or compensates her if she cannot marry.

But friendship also has other connotations in the novel, sometimes signaling a relationship not constituted as internal to and in support of a heterosexual system but rather in excess of it. Explicitly romantic and implicitly erotic, this sort of female "friendship" provides—like those in service of heterosexuality—companionship and emotional intimacy, but it replaces rather than prepares for a heterosexual marriage. As Enid explains to Sylvia:

"The fact remains that you come first. You are my friend. I have so many friends, I cannot count them. And he, the impossible he, would have to be the first friend on the list, which he cannot be, since that is your place."

She lowered her voice and added:—"It is twelve years now—did you know it?—since we began to be friends." (353)

This statement distinguishes among various types of friends. Enid's "many friends" suggest the more commonly understood use of the term, but when Enid dates the origin of her friendship with Sylvia, the term takes on an added valence. Sylvia's brother acknowledges this when he responds to the suggestion that Sylvia is in love with a man by laughing and stating, "No fear of that. Too much Enid" (224).[32]

The excess element of this friendship is erotic desire, present in a veiled

representation that threads its way through the narrative. A chapter ironically titled "Two Old Maids" exemplifies the way in which the representation of Enid and Sylvia's relationship mingles the camaraderie of friendship with a romantic and erotic charge. The chapter recounts the women's
bedtime conversation, as Enid brushes and braids Sylvia's hair and the
two discuss their arrival in New Orleans. The scene underscores their intimacy, representing it as sensual and female-specific. But Converse adds
an extra charge to the scene: when Sylvia admits to being struck by Jocelin's face, Enid gasps, and the narrator reports, "'that I should live to
hear you say you were haunted by the face of a man!' she gurgled indis-
tinctly against her friend's knee," going on to make a joke about the size
of Jocelin's nose (56).[33] Although the women have separate (adjoining)
rooms, the chapter ends when Enid comes to put Sylvia to bed: "Enid had
her arms about her, and was saying a great many things very softly in the
dark" (63), a scene that allows for multiple interpretations.

Both the novel and Enid herself persistently and explicitly locate Enid
in the place of lover toward Sylvia, as when Enid acknowledges her jealousy of Jocelin. When Jacques suggests that Enid warn Sylvia not to fall
in love with the dissipated Jocelin, for instance, Enid responds furiously,
then apologizes by saying, "it was not quite safe to tell me that the one
who is dearest to me in all the world was in danger of giving her love to
another,—and such a despicable other!" (188). When Jacques dismisses
her jealousy, offering her a conventional reading of female friendships as
a preparatory stage in a girl's life, she will not be swayed:

> "But," he replied, looking rather amused, "it isn't the same thing at all. There
> wouldn't be any disloyalty in her doing it [falling in love with Jocelin]. Friendship
> is one thing, love is another. It is my experience that a love affair makes a woman
> rather more interesting to her women friends,—gives them something to talk
> about. All women expect to marry."
> "I do not expect to," said Enid. "My life has other work in it. And my friend
> is sufficient for me. . . . If you loved a woman you would not listen to such an in-
> sinuation any more than I do."
> "Your loving a woman and my loving a woman are entirely different matters,"
> said Jacques.
> "You do not understand," she persisted. (189)

Jacques's insistence on clearly drawn lines between love and friendship,
between a man's and a woman's love for a woman, make him unable to
"understand" Enid's love for Sylvia as romantic and erotic.

In the end, however, Jacques comes to recognize Sylvia as a rival, even
while he still cannot accept the ramifications of such a love. Interestingly,

when Jacques confronts Sylvia, Converse has him object to Enid's devotion to Sylvia not because Sylvia is a woman, but because Sylvia does not reciprocate Enid's love, a curious moment indicating a recognition of the romantic and erotic charge of a female friendship without a pathologizing of that charge. At the same time, however, even as Jacques recognizes the power of Sylvia's "influence," he also continues to deny it, telling Sylvia, "You fill her life, she says, so that she has no need of the other kind of love. It is a thing improbable, but she says it is true. Evidently I do not understand women" (344). This moment of disavowal, however, only attests to his recognition of Sylvia as romantic rival.[34]

Here as elsewhere the novel offers complicated and even contradictory representations of Enid and Sylvia's Boston marriage. Even as Converse produces a novel celebrating this form of female relationship, her language and her structuring of the friendship put her in conversation with the more pathologized model of the sexologists. Enid conforms to many aspects of Ellis's and Krafft-Ebing's models of the congenital invert, particularly in her female object-choice and her indifference to men. The novel repeatedly stresses the latter, as when the narrator describes Enid's interpretation of her friendship with Jacques as "devoid of all sentimentality; they were merely good comrades" (134). Jacques, with heterosexual instinct, recognizes Enid's lack of interest in men:

He liked Enid. She did not burden him with a sense of responsibility. It was still an astonishment to him that she obviously never expected him to make an effort to entertain her, but it was a relief as well. He did not know that he entirely approved this frank though unspoken avowal that the attentions of his sex were matters of complete indifference to her; it was not quite in accord with his ideas of feminine modesty; but, after all, it was convenient when a man came home tired and hungry after a hard day's work. (84–85)

However, Converse also makes a point of not representing Enid as simply a desireless old maid:

"Don't you think," faltered Sylvia, "that although you have the sorrows of humanity at heart, sometimes you are a little impatient of the sorrows of particular men?"

"Yes," answered Enid; "I do think so, but not of particular women." She laughed as she said this, and leaning over, kissed her friend. (122)

Sylvia, of course, as that particular friend, can be read across a spectrum of meanings.

Like a congenital invert, Enid does not play the social role of "woman," and Jacques comes to value the fact that he can talk to her "as if she were a man" (131). But in fact, unlike the congenital invert, Enid is not quite playing the "man" either (she does not, for instance, smoke cigars or cross-dress). Converse recodes both the gendered behaviors and the physical traits that the sexologists claim as masculine, so that even when Enid exhibits these traits, they are represented as making her more, not less, feminine. Ellis's active invert, the "mannish" woman, is defined both by a propensity for dressing and acting like a man, and by physical elements: her "brusque, energetic movements, the attitudes of the arms, the direct speech, the inflexions of the voice, the masculine straightforwardness and sense of honor" (143) and the fact that her "muscles are everywhere firm, with a comparative absence of soft connective tissue; so that an inverted woman may give an unfeminine impression to the sense of touch. Not only is the tone of voice often different, but there is reason to suppose that this rests on a basis of anatomical modification" (144). Her mannishness is mapped onto both her behavior, coded as masculine, and her very physiology: both her body and the way she carries it—what she does with it—mark her difference from "normal" women.

Enid, in contrast, may enact the New Woman's independent behavior, but her independence is represented (borrowing the strategy of the women who reworked the ideology of separate spheres to justify women's entry into the public sphere) as a logical outgrowth of a female world and an American bent for self-reliance and self-development. Her body, on the other hand, is the site of the intersection of discourses. Converse opens "Two Old Maids" with a lengthy description of Enid that seems purposely located to contradict the explicitly raised image of the old maid and the implicit image of the "deviant":

Enid always had to spend a long time arranging her hair at night; it was such heavy hair, like a mane, burnished bronze, with a big ripple along its length now and then. Enid was tall and broad and strong; her skin was smooth; her flesh was firm; her eyes were brown and clear, with golden lights in them, like the lights in her hair.

She stood before the mirror to-night, her wrapper falling straight down around her, one arm, half bare, holding a mass of clinging hair above her head. She was a beautiful woman. (53)

Enid's size and strength as well as her "firm" flesh might link her to the mannish congenital invert. Instead, these qualities, in conjunction with the passage's statue imagery, link her to the virgin huntress Diana of the book's title—the victorious one—the goddess who, as Sarah B. Pomeroy points out, "retains control over herself; her lack of permanent connection to a male figure in a monogamous relationship is the keystone of her

independence" (6).[35] Sharing this independence and the unavailability to
men that it implies, Enid is also physically modeled on Diana. The narrator summons this allusion by referring to "the statuesque pose of her
[Enid's] head and the large, classic correctness of her profile" (235).
Moreover, both the description of Enid's hair, traditional marker of femininity and feminine sexual allure, and the depiction of her above as a
tableau of "woman before a mirror," employ conventional female tags,
marking her both as "beautiful" and, as the narrative later describes her,
"statuesque" (53). Although the narrator's assertion that Enid is "a beautiful woman" might seem a defensive repudiation of sexological models,
the representation of Enid's body does not simply rehearse sexological
models, it also reworks them, drawing on images of the "mannish" body
of the congenital invert but appropriating them as female and making
them the basis of a new formula for female beauty.[36]

Sylvia's character closely resembles that of the sexologists' passive invert, although as critics have noted, the passive invert is so nearly indis-
tinguishable from the "normal" woman that the category is less useful or
distinct than that of the active invert. Sylvia, the model of a sympathetic,
physically weak woman, with her face "quiet with the rapt stillness of
constant receptivity" (46), and with her "transparent" skin (60), is sensitive to all and elicits treatment as "something a little finer than mortal
clay" (133), but this might just as well describe the ideal heterosexual
American woman. Interestingly, as a result of this overlap, Sylvia, like the
sexologists' passive invert, receives less narrative attention than her
mate.[37] In fact, it is less her role within the plot than her structural positioning that is of interest to me here: specifically, her positioning at the
crossroads of homosocial/sexual and heterosexual desire.

Insofar as Converse borrows from the sexologists in eroticizing the
Boston marriage, she also borrows, to a certain extent, their framing of
erotic desire as heterosexual. At first glance Sylvia's relationship with Enid
is structured like those of the passive and active invert, with Enid as the
active desiring (coded masculine) subject and Sylvia as the passive desired
(coded feminine) one. Sylvia's failure to recognize the depth of Enid's
devotion until it is articulated to her by Jacques might be read as an instance of this heterosexual model, an articulation of the sexologists' division of erotic labor. Sylvia sees Enid as a woman and hence cannot ascribe
active desire to her; Enid's desire only becomes visible to Sylvia as erotic/
romantic after it is articulated by a man.

Sylvia, however, does not change her view of Enid after recognizing
her desire and so might be read as following the narrative's point of view

in seeing as feminine the character traits conventionally coded masculine (desire, independence, public-mindedness, etc.). In fact, the novel as a whole interrupts and dismantles this sexological model of active male/passive female, making it impossible in the end to define Enid and Sylvia's relationship in these terms. This is because of the way this model assigns desire and because it structures its subject positions as an absolute dichotomy. Sylvia, although ostensibly occupying the passive, receptive position, is assigned an active desire for the ostensibly desiring man, Jocelin. Sylvia recognizes her feelings for Jocelin as a "temptation" that has taught her "what it is to desire the things of the flesh," as she so biblically puts it (259), a comment that suggests this is the first time she has occupied the position of the desirer.[38] Although her attraction to Jocelin seems to mark her as that sort of "pseudo" invert who might be "cured" by exposure to the heterosexual world, Enid's laughter at living to hear Sylvia admit a fascination with a man (56) implies that such a fascination is anomalous. More importantly, Converse's mixing up of the sexologists' neat alignments of sex, gender, sexual role, and sexual orientation (i.e., the model that would align female, feminine, passive receptive, and heterosexual) suggest a prying apart of these naturalized categories, a refutation of the sexologists' claim that, as Chauncey describes it, "a woman could not invert any aspect of her gender role without completely inverting that role" (91).

Perhaps the clearest representation of this destabilizing of alignments appears in a description Enid offers of her relationship with Sylvia, which at first seems to construct the two women as active and passive inverts, but on closer examination collapses those terms entirely:

We are a partnership, Sylvia and I. I am the man about town, the planner, the promulgator. Sylvia sits in the counting-room and cashes the checks, and she is to keep the record of events, and lay the affairs of the firm before the public in good literary form. You don't really know anything about Sylvia. I'm the showy person, but Sylvia takes all my little theories and turns them inside-out before my eyes, and clothes them in metaphor and metre. (145)

Although Enid begins by representing herself as the "man about town" and Sylvia as the woman behind the scenes, in one sense both Enid and Sylvia are imaged as occupying a space traditionally coded male. Both become public creatures rather than domestic ones; both are partners in the "firm," one acting as manager, one as accountant. The writer/accountant Sylvia is still contained in an enclosed space, still occupied with good form and public decorum, while Enid as the flashy man about town remains publicly private, unreadable, and indebted to the writer who both constructs Enid's theories for her and constructs her own texts through the help of Enid. This conceit foregrounds the identification of the two women and brings us back to one of the most radical ramifications of the New Woman phenomenon and its manifestation in the Boston marriage: the specter of women acting independently of men and in the public sphere, composing a social unit made up of homogeneous rather than heterogeneous terms.

But Converse goes beyond simply adding her representation to the cultural discourse on female-female relations. Her novel suggests not only that the Boston marriage is a healthy and potentially erotic relationship option for women but also that it embodies the best of American values as a whole. In contrast to both the Southern model of degeneracy and the Southern model of domestic tyranny, the Boston marriage becomes an embodiment of national virtues and a model for the future, a future in which women, freed from the constraints of heterosexual family life, dedicate themselves to the good of the nation. A conversation between Jacques and his father, the patriarch of the Dumarais family, establishes this model as represented by Enid:

> "Why is it that you set your heart upon the impossible woman [Enid], Jacques? She is of the race of Jeanne d'Arc, this Northern girl, in her voice, her bearing, her beliefs. This kind is not to be possessed by one man; she belongs to a cause, to the people. . . . Fortunately, they are the exceptions."
>
> "Not so much as you think. There are dozens of them in the North. She told me so herself. They are increasing every day," said Jacques moodily. (296–7)

This conversation reproduces associations of region, gender, and sexual orientation made elsewhere in the text, for Jacques's father goes on to advise him that he should choose a wife from among the New Orleans women, women who will "keep this house, and mend your clothes, and bring your children into the world" in a way that Enid never would (297). New Orleans and the South once again signify romance and operate as the locus of heterosexual love and family formation, in which women "belong" to their husbands and serve the family. But in addition to linking Northern women to social activism and the unmarried state, this passage broadens out to propose Enid as belonging to the "people," a nonregionally specific image that might be read as the nation. Supporting this interpretation is the fact that Jacques's father figures Enid as "Jeanne d'Arc," a (French) national symbol. Just as Jacques's French (not creole) energy paradoxically marks him as especially American, Enid's status as unmarried French crusader for the people marks her as the representatively Northern and hence American model of the future.[39]

Within the logic of the novel Enid's representative status calls for the disruption of the heterosexual family unit, a disruption depicted less as a loss for the women involved than as simply the next step in the evolution of the people, a step that produces both widespread social change and new formations of family among women. The novel undertakes the working out of these formations, depicting Enid and Sylvia as satisfied with their decision to abandon conventional roles even though they have to struggle to create new ones. Early in the novel the narrator implicitly comments on this process, noting that "Enid averred once that, with a married woman, husband and children, the particular, the personal relationships, must come first, but that the unmarried woman, who consecrates herself to a cause deliberately, gives up the personal claims; it is a part of the sacrifice. Shortly after making this statement, Enid came South with Sylvia" (76). Going South begins the testing of Enid's willingness to make this "sacrifice," as Sylvia metaphorically enters the region of heterosexuality and is tempted by it, forcing Enid, as she looks on helplessly, to recognize that, in fact, she has not given up her "personal claims" to Sylvia.

But the novel does not force Enid to give up Sylvia in order to work for social progress. It refuses to cast the Boston marriage as an inverted or degenerate relationship beyond the pale of American culture and progress, representing it instead as allowing for both a "cause" and "personal claims." The novel does, however, force both Enid and the reader to rework notions of what counts as happily-ever-after. Reworking old models, it turns out, means more than simply substituting a homosocial/sexual dyad for a heterosexual one. It also involves reconfiguring the relations between personal and public, home and work, and individual and social and then recognizing all these areas as implicated in a woman's happiness.[40]

Through a conversation at the book's end, Converse self-consciously suggests this reconfiguration, implying that while hers may not be a conventional fictional ending, it is an ending that represents the lives of women in Boston marriages and one that is increasingly being represented in fiction. After Sylvia has told Enid that she is going to put her into her next book, Enid protests by saying, "I should not go well in a book: I'm too old, and there's nothing romantic about me; I'm stodgy" (360), thus emphasizing the distance between her and the conventional heterosexual romantic heroine. Sylvia, however, professes to "know better," reclaiming "romantic" as a description of a woman in a Boston marriage. The scene continues to posit a counter-narrative to those offered in conventional novels:

"I know better!" Sylvia contradicted her, and, after a pause, mischievously, "Shall I make you marry him—in the book?"

"Yes, if you like! It would be quite as true to life as the other way, and the public are more used to it. But some times, Sylvia, I don't marry,—even in books." (360)

Enid's rejoinder foregrounds the literary as her "I" comes to signify all the women of the Boston marriage and their literary representations. Writing becomes a part of Enid and Sylvia's relationship, as one New Woman writes about another. Sylvia's writing is nurtured by Enid not only through Enid's caretaking of Sylvia, but also through Enid's furnishing Sylvia with subject matter. As in the relationship between Jewett's two protagonists, both power and desire between the two women circulate in part through the writing, both articulated by and displaced into Enid's appearance in Sylvia's book, as public and private spheres are reconfigured in the world of the Boston marriage.

Narrative representation, Enid implies, has begun to include the New Woman's reality, now offering the plot of the Boston marriage in addition to conventional marriage plots (such as Roma Campion's). This claim can be taken as a gesture to the broader literary context in which *Diana Victrix* appeared. By the 1880s onward representations like Sarah Orne Jewett's in *The Country of the Pointed Firs* (1896) offered critiques of the heterosexual marriage plot through what Boone calls "form-breaking counterplots that dare to reenvision and rewrite the traditional plot of personal desire" (21), whereas novels such as Henry James's *The Bostonians* (1886) attacked the Boston marriage. In whatever light they appeared, then, some women in the American novel were not marrying and were appearing in plots that often involved the yoking of regional, national, and sexual identity.[41] James's journal entry of April 8, 1883, articulates the national inflection of this literary phenomenon: referring to *The Bostonians* he writes that the "relation of the two girls should be a study of one of those friendships between women which are so common in New England. The whole thing as local, as American, as possible, and as full of Boston: an attempt to show that I *can* write an American story" (19).[42]

The "American story" of the "relation of the two girls" is precisely what *Diana Victrix* provides. Vida Scudder called women's friendships "material for many novels not yet written" (221), but *Diana Victrix*, like other novels of the period, not only focuses on women's friendships but puts them at the heart of American culture. Rewriting sexological narratives of inversion to locate the white middle-class women of the Boston marriage comfortably within American values, Converse defends the romantic and erotic elements of such relationships while scripting them as not degenerate but rather a step forward in the evolution of the nation. Borrowing from the vocabularies of degeneration theory and the racial discourse of her day, she valorizes the model of sameness on which the Boston marriage is based and links it to an undiluted commitment to the nation, a narrative move that operates on several levels. On one level, the novel challenges the sexological discourse that pathologizes the Boston marriage as a form of "inversion" and conceives of erotic desire only in terms of heterosexual difference. At the same time, this interruption of the coding of individual women's bodies and their desires functions on the level of the nation, where similar debates over difference were being played out in terms of regions and races. As I will argue in the next chapter that Pauline Hopkins's *Contending Forces* does, *Diana Victrix* stands as a contribution to discourses of national identity that figured America as a national body made up of disparate and contentious parts (North/South or black/white). But unlike Hopkins, who directly confronts race and locates the future of the nation in a "mixed blood" and mixed region heroine, Converse complicates but ultimately reinscribes a regional hierarchy of value—North over South—in her attempt to link the Boston marriage to the privileged site of national identity. Simultaneously, she seeks to evade the issue of racial hierarchy, sidestepping it through her discussion of the creole as a conflict of cultures rather than of races. Located at the crossroads of the central cultural debates of Converse's time and in the midst of a literary context engaged in these debates, *Diana Victrix* stakes a claim to the novel's ability to contribute to the cultural work of nation-building, offering a version of America in which degenerate citizens like Jocelin slowly fade away as the New England woman's woman, like Joan of Arc, optimistically leads her country into a brighter future. In doing so, Converse rescripts both the American novel and the future of the nation. Far from being a degenerate type on the margins of her society, the woman of the Boston marriage plays the starring role in a drama of national identity, cast in this part specifically because she is the heroine who doesn't marry, "even in books."

3 Slavery, Sexuality, and Genre

PAULINE E. HOPKINS'S NEGOTIATIONS OF
(AFRICAN) AMERICAN WOMANHOOD

> . . . the names by which I am called in the public place ren-
> der an example of signifying property *plus*. In order for me
> to speak a truer word concerning myself, I must strip down
> through layers of attenuated meanings, made an excess in
> time, over time, assigned by a particular historical order, and
> there await whatever marvels of my own inventiveness. The
> personal pronouns are offered in the service of a collective
> function.
> —Hortense J. Spillers

Slavery, Sexuality, and Representation

Hortense Spillers's words, taken from her "Mama's Baby, Papa's
Maybe: An American Grammar Book," point to the importance of self-
representation for contemporary African-American women writers, and
to the urgency of the need to articulate identity through a discourse
which, if not one's own, might be temporarily appropriated as such. Implicated in this process, her statement suggests, is a confrontation with the
"attenuated meanings" assigned to African-American female identity by
the American "historical order." Spillers's formulation and the important
article from which it is taken chart a relationship between African-American female identity and history, putting into relief the historical impact of
slavery on the formation of African-American identity and linking the individual subject formation of the African-American woman to the (re)for-
mation of a national identity. Placing Spillers's argument itself into a historical context, we can use her formulation to help us understand both
post-Reconstruction African-American female writers' efforts toward
self-representation and, at the same time, the *literary* history that has read
(or misread) these writers. Moreover, Spillers's work can also help us understand how such self-representation alters the landscape not only of
these writers' historical order but also of their imagined collective future

nation. Spillers contends that within slavery, even prior to differentiation on the basis of gender or sex, there operated a differentiation between human and nonhuman, what she calls "body" and "flesh" (67). I would suggest that African-American women writers like Pauline E. Hopkins (1859–1930) used the sentimental novel form and specifically the figure of the mulatto heroine, not only as a means of extracting themselves from the category of "flesh" in order to claim human subject status but also as a means of extracting themselves from the category of "body," in the sense that the body had come to signify for African-American women a stereotype of the sexually voracious and immoral female sexed body.

Hopkins, like many turn-of-the-century African-American women writers, was engaged in multiple but overlapping arguments with historical constructions of African-American womanhood, struggling in her novel *Contending Forces* (1900) to avoid being reduced to the body while also struggling to recode that body. For African-American women writers specifically, of course, history dictated more than one of what Spillers has dubbed an "attenuated meaning" for sexuality: under slavery African-American women were both stripped of the role of mother and burdened with the role of the hyper-erotic. African-American women in the post-Reconstruction period were thus forced, on the one hand, to confront not only the dominant white ideal of the Cult of True Womanhood but also its inverse image: the stereotype Mary Helen Washington describes as the "immoral," "licentious and oversexed" black woman with "insatiable appetites" (73).[1] On the other hand, Hopkins and her contemporaries were not only engaged in a conversation with old images, they were also involved in debating those images' current meaning within an evolving race discourse of the 1890s. As Susan Gillman has so persuasively pointed out, the turn of the century saw "a full-scale national effort to reinterpret slavery, the Civil War, and its aftermath, usually with the goal of healing sectionalism and fostering national reconciliation, which meant a glossing over or active denial of the slave's experience" ("The Mulatto" 243). Coming to terms with her historical order for Hopkins thus entailed both insisting on its very existence and refiguring it through a fictional narrative. Rewriting an erased history specifically through figures of African-American womanhood—primarily mulatto members of the bourgeoisie but also the working-class business woman—Hopkins produced a new version of African-American womanhood and simultaneously made it clear that "America" had always included her, even if in an elided form. Like Florence Converse, then, Hopkins understood America to be a nation constituted by multiple and disparate parts—both racially and regionally—but unlike Converse, who resolved the tensions among these parts by envisioning a future based in sameness, Hopkins imagined a heterogeneous national identity. Ultimately, her novel depicts African-American women as embodied human Americans in two ways: first, by grounding representations of a raced, gendered, regionally-inflected identity in a reworked notion of erotic and maternal desires; second, by reading that emergent identity as a figure for the complexity of American national identity, emblematic both of African-American community and of a broad national culture of which that community is a constitutive part.

The terms of this attempt are clearly complicated and involve a reevaluation of the very grounding notions of gendered identity. Hortense Spillers points out that, given the legacy of slavery, "we could go so far as to entertain the very real possibility that 'sexuality,' as a term of implied relationship and desire, is dubiously appropriate, manageable, or accurate to *any* of the familial arrangements under a system of enslavement, from the master's family to the captive enclave. Under these arrangements, the customary lexus of sexuality, including 'reproduction,' 'motherhood,' 'pleasure,' and 'desire' are thrown into unrelieved crisis" (76). This crisis of "the customary lexus of sexuality" was inherited by postbellum African-American writers like Hopkins, who struggled both in her fiction and in her work at *Colored American Magazine* to find the words and the literary forms to articulate what had not been sayable under slavery.

Hopkins herself viewed fiction as the most effective narrative vehicle for her political goals, the vehicle most likely to effect a shift in this "lexus of sexuality." In her preface to *Contending Forces* she explicitly links her choice of narrative form to her motives for writing the novel. She begins her explanation with a disclaimer common to nineteenth-century women's fiction in general, stating, "In giving this little romance expression in print, I am not actuated by a desire for notoriety or for profit, but to do all that I can in an humble way to raise the stigma of degradation from my race" (13). Like many American women writers of the period, she deflects a charge of greed or personal pride and emphasizes the moral and didactic motivations behind her writing. Like her specifically African-American predecessors, she goes on to identify racial "uplift" as her goal, a goal that *Colored American Magazine*'s editors reiterated in attributing to Hopkins "a heartfelt desire to aid in every way possible in uplifting the colored people of America, and through them, the world" ("Editorial and Publishers' Announcements" 64). While Hopkins devoted four years to this goal in working for *Colored American Magazine* as both contributor and editor, her faith in fiction as the preferred means of achieving this goal is clear from her assertion in her preface that[2]

the colored race has historians, lecturers, ministers, poets, judges and lawyers,— men of brilliant intellects who have arrested the favorable attention of this busy, energetic nation. But, after all, it is the simple, homely tale, unassumingly told, which cements the bond of brotherhood among all classes and all complexions.

   Fiction is of great value to any people as a preserver of manners and cus- toms—religious, political and social. It is a record of growth and development from generation to generation. *No one will do this for us; we must ourselves de- velop the men and women who will faithfully portray the inmost thoughts and feelings of the Negro with all the fire and romance which lie dormant in our his- tory,* and, as yet, unrecognized by writers of the Anglo-Saxon race. (13–14, em- phasis in original)

Hopkins here identifies the need for self-representation and for reclaim- ing and redefining the terms used to define African Americans. She links this need, through fiction's uses, to community-building. In order to envi- sion a collective cultural identity, she implies, one needs representations of the self. Thus, her fiction stands not only as a supplement to "Anglo- Saxon" self-representations or even as a corrective to prior misrepresen- tations of the African American by the "Anglo-Saxon race" but also as an independent moment in the present of African-American culture, a pre- sent moment necessary to the envisioning of that culture's future within American society.[3]

   The figure who bears the weight of that future in *Contending Forces* is the African-American woman, most centrally the mulatto heroine, Sap- pho, a fragmented self whom the plot moves toward unifying. By bring- ing into concert the racial, gender, and regional components of Sappho's identity, the novel not only displaces the racist literary and cultural her- itage that linked African-American women's sexuality to rape but also emphasizes this African-American woman's integrity as a human being, as well as the power of her unique status *as* an African-American woman.[4] Sappho's character thus operates for Hopkins on several levels at once: she is the heroine of the domestic plot; she is a figure of the reunification of the black community in post-Reconstruction America; she is a figure of the reconciliation of black and white America; and, finally, she is a figure of national reunification through the discourse of North and South in which her character is steeped. While Hopkins registers the complexity of American cultural politics by sending her heroine abroad at the novel's end, she goes abroad with her new family to open a school for "Negro youth of ability and genius" (386), a motive that reinscribes her in a project of racial uplift. What Hopkins produces, then, is a political intervention in American race discourse, a new narrative with new kinds of heroines, a narrative that reworks racial and gendered identity to claim a narrative space for a new version of African-American womanhood.

Reading the Sentimental

Hopkins, having been virtually ignored by literary critics for most of the twentieth century, has in recent years been rediscovered, largely through the work of African-American feminist critics and aided by the republication of her works in the Schomburg Library editions from Oxford. Critics have situated the work of the end-of-the-century African-American women such as Hopkins and Frances E. W. Harper within the literature of racial "uplift," a literature that often used the vehicle of the sentimental novel, producing heroines who celebrate domesticity, marriage, and motherhood, and who reflect a dominant white model of virtuous, middle-class womanhood. Many early critics of African-American fiction disparage writers like Hopkins for their use of the sentimental novel, either because these authors use the sentimental novel form at all—a form long dismissed as "feminine" and trivial—or because they attempt to use it as a form of political protest. In this first line of criticism, the sentimental novel is viewed as a degraded form, a white literary convention that inculcates white bourgeois values, so that Hopkins becomes guilty of buying into white ideology and using a white literary form to argue for assimilation. In the second, related line of criticism, the sentimental novel is both a degraded form and one that Hopkins and her sort misuse by trying to import an overlay of political protest. Early critics have thus taken Hopkins (and other nineteenth-century African-American novelists) to task, arguing variously that the sentimental novel is bad art, white art, bourgeois art, or all three, and that it is, moreover, incompatible with political protest fiction.

More surprising, however, is a continued denigration of Hopkins by certain contemporary African-American critics and canon makers. Richard Yarborough, for instance, in his introduction to the prestigious Schomburg Library edition of *Contending Forces*, constructs a dichotomy between the "sentimental romance" and "political fiction." Implicitly equating protest fiction with Realism, he reads *Contending Forces* in terms of early African-American fiction writers' efforts to "discover a vehicle that would satisfy their urge toward realism without undermining their adoption of popular literary forms" (xxxvi). Even more curious than this as-

that was constituted in part by the absence of black women authors and heroines from its pages: True Womanhood was, by definition, not African-American. Further, to chronicle an African-American True Woman whose identity was based partly in erotic desire constitutes a double reshaping of the sentimental novel. Such a heroine embodies both non-white and non-passionless virtue. Hopkins thus doubles the stakes in representing female erotic desire through her struggle concurrently to refute and to offer an alternative to both the passionlessness of the model of True Womanhood and the lasciviousness of the stereotype of the African-American woman. Moreover, by offering at least a limited depiction of both heterosexual and homosocial female desire, Hopkins further expands the representational range of female desire within her portrait of African-American female identity.

Meanwhile, by rewriting the "mulatto" narrative to foreground white male rape, rather than African-American lust, as the source of miscegenation, Hopkins offers her contribution to the discussion of the "race question," a question at the heart of turn-of-the-century American culture. The mulatto was, of course, a character frequently invoked in Postbellum fiction by both black and white writers, a figure whose "mixed blood" seemed to literalize the cultural dilemma of how the two races were to coexist in America. The mulatto was seen by nineteenth-century readers as embodying the possibility of racial intermingling or even, in the hysterical "plantation fiction" of Thomas Dixon, for instance, the possibility of a "threat" by African Americans to white cultural hegemony. As William L. Andrews frames the issue, to "countenance miscegenation or the relaxation of political, economic, or social barriers to it was to threaten the principle of racial purity on which not only Southern race pride but social and political order in the post-war South were based," with the result that "the issue of black rights did not come down to a matter of abstract politics but rather of sexual politics in which miscegenation became the ultimate political act of triumph for blacks over the restraints of Southern civilization" (14). Andrews's statement allows us to see that miscegenation was itself a symptom of racial conflict coded in sexual terms. In its most virulent application, postbellum and post-Reconstruction white supremacists used the threat of miscegenation as justification for the lynching of black men, by means of a redefinition of miscegenation in terms of black male rape of white women. Thus, white supremacists transferred the site of miscegenation from its historical origin—the rape of slave and ex-slave black women by white men, before, during, and after the Civil War—to a new site, a phantasmagorical site on which dangerous postbellum black men ravished white Southern womanhood in an effort to topple white power, while mulattos "passed" as white in order to infiltrate and corrupt white society.

Hopkins counters this post-Reconstruction racist white supremacist appropriation of the mulatto figure and simultaneously resists a Booker T. Washingtonian politics of emulation by resituating the mulatto in the context of master-slave relations. Using rape in place of "passing" as a figure for relations between the races, Hopkins self-consciously underscores the ways in which the white American imagination had linked sexuality to racial identity and had, moreover, figured a racial "threat" in sexual terms.[11] Thus, she both addresses and redresses the discursive terms used to construct African-American womanhood and in so doing exhibits not a post-Reconstruction African-American drive toward assimilation but rather an emphasis on the historical construction of race relations and how they are sexually configured. As Hazel V. Carby notes, "Hopkins wanted to emphasize those sets of social relations and practices which were the consequence of a social system that exercised white supremacy through the act of rape" (*Reconstructing* 140).[12] To this end the mulatto, as what Ann duCille calls "both a rhetorical device and a political strategy" (7), was clearly an ideal narrative choice.

Essentially Reconstructed Womanhood and the Moral Geography of the Nation

The main plot of *Contending Forces* focuses on the "mulatto" Smith family—Ma Smith, her daughter Dora, and son Will—and on life in their post-Reconstruction, middle-class, Boston boardinghouse. The novel opens, however, earlier in the century with an account of how the Smiths' white ancestors, the Montforts, fell from being Bermuda slave owners to American slaves. Their two sons eventually escaped slavery to marry, one into a free black Northern family and the other into an aristocratic white English family. This opening section provides background for the main plot and also signals the importance of history in this narrative. Furthermore, as Carla Peterson reminds us, it "clarifies the relationship between British imperial domination and the American slave system, between external and internal frontiers" (181). While part of the plot traces the reuniting of the lost British side of this family with the American side, the main plot, set in post-Reconstruction Boston, traces the courtships of the two mulatto heroines. The first courtship is that of Dora Smith and her two suitors: the eventually rejected villain John Langley and the ultimately victorious and noble Dr. Arthur Lewis. The second courtship is between Will Smith and the mysterious Sappho Clark. Simultaneously, the novel charts the growth of a homoerotic friendship between Dora and Sappho as part of a broader focus on African-American female community. An important subplot runs side by side with Dora and Sappho's stories, a plot centered on a working-class character, Ophelia Davis, and her relationships with her business partner Sarah Ann White and her suitor, the Reverend Tommy James. Though the novel concludes by bringing together all three heterosexual couples, the two main heroines confront the history of American race relations along the way. In order to make possible a future, Sappho, in particular, must deal with her past—her status as an "impure" woman and unwed mother as a result of her rape by her white half-uncle. Much of the plot thus concerns the working out of historical legacies and blood lines as affected by slavery.

While Hopkins's novel chronicles in detail the lives and loves of two mulatto heroines, Dora and Sappho, it is in the depiction of the women's sewing circle, in the chapter of the same name, that Hopkins's general picture of African-American female identity and community emerges. The narrative space devoted to this circle, along with that devoted to the church fair, represents Hopkins's most sustained characterization of women working collectively for a larger social good. The circle itself constitutes a version of female community, both political and social. Recent critics have called attention to this chapter for its portrait of the women's club movement and the domestication of political issues that this movement entailed.[13] In the sewing circle, literally, the domestic realm of the sentimental novel becomes the forum for political debate, as the women meet to sew and "to go over the events of interest to the Negro race which had transpired during the week throughout the country" as well as to listen to Mrs. Willis give "a talk upon some topic of interest" (143). Significantly, the political discussion of the week itself focuses on African-American female identity and its relation to community.

Hopkins embodies this very question in the character of Mrs. Willis. As the woman of the public sphere, Mrs. Willis is Hopkins's spokesperson on the "Woman Question," but she also evokes an anxiety in Hopkins's narrative because of her public position. Left a widow without financial support, Mrs. Willis is forced to

hunt for the means to help her breast the social tide. The best opening, she decided . . . was in the great cause of the evolution of true womanhood in the work of the "Woman Question" as embodied in marriage and suffrage. She could talk dashingly on many themes, for which she had received much applause in by-gone days, when in private life she had held forth in the drawing-room of some Back Bay philanthropist who sought to use her talents as an attraction for a worthy charitable object, the discovery of a rare species of versatility in the Negro character being a sure drawing card. . . . The advancement of the colored woman should be the new problem in the woman question that should float her upon its tide into the prosperity she desired. And she succeeded well in her plans: conceived in selfishness, they yet bore glorious fruit in the formation of clubs of colored women banded together for charity, for study, for every reason under God's glorious heavens that can better the condition of mankind. (146–47)

Although Mrs. Willis thus embodies what the dominant culture would have seen as the self-glorification and self-aggrandizement—the exploitation of the public for private gain—dangerously inherent in woman's entrance into the public sphere, she also views public discourse as a means of curing society's ills. She justifies her entrance into this discourse on moral grounds, so that self-interest and collective benefit become completely harmonious. The "race question" and the "woman question," so central to Hopkins's day, also collide in Mrs. Willis: by working for the "advancement of the colored woman" Mrs. Willis serves both woman and the broader cause of "Negro uplift."

Mrs. Willis's presence in the novel can also be read as Hopkins's assertion of the inextricability of public and private spheres as well as the African-American woman's ongoing presence in both. If Mrs. Willis has carried her private "drawing room" skills into public, Hopkins suggests that even her past drawing room use of them was in a sense a public use, for it served a public "charitable object." Implicitly, too, one can read this as a statement of African-American women's (invisible) presence in white American culture. Given that the audience to whom the "Back Bay philanthropist" displays Mrs. Willis views an articulate African-American woman as a "rare species," we might assume that audience to be white.

Hopkins uses Mrs. Willis and the sewing circle to stage a discussion of the "place which the virtuous woman occupies in upbuilding a race" (148), a discussion that provides Hopkins with the opportunity to define a virtuous woman and to foreground the importance of African-American female sexuality in American historical constructions of race. Mrs. Willis opens by raising the specter of the immoral, sexually lascivious African-American woman, charging the young women of the circle with the responsibility of "refut[ing] the charges brought against us as to our moral irresponsibility, and the low moral standard maintained by us in comparison with other races" (148). This refutation is a common enough sentiment for African-American writers of Hopkins's day. What is more uncommon is the means by which the women are to muster their defense of their sex. When Sappho asks if "the Negro woman in her native state is truly a virtuous woman" (148), Mrs. Willis asserts that "Travelers tell us that the native African woman is impregnable in her virtue," and when Dora suggests that they have sacrificed that virtue in the acquisition of "civilization," Mrs. Willis clarifies her position still further by stating, "No, not 'sacrificed,' but pushed one side by the force of circumstances. Let us thank God that it *is* an essential attribute peculiar to us—a racial characteristic which is slumbering but not lost. . . . But let us not forget the definition of virtue—'Strength to do the right thing under all temptations.' Our ideas of virtue are too narrow. We confine them to that conduct which is ruled by our animal passions alone. It goes deeper than that—general excellence in every duty of life is what we may call virtue" (149). Hopkins here goes beyond merely defending African-American women's potential to emulate a white model of True Womanhood to lay claim to both an inherent "animal passion" and a wide-ranging, inherent, essential purity specific to African womanhood. Further, Hopkins's use of "impregnable" signals implicitly what will be later articulated explicitly: that African-American women in the past cannot be held responsible for what the dominant culture would term their "compromised" moral state. That is, we must read "impregnable" not in literal terms: if African women are generally "impregnable," African-American women, although physically pregnable by their masters, remain at the same time *morally* impregnable.

Sappho's movement through the novel may in great part be charted by her progress toward learning this lesson. This question of moral culpability for rape is raised early in the novel by Sappho, herself the victim of a white man's rape, when she asks Mrs. Willis if "Negro women will be held responsible for all the lack of virtue that is being laid to their charge today? I mean, do you think that God will hold us responsible for the *illegitimacy* with which our race has been obliged, as it were, to flood the world?" (149, emphasis in original). Her use of "obliged" here signals her confusion on this issue, obligation locating causation in duty rather than coercion or force. Echoing Sappho's religious terms of justification, Mrs. Willis claims in response that "we shall not be held responsible for wrongs which we have *unconsciously* committed, or which we have committed under *compulsion*. We are virtuous or non-virtuous only when we have a *choice* under temptation" (149, emphasis in original).[14] Mrs. Willis thus draws on an American liberal humanist tradition in which the human is assigned responsibility for his/her individual acts, but she offers a reworking of an Emersonian self-reliance argument by claiming that individual responsibility can only be ascribed if individual agency is present first. The power and agency inherent in the "choice" of sexual activity brings us back to Spillers's distinction between the body and the flesh, for it is only the slaveowner, defined as human, who has the choice. Hence, choice becomes one way of distinguishing the human subject from the enslaved object.[15] And yet, even as Mrs. Willis defines the power to choose as essential to humanity, she retains a gendered white bourgeois model of humanity and specifically of female purity—women who choose "temptation" *have*, in these terms, committed a "wrong." But through religious rhetoric and a claim of essential purity Mrs. Willis exempts the victimized African-American women from blame—this is a wrong for which the women are not responsible.

At the same time that Hopkins delineates this "naturally" pure African-American woman, however, she also attributes to her a natural "passion," defining passion as broadly as she does virtue but with somewhat more ambivalence. In the sewing circle discussion the connotation of passion is somewhat negative, in reaction to the historical construction of African-American female erotic desire, a construction used in the interests of dominant white culture to excuse white male "passion" in the form of rape. At this point in the novel passion is coded as Christian sin and returns the women to the question of responsibility. Sappho, unable to distinguish what a woman can and cannot control, cannot define agency and hence cannot assign responsibility. She asks Mrs. Willis, "how are we to overcome the nature which is given us? I mean how can we eliminate passion from our lives, and emerge into the purity which marked the life of Christ? So many of us desire purity and think to have found it, but *in a moment of passion, or under the pressure of circumstances which we cannot control*, we commit some horrid sin, and the taint of it sticks and will not leave us, and we grow to loathe ourselves" (154, emphasis added). The passive voice of "the nature which is given us" signals Sappho's confusion and allows for two readings of this passage. One might read this "nature" as the stereotype of lascivious and uncontrollable erotic desire assigned to African-American women by dominant culture, or one might read it as an innate erotic desire "given" to African-American women by God or Nature. The ambiguity of the passive voice marks, I would argue, Hopkins's narrative comment on the subject, just as Sappho's confusion indicates the degree to which the former reading replaces the latter in the dominant culture's construction of African-American womanhood. Sappho reads passion as lust, that which prevents access to a life like Christ's.

More strangely, she conflates desire and coercion, as Sappho's rhetoric collapses the autonomous agency of a woman's passion with the sexual victimization resulting from sexual assault (the "circumstances which we cannot control"). In this logic the difference between chosen and unchosen sex disappears, all sex is a "sin," and women are always culpable. How to refute this version of passion stands as one of the central projects of *Contending Forces* and an obvious moment of political intervention on Hopkins's part.

In answer to this, Hopkins, through the voice of Mrs. Willis, broadens the definition of passion to include not only "animal passions" (149) but also any sort of governing interest. Here Hopkins both grants women an essential "passion"—both sexual and nonsexual—and cautions against its dangers, counseling self-control. "Passion," Mrs. Willis explains, " . . . is a state in which the will lies dormant, and all other desires become subservient to one. Enthusiasm for any one object or duty may become a passion . . . in some degree passion may be beneficial, but we must guard ourselves against a sinful growth of any appetite. All work . . . needs a certain amount of absorbing interest to become successful, and it is here that the Christian life gains its greatest glory in teaching us how to keep ourselves from abusing any of our human attributes" (154). Both passion as sexual desire and passion as a metaphor for obsessional interest are contained here through the imposition of Christian self-control, the same self-control conventionally recommended to contain the abuse of "human attributes." Thus, Hopkins grants her heroines innate desires and desires that are not innately wrong or corrupt, but she also demands that they be strictly monitored, limited, and turned to the moral good of the race. As I will argue below in relation to homosocial desires, heterosexual desires are acknowledged without condemnation but are simultaneously strictly regulated.

Hopkins further suggests that African-American women, by virtue of their innate "purity," are responsible for teaching their male companions this redefined notion of passion. When Sappho tells Mrs. Willis a veiled, slightly reworked version of her own story—the "fallen woman" who married a good man who did not know of her past—she asks if it was the woman's duty to tell the man her history. "'I think not,' replied Mrs. Willis dryly" (156), again speaking for Hopkins, whose use of "dryly" here may be taken to indicate her skepticism about men's moral development and their ability to see beyond conventional received representations of African-American female desire. Mrs. Willis goes on to tell Sappho that "most men are like the lower animals in many things—they don't always know what is for their best good. If the husband had been left to himself, he probably would not have married the one woman in the world best fitted to be his wife. I think in this case she did her duty" (156). Hopkins implies that the hapless husband—whatever his race—would have been likely to rehearse a white dominant order's narrative of the fallen woman and that it is thus the duty of the African-American woman to insist on a narrative that redefines her passion and writes her into the story in a new way. Solidarity among women counters what Hopkins sees as male ignorance across racial lines.[16]

But Hopkins's work is not merely an essentialist echoing of Progressive Era rhetoric of Woman's inherent moral superiority and the social reform work that it was used to justify. Rather, her depictions of African-American womanhood are deeply grounded in American history and explicitly linked to historical relations that cross race, regional, and gender lines. The depictions also show how these lines are hopelessly intertwined. American history thus becomes a central player in Hopkins's work, producing a legacy of "contending forces" for African-American women in which structuring oppositions of American life—North/South, black/white, male/female—overlap, stand in for one another, and form a metonymic chain that leads to and ultimately constitutes American national identity. Hopkins's contributions to *Colored American Magazine* consistently display this sophisticated understanding of the ways in which gender and regional alignments cut across race and are simultaneously inflected by it. An article appearing in her "Famous Women of the Negro Race" series entitled "Club Life Among Colored Women," for instance, chronicles the women's club movement Hopkins was to write about in *Contending Forces*. In this article she depicts the white women's club movement's betrayal of the black women's club movement, tracking "the race battle in women's clubs" (274) as it was played out at the Sixth Biennial of the General Federation of Women's Clubs in Los Angeles, a battle that resulted in a vote that "practically closes the federation to colored clubs" (275). Hopkins initially reads this vote as a result of white Northern women deferring to white Southern women in order to maintain unity among the ranks of the white club members. She quotes, for example, the opinion of one Mrs. Dimies T. Denison, a white member from New York, who notes that the "Civil War is past; the old wounds have been healed; the North and the South have been reunited, and we cannot afford to take any action that will lead to more bitter feeling. The South is strongly represented in the Federation, and the effect on those members is obvious if colored women are admitted on a social equality with white members. We must not . . . do anything that threatens disruption of the Federation"(275). Racial Othering here does the work of white national reunification: the North and South can be unified only if they are understood to mean white and then pitted against the African American. Despite Mrs. Denison's claim, it is clear that even at this historical moment the North and South are *not* reunited: race continues to do this cultural work. Region and race here block female solidarity in a structure of affiliations pre-dating the Civil War.

Hopkins at first responds to this argument in kind, using the North/South axis as a means of establishing African-American club women's right to equality within the Federation. Equating the North with liberty and the South with racial prejudice and oppression, Hopkins claims, "thrice before in the history of our country the 'spaniel' North has grovelled before the South, but, thank God, the time came when the old New England spirit of Puritanism arose and shook its mane and flung off the shackles of conservatism" (277). The evocation of the New England "spirit of Puritanism" allows the defense of a specifically African-American female liberty to broaden into a more generalized American spirit of independence. Hopkins thus replaces a vision of regional factions with one of national panracial unity, a unity paradoxically regionally embodied by New England and rhetorically summoned here and elsewhere in *Contending Forces* through images of American patriotism and particularly through the incipient sense of national identity that provoked the American revolution.

But in her assessment of the women's club movement Hopkins goes beyond this race- and region-based analysis to offer an astute reading of the Southern women's motives, a reading that adds gender into the equation and ultimately points to white Southern men as a force dividing women, both on a North/South axis and on an Anglo-American/African-American axis:

We grant that the Southern woman has given us a terrible blow. . . . Granted conditions are hard for a certain class of Southern white women; but the results of profligacy are the same in any case no matter whether white or black are the partners. Certainly the rapid life of society everywhere at present, among white and black, is not suggestive of absolute purity, and the black is no worse than his environment. . . .

But if this thing [white men sexually exploiting African-American women] be true . . . it is but the result of conditions forced upon a helpless people, and not their choice. . . . Meanwhile, tears and sorrow and heart-burning are the Southern white woman's portion and like Sarah of old, she wreaks her vengeance on helpless Hagar. Club life has but rendered her disposition more intolerable toward the victims of her husband's and son's evil passions. (277)

In a tradition dating back at least as far as Harriet Jacobs, Hopkins thus traces Southern white women's animosity toward African-American women to the system of sexual oppression in which they are both implicated: the "thing" that Hopkins posits as "true" is the fact of white male exploitation of African-American women under slavery and white women's complicity with white men in the subsequent blaming of the victim. Racial solidarity overrides gender solidarity despite the fact that both African-American and white women are, to varying degrees, controlled by white men, and the public spaces provided by club life only serve to heighten white women's loyalty to dominant sources of power. History here inextricably links African-American and Anglo-American women within a larger discourse of American nationality. As Spillers points out,

we could say that African-American women's community and Anglo-American women's community, under certain shared cultural conditions, were the twin actants on a common psychic landscape, were subject to the same fabric of dread and humiliation. Neither could claim her body and its various productions—for quite different reasons, albeit—as her own . . . we cannot unravel one female's narrative from the other's, cannot decipher one without tripping over the other. (77)

Hopkins's work here and in her fiction establishes this claim, bearing witness to the complex and interrelated set of forces—race, region, gender, and their intersections—that determine the shape of late-nineteenth-century American identity. Insisting that we can only "decipher" American narratives by recognizing African-American women as a structuring figure within them, Hopkins ends her account of the Federation meeting by urging, "Never until we welcome the Negro, the foreigner, all races as equals, and welded together in a common nationality, will we deserve prosperity and peace" (277).[17]

In *Contending Forces* the vehicle through which Hopkins ultimately imagines a "common nationality" of unified regions is gender. Both on the level of character and through the defining of regions through the image of woman, Hopkins locates African-American womanhood—in various forms—as central to the work of cultural reunification and American national identity. Dora and Sappho's friendship provides the most obvious instance of Hopkins's discussion of "Negro Life North and South." Dora embodies the spirit of liberty that the Maine-born and Boston-raised Hopkins attributes to the North: "into Sappho's lonely, self-suppressed life the energetic little Yankee girl swept like a healthful, strengthening breeze" (114), the narrator comments, aligning Dora with Boston and "Northern life" (114). In "Club Life Among Colored Women" Hopkins explicitly marks the North as superior to the South (a distinction obviously aligned with the regions' pasts as free and slave-holding), stating that the "claim of the North to govern has been in the past that civilization here is nobler than in the South, and we believe this to be still an axiom" (277). Liberty, a constitutive American value, produces this nobility, Hopkins implies in *Contending Forces*, claiming, for example, that the "Negro" in Boston "reflected the spirit of his surroundings in his upright carriage, his fearlessness in advancing his opinions, his self-reliance, his anxiety to obtain paying employment that would give to his family some few of the advantages . . . , his love of liberty, which in its intensity recalled the memory of New England men who had counted all worldly gain as nothing if demanding the sacrifice of even one of the great principles of freedom" (114–5). As a representative of the city where "in the free air of New England's freest city Sappho drank great draughts of freedom's subtle elixir" (115), Dora is the end point of a chain of signifiers linking Boston, New England, the North, freedom from slavery, and the independence of spirit representative of American national identity. Added to this chain throughout the novel is also the commitment to work both for the improvement of women and for racial uplift, as implied in Hopkins's specific description of Mrs. Willis as Northern, as "one of many possibilities which the future will develop from among the colored women of New England. Every city or town from Maine to New York has its Mrs. Willis" (144). Invoking both the North's abolitionist past and New England's Revolutionary principles, Hopkins privileges the North, implicitly looking to a Northern audience for support in the cause of racial justice.

Predictably, while Hopkins aligns the work of racial uplift with black Northern women and a spirit of independence with Northern women of all races, she codes the South as backward and racist, depicting the South as the site of reactionary and often violent racial politics, and she often downplays Boston's racist employment practices in order to emphasize Southern lynching and rape.[18] Simultaneous with this mapping of American moral geography, Hopkins offers a gendering of region, often imaging the South as female. In a typical example Hopkins concedes that there is prejudice in Massachusetts, but she argues that it is "prejudice which is fed every day by fresh arrivals from the South and by intermarriage between Southern women and the sons of Massachusetts" (224). She then goes on to combine the gendering and moral coding of regions by invoking the stereotype of the exotic, sensuous South in contrast to a more Puritan legacy in the North, a set of stereotypes that she both rehearses and ultimately, through the figure of Sappho, resists. White southern women come to represent the region and its racism, as in the example above, but the region is also credited with producing in both white and African-American southern women a regionally based, specifically sexual immorality not unlike that attributed by Florence Converse to creole New Orleans. Ophelia Davis and Sarah White, the two laundresses in Ma Smith's boardinghouse, for instance, assume that Sappho is from the South because of her great beauty, speculating that Louisiana is her home. Confirmed in this judgment by Sappho, Mrs. White crows, "I knowed it. . . . Ol' New Orleans blood will tell on itself anywhere. These col'-blooded Yankees can't raise nuthin' that looks like thet chile; no, 'ndeed!" (108). Meanwhile Dora complains that her suitor John Langley "said that he had not met a decent-looking woman who was Northern-born, and that when he did see a pretty colored girl on the street he knew without asking that she was a Southerner" (180). Langley himself takes this notion of regional beauty to its furthest extreme, conflating it with sensuality and moral laxness. The narrator notes that Langley had observed in Sappho a "coldness more in accordance with the disposition of women of the North than with that of one born beneath the smiling skies of the languorous Southland" (227). In confronting Sappho with her past, Langley not only blames the victim but frames her status as regionally based. Replying to her protest that she was an "innocent child" when raped, he comments, "I know . . . but girls of fourteen are frequently wives in our Southern climes, where women mature early. A man as supercilious as Will in his pride of Northern birth could take no excuse, and would never forgive" (319). Langley here implies both that Southern women are sexually precocious in comparison with Northern women and that Northern men hold "their" women to higher moral standards than Southern men do, a judgment that Hopkins tacitly confirms in having Sappho, after her past has been revealed, flee to New Orleans because, in Sappho's words, "my case will not be noticed, because it is not uncommon" (344).

Although the South is credited with racial evils and moral impurities, Hopkins does not settle for simply projecting all of the country's evils onto the South: the North may be liberty loving, but it also reveals racism deeply inscribed in both its economic practices and its social ones. Thus, while Hopkins structures the novel in part around a North-South divide, she also articulates a racial divide, calling for unity among blacks, Northern and Southern, against racist whites nationwide. Ma Smith reminds Dora "that sectional prejudice has always been fostered by the Southern whites among the Negroes to stifle natural feelings of brotherly love among us. Dissension means disunion" (181). As a free-born Northern African American, Hopkins was well aware that axes of race and region intersect in American culture but are not identical.[19]

Meanwhile in case any reader has missed her point, Hopkins has Ophelia Davis, one of her working-class characters, an ex-slave now enjoying the "liberties" of Boston, compare race relations North and South through a discussion of her originally Southern ex-employer. Davis comments, "Lor', chile, but Mis' Mason's a lady borned; she don't know how to be like some o' yer Northern people. Sho! these ladies up here are so 'fraid thet the black'll rub off. Down South the big white folks has nussed so meny black mammies that they don't know nuthin' else fer their chillun. It don' matter how black you is ef yer willin' to keep in the mud. Up here it's diffurunt; you can do all right and live all right, but don't put yer han' on a white man or woman, or they'll have a fit fer fear the black'll rub off" (192). Hopkins here delineates the many faces of racism, underscoring that economic and social equality or proximity are not inherently linked: Northern blacks might have greater economic stability than Southern blacks living "in the mud," but at the same time there might be a greater social distance between races in the North than in the South.[20] At the same time, Davis's discussion of "white folks" further serves to underscore once again the presence of the African-American woman in every area of American life, standing in intimate relation to dominant white culture both as the mammy of the Southern past and as the worker of the Northern present.

Erotic Charges and Social Debts

Ophelia Davis's commentary, in fact, often provides the novel with this sort of insight, so that she occupies a more important place in *Contending Forces* than is apparent at first glance and might be read as condensing a number of issues central to the novel. As an ex-slave now occupying the place of a working-class free Northern woman, Ophelia Davis, like Sappho, embodies the meeting of North and South and also stands as representative of the African-American woman in relation to both a female community and a male suitor. Even more significantly, as a business woman she provides a counter-example to that of Mrs. Willis of the African-American woman in public. Richard Yarborough, in his introduction to *Contending Forces*, argues that "Hopkins's own elitist views mar her treatment of lower-class black characters like Sarah Ann White and Ophelia Davis" (xli), but I would suggest that Ophelia Davis (and, to a lesser extent, White) provides Hopkins with one of her most important sites of intervention into both the racial discourse and a discourse of sexuality of her day.[21]

With her old friend Sarah Ann White, Ophelia Davis leaves her native Louisiana after the Civil War, seeking "the blessings of liberty in the North" (104). Although Hopkins does not give much narrative space to their relationship, she does explain that they are friends "of long standing" and that once in the North they go "into partnership in a laundry" (104), a business that proves very successful. Business partners and friends, they exemplify the kind of African-American female community that Hopkins advocates, a community that grows from an American emphasis on individual capitalism but yet fosters affection and support among its members. This model is replicated in the scenes of Mrs. Davis's rivalry with one Mrs. Robinson at the church fair. They compete for a piano and for the largest profit made at a refreshment table, flinging challenges back and forth. However, when Mrs. Davis finally beats out her church rival in a spirited fashion, she gives Mrs. Robinson the prize and asks the officiating pastor to "tell her we's quits, an' I fergive her fer all her mean feelin's to me" (218).[22] Hopkins rewards Mrs. Davis's commitment to community not only by giving her the successful laundry and church competition but also by setting her up as successor to Ma Smith, for it is Mrs. Davis who takes over Ma Smith's boardinghouse when Ma Smith gives it up to go live with Dora and her new husband at the novel's close.

Hopkins also writes Mrs. Davis into a heterosexual courtship plot, a subplot that can be read in a number of ways. On one level this courtship plot stands as a foil to those of Sappho and Dora. Mrs. Davis's romance with the Rev. Tommy James is notable in this sense because it is the least bourgeois and most embodied of the novel's three courtships and because, as a result, Ophelia Davis stands at a greater distance than the other two heroines from the space of True Womanhood. She is hardly the conventional bourgeois heroine. A businesswoman, she does not occupy only the private sphere and works for herself rather than for racial uplift.[23] She is considerably older than James, and in both age and physical appearance she does not meet the standards of the sentimental heroine. Mrs. Davis is a heavy woman rather than a frail beauty, and her dignity is repeatedly undercut by both her friend Sarah Ann White and by the narrative itself. James's proposal, for instance, occurs after the two have had a bicycle accident, an undignified event that Mrs. Davis describes in much detail to Ma Smith. After proudly describing both her own and James's clothing,

Mrs. Davis notes, "Everybody was a-lookin' an' a-gappin' at us. Sarah Ann says it was 'cause we looked like a couple o' jay birds stuffed" (367), then goes on to describe the accident itself and its effect on her:

As fer me, I tore my gloves, los' my hat, an' busted a new pair o' corsets right off me. Besides thet, I nearly swallered my upper teeth, an' I lost my bangs. They picked me up an' carried me into a house they was a-buildin', an' give me a chance to fix myself up a bit. But I 'clar to you them corsets was no good never after thet; an' it cost me ten dollars to fix thet upper set o' teeth so I could wear 'em agin; I never have seen them bangs sence. (367–68)

Just as this is clearly not the conventional bourgeois heroine, the Davis-James union is not the conventional bourgeois marriage. Although they do feel affection for each other (as fiction of the period prescribes for partners in a good middle-class marriage), theirs is neither a marriage grounded in erotic passion nor a marriage dedicated to racial uplift. James, in considering his feelings for Mrs. Davis, reasons that while "she was old enough to be his mother . . . she had many good points to be considered. She was a good worker, experienced in married life and ways of making a man comfortable. Then her savings must be considered. When Tommy reached this last point he always felt sure that she was the most desirable woman in the world for a young minister" (161). A marriage based neither in a spiritual bond nor in a bond of passion, the Davis-James marriage reads a bit like a business merger, albeit an affectionate one. Mrs. Davis describes their future plans in business terms: "The society he's been preaching fer Sundays is goin' to give him their church, and I'll keep the laundry a-goin' an' rent rooms" (365). Read as a foil to the marriages of Sappho and Dora, then, Mrs. Davis's marriage carries with it neither an erotic charge nor a sense of social debt and offers a working-class model of African-American marriage in contrast to the two main heroines' bourgeois courtships and marriages. As such, Mrs. Davis has Hopkins's approval and although she does provide the comic relief of the novel, I would hold that ultimately she is both a sympathetic character and one whose prosperity signals her virtue.

Mrs. Davis's relationship with the Rev. James can be read, however, not simply as a foil to the other heroines' heterosexual courtship plots. It is also juxtaposed in the novel to her relationship with Sarah Ann White, a narrative doubling that has recently begun to receive critical attention. Carla Peterson reads the courtship between Mrs. Davis and the Rev. Tommy James as the novel's most successful attempt to reconcile the contending forces within the African-American community. She sees their relationship as offering "a movement toward gender equality" as well as "the continuation of a long tradition of collective action within the black community" (194). What Peterson does not note, however, is that the same might be said of Mrs. Davis's relationship with Sarah Ann White. Mrs. Davis's relationship with White and her emphatically nonerotic heterosexual relationship offer both to the character and to the narrative many of the same beneficial refigurings of an African-American heroine who has a private life but also occupies the public sphere. This analogy might be extended. Siobhan Somerville, in a discussion of homoerotic desire in *Contending Forces*, describes the Davis-White relationship as "at once affectional and economic—not unlike heterosexual marriage" (156), particularly, I would add, a heterosexual marriage with as little erotic charge as the Davis-James one. This comparison is supported by Mrs. Davis's prolonged description of Mrs. White's opposition to James's suit, a description that culminates in Ophelia Davis asserting, "Sarah Ann an' me'll have to part after I'm married, she's that jealous" (365), a jealously that implies competition between Mrs. White and the Rev. James for Ophelia Davis's affections. Somerville argues in relation to this scene that the fact "that their 'breakup' involves jealousy and protectiveness is also evidence that she [Hopkins] wanted in some way to express the passion existing between these women. . . . Like Dora, Davis is compelled by cultural custom to agree to marriage in spite of her indifference to her fiancé and her passionate attachment to her female companion" (159). Although I would argue that the novel leaves open the question of a specifically romantic/erotic "passion" between Ophelia Davis and Sarah Ann White, it certainly represents them as bearing toward each other the sort of passion Mrs. Willis defines early in the novel as "absorbing interest" (154). More explicitly, Hopkins offers their relationship prior to the Davis-James romance as a model of a supportive female community that moves between public and private spheres. It stands as a representation of the historical relationships between women that Smith-Rosenberg and other historians have read as culturally sanctioned, intense relationships between women that were seen as preparatory to marriage but often continued beyond a woman's marriage.

At the same time, Somerville's comment suggests a comparison between Ophelia Davis and Dora Smith that is fruitful on several levels. Most obviously, perhaps, in comparison to Ophelia Davis's courtship with the Rev. James, Dora's courtship plot emerges as the plot of African-American True Womanhood. Mrs. Willis's model of innate desire displaced into cultural service structures Dora's marriage to Dr. Arthur Lewis. Claudia Tate has persuasively argued that marriage in general operates as liberational in nineteenth-century African-American women's sentimental texts, as a new civil right that confirmed the ex-slave's legal status as human rather than chattel. It also, of course, confirms a model of humanity that is specifically bourgeois and replicates the ideal of purity and nonerotic True Womanhood. Within this model "courtship is devoid of all ardent sentiment that does not arise from noble admiration. Respect kindles love, and mutual commitment to advancing the race engenders love" so that "the emphasis falls on explaining how the couple plans to live out their married life actively engaged in working for racial progress" ("Allegories" 117). Dora clearly fits this pattern. Her first engagement, to John Langley, is coded by the narrator from the start as doomed. At Langley's introduction into the plot we are told that he lacks Will's "strong manhood and honesty of purpose" (90) and that, moreover, he is a "North Carolinian—a descendant of slaves and Southern 'crackers'." The narrator goes on to identify this lineage as "a bad mixture—the combination of the worst features of a dominant race with an enslaved race" that produces in him "a carefully concealed strain of sensuality" and "a mercenary streak, which made love of money his great passion" (91).[24] Unwilling to work for racial uplift, he is too selfish to be a fit mate for Dora, the narrative implies, whereas Dora (as a Northern woman, one might infer) lacks passion enough for Langley. But Dora is vaguely dissatisfied with her engagement to Langley even before she recognizes his moral failures. Even early in the novel, before she explicitly realizes and articulates her commitment to working for racial uplift, Dora sees that passion cannot be the motivation for her marriage. She admits of John, "I like him well enough to marry him, but I don't believe there's enough sentiment in me to make love a great passion" (119). It is clear, moreover, that her passionlessness is not merely a case of not yet having met the right man. Dora also lacks passion for the man marked by Hopkins as her rightful husband, a man Dora describes as not "a fascinator, or anything of that sort; he's just good" (123). Dora's description of Arthur Lewis further de-eroticizes him by locating him as a symbolic brother: "We were children together," she tells Sappho, adding, "I never think of him except as old Arthur, who used to drag me to school on his sled" (123). Tate notes that domestic novels "almost categorically assert the sibling model of ideal love," arguing that, as a result, the novels "silence the expression of sexual ardor and engender romantic idealism" (*Domestic Allegories* 176). This is certainly true of Hopkins's representation of Dora's marriage to Lewis. Dora is, however, filled with "respect" for Lewis (360), a character who runs an industrial school in Louisiana (and is modeled on Booker T. Washington), and she agrees to marry him based on a feeling of "peace and contentment" (361). Like Frances E. W. Harper's heroine, Iola Leroy, Dora enters a marriage of spiritual partnership, leaving with her new husband for "his far-off Southern home to assist him in the upbuilding of their race" (381).

Dora, then, like Ophelia Davis, lacks erotic passion for her husband. But unlike Mrs. Davis, Dora is provided, as an implied substitute for this passion, with a "passion" in the form of governing interest toward "the upbuilding of their race." This is a substitution the novel codes as entirely appropriate and as defining Dora (in contrast to Mrs. Davis) as the idealized African-American middle-class lady. This version of African-American True Womanhood replicates the erotic passionlessness of the dominant white model combined with an imperative to community service and is offered as one possible role for the African-American woman of the future. At the same time, however, this lack of erotic passion is also coded as problematic, as when Dora quite explicitly tells Sappho, "What troubles me is having a man bothering around . . . after you marry a man, he's on your hands for good and all" (121) then adds, "Then I get tired of a man so soon! . . . I dread to think of being tied to John for good and all; I know I'll be sick of him inside of a week" (121–22). She also notes that her lack of a sense of eternal love makes her feel "*unsexed*" (122, emphasis in original). In this context passion is constitutive of the (hetero-) sexing of a woman and seems to mean both heterosexual romantic love and a sense of individuated desire, whether emotional or physical. In implying that a properly "sexed" African-American woman would feel passion, Hopkins rehearses conventional white models of femininity (in ascribing romantic love to woman's realm) and challenges them (in calling for erotic desire in this refigured model of True Womanhood), a seeming contradiction linked to her reclaiming of both romantic love and erotic desire for the African-American woman.

But in fact, this contradiction can be understood if viewed in the broader terms of Hopkins's recasting of African-American womanhood, a recasting that allows not simply for several forms of passion (both erotic and a broader sort of governing interest) but also for several locations for passion. Not only does Dora feel a noerotic passion for racial uplift, it would also be a misreading to argue that Dora is completely lacking in erotic passion. This regulatory vision of female desire erased or displaced into moral service does not represent the final word on passion in Dora's case (or in Sappho's, as I will argue).[25] More accurately, one might say Dora lacks heterosexual passion: she feels a strong, albeit undefined, attraction to Sappho. Dora, we are told, "did not, as a rule, care much for girl friendships, holding that a close intimacy between two of the same sex was more than likely to end disastrously for one or the other. But Sappho Clark seemed to fill a long-felt want in her life, and she had from the first a perfect trust in the beautiful girl" (98). She has "a great fascination" (97) for Sappho, and the two become "fast friends at once" (98), after which "the two girls were much together" (114). Although Hopkins does not fully develop the relationship between Dora and Sappho, her statement that Sappho fills a "long-felt want" in Dora's life, as well as her choice of Sappho as the name of her heroine, suggests a homoerotic bond between the two women, inviting a reading of this friendship as proto-lesbian. Given that Hopkins was raised in and set her novel in the home of the "Boston marriage," she may well have been offering this friendship as a model of a world in which women's affectional ties (whether physically enacted or not) were often seen as equally, if not more, important and sustaining as their ties to men.[26] Somerville argues that "Hopkins portrays female couples as potential sites for the expression of desire and identification, at the same time that she contains their threat to the narrative's overall heterosexual trajectory. Hopkins contains these eruptions of homoeroticism" (159). I would refine this formulation to suggest that although Dora's belief that "girl friendships . . . end disastrously" (98) locates Hopkins's novel within the historical moment when female-female desire is increasingly being pathologized, her narrative, like Jewett's, evades this construction by depicting Dora's homoerotic passion in the earlier historical terms of romantic friendship. As a result, this desire is sanctioned by the narrative, where it bolsters rather than challenges the heterosexual plot. As such, it both draws on older models of female-female desire and specifically inflects them racially, producing a portrait that refigures both African-American female identity and representations of African-American female desire by virtue of its location at the crossroads of the discourses on sexuality and race at the turn of the century.

The most complicated example of refigured desire in the novel, however, is Sappho. That Sappho's character will be the location of Hopkins's fullest examination of sexuality's relation to African-American womanhood is clear from the very introduction of the character to the plot. In a scene remarkably reminiscent of one in *Diana Victrix*, the Smith family discusses their new boarder, and Will speculates that she will be "a rank old maid with false teeth, bald head, hair on her upper lip" (96), an image that, like Jacques's description of Enid and Sylvia, translates the economic and social independence implied by Sappho's status as boarder into a challenge to norms of femininity and heterosexual desirability. In fact, however, while Sappho (like Enid and Sylvia) does challenge gender norms, she does so not in the terms Will predicts: she is beautiful and attractive to both Dora and Will. Instead, the specifically homoerotic element of Sappho's character disrupts racialized gender norms in less predictable ways, in part by drawing on several of the discourses most centrally at issue in the novel. In terms of the sexual discourse of the day, Sappho's character is disruptive simply because of the homoeroticism implied by her name. Somerville reminds us that by the end of the nineteenth century, older understandings of the historical Sappho as either a courtesan or a bodiless model of love were shifting to an aligning of her with female homosexuality, whereas the discovery of a new papyrus in Egypt opened the possibility that "the figure of Sappho may have suggested not only codes of gentility and a model of an intellectual and artistic woman, but also a potential link to a specifically African past" (146–47). This configuration of meanings suggests a homoerotic element to Sappho's character but has several other ramifications as well. By ascribing homoerotic desire to its model of the ideal African-American woman, the novel firmly locates the homosocial within the idealized African-American bourgeois community and implicitly sanctions its presence there. Whether one reads the original Sappho as the forerunner of the modern lesbian or merely as the leader of a spiritual community of women, Hopkins's use of the name to signify friendship, love, and community among women—as well as a homoerotic bond between Sappho and Dora—provides the reader with one more representation of African-American female community and yet another space for a refiguring of African-American female desire.[27] Moreover, by specifically inflecting female homoerotic desire racially as African-American, the novel also suggests that the range of female-female relations available to nineteenth-century women operated across race lines to a degree not yet fully explored by historians, who have tended to read these relationships simply as white.

Certainly, Sappho and Dora's relationship stands as a model of female community in the book—throughout the novel Sappho and Dora trust in and support one another in the face of duplicitous lovers and blackmailers—and serves as a precursor to the heterosexual marriages they will both make. So that just as the sewing circle discussion allows a space for female (implicitly heterosexual) passion but argues that it must be monitored and contained, the novel itself allows a space for homoerotic female passion but similarly contains it in the space of romantic friendship. But Sappho and Dora's relationship can also be read, like Sappho's heterosexual marriage, as a narrative means of unifying the regional divides of North and South. Indeed, Dora, much more explicitly than Will, is represented as embodying the spirit of the North, of Yankee independence, while Sappho, of course, represents the legacy of the South, specifically the enslaved African-American South. This representation—African-American homosocial desire as the mechanism for resolving sectional tensions—offers perhaps the most radical vision of the novel despite its brief appearance and its narrative supercession by the more conventional heterosexual marriage reunification narrative.

"Impregnable" Erotic Virtue and Mulatto Mothers

Ann duCille reads Mabelle's choice of "Sappho" as her new name as "link[ing] her metaphorically to the lesbian poet of the same name" and as indicating that "she denies . . . the sexual dominance of men" (42), a claim that seems true although not sufficient. The text as a whole, that is, not only does not code the rejection of male sexual dominance as lesbian, it also actively promotes a representation of heterosexual female desire grounded in the same rejection of dominance. This form of desire is most explicitly represented in Sappho's relationship with Will, where Hopkins grants Sappho a passion that is actively erotic, non-victimized, and marked as positive. The narrative clearly shows Sappho as bearing erotic desire for Will, the hero marked out by the narrative as Sappho's rightful husband, and in the end Hopkins sanctions that desire by bringing the two together in marriage. This recoding of the body and desire is accomplished through an emphasis on choice rather than coercion. After Sappho has fled Will to spare him her sexual "disgrace," she reclaims her son and finds a comfortable position as governess/companion yet remains unhappy. The narrator explains that Sappho "tried not to allow herself to think upon the past; but when night came she lay awake hungering for the sight of a face, the touch of a hand, the glance of an eye. Sometimes the craving grew almost too powerful to be resisted, and once she started to dress, resolved to return to Boston, find Will, and trust all to his love" (354). Such desire, originating in Sappho rather than forced upon her, is clearly both erotic and sanctioned by Hopkins, offered as yet another prototype of a model marriage.

Like Dora's and Mrs. Davis's marriage, Sappho's marriage does not relegate her to the private sphere. Lois Lamphere Brown argues that Sappho does not end up "ensconced within . . . African-American communities" and that "Hopkins denies her American mixed-race characters the strength derived from immersion in work relating to racial uplift" (59), but in fact the narrator tells us that Sappho and her new husband, like Dora and her husband, plan "to work together to bring joy to hearts crushed by despair" (401). The new family does leave the U.S. for Europe at the novel's end but with the goal of serving the African-American community from abroad. The narrator tells us that the "ambition of his [Will's] life was the establishment of a school which should embrace every known department of science, where the Negro youth of ability and genius could enter without money and without price . . . he would be a father to the youth of his race" (386). Thus, although Will and Sappho are distanced from their community geographically, they remain linked to it ideologically.

Ultimately, it is Sappho's marriage that brings together her erotic desire and her desire to work for racial uplift, and these desires' conjoining in her marriage locates her in both public and private spheres at once. However, this narrative closure only guarantees a position the plot has accorded Sappho from the start. Hopkins insists on this dual location for Sappho throughout the novel, a duality paralleled and underscored by the narrative's use of her mulatto identity. Sappho is the mulatto version of the white bourgeois heroine, "tall and fair, with hair of a golden cast, aquiline nose, rosebud mouth, soft brown eyes veiled by long, dark lashes which swept her cheeks . . . a combination of 'queen rose and lily in one'" (107). Men and women alike are struck by her beauty, and she is quiet and reserved, a living refutation of the stereotype of the immoral, sexually unrestrained African-American woman. Although she is a domestic ideal, she is also a New Woman, a stenographer who "picks up a good living at home" with her typewriter (89). Clearly a model for the independent woman, she has, as Mary Helen Washington notes, "one of the first nonnurturing professions black women have in fiction" (80), a profession that Hopkins herself relied on at various points in her life. In addition, Sappho secretly supports dependents and is capable of arranging her own affairs, from renting a room in Ma Smith's boarding house to taking a long train journey alone. In her friendship with Dora, she discusses politics, proving that the domestic can be the sphere of politics and explicitly dismissing Arthur Lewis's Washingtonian position of conciliation in favor of Hopkins's own support of Du Bois's position (a position also represented in the novel by Sappho's future husband, Will). Learning that Lewis "thinks that women should be seen and not heard, where politics is under discussion," Sappho, not short on opinions, labels him an "insufferable prig" (126). Ultimately, her movement back and forth between, and her conflation of, the public and private realms effectively blurs the lines not only between these realms but also between various races and regions in America.

Of course, as part of this process, Sappho must traverse miles, years, and seemingly endless pain. This journey, as much as its happy ending, constitutes Hopkins's repositioning of African-American female identity within American culture. In Sappho, Hopkins has created what Spillers describes as the African-American woman's position in general: "a meeting ground of investments and privations in the national treasury of rhetorical wealth" (65). And as both victim and survivor, Sappho serves as a synthesizing force. In the end it is Sappho who is the meeting ground of North and South; Sappho, who is really Mabelle Beaubean; Sappho, who is Southern-born but Northern-settled; Sappho, who as the victim of Southern racial violence is cast as the Fallen Woman but who also embodies Northern purity and liberty; Sappho, who enacts both nurturing homosocial bonding and normative heterosexual bonding; Sappho, who through her marriage to Will helps form a couple whose very names alert us that they are Hopkins's ideal pair, the two who unite the will-power of the head with the love of the heart; Sappho, who in the end stands for both racial and gender solidarity, as well as the promise of national reconciliation.

In the narrative of Mabelle's rape and its aftermath, Hopkins establishes the complex nexus of forces shaping African-American women's identities, drawing race, gender, region, and historical legacy into play on the body of the African-American woman. Carby reads Sappho as Hopkins's "paradigm of the historical rape of black women" (*Reconstructing* 138): viewed in this light, Sappho provides the narrative space for the voicing of an African-American woman's elided history. Her story not only establishes her as guiltless, "a victim! an innocent child!" (219) but also demands that the African-American woman, even the raped, unmarried mulatto mother, be accorded full human and female subject status. This accession to full human female status requires that Sappho come to terms with the historical legacy that imposes the erotic and the reproductive functions on the African-American female body while at the same time alienating that body from the cultural privileges of the maternal. It thus demands a rewriting of the story of African-American women in American culture.

After the mulatto child Mabelle is abducted, raped, and left pregnant in a brothel by her white half-uncle, the half-uncle explains himself to the grief-stricken father by stating, "whatever damage I have done I am willing to pay for. But your child is no better than her mother or her grandmother. What does a woman of mixed blood, or any Negress, for that matter, know of virtue? It is my belief that they were a direct creation by God to be the pleasant companions of men of my race. Now, I am willing to give you a thousand dollars and call it square" (261). This statement quite explicitly follows the ideology of slavery in its representation of African-American women, articulating (as does Grace Montfort's story) the very view Hopkins rewrites. In its terms Mabelle "follows the condition" of her mother, a "quadroon" (258), and is to be considered by the white man as chattel, property, not as a human and not as even part white. As a non-white woman, she cannot embody the white bourgeois ideal of female virtue, but she must, rather, occupy the space of the lascivious black woman. As such, Mabelle/Sappho is fair game for white male lust and her half-uncle considers himself exceedingly fair in offering a good price for her "virtue." The scene stands as a searing indictment of the sexual politics of slavery and, further, indicates that these sexual politics have outlasted the legal system of slavery in the United States. Sappho's rape, echoing Grace Montfort's symbolic rape, shows that if the laws have changed since the Civil War, the ideological beliefs and investments fueling them have not.[28]

Rape, of course, is linked in America to lynching, both historically and in terms of Hopkins's narrative. Alleged rapes of white women by black men served to deflect attention from the real rapes of black women by white men, and, further, were used as the justification for the lynching of black men. Ronald Takaki reminds us that, symptomatic of what he labels a "hardening of racial repression," the United States had "an average of about 188 lynchings a year . . . during the 1890s," a figure that helps to suggest the extent of this political violence (*Iron Cages* 214). Jacquelyn Dowd Hall identifies lynching as a form of "ritual violence" and "psychological intimidation" and links this to a similar political usage of rape in the post–Civil War United States (329, 330). Will Smith, Hopkins's Du Bois character and one of her favored mouthpieces, directly addresses this political significance, stating, "lynching was instituted to crush the manhood of the enfranchised black. Rape is the crime which appeals most strongly to the heart of the home life. Merciful God! Irony of ironies! *The men who created the mulatto race, who recruit its ranks year after year by the very means which they invoke the lynch law to suppress*, bewailing the sorrows of violated womanhood!" (270–71, emphasis in original). Lynching and rape both operate here as acts of racial terrorism whereby African-American men and African-American and Anglo-American women are kept subservient by the threat of violence, a threat that simultaneously reinforces white male privilege.

In addition, rape, as a political weapon, strips the African-American woman once again of her right to control her body, both in terms of sexual actions and in terms of "motherhood." Rape robs the African-American woman of a voluntary and non-alienated relationship to her offspring, placing her in the same cultural space as her enslaved forebearer. Because the rape of a woman, in the ideological terms of the time, disqualified her from the right to occupy the domestic ideal of True Woman and mother, the rape of African-American women by white men can be seen not only as a violent denial of the women's human status but also as a disruption of the African-American family. Hopkins counters this use of rape by reworking the notion of redemptive maternity and domesticity. If, as Claudia Tate has argued, marriage was a liberatory event for a newly freed African-American people, one must also read the creation of a domestic sphere as equally liberatory and radical for the African-American woman. Stripped of maternal and familial rights in slavery, the African-American woman must of necessity have viewed these rights as more than just a white bourgeois space. Given that slave women had no legal right to their children, who were routinely torn from their mothers to be sold as valuable property by their white, male owners and sometimes fathers, maternity would necessarily have meant something structurally and affectively different for late-nineteenth-century African-American women than what it meant for white women. Thus, claiming maternal and familial rights could be viewed as a form of empowerment even if an empowerment strictly within the narrow terms of a middle-class liberal humanism. In this light Hopkins's use of the seemingly conventional trope of redemptive maternity becomes not so conventional.

Hopkins's original use of the trope employs a predictably Christian rhetoric. When Sappho has been exposed as Mabelle Beaubean by the villain Langley and has fled from Will, she is suddenly struck with regret at her abandonment of her illegitimate son. The narrator tells us that Sappho "fancied . . . that Conscience spoke in condemnation of her neglect of her child. She had felt nothing for the poor waif but repugnance. Her delicate nervous organization was naturally tinged with superstition, and she felt that God had sat in judgment on her willingness to forget her child. . . . At length she rose from that seat resolved that come what would she would claim the child and do her duty as his mother in love and training. She would devote her life to him. They would nevermore be separated" (342). This is a straightforward use of redemptive maternity, an invocation of a moral mother-love and its transformative powers. Indeed, once Sappho acts on this decision, she finds that the "mother-love chased out all the anguish that she had felt over his birth" (346) and that "this new and holy love . . . was the compensation for all she had suffered" (347).

Hopkins codes this redemptive love not merely as imitative of a white woman's model but also as an answer to the disruption of the family effected by slavery. It is here that Sappho's status as a mulatto emerges as crucial, for this status not only challenges racial ideologies of Hopkins's day but also, in the context of the novel, forces a refiguring of both the family structure itself and the American culture it helps to constitute. Putting "black," "white," and "mulatto" into a familial relation enables Hopkins, through the vehicle of Sappho and her relationship with her child, to explore the African-American woman's relation to family, patriarchy, and the white fathers—her own, her child's, and society's.

In the racist ideologies of Hopkins's day, the "one drop" theory continued to prevail, holding that even a single drop of black blood made one black. Originally constructed in response to white owners' rape of enslaved women, this theory obviously operated as a rationale for the slave "following the condition of the mother" and hence increasing the owner's wealth and labor force. Even at the end of the century the mulatto continued to be aligned with the African-American community. As Claudia Tate points out, the mulatto figure served for turn-of-the-century African-American writers as a figure of inclusion, as "a generic term for designating the emancipated population and their heirs" (*Domestic Allegories* 146). Hopkins, like many of her peers, uses the mulatto as representative of the African American: emphasizing the mulatto's omnipresence in American culture, for instance, Hopkins has Mrs. Willis assert that "It is an incontrovertible truth that there is no such thing as an unmixed black on the American continent . . . out of a hundred apparently pure black men not one will be able to trace an unmixed flow of African blood since landing upon these shores" (151). Hence, for Hopkins, unlike for Jewett or for Converse, a "mixing" of blood and/or community—be it racial or national—is not only not degenerative; it is inevitable. Indeed, such a mixing represents the future of the nation, a vision that resembles, as I will argue, that of Sui Sin Far.

Tate reminds us that viewing mulattos as "racially ambivalent African Americans who rely on their light skin color to bolster their self-esteem and bourgeois ambitions" and seeing the mulatto "not as representative of but antagonistic to the black population" is a twentieth-century interpretation that differs significantly from Hopkins's and her contemporaries' reading of the figure (*Domestic Allegories* 146, 147). Tate's description of the more negative twentieth-century reading of the mulatto is enacted by Houston Baker, who reads the mulatto in a way that identifies the figure as white, or at least would-be white. He argues that "subject-hood in the nineteenth-century daughters' [in which he includes Hopkins] texts comes to imply . . . more than simply a literate mediational voice; it finally comes to mean an implicit approval of white patriarchy inscribed in the very features of the mulatto character's face. The nineteenth-century daughters' departure recapitulates, then, the dynamics of the daughters' seduction" (25).[29] Baker appears to see only the legacy of the white father's face in the mulatto's face, rather than the complexity of that face, thereby relegating the mulatto to the category of would-be or failed whiteness. This reading, even if taken as a metaphor, erases both the mulatto's individual identity (as anything more than the father's daughter) and the very constitutive fact of her racial identity: her *combination* of black and white "blood" (and the mixed cultures that this combination symbolizes). What this view shares with its nineteenth-century predecessor is a tendency to lapse into the binary opposition that the mulatto figure calls into question. The pressure to locate the mulatto as exclusively a part of either the "black" or the "white" community undermines the figure's potential as a third term, a complicating space in the geography of American racial fictions.

This space, a national terrain that encompasses fictions of "pure" racial categories but also supersedes them, is articulated by legal scholar Patricia J. Williams. Williams talks about discovering, on the eve of beginning law school, that her great-great grandfather, the slave owner who had raped his eleven-year-old slave Sophie (her great-great grandmother), came from a family of lawyers. Williams's mother tells her this to calm her fears about law school, asserting, "in a voice full of secretive reassurance," that Williams has the law, as she recounts, "in my blood" (216). Although this story empowers Williams by allowing her to reclaim a lost part of her heritage, a powerful part, it also, as she points out, asks her to deny another part: the disempowered little slave girl. In attempting to think through the effects of having two "bloods," Williams spells out the complicated nature of her enterprise, noting that "reclaiming that from which one has been disinherited is a good thing. Self-possession in the full sense of that expression is the companion to self-knowledge. Yet claiming for myself a heritage the weft of whose genesis is my own disinheritance is a profoundly troubling paradox" (217). This is a paradox, I would suggest, that plagues Hopkins as well as her twentieth-century sisters, and that Hopkins addresses both by having Sappho represent and be a part of the African-American community and by having Sappho represent a complex combination of races, regions, and desires that constitutes American culture as a whole.

Hopkins achieves this through her representation of Sappho's relation with her son. As Sappho goes to reclaim her son from her aunt, the narrator records her thoughts in revealing rhetoric: Sappho "gazed on the innocent face with mingled feelings of sorrow and regret as she thought of the lonely, loveless life of the child. She had been so wicked to put him from her. It was her duty to guide and care for him. She would do her duty without shrinking. . . . She gazed with new-found ecstasy at the rosy face, the dimpled limbs, and thought that *he was hers*. Her feeling of degradation had made her ashamed of the joys of motherhood, of *pride of possession* in her child. But all that feeling was swept away" (344–45, emphasis added). Although at first glance it looks as if, in putting "him from her," Sappho has unwittingly replicated the separation of slave mothers and their children, a denial of both her mother rights and duties, in fact, there is an important difference between the two acts. Indeed, Sappho can be read here as resisting slavery's model of maternity: Sappho *chose* to put her son from her, rejecting the white man's child. She has exercised an agency not available to an enslaved woman, using it to reject the manifestation of her oppressor's power. Reclaiming her son then becomes a similar act of resistance, because it too is based on choice, a choice Sappho makes to reclaim the child as hers, not her rapist's. She identifies the joys of motherhood as involving "possession," the knowledge that her son is "hers." To use the metaphor of blood, one might say that Sappho at first sees only her son's "white blood," and so rejects him, but then comes also to recognize his "black blood"—he was "hers"—and so reclaims him. But the latter recognition does not cancel the former; in reclaiming this child, Sappho acknowledges his origins and thus both his "black" and "white" blood, his status as a mulatto.

Thus, she rejects a disenfranchisement of the emotions, claiming her legal, moral, and emotional bond to her son, the fact that he "belongs" both to and with her. As a result, the novel offers a revised version of motherhood. Sappho reclaims not merely an illegitimate mulatto child but an illegitimate mulatto child born of rape. Unchosen maternity—motherhood resulting from rape—is thus transformed from its status as a sign of dispossession. Through reclaiming both her son and her right to occupy the space of the maternal, Sappho transforms unchosen maternity into an assertion of self and kin. Refusing the white father's narrative (as here articulated by her white uncle/her son's white father), Sappho acknowledges her relation to her past and the white father in it but reconceives its significance. The mind/body split caused by the rape—the body creating a child that the mind rejected—is thus healed by this new version of maternity, a white bourgeois model of maternity now expanded to include the "fallen woman" and the African-American woman. Thus, the resolution of illegitimate child plot not only does not demand the mother's death, it does not follow the conventional narrative movement toward the punishment and repentance of a sinning woman. In fact, to the extent that Sappho must repent, it is her casting off of her son that is at issue, not her "fall." In the most radical aspect of the novel's refiguring of maternity, the narrative in general and Sappho and her community in particular now understand her rape, as Will puts it, as "the monstrous wrong committed against" her (396), an outrage or a crime but certainly not a moral failing on Sappho's part or a personal flaw that would block her access to motherhood. That Hopkins ends her narrative by making Sappho both wife and mother—rewarding her with her destined partner Will—only reinforces both Sappho's status as virtuous woman and her place within her new family structure.

Of course, a discourse of maternal "possession" in this context must also always raise the specter of the slaveowners' "possession" of the slave. Critics such as Spillers and Tate remind us that the structural lack of the black father under slavery and his replacement by the white slaveowner have had profound implications for the notion of "family" among African Americans (Spillers 66, 80; Tate, "Allegories" 121 and *Domestic Allegories* 121, 162). Tate concludes from this that "the mother's law is dominant" ("Allegories" 121), a reading that certainly describes the privileged status of motherhood in *Contending Forces*. Clearly, the absence of the all-powerful patriarchal father changes the nature of the family. The Smith family, even when all its long lost members are reunited at the novel's close, contains no fathers. This absence, Tate suggests, "diminishes the importance of excessive patriarchal demands for feminine piety, purity and property, as well as mitigates feminine prescripts for absolute deference to male authority" ("Allegories" 121), both of which reinforce an increased maternal power. If this new version of motherhood is privileged, however, it is also, by virtue of its power, potentially dangerous, a position of authority that might be either used or abused. The lingering linguistic traces of slavery in Hopkins's description of maternity might thus be read as the sign of the dispossessor in the mulatto mother's heritage and thus as a warning, a caution against the misuse of a newly acquired power. We might also read it as a reminder that the liberatory

SLAVERY, SEXUALITY, AND GENRE 129

force of claiming the white bourgeois heterosexual family structure grows out of an embodied, historically specific position. In turn-of-the-century America, at a moment when Jim Crow laws were shutting down the possibility of real legal equality for African Americans, the family and the cultural arena more generally offered radical possibilities. But these radical possibilities carried with them the weight of other times and spaces wherein the family operated (and continues to operate) as a conservative and even oppressive structure. Even in the present of the novel, the liberatory force of claiming the heterosexual family comes at the cost of relegating the homosocial to the past: Dora's relationship with Sappho must give way to the heterosexual plot line, so that although the two remain close friends, the homoeroticism of their relationship, while present, is muted in the narrative by the attention given the heterosexual romance plot.

There are thus several levels of discourse occurring at the same time in Hopkins's discussion of the strong African-American mother. Hopkins refigures a white bourgeois model of True Womanhood in several ways by taking the Others against whom this model defines itself and incorporating them into the model. She expands the notion of True Womanhood to include the "fallen woman" (conventionally represented as the True Woman's polar opposite in terms of class and sexual purity), the African-American woman (conventionally the model's opposite in racial terms), the woman with both homosocial and heterosexual desire, and the mulatto mother. Although Hopkins here remains within the white bourgeois discourse on womanhood, her recasting of the strong mother uses a bourgeois model to radical ends and marks, within this historical context, a new step in the representation of African-American female identity. At the same time, however, this challenge to dominant gender ideologies can and has been appropriated—both in Hopkins's day and in ours—by the dominant culture and used against African-American women. For in a culture that privileges the father (both symbolic and literal), a family structure that lacks a father and offers a strong mother is always open to attack.[30]

Hopkins's contribution to the "race question" of the turn of the century ultimately produces a hopeful vision, in a "Romance . . . of Negro Life North and South," that works for the "uplift" of her race in general, and also concentrates more specifically on refiguring and relocating African-American female identity. Inheriting a veritable national thesaurus of terms for both black and white womanhood, Hopkins reclaims both passion and virtue for the African-American woman, redefining both in terms that relocate them within, rather than at odds with, conventional notions of "pure" American womanhood. By using the sentimental novel to confront the historical effects of rape on African-American female identity, Hopkins powerfully refocuses the sentimental's categories of home, family, domesticity, and marital love, appropriating on behalf of the African-American mulatto a reworked version of maternity and family and thus a new location in American culture. Embodying regional relations in the figure of a heroine who simultaneously recasts racial relations and the meaning of True Womanhood, Hopkins deploys her heroine in a manner similar to that of Ruiz de Burton. And like Ruiz de Burton, to whom I will now turn, Hopkins uses her heroine thusly in order to locate the Othered woman within the imaginative boundaries of the nation. Hortense J. Spillers looks to the future with the statement that "actually *claiming* the monstrosity (of a female with the potential to 'name'), which her culture imposes in blindness, 'Sapphire' might rewrite after all a radically different text for female empowerment" (80), a comment that implies that African-American (and, implicitly, other disenfranchised) women might finally be able to claim a space in discourse and history, articulating their own lives and selves rather than being the objects represented by someone else's narrative. Hopkins, by reworking the sentimental novel to provide a space for Sappho, Dora, and Ophelia Davis, begins to do just that.

4 María Amparo Ruiz de Burton's Geographies of Race, Regions of Religion

> . . . by the time the little girl is twenty, she will be very rich, and people wouldn't call her Indian or nigger even if she were, which she is *not* . . . she will be very beautiful, as that black skin will certainly wear off.
> —Dr. Norval, *Who Would Have Thought It?*

> The majority of my best friends are Americans. Instead of hate, I feel a great attraction toward the American people. Their sentiments, their ways of thinking suit me.
> —Don Mariano Alamar, *The Squatter and the Don*

Land, Race, and the Californios

Across the continent from Hopkins but no less imbricated in American racial discourse, Californio María Amparo Ruiz de Burton (and her fiction) might be said to be located on the faultlines of American imperialism. As a daughter of the land-owning ruler class in Mexican Alta California, Ruiz de Burton (1835–95) lived through the U.S. conquest of California in 1848 and the subsequent disenfranchisement of the Californios, who lost most of their land, power, and cultural capital as Anglo America rewrote the "Dons" into the role of "greasers." A victim of imperialist rescripting of both transnational relations and United States national borders, Ruiz de Burton thus had personal experience of American colonial expansion and the workings of Manifest Destiny, both of which she would explore in her fiction. Her two historical romances, *Who Would Have Thought It?* (1872) and *The Squatter and the Don* (1885), interrogate the meaning of *American* through a double-pronged cultural intervention aimed, first, at critiquing the historical record's account of the Californio/Mexican relationship to the United States and, second, at recasting such a relationship for the future. Such a recasting, beginning with a critique of the U.S. policies of Manifest Destiny and capitalist expansion, refigures the Californios as citizens within the cultural imaginary of the nation. To do so, Ruiz de Burton's novels—grounded in both Mexican discourses of race and class as well as U.S. discourses of race and region—rely ultimately on the figure of woman and her naturalized domestic sphere.

Genaro Padilla has argued that in nineteenth-century Mexican-American autobiographies, "nostalgia is a realization that there are future stakes involved in the reconstruction(s) of the past. To remember is not only the act of not forgetting but an act of not being forgotten" (325); his work and that of Rosaura Sánchez on the Californio *testimonios* has established that these narratives were an attempt by Californios to contest the dominant Anglo-American historical record.[1] Ruiz de Burton's novels—critiques of Manifest Destiny and the fate of the Californios post-1848—work toward a similar political end. In the 1848 peace treaty of Guadalupe-Hidalgo, the United States government, having taken approximately a third of Mexico's territory, including Alta California, promised full rights of citizenship to the Californios, but through a series of congressional acts, the United States in effect stripped the Dons of land ownership rights by calling into question all of the Californios' land claims. Under the Land Act of 1851, the Dons were compelled to submit their land claims to American governmental verification. All claims were presumed invalid until proven otherwise, and the land was declared open for settlement by Anglo-American settlers. While the Board of Land Commissioners finished hearing the claims in 1856, appeals to U.S. district courts and then to the Supreme Court dragged on for years.[2] Ruiz de Burton herself experienced this: Kathleen Crawford notes that once Ruiz de Burton was widowed, land claims "would embroil her in endless litigation that would cease only with her death" (205).[3] Meanwhile Anglo-American squatters from the 1850s forward, encouraged and enabled by American law, took large areas of land from their former owners and ultimately most of the Dons lost their land as Congress looked on at the completion of the work of Manifest Destiny.[4]

José David Saldívar is right to set Ruiz de Burton's work against the context of the Californio *testimonios'* versions of this "monumental historical past" (171), but Ruiz de Burton's use of the novel has the advantages of offering her a wider audience than that of the (for the most part) unpublished *testimonios* as well as (unlike the *testimonios*) unmediated control of her own text. Importantly, it also allows for the projection of a fictional future in which the Californios might play a new role in the drama of "American" identity. Doris Sommer's work on one political use of the novel has shown how in the foundational novels of Latin America, marriage "provided a figure for apparently nonviolent consolidation during internecine conflicts" (6) as both Latin American and European foundational novels "sought to overcome political and historical fragmentation through love" (26). Recalling *Contending Forces*'s use of the marriage between the Southern Sappho and the Northern Will as a figure for national reunification, we might read certain late-nineteenth-century American novels as doing similar cultural work. Antonia Castañeda, in her impressive survey of the historiography of Spanish-Mexican women, for instance, notes that the image of the "chaste, industrious Spanish beauty who forsook her inferior man and nation in favor of the superior Euro-American became embedded in the [Anglo-American] literature" of the Mexican period as well as the subsequent popular historical accounts of the second half of the century (10), a representation that clearly uses the romance as a vehicle to naturalize Anglo-American conquest of Mexican land. Within the context of this political use of the novel, we can read Ruiz de Burton's historical romances as employing the figure of woman and her naturalized domestic sphere to suture seemingly irreparable national, regional, ethnic, and even religious divides in order to posit an American future that includes the Californios.

But the figure of woman is never an unmarked one: Castañeda's description of the "Spanish beauty" points to another discourse central in structuring Ruiz de Burton's representations. A historical discourse of intertangled class and race/ethnicity inflects this fiction, resulting in part from the fact that California, even by Ruiz de Burton's day, had a long and complicated colonial history, a history that collided with and inflected the Anglo-American colonial enterprise in California.[5] The historical developments that culminated in the rancho system are important to nineteenth-century American history in general and to Ruiz de Burton's position in particular, but what is of perhaps even more long-lasting significance here is the nexus of class, racial, and ethnic discourses that informed the rancho system and the Californio position within it. Negotiating difference—both establishing and denying it—was a problem for the ruling class *gente de razon* from the start of the Spanish period, as it always is for the Creole descendants of a colonial power. As one critic argues, ethnicity goes beyond merely indicating a social group with distinct characteristics but is rather "a sense of identity established by awareness of difference, and this awareness of difference comes in turn through a history of displacement" (Sennett 198). This was certainly the case for the *gente de razon*.[6] From the eighteenth century onward the *gente de razon* turned to fictions of blood to establish a more essentialized and unshakable ground for their privilege, placing increasing importance on their "purity" of Spanish blood both as a way of differentiating themselves from the *indios* and as a way of arguing their equality to their mainland Spanish peers. These fictions of blood—what Ramón A. Gutiérrez and Genaro M. Padilla identify as "largely cultural fictions used to create social boundaries and hierarchies of prestige" (19)—continued into the nineteenth century. As Rosaura Sánchez puts it in *Telling Identities*, "in Alta California, the discourses of caste and notion of 'purity' of blood came with the colonists and continued to hold sway throughout the Mexican period" (56).

Certain analogies are clear between this racial discourse's setting "pure" Spanish blood against "mixed" and/or "*indio*" blood and the concurrent U.S. discourse's posing "purity" of "white" against "mixed" or "black" blood.[7] But the racial politics of the Mexican period did not simply run parallel to the United States East Coast politics of race; they also involved intersecting transnational colonial discourses. As contact with the U.S. increased through the course of the nineteenth century, and as the Mexican ruling class came to be located more and more in relation not only to other Mexicans but also to Anglo Americans, cultural hierarchies became increasingly complicated in light of a developing clash of national vocabularies. For if social/racial/ethnic/class distinctions were internal issues for Mexico, these problems were also exacerbated by the Anglo encroachers, whose program of Manifest Destiny was served by seeing all Mexicans as the same, as well as by frequently conflating all Mexicans with Native Americans. U.S. rhetoric consistently figured Mexicans as an impure, mongrel race whose mixed blood left them nationally inferior to the U.S., racially scarcely distinguishable from Indians, and consequently wholly incapable of self-rule. James Buchanan, for instance, asserted in 1845 that "our race of men can never be subjected to the imbecile and indolent Mexican race" whereas Walt Whitman asked in 1847, "What has miserable, inefficient Mexico . . . to do, with the great mission of peopling the New World with a noble race?" (quoted in Horsman 217, 235). This casting of Mexico as fair game for U.S. expansion depended in great measure both on the conflation of Mexicans with Indians and on the representation of Mexico as constituted by what the editor of the *Cincinnati Herald* called "degraded mongrel races" (quoted in Horsman 238). In 1848, for instance, Senator Sam Houston opposed the Treaty of Guadalupe-Hidalgo, arguing that "the Mexicans are no better than Indians, and I see no reason why we should not go on in the same course now and take their land" (quoted in Weber 100). In 1846 the *Augusta Daily*

Chronicle described Mexico as "a sickening mixture, consisting of such a conglomeration of Negroes and Rancheros, Mestizoes and Indians, with but a few Castilians" (quoted in Horsman 239).[8]

As a result of this rhetorical locating of Mexico and its citizens, what had been a pressure on the *gente de razon* during the Spanish period—to negotiate an identity located in a Creole space between the Spanish and the indigenous peoples of Mexico—increasingly gave way in the Mexican period to a pressure on the ruling class to distinguish itself from the racist and disparaging Anglo-American images of Mexicans. In response to this pressure, as Leonard Pitt explains, "the local nomenclature changed, until the native-born ceased calling themselves *Españoles* or *Mexicanos* and began to insist on the name Californios" (7), with the term signifying what McWilliams calls "high-class Mexicans . . . a special category of 'native Californians'" distinct from "lower-class" workers (55). As a term that identifies a people through their relationship to a place (and, implicitly, the land which they owned there), *Californio* resonates with the land issues that were to be so central to the fate of both the Californios and the state of California. At the same time, as a term that was understood as identifying a people implicitly in terms of race/ethnicity (as against the *indios*), the term condenses class and national identity, categories at the heart of the colonial undertaking.

Just as becoming citizens of the new state of California reconfigured rather than resolved the terms of Californios' conflicted position in relation to American centers of power, their figurative relocation within national borders also reconfigured rather than erased the Californios' relationship to the structuring American discourses of race and region. For although the Civil War was over by 1872, when Ruiz de Burton published her first novel, the racial and regional divides it embodied had already long shaped representations of Mexicans and Californios on the far side of the border. It would continue to shape representations of them once they were inside the border, in national discourses that lasted the duration of the century and that defined who counted as savage, who as civilized, who as American, and who as Other. Hence, Ruiz de Burton's cultural location was not simply doubled—as part of both Mexican and Anglo-American pasts and presents—it was also one that provided her with complex and interwoven discourses of race, ethnicity, class, and gender on both sides. Both discourses simultaneously structure her fiction, at times interrupting or contradicting each other—as in representations of the Californios as simultaneously colonizers and colonized—at times overlapping with each other—as when a Californio discourse of racial purity enables her characters' entrée into a U.S. discourse wherein citizenship depends on whiteness.

Who Would Have Thought It? and *The Squatter and the Don* reflect these doubled discourses in both their critiques of the U.S. and their reformulations of Californio/Mexican relations to post-1848 America. Ruiz de Burton's critique focuses centrally on issues of land (a central topos of imperialism), whereas her reformulations draw more heavily on vocabularies of race. Land is at issue in *The Squatter and the Don* specifically in terms of the California land taken from the Californios; more generally, it is at issue in both novels in terms of American regions' relations to national identity and transnational affairs. That land would be so central to Ruiz de Burton is hardly surprising, both because of the mass loss of land sustained by the Californios at the hands of the Americans and because, in "the symbolic processes through which the United States constitutes subjects," (59) as Priscilla Wald has noted, "the natural right to own property is a critical component of the definition of personhood" (63). In her first novel Ruiz de Burton dismantles the myth of New England as representative of national culture and as the source of universal American values, using both the geographic division of North/South and the racial division of the color line to expose America as an always regionally and racially multiple nation in which the relationships of internal parts to the nation are intimately linked to the relations of the nation to the world. At the same time, by introducing a character representative, in broad terms, of both the "West" and "Mexico," Ruiz de Burton disrupts a Civil War regional model of America as North/South and simultaneously locates that particular sectional divide in relation to the American geopolitics of imperial expansion. In her second novel Ruiz de Burton leaves the East Coast behind to focus explicitly on California and the plight of the Californios. Written as a protest against the American government's treatment of the Californio landowners in the period following California's annexation by the United States, *The Squatter and the Don* addresses an "American" history of colonial expansion via a policy of Manifest Destiny. By shifting the locus of "America" from New England to Southern California and the salient geographic distinction from North/South to East/West, Ruiz de Burton, in *The Squatter and the Don*, rewrites that "American" history.

Fundamentally linked to this critique of imperialist deployment of land is Ruiz de Burton's formulation of a future location for Californios in U.S. culture, a formulation enacted through women, located in the domestic plots of the novels, and crucially grounded in both Californio and

U.S. racial discourses. Whether she is directly concerned with East Coast American relations of "black" and "white" (as in *Who Would Have Thought It?*) or focused on differentiating the Californios from both Mexicans and Indians (as in *The Squatter and The Don*), Ruiz de Burton remains deeply embedded in her doubled racial discourses, and it is from within them that she reworks Californio and American national identity. Although on the one hand she critiques anti-black racism through a savagely ironic depiction of New England Abolitionists in her first novel, both novels articulate a Californio racial hierarchy and a U.S. one that came in certain ways to absorb the Californio one in the post-1848 period. That is, Ruiz de Burton rehearses the Californio claim to purity of Spanish blood—read here as "white." This strategy not only replicates a historical use of the claim to disavow a mestizo heritage, it also becomes evidence of Californio eligibility for American identity.[9]

This second use reflects U.S. assignment of legal racial status to the newly incorporated California Mexicans. Unlike the Chinese or the Indians, Mexicans were legally defined white and thus extended citizenship rights. Although this legal status offered the Californios some protections—their men got the right to vote, for instance—cultural meanings assigned by Anglo-America to the California Mexicans to some extent replicated Californio hierarchies while recasting them within U.S. racial hierarchies. Hence, as Tomás Almaguer reminds us, although the Californio claim to descent from European elites "facilitated the assimilation of segments of the upper class into European American society. . . . In sharp contrast, the Mexican working class was generally viewed like other racialized groups. . . . Unprotected by the status European ancestry afforded the *gente de razon*, they were much more vulnerable to having their political and legal rights violated with impunity" (46). Moreover, although Californios were at least legally defined as white, as John M. González reminds us, "they also helped block citizenship status for the indigenous peoples who had created the wealth that had purchased whiteness" (32). Racial identity thus functions here as utterly interwoven with class status, because legal racial categories function as only a part of the larger racial formations. While U.S. racial formations here replicate the class divisions of Californio culture, the culture of U.S. racism left even the privileged Californios on dubious ground.

By arguing in both her novels that the heroines (one a Californio and one a Mexican from Sonora who represents both Mexicans and, more figuratively, the Californios) are of "pure" Spanish blood, Ruiz de Burton thus deploys both Californio and U.S. racial hierarchies to make a case for admitting the Californios to the category of "American." Both in this call for the reformulation of "American" identity and in the critique of the politics of American imperial expansion that accompanies it in the novels, we can track the complex intersections of Ruiz de Burton's double locations, the interruptions, intersections, and conflicts between the discourses of these locations, and, finally, the ways these forces shape her vision of the interconnections among sectional and transnational discourses of American life.

New England and/as the Nation

Ruiz de Burton had personal experience of what Amy Kaplan calls the way "international relations reciprocally shape a dominant imperial culture at home" (14): both because of her position as Californio and because of her marriage to the Anglo United States Army Captain Henry S. Burton, Ruiz de Burton learned a great deal about the consolidation of American regions and the negotiations of racial politics. In 1859, when her husband was assigned to duty in the Union Army, she accompanied him east. She remained on the East Coast until her husband died in 1869, and so experienced the Civil War and the racial tensions surrounding it firsthand. Out of this clearly formative experience she produced *Who Would Have Thought It?*, a searing indictment of American politics during the Civil War period. The novel is noteworthy not only as perhaps the first novel in English by a Californio woman but also as a critique of United States imperialism and an intervention into the geography of U.S. race relations, both regional and national. As Rosaura Sánchez and Beatrice Pita put it in their introduction to *The Squatter and the Don*, Ruiz de Burton's first book is "a bitingly satirical novel, a caustic parody of the United States during the period of the Civil War" (11). Set mainly on the East Coast (in New England and in Washington, D.C.), the novel provides a critique of New England's claim to ideological centrality within the American imagination, then goes on to use New England's regional status as the basis of a discussion of the relation between region and nation and then of the relation between nation and foreign space; that is, of both intranational and transnational relations. Along the way the novel reshapes conventional Civil War American models of race and region, rehearsing dominant American discourses of "black" vs. "white" blood and the structuring geographical discourse of North vs. South but only to interrupt these discourses by insisting on a recognition of the broader landscape of American imperial expansion. As is also true in *The Squatter and the Don*, this process is ultimately connected to Ruiz de Burton's deployment of gender as played out in the figure of the woman.

The novel's plot, focusing on the New England Norval family and their fortunes just before and during the Civil War, is set into motion by New England geologist and doctor Dr. Norval's travels in California, where one of the "specimens" he collects is a little Mexican girl whose aristocratic mother survives the "horror" of having been kidnapped from Mexico by Indians only long enough to implore Dr. Norval to "save" her daughter Lola.[10] Norval promises to raise the girl and so brings her home to New England, along with the fabulous wealth that her mother, Doña Theresa Medina, has given him. Despite ongoing efforts by Mrs. Norval to swindle Lola out of her fortune, the doctor invests most of the wealth in Lola's name, but even the small part he keeps as payment for rescuing her is enough to make the Norval family wealthy. The plot tracks Lola's coming of age and her romance with Julian Norval while simultaneously tracking the fortunes of the Norvals and some of their neighbors (notably the minister Hackwell and the Cackle family) during the Civil War. The political/historical plot allows Ruiz de Burton to critique the workings of the United States government and the nepotism fueling war politics. At the same time, through the vehicle of Lola, Ruiz de Burton superimposes an East/West geographical divide on the North/South model and brings the Mexican/Californio into U.S. racial discourses of the day. As a result she underscores the links between internal and international U.S. concerns with race and imperialism, region and nation, complicating an internal issue of "color" by introducing the external cultural Other.

Who Would Have Thought It? draws this complicated map in part by tracking multiple American regions. In doing so, Ruiz de Burton avoids the simplistic dualism of what Werner Sollors calls the region "in contrast to the mental construct of the 'non-region' or 'un-region'," a reductionist dualism that results in "the forced homogenization not only of the non-region not studied but also of the investigated region itself" (177). The novel resists this homogenization both by challenging the notion of New England as an American ideological center against all other regions— New England as the essence of America—and by the narrative use of Lola, the novel's "Mexican." Perhaps as a result of Ruiz de Burton's experience as a Californio outsider inhabiting the East Coast at precisely the moment of its deepest sectional fragmentation, her novel avoids simply representing the nation in terms of either "North" and "South" (because Lola cannot be said to belong to either of these categories) or of "East" and "West" (because the "East" is already subdivided into New England, the South, and even, arguably, Washington, D.C., as its own region), but instead produces a representation of a nation comprised of multiple regions in complicated relation to each other. Further, as Sui Sin Far was later to do, Ruiz de Burton reverses the movement of other California narratives—"frontier" tales and tales of the Forty-Niners—which locate California as the far reaches of the nation, the endpoint of an East-to-West pattern of migration. Instead, her heroine moves West to East, implicitly calling into question the established relation of national margin to center.[11]

Ruiz de Burton emphasizes the variety of diverse American regions by setting the novel during the Civil War, a war that made painfully obvious the fact that the regions had differing goals and ideals. Hence, the novel challenges New England as synecdoche of the nation in part by representing it as only one region among many. In addition, Ruiz de Burton goes beyond mere geographical reporting to argue that the regional values of New England are inadequate for a national ideal because they are too narrow: she dismantles a dominant notion of New Englanders as the upstanding, emotionally repressed, duty-bound Protestants who support Abolition out of their abiding commitment to justice and freedom, representing them instead as provincial, narrow-minded, racist, xenophobic, and hypocritical.[12] She thus takes the American rhetoric of liberty and justice for all and applies it as a measure to New England, revealing that the New England model of American identity does not meet the standards of American national ideals. Focusing this critique through the lens of gender, Ruiz de Burton assesses the American ideal of the Cult of True Womanhood, showing that both the model itself and its New England representatives also fall short of national ideals.

A representation of New England as a provincial enclave that defines itself against an excluded and denigrated Other runs throughout the novel. Against the backdrop of the Civil War the New England characters define themselves, of course, as the North opposing the South. The community's censure of Dr. Norval as a typical New Englander underscores this point. The narrator voices the "mind of New England"'s opinion thusly: "The doctor might say what he pleased about loving his country too well to have too much partiality for *one section*. They, the New Englanders, knew better; and if the doctor had not felt too strong a partiality for the wicked South he would have stayed quietly at home, and then have gone and thrashed them back if they rebelled" (64, emphasis in original).[13] The New Englander's sectional bigotry expresses everything Ruiz de Burton

wants to condemn in regional loyalty and is a fairly predictable representation of the divisiveness of Antebellum regional identity. But Ruiz de
Burton takes this sense of provincial and exclusionary identity further, beginning in the book's very opening pages, where Ruiz de Burton uses the
minister Mr. Hackwell—whose name signals Ruiz de Burton's opinion of
him—and one Mrs. Cackle—a caricature town busybody—to embody
the worst of New England on a grand scale. Dr. Norval's return from a
trip to California provides the occasion for a diatribe on what his New
England community sees as his faults, as voiced by Hackwell quoting
Mrs. Cackle. She claims that Dr. Norval's faults all

have their root in the doctor's most unnatural liking for foreigners. That liking
was the cause of the doctor's sending his only son Julian to be educated in Europe—as if the best schools on earth were not in New England,—and Heaven
knows what might have become of Julian if his heroic mother had not sent for
him. He might have been a Roman Catholic, for all we know. That liking was also
the cause of the doctor's sending Isaac to be a good-for-nothing clerk in sinful
Washington, among foreigners, when he could have remained in virtuous New
England to be a useful farmer. And finally, impelled by that liking, the doctor be-
took himself to California, which is yet full of *natives.* (11, emphasis in original)

This passage voices the provincial and arrogant view that Ruiz de Burton
satirizes throughout the novel of New England as the center as against a
variety of others: New England functions as both the region to be preferred to all others (especially Washington, D.C.) and as a synecdoche of
the United States itself (America as superior to Europe for education).
The Other here encompasses the religious Other (the Catholic), the regional Other (both California and Washington, D.C.), and the national
Other (the European), all of which are conflated. Later Mrs. Norval adds
race into this group, arguing that "there is no reason why Julian should
not marry one of his own race and religion. I hate foreigners and papists"
(92). Her syntax links non-white, non-Protestant, and non-American, a
cluster Mrs. Norval will eventually explicitly connect to Californios and
Mexicans, claiming, "of course no good could come of his unnatural liking for foreigners, and of all foreigners the last of all, Mexicans" (218).

Taking apart this formulation, which privileges New England and collapses everything else into non-New England, is one of the central projects
of *Who Would Have Thought It?*, a project facilitated by the fact that the
formulation turns out to contain the key to its own deconstruction. This
key lies in its interconnections among regional, national, and transnational relations, connections that Ruiz de Burton displays throughout the
novel as a corrective to the insular New England view. When Mrs. Cackle

notes that in punishment for his liking of foreigners the doctor was nearly "roasted by the natives" (11), for instance, Mr. Hackwell continues,

Whereupon, in behalf of truth, I said, "Not by the natives, madam. The people called '*the natives*' are mostly of Spanish descent, and are not cannibals. The wild Indians of the Colorado River were doubtless the ones who captured the doctor and tried to make a meal of him." "Perhaps so," said the old lady, visibly disappointed. "To me they are all alike—Indians, Mexicans, or Californians,—they are all horrid. But my son Beau says that our just laws and smart lawyers will soon '*freeze them out.*' That as soon as we take their lands from them they will never be heard of any more, and then the Americans, with God's help, will have all the land that was so righteously acquired through a just war and a most liberal payment in money." "Ain't that patriotism and Christian faith for you?" added Mr. Hackwell. (11, emphasis in original)

Through Mrs. Cackle, Ruiz de Burton satirically voices both the argument of Manifest Destiny (an argument that Ruiz de Burton will take up in greater detail in *The Squatter and the Don*) and that argument's dependence on a conflation of all others—"Indians, Mexicans, or Californians." The statement also reveals how the American colonial project— whether represented as internal or external expansion—is grounded in the same ideological system of "Christian" patriotism that allows the sanctimonious New Englander to maintain a sectional view of the nation with New England as the center. Ruiz de Burton's irony here ultimately affirms that a sectional vision of the nation is inevitably connected to relations of the nation to other nations.

(Not) New Englanders and the Color Line

Resisting an expansionist conflation of all others, however, the passage also draws, "in behalf of truth" a distinction between the "natives . . . of Spanish descent" and the "wild Indians," a distinction that Ruiz de Burton is at some pains to establish in *The Squatter and the Don* and that is also at issue in *Who Would Have Thought It?* through the figure of Lola. Lola Medina, in fact, is the narrative site where discourses of race, color, region, religion, nationality, and gender intersect. The introduction of this Western/Mexican body disrupts both North/South regional and black/ white racial American binary models. Religiously, regionally, and nationally Other, Lola's "difference" gets played out during her sojourn in New England mainly through color. Ruiz de Burton employs a nineteenth-century racial discourse but complicates the East Coast version of the color

line that informed the institution of slavery (black against white) by introducing not just the "Indian" but also the "Mexican" of "pure Spanish
blood." The novel uses dominant U.S. racial categories ambivalently, interrupting the black/white color line by introducing a Mexican child, but
ultimately reinscribing racial dichotomies by making a claim for Lola as a
white "lady" of Spanish blood. Similarly, although the novel criticizes the
racism of the North, it fetishizes whiteness, implicitly countering Anglo
representations of Mexicans as a "mongrel race" by enacting a Californio
racial hierarchy. This hierarchy circulates in the novel by displacing U.S.
racist constructions from the "Mexican" onto the "Indian," eliding multiple and complex tribal affiliations by collapsing all tribes into the category
of the Indian Other.[14] Ultimately, *Who Would Have Thought It?* demands
not that Lola be accepted as precisely American but that she be acknowledged white, a racial status that functions here as a metaphor for culture,
class privilege, and a sophisticated European heritage, all of which make
Lola, as a cultured Mexican lady, a fit mate for the American hero Julian.
Ruiz de Burton thus uses both Californio and U.S. racial discourses and
links them to ethnic, regional, and national identity, implicitly linking the
racial politics of the Mexican-American War to those of the Civil War.
Proposing a solution specific to neither the Californios' problems nor the
racial conflicts embedded in the Civil War, the novel engages both but displaces them onto transnational relations, recoding both national sectional
problems and transnational ones in a romance plot.

The novel engages these issues first and foremost through its representation of Lola's color, explicitly read by the novel's characters as an indicator of her race but metaphorically also serving as an indicator of her ethnic, economic, and national identity. Lola literally changes color through
the course of the novel, in an extraordinary plot device involving a skin
stain that paradoxically allows Ruiz de Burton to expose the hypocritical
racism of New England and defend the Californios and Mexicans against
this racism, while at the same time not attacking the American racial hierarchy itself.[15] Lola is introduced in a chapter entitled "The Little Black
Girl," where her color is remarked upon over and over by the Norval
family. She is, the narrator tells us, "very black indeed" (16), a fact that
prompts Mattie, one of the Norval daughters, to identify her as a "nigger
girl" (16). Following this racial assignment, Mrs. Norval rhetorically reduces Lola to an animal, referring to the doctor's stone collecting to assert
that "he, I fear, having exhausted the mineral kingdom, is about to begin
with the animal, and this is our first specimen" (16), a sentiment taken to
its extreme in the Norval daughter Ruth's claim that the "next specimen

will be a baboon . . . for Papa's samples don't improve" (16). The family examines and discusses Lola like the metaphoric object she has become. Ruiz de Burton voices white obsession with and revulsion over "blackness" through the characters of Mrs. Norval and her daughter Ruth—the two Norvals most discredited by the narrative as narrow-minded and self-ish, clearly representative of the New England positions that the novel most condemns. At the same time, Mattie and her aunt Lavvy, two New Englanders who occupy more moderate positions and enjoy slightly more authorial approval, also examine Lola, noting that she is pretty, with "magnificent eyes . . . red and prettily-cut lips" (16). But Lavvy notes that Lola does not have "negroes' lips" (16) while Mattie observes that "the palm of her hand is as white as mine,—and a prettier white; for it has such a pretty pink shade to it" (17). Their defense of Lola thus employs the same racist racial binaries as the others' attack does: in their construction Lola is pretty insofar as she approaches white.

From looking at Lola, Ruth concludes that Lola's parents were "Indian or negroes, or both. . . . Anyone can see that much of her history" (17). But the narrative makes clear that the only way these characters can "see" Lola's history is by reading her Mexican body through preexisting U.S. racial codes—white/black/Indian—as Lola becomes a screen on which the characters project various available American racial and cultural stereotypes. From an opening assumption that she is black, the family allows for the possibility that Lola is Indian, because the doctor has brought her from the West, a racial possibility that is slightly but not much better in the family's eyes than the possibility that she is black.[16] Ruth, for instance, says, laughing, "I suppose her name is Rabbit, or Hare, or Squirrel; that is, if she is Indian" (20) and Lavvy announces, "Indians are as proud and surly as they are treacherous. . . . I suppose she is a mixture of Indian and negro" (20). These comments illustrate both the catholicity of the Norvals' racism and the pre-existing categories that structure it: Lola, as "not white," must be either black or Indian.

Foregrounding these categories allows Ruiz de Burton initially to satirize New England abolitionism. Although Mrs. Norval, for example, is described by her husband as "a lady of the strictest Garrisonian school, a devout follower of Wendell Phillips's teachings, and a most enthusiastic admirer of Mr. Sumner," he contrasts "these facts with the reception she gives this poor little orphan because her skin is dark" (18).[17] The neighbors similarly speculate on Lola's origins and race, noting that the doctor has stated that Lola "has neither African nor Indian blood in her veins" (46). The conversation continues,

"If she had, Mrs. Norval would not take the girl in her carriage. Mrs. N. ain't that sort of person," said old Mr. Cackle.

"Mrs. Norval is a great abolitionist, and doesn't mind negroes. Besides, doesn't Lavvy take her poodle too?" Mrs. Hammerhead remarked.

"Mrs. Norval is a good abolitionist in talk," replied Miss Lucretia Cackle, with a sneer; "but she ain't so in practice" (46–47).

The novel thus locates Mrs. Norval as representative of her community, for if the gossips can see the racism underlying Mrs. Norval's support of abolitionism, their rhetorical equation of "negroes" and "poodles" simply replicates it.

In one sense, then, the novel's representation of the white New Englanders exposes and critiques racial hierarchy as a founding term of American culture. At the same time, however, while none of the New England characters calls racial hierarchies into question, neither ultimately does the narrative as a whole. Dr. Norval, Lola's great champion throughout the novel, defends her on the basis of her "white" blood and her money, voicing a defense of the Californio/Mexican at the expense of the black and the Indian. He tells Mrs. Norval, "once and for all, let me tell you that the blood of that child is as good as, or better than, yours or mine; that she is neither an Indian nor a negro child" (25). Hardly a challenge to dominant American racial hierarchies, this is merely a defense of Lola as white, a reenacting of a Californio disavowal of mestizo "blood" through a claim to "pure" Spanish blood. Similarly, although Lola objects to Julian's seeing her as "Indian or black" (100), she objects not to the racial hierarchy implicit in this evaluation, but rather to its application to her, telling him, "I could not bear to think that to you, too, I was an object of aversion because my skin was black. And yet I was too proud to tell you that the blackness of my skin would wear off; that it was only stained by the Indians to prevent our being rescued. My mother also was made to stain her lovely white skin all black" (100). In keeping with a Californio racial discourse that elevated "pure" white/Spanish blood while collapsing tribal distinctions and racially Othering all Indians, Lola does not call into question the racial politics of the color line. Like her creator, she merely wants to locate the Mexican on the privileged side of that line.[18] Analogously, one might see the time expended by Ruiz de Burton on Lola's family history as yet another defense of Lola's racial parity with the New Englanders. The doctor's tale establishes what are clearly Lola's two salient traits: she is vastly wealthy and her "blood is pure Spanish blood" (28). In a comment that both identifies race as a class-mediated social construction and, paradoxically, grounds it in a bodily essence, he notes, "by the time the little girl is twenty, she will be very rich, and people wouldn't call her Indian or nigger even if she were," but then goes on to add "which she is *not* . . . she will be beautiful, as that black skin will certainly wear off" (27 emphasis in original).

Which, in fact, it does. In the novel's most incredible narrative device, as Lola grows up, her color begins to change, a change appearing as spots on her skin. One theory offered as explanation by Mr. Hackwell is that "Lola must belong to a tribe of Mexican Indians called 'Pintos,' who are spotted" (78), a comment that more or less equates Mexicans and Indians and locates them (and Lola) on an intermediary level between black and white, just as Lola's skin color is somewhere between black and white. Alternately, Mrs. Norval wonders if the spots are "some sort of cutaneous disease," (79) and fears "being infected" by Lola's spots (79), a not very subtle metaphor of white fear of racial "difference."[19] Eric Lott has shown how blackface minstrelsy, "a dramatic spectacle based on an overriding investment in the body" functioned in the Antebellum period (and even after) as "a ground of American racial negotiation and contradiction" (6, 30). As a narrative device, Lola's color and specifically her spots function (like the portraits of the racist New Englanders) in an analogous way. A critique of American racial politics, what Lola's spots signal is the instability of race as a category, turning her body into a parody of notions of purity of blood, an ironic inversion of countless nineteenth-century mulatto heroines who start their plots as privileged white ladies only to be revealed as having the "one drop" of blood that relocates them as black.

Rosaura Sánchez and Beatrice Pita argue in their introduction to *Who Would Have Thought It?* that the novel's "performance of blackface" underscores "the deceptions and hypocrisy of the New England community" and thus functions as a means of "censuring abolitionist racism" (xxi). Although they read Lola's whitening as "working out social contradictions while at the same time containing them" (xxi), I would suggest that their notion of containment here needs more emphasis. Just as minstrelsy voiced "dissension as much as domination" to what Lott calls "a peculiarly American structure of racial feeling" (37, 18), Lola's spots—and the narrative attitude toward them—serve simultaneously to reinscribe the very notions of essentialized racial identity that they expose as precariously and culturally constructed. Nowhere is this clearer than in the love plot of the novel, where race, region, and nationality intersect to determine Lola's happy ending. Lola fears that Julian's (mis)perception of her race will block their love, while the narrator depicts Julian as being able to see "beyond" the spots to the real Lola—the white Lola—within. When

Mrs. Norval uses the symbol of Lola's racial difference to attempt to block Julian's love, for instance, calling attention to the spots in a way that turns Lola "crimson with shame and resentment" (91), the strategy backfires, for in examining the spots "Julian looked at Lola's eyes and lips, and he forgot all about the spots. His gaze became fixed on hers, and a thrill went through his whole frame from the little soft hand he held in his" (91).[20]

At this point the narrative begins to read less like a parody of the plot of the tragic mulatta than an inverted version of it. One might read race as the impediment to the lovers' union, much as it functions in novels of the period dealing with the "tragic mulatto" and the issue of "miscegenation" between black and white. But although this plot has a happy ending, that ending rehearses rather than challenges dominant racial codes, for what Julian recognizes and what resolves the "problem" of the lovers' racial difference is the revelation that Lola is white. Lola's spots are temporary, the racial difference illusory. When the spots disappear, the narrator states explicitly, "Lola's skin was white and smooth, and she was very pretty" (79). So that although on one hand Lola's spots serve to underscore the arbitrary and constructed nature of race, they simultaneously reinscribe racial dichotomies, reenacting an American repression of the mulatto or the mestizo. Lola's impending marriage to Julian at the novel's close is used by Ruiz de Burton to signal neither the happy healing of U.S. regional Civil War divisions nor the harmonious solution of the American "race" problem via intermarriage.[21] Instead, this domestic plot's solution and its dependence on whiteness encapsulates the contradiction inherent in *Who Would Have Thought It?*'s racial politics. For although the history of Lola's skin color underscores the instability of U.S. racial categories, the narrative's fetishization of what it represents as her essential whiteness performs the very repression of the mestizo/mulatto upon which American notions of racial purity depend while simultaneously bringing a Californio insistence on ruling-class "purity of blood" into a U.S. racial discourse. But this reading of Lola's marriage to Julian—a reading focusing on its meaning on the intranational/regional level of racial politics—needs to be accompanied by a reading that focuses on the marriage as a figure for the solution of the international "problem" of the proper relationship between the U.S. and Mexico.

The novel encourages a reading that links intranational and international contexts by linking Lola's nationality and race, explicitly marking her as Mexican and as white, in a representation that contests U.S. racist depictions of "Mexican" but does so from within both Californio and dominant U.S. racial discourses. This representation defends "Mexican" as the upper-class, white, cultured descendent of the European (Spanish) elite, as in the following:

"Talk of Spanish women being dark! Can anything be whiter than Lola's neck and shoulders?" added Mattie, addressing all.

"Lola is not Spanish; she is Mexican," said Ruth.

"I think Lola might teach us the secret of that Indian paint that kept her white skin under cover, making it whiter by bleaching it. I would bargain to wear spots for awhile," said Emma. (333)

That Mattie, a comparatively favored character, identifies Lola as "Spanish" echoes both a Californio and, later, an Anglo-American deployment of the term. Antonia Castañeda reminds us that in "accounts of Mexican California (1822–1846), the popular historians divide women into two classes: 'Spanish' and 'Mexican' . . . women from long-time Californian elite, land-owning families . . . were called 'Spanish.' Women from more recently arrived or non-elite families were called 'Mexican.' 'Spanish' women were morally, sexually, and racially pure; 'Mexican' women were immoral and sexual and racially impure" (9). In this context Ruth's comment might be read as one more insult flung at Lola, a reinscription of "Mexican" as inferior to "Spanish." But by ascribing this comment to the discredited Ruth, the passage in effect defends both Mexicans as a people and Lola as an individual. Lola is thus defensively represented not merely as white, but as the beautiful and desired model of elite and cultured white womanhood.[22] This representation of Lola and, by extension, of her family as descendants of a European elite functions in the novel, as Anne E. Goldman points out, to "undermine conventional Anglo American representations of Mexicanos on both side of the newly defined border" (75). It also allows Lola's marriage to symbolize both the international union of Mexico and America and, more figuratively, the intranational union of Euro-American and Californio, all on the basis of racial sameness. That these two meanings can be brought together in one image reveals the extent to which U.S. racial discourse informs American relations with those across its national borders.

Patterns of Womanly Virtues: New England Matrons and Failed Ideals

It is not only through the novel's representation of Lola that Ruiz de Burton dismantles the centrality of New England. In the novel's examination of the Cult of True Womanhood, more generally, gender becomes a lens through which Ruiz de Burton's critique of America is filtered. She shows first that this allegedly national ideal is regionally inflected; second, that its regional representatives do not embody the ideal as closely as does the Mexican woman; and third, that the ideal itself is flawed, limited, and limiting. In all parts of this critique Ruiz de Burton underscores the importance of gender as a structuring influence in national identity.

Much of this critique is accomplished through the contrast between Lola's mother, Doña Theresa Medina—the embodiment of a good mother's innate and unshakable devotion to her children—and Mrs. Norval—the representative New England mother who does not live up to the ideal and so cannot adequately embody American ideal femininity. While nursing her son Julian (wounded in battle in the Civil War), for instance, Mrs. Norval rages at not being able to nurse the also-wounded Mr. Hackwell (with whom Mrs. Norval is in love), at which the narrator comments, "the stately matron, always quoted by all her own and the surrounding villages as a pattern of womanly virtues, and as a *pink of propriety*, indulged in abusive language! She was alone, though, or at least nearly so, for she considered her half-dead son as incapable of hearing her, and in fact she had forgotten him for those few moments" (134, emphasis in original). Her own illicit erotic desire for Hackwell not only takes precedence over her maternal feelings, it even prompts her to forget about her son entirely.[23]

In contrast, while Mrs. Norval is too distracted by her desire for Hackwell to pay attention to the son who appears to be dying, Doña Theresa Medina is willing to sacrifice her own life to save her daughter. Dr. Norval's account of Lola's mother's story, itself drawing on the rhetoric of a conventional captivity narrative, emphasizes the mother's devotion to her daughter in what becomes little short of a hagiography. When the doctor meets Doña Theresa, she has been held captive by Indians for ten years but "had made an oath to the chief not to try to escape, because in that way he would relax his vigilance, and she be enabled to send her little girl away" (35). Indeed, she goes on to say that she cannot face her real family "after ten years of such life as had been forced upon her; that she only wished to save her daughter from a similar fate, and then to lie down and die" (35). The doctor recounts that after he agreed to help her, he noticed that the "prospect of being forever separated from her child was rapidly killing her, and she knew it full well. But such was the self-sacrificing devotion of that lady, that sick and weak as she felt, with a sinking heart and no hope for herself, she never swerved from her purpose to set her child free, and then, literally, lie down and die" (36). This she does as soon as the doctor succeeds in arranging Lola's escape.

Both the form and the content of this narrative thus serve to reverse the disqualifying of the Othered women from the position of idealized American mother. The form echoes both the structure of the captivity narrative and the abolitionist rhetoric of novels like *Uncle Tom's Cabin* and slave narratives like that of Harriet Jacobs, while the story thematizes the willingness of a mother to die in order to gain her child's freedom. At the same time, the narrator's difference from the conventional narrators of captivity narratives is significant as well. Unlike those narrators, Doña Theresa does not gain from her period of captivity a greater understanding of or sympathy for her captors. She feels irreparably sullied by her contact with them, filled with "shame" at what she describes as her "degradation" (202). In rhetoric that rehearses a Californio Othering of Indians, the narrator reads a portrait of the dead Doña Theresa as saying, "I was always pure, for my soul did not sin, although I was insulted by a savage. I was a martyr; now an angel" (202). This imagery of conflated purity, whiteness, and Californio womanhood against dirty, savage Indians is articulated most explicitly by Dr. Norval when he describes his final encounter with Lola's mother on the eve of his rescuing Lola:

In a miserable Indian hut lay the dying lady. The surroundings were cheerless enough to kill any civilized woman, but the bedclothes, I noticed, were white as snow, and everything about her was clean and tidy. She smiled when she saw me, and said, "Thank God, Lolita is away from those horrid savages! Please do not forget that she must be baptized and brought up a Roman Catholic." (36)

That Dr. Norval is the character to offer this account underscores the degree to which the Californio racial hierarchy that privileges whiteness dovetails with an Anglo-American racial hierarchy.

That this dying woman is a Mexican Catholic who insists on her daughter's Catholic education further reminds us that the criteria of qualification for the ideal of Republican Motherhood included not only race and nationality, but religion as well. In this portrait of Catholicism Ruiz de Burton flags the extent to which legacies of Puritanism inform American national identity and are consolidated through anti-Catholicism.[24] Jenny Franchot has shown how an "animus against Romanism was a central determinant in colonial Puritan identity" (xix), contending that Catholicism "performed an integrative function crucial to New England's pursuit of national primacy" (xix–xx) and pointing out that geographically the West was often linked to Catholicism because of the historical presence of Spain and the ongoing American fear of Spanish influence there (100). Situated against this wide-ranging American anti-Catholicism, Lola's and her mother's Catholicism serves as a reminder of the degree to which Protestant discourse both constructed itself against a Catholic Other and simultaneously swerved toward Catholicism in its construction of a maternal ideal based on a form of secular mariology. Doña Theresa as sacrificial mother implicitly involves Catholicism, raising the specter of the prototype of the sacrificial mother: the Virgin Mary. Ironically, then, the Virgin Mary, through the theory of transitivity, might be said to be the prototype of the American mother.[25] Ultimately, the contrast between Doña Theresa and Mrs. Norval is important for its bringing together of regional and religious issues and is typical of the novel's use of a North/South axis to comment implicitly on a Californio issue. That is, the comparison should be read not merely as a critique of the New England mother but also as an implicit defense of both Californio Catholicism and motherhood, a defense made from within dominant "American" culture and using dominant "American" principles.[26]

The novel thus reworks the category of True Womanhood by revising just who is eligible for it: the Othered woman here fits the ideal better than the New England lady. At the same time, Ruiz de Burton suggests that the ideal itself needs to be reworked: not only does eligibility need to be broadened but the actual terms of the ideal are limited and limiting. Here too Ruiz de Burton locates her discussion at the intersection of region and gender, starting from a discussion of repression as a New England trait that Ruiz de Burton critiques as the unnatural response to the natural existence of emotion (especially although not exclusively in women). Dr. Norval, for example, recalls "caresses" from his children as a thing of the past, "before their mother had scolded them, with cold dignity and great propriety, into learning to curb all emotion and check all show of feeling" (116–17). The novel offers various reactions to this training, but all point to the conclusion that repression is at best unsuccessful and at worst hypocritical.[27]

The critique of a specifically New England form of repression is sustained throughout the novel, but this regional analysis is also complicated by being linked to an analysis of sexual politics by way of an interrogation of passionlessness as a part of proper womanhood. Ruiz de Burton challenges this representation in part through Lavvy, who although a "spinster" is not passionless: she loves her canaries and also nurses a thwarted erotic desire for Hackwell. Less conventional in terms of nineteenth-century women's novels than this protest against the dismissal of the unmarried woman, however, is Ruiz de Burton's depiction of Mrs. Norval and her illicit but consuming passion for Hackwell. The novel treats Jemima Norval's unsuccessfully repressed desire with ambivalence. Although Ruiz de Burton's tone is often sarcastic and critical of Mrs. Norval herself, it also shifts to sympathetic and suggests that Mrs. Norval and her passions are the victims of oppressive New England values:

the cold selfishness and unloving impassability of her previous nature had preserved her young, as the ice she used to put around her turkeys to pack them for the Boston market kept those fowls fresh. . . . She had had only one passion,—her religious bigotry,—which had inspired her with a strong hatred towards everything and everybody that was not Presbyterian. She had felt but one ambition,—that of saving, saving, saving,—putting away more pennies and five- and ten-cent pieces than any of her neighbors. Aside from these two feelings, which alone could be said to have had in her strength enough to be called passions, there had been no other to shake her soul. (231)

While the narrator casts Mrs. Norval as a selfish, greedy, religious bigot, there is also a suggestion here that she is to be pitied for the constricted existence produced by the repression of all natural emotion. Elsewhere, drawing on the language of the sentimental romance, the narrator comments, "Ah me! such is poor humanity! Cast not a stone—no, not a little pebble—at the madam, for, after all, she was very womanly when she was so absurdly silly. And who is not silly when truly in love?" (136). This gesture of sympathy becomes even more pronounced later in the novel, when the narrator describes Mrs. Norval's heart as "thawed" and notes that Mrs. Norval "loved this new state of being. She had so far degenerated that she regarded her youth as misspent, her life a blank, until she loved Hackwell, until she was past forty. Poor woman! to have been a chrysalis all her days! Who would not excuse this avalanche of the snows of forty years?" (173). Sánchez and Pita argue in their introduction to the novel that the narrative deals "half-compassionately and half-moralistically" with Mrs. Norval's passion (xxxiii), a reading I would support: despite the judgment implied in the use of "degenerated," the narrator's tone is clearly sympathetic, the imagery of the thaw locating Mrs. Norval's passion as natural and suggesting a movement from the death of Winter to the life of Spring. This use of figurative language draws on the rhetoric of romance and insists that the reader empathize with what the novel codes as a universal, essentialized experience: erotic desire.

This compassion toward a character otherwise roundly satirized in the novel is striking and makes sense only if understood as signaling the complicating of regional categories with gender politics. That is, while Mrs. Norval functions as a whipping boy through much of the novel because of her provincial New England views, as the repressed New England matron she also provides Ruiz de Burton with a perfect space for the discussion of explicitly erotic female desire. As the use of figurative language (especially the imagery of snow and ice) in the passages above indicates, Mrs. Norval's is an erotic passion and one culturally coded as improper in good American women. Describing Mrs. Norval's reaction to Hackwell's putting his arm around her, for instance, the narrator comments,

She felt a thrill through her entire frame, just as might have felt one of those creatures—whom she so abhorred—who go to parties in low necks and short sleeves, and go to theatres, and, in their wild chase after worldly pleasures, do court such thrills. She, a strict hater of popery, a pious, proper churchwoman, felt just the same. And who was the man who had the power thus to thrill her whole being and set her heart throbbing in such unmatronly, unpresbyterian tumult? No other than her spiritual advisor. (173)

The "mature inamorata" (173) goes on to tell Hackwell, "you are mine, my own in every respect,—my lawyer, my lawgiver, my lord, my all. If I were like some of those irreverent women with foreign loose notions, I would say, my God on this earth. Come to me; your caresses take away my strength" (174). Goldman argues that "it is her own authorial remove from the Presbyterian matron that allows Ruiz de Burton to raise this erotic possibility for women" (66); I would contend, moreover, that as this mapping of female eroticism onto regional and religious discourses displays, what makes Mrs. Norval not simply a possible vehicle but indeed the perfect vehicle for this discussion is the fact that she *is* a matron, a Presbyterian, an American woman feeling passion; not a low-necked-dress-wearing, party-going, Catholic foreigner at all. Here Ruiz de Burton is in conversation both with the dominant construction of American Womanhood and its flip side. The dominant construction represented the ideal American lady (the white, middle-class, Protestant lady allegedly embodied by New England women like Mrs. Norval) as lacking erotic desire, whereas the opposite of this dominant construction projected that lady's disavowed desire onto the figures of the woman of color, the working-class woman, the "savage" "native" woman, or, when it was necessary to move beyond the exclusively American arena, the foreign woman. Hackwell brings this intersection of race, region, and sexuality into sharp focus when he says of Mrs. Norval, "Who would have supposed such a Vesuvius covered over with New England snows, eh? A Yankee Popocatepetl!" (177). The image of the Mexican volcano covered with New England snows perfectly articulates Ruiz de Burton's reworking of female erotic desire: the prim New England matron is filled with the eruptive passion usually displaced onto the Other woman.[28]

Mrs. Norval's desire and the narrator's sympathy for her open up a space in the novel for a tentative recoding of female erotic desire as positive. Given the narrator's tone it is clear that rather than simply condemning Mrs. Norval on the basis of her passion, the novel is challenging the binary terms of this model of womanhood itself: the good passionless woman and the bad erotic woman. That Ruiz de Burton launches this challenge through the image of the New England lady rather than through the image of the Othered woman brings her doubled narrative rewards. Sánchez and Pita point out that "the novel overturns the stereotypical description of passionate Latin women by mockingly describing the repressed passion of a good Puritan woman" (xxxiii); I would amend this claim slightly to argue that by using the figure of Jemima Norval for an interrogation of female passion, Ruiz de Burton both challenges the stereotypical depiction of "passionate Latin women" and its inverse, the passionless Anglo matron, thus obliquely calling into question the terms of construction itself.

While the depiction of Mrs. Norval redirects a rhetoric of passion from the Latin woman to the New England lady, the novel further challenges the terms of womanhood by cautiously characterizing Lola as innately passionate but by recoding that passion as innocent and pure. Like Pauline Hopkins, for instance, who contests dominant alignments of pure womanhood with whiteness through representations of African-American female heterosexual virtue and muted erotic desire, Ruiz de Burton attempts to recode passion as positive here. The narrator describes Lola's response to Dr. Norval's decision to leave on a long trip to Africa, for example, in these terms: "Lola, prompted by an irresistible impulse, went up to her beloved guardian, and, throwing her arms around his neck, burst out crying, pouring on him a shower of most emphatic kisses" (83). This display prompts Dr. Norval to consider his children's lessons in repression, a comparison that rhetorically positions Lola as his child and figures both her and all children's emotions as natural and innocent. "Why could not his daughters be affectionate like this poor little orphan?" he goes on to ask himself, answering, "because their mother hated anything like a show of affection, and imperiously prohibited it. . . . Lola was the only creature who showed any affection for him" (84). The narrator ends this description of the little girl sitting on the doctor's knees by observing

They had been thus clasped in each other's arms for some time, when they were startled by a voice at the door saying,—

"Pretty business, doctor, you are discussing with your little Indian!" And the tall form of Mrs. Norval appeared in the door-way. (84)

While Ruiz de Burton defends the expression of emotion as a positive thing in this passage, she also (through Mrs. Norval's linking that passion to an essentialized racial identity) rehearses a stereotype of the Other— the "little Indian"—as inherently passionate, in an image that conflates passion, savagery, childishness, and incestuous desire. Similarly, when Lola and Julian declare their love, the narrative attributes her passion to an essentialized nature that is implicitly aligned with ethnicity by being juxtaposed with a discussion of Lola's race/ethnicity. Immediately following the moment when Lola tells Julian "in her impetuous, passionate language, how she had loved him all the time, even when she saw he was in love with Emma, and how she had cried in the misery of her heart because she thought he despised her" (100), she tells him the story of her skin color and the Indian dye, an account that complicates the yoking of Lola's passion and her color and ethnicity. Initially, Ruiz de Burton appears to invoke stereotypes of the "hot-blooded" Latin with an undercurrent of the generalized stereotype of the savage, passionate racial Other. Lola's account of the dye, an account that functions to insist that she is white, Mexican, and not-Indian, however, doubles back the representational claims of this passage. For while this account ascribes desire to the Mexican, it also attributes it to the racially white, symbolically conflating the Mexican and the Euro-American under the sign of desire and perhaps underscoring the difficulty involved in any attempt to dismantle dominant U.S. constructions of womanhood and their reliance on racialized binary oppositions of purity and impurity.

Perhaps not surprisingly, given this, the narrative is more effusive in the description of Lola's daughterly love and gratitude to Dr. Norval than in its representation of her romantic passion for Julian. Although the narrator describes and allows Lola to express her romantic love for Julian, the narrative never *directly* represents her as bearing erotic desire, an instance of narrative caution sharply in contrast with the representation of Mrs. Norval. Hence, Ruiz de Burton defends female erotic desire by explicitly attaching it to the white New England lady but avoids representing that recoded desire in the Othered women, sidestepping a danger of simply reinscribing the dominant culture's stereotypes of the exotic, erotic Other on the level of plot only to replicate it in the imagery of the narrative.[29]

Good American Girls, Wonderful Deeds, and the Nation

Ultimately, gender becomes the means in *Who Would Have Thought It?* of bringing together several ongoing issues. Norms of femininity are linked to and become representative of regional and even national norms, as Ruiz de Burton launches her critique of U.S. national politics through the figures of women. At the same time, she links models of American femininity to regions and uses them to query the relation between public and private spheres, as well as between region and nation and between government and nation, setting up a grid of interlocking determinants of American identity. In a telling moment early in the novel Ruiz de Burton describes a particular Sunday as "the anniversary of some great day in New England . . . —some great day in which the Pilgrim fathers had done some one of their wonderful deeds. They had either embarked, or landed, or burnt a witch, or whipped a woman at the pillory, on just such a day" (62). With this image of embarking and landing, this caustic aside first implicitly invokes and conflates the Pilgrim settlement of New England and the history of Euro-American colonial expansion, and then links both to the punishment of the "hysterical" or disobedient woman. This linking of American public, political "wonderful deeds"—the success of colonial expansion, the pursuit of freedom—to the containment of women sets up a chain of associations that reminds the reader that the policy of Manifest Destiny fueling America's involvement in the Mexican-American war, the Abolitionism under dispute in the Civil War, and the relegation of women to the private, domestic sphere all coexist and support one another within an ideological system where national power emerges from subjects differentially (dis)empowered according to their sex, race, region, and national identity.

Perhaps the most explicit interweaving of these threads is in the novel's account of Lavvy, Mrs. Norval's spinster sister. In the opening of *Who Would Have Thought It?* Lavvy fills the space, familiar in nineteenth-century women's fiction, of the superfluous spinster. She is one of the country's "old maids . . . past thirty-two" (107). Sister to Mrs. Norval, she lives with the Norval family, tending her canaries and ridiculed as unfashionable. But when the war begins, Lavvy, like so many of her historical counterparts, volunteers as a nurse and so enters the public sphere, moving to Washington, D.C., to oversee a hospital ward. Perfectly capable, Lavvy, the narrator notes, "wanted nothing better than plenty of employment for her exuberant moral energies and redundant force of will"

(104). She finds that employment in nursing and then in searching for her brother Isaac, who is lost in a Confederate war camp. This latter occupation brings her into contact with Congress, a plot development that allows Ruiz de Burton to bring together a critique of separate spheres, an implicit critique of the position of the Californios, and an assessment of the relation of the government to the nation.

On one level Lavvy's plot serves as the basis of a critique of dominant gender relations as articulated in the concept of separate spheres. Lavvy's search for information on Isaac takes her to various army and congressional offices where for the most part she is ignored, put off, patronized, dismissed, and generally treated, because of her sex, as if she were simpleminded or of no importance. After being told to wait at the Secretary of War's office, she falls into a meditation on the nature and ranking of male and female spheres. She observes, the narrator tells us,

that no matter how much a woman, in her unostentatious sphere, may do, and help to do, and no matter how her heart may feel for her beloved, worshipped country, after all she is but an insignificant creature, whom a very young man may snub, simply because he wears very shiny brass buttons and his uncle is in Congress. "What a miserable, powerless thing woman is, even in this our country of glorious equality! Here I have been sitting up at night, toiling, and tending disgusting sickness, and dressing loathsome wounds, all for the love of our dear country, and now, the first time I come to ask a favor,—*a favor*, do I say? No. I come to demand a right,—see how I am received!" (106, emphasis in original)

Lavvy's comments and predicament underscore the reality that separate spheres may be separate, but they are never equal. As the narrator observes later, "Lavvy was no advocate of 'woman's rights.' She did not understand the subject even, but she smiled sadly, thinking how little woman was appreciated, how unjustly underrated. *She* could obtain *nothing* from the government" (129, emphasis in original). This treatment echoes Ruiz de Burton's own when she tried to get her Army widow's pension increased in 1884. Asking a male friend in Washington to intervene with the Senators on her behalf, she writes, "please speak to both [a senator and a general]. There is no use in my writing to them. I am so unimportant for them to do any more than throw my epistle in the wastebasket. Particularly the Senator" (Letter, 1884).[30] Implicit in this letter and in the novel's analysis of gendered spheres of American life, of course, is a clear advocacy of women's rights: a demand for the acknowledgment and appreciation of "woman's" work, a protest at women's public, political powerlessness, and a recognition that this powerlessness of a whole group of patriotic Americans shows that the myth of America as a "country of glorious equality" is simply untrue.

The image of Lavvy ignored by the government functions on another level as well, because by 1872 it was clear that America had not proven to be a "country of glorious equality" for the Californios either. Read metaphorically, Lavvy's scenario also describes the plight of the Californios in the aftermath of annexation and the Land Law of 1851. As *The Squatter and the Don* would go on to dramatize at some length, the Dons' attempts to get the attention of the American government proved to be no more effective than Lavvy's, and their reception, when they came "to demand a right," turned out to be just as cold.[31] Amy Kaplan points out that "imperialism as a political or economic process abroad is inseparable from the social relations and cultural discourses of race, gender, ethnicity, and class at home. The binary opposition of the foreign and the domestic is itself imbued with the rhetoric of gender hierarchies that implicitly elevate the international to a male, public, realm, and relegate the national to a female, private sphere" (16). Reading Lavvy as symbol of the Californios underscores this link between imperial, foreign, and domestic while also exemplifying Kaplan's description of gender as a structuring hierarchy in national affairs.

These connections, suggested by Ruiz de Burton's use of the figure of female powerlessness emblematic of Californio powerlessness, further raise the question of the government's relation to "the people" and to the ideal of the nation. Throughout this section of the novel Ruiz de Burton consistently paints Lavvy as the little honest individual forgotten by, and powerless in the face of, the large anonymous government, a government that is neither honest nor concerned about its people.[32] In commenting, "poor Lavvy! she had no experience about asking favors of great men. She had believed all she had read in printed political speeches delivered just before election times" (106), the narrator locates Lavvy as a loyal citizen whose faith is betrayed by a government that does not embody her patriotic ideals. Hence, while ostensibly supporting patriotic American national ideals, Ruiz de Burton attacks the American government, painting it as patriarchal, non-democratic, expansionist, and oblivious to the rights and desires of even its own people. By focusing her criticism on the government instead of on the ideal of the nation, Ruiz de Burton voices her critique obliquely, disavowing it by characterizing the country's flaws not as fundamental problems but as merely the results of a government that has strayed from its true ideals.[33] This strategy links her again to nineteenth-century Mexican-American autobiographers, who, Genaro Pa-

dilla asserts, "mouthed a rhetoric of democratic ideals but practiced unrelenting hostility in its relations with them" (310), a political strategy
employed here.

Ruiz de Burton launches her critique of masculine state-building and
its violence by repeatedly portraying the government as indifferent to the
needs of the people. She then juxtaposes Lavvy's voice of the naïve patriot
and the narrator's more cynical commentary, tracking their responses as
a way of measuring the gap between the real and the ideal nation.[34] Lavvy
initially voices the belief of the innocent American who assumes an identity among the people, the government, and the nation. Unable to believe
that the government is less than the highest representative of the nation,
she struggles to believe instead that she has misinterpreted the government's behavior. Wondering why her brother has not been part of a pris-
oner exchange, for instance, Lavvy asks, "can it be possible that he
has been forgotten? I can't believe it. . . . It can't be! Our government
wouldn't forget him. It seems so, but it can't be so" (108–9). Invoking
the gendered topos of male state-building through war and woman as
mourner of the lost, Ruiz de Burton offers a critique of both Civil War
politics and American imperialism. The irony of Ruiz de Burton's tone becomes explicit in a scene where the pompous Mr. Blower tells Lavvy that
the government will end the war more quickly by leaving Northern men
(like her brother Isaac) imprisoned in the South, because, according to
this logic, the more prisoners the South has to feed, the faster its army
(and the prisoners) will starve and will be forced to surrender. This advocacy of indirect killing of the Union's own soldiers—an oblique reference
to the U.S. treatment of Native Americans, Mexicans, and other imperial
conquests—is too much for Lavvy's "little head," but when she responds
in "silent amazement," Blower continues, "I see you don't grasp the idea.
Of course, ladies can't well grasp great ideas, or understand reasons that
impel men in power to act at times in a manner apparently contrary to
humanity, to mercy, to justice" (113–14), a fact he accounts for by observing, "you, of course, reason like a lady" (114). He then dismisses her
by kissing her hand and telling her, "You are a good girl, and an honor to
your country. If you understood this policy, I am sure you would approve
it. But it is not to be expected that *ladies* would exactly appreciate those
ideas, they being beyond their sphere of thought" (115, emphasis in original). Lavvy, "like a good American girl," then goes on innocently to appeal to the ideal of the nation, asking Mr. Blower, "do THE PEOPLE of
the United States,—I mean *the loyal people*,—do they approve of their
brothers being left to starve in the South?" (115–16, emphasis in original),

a question that locates authority in "the people" over the corrupt government.[35] This scene thus brings together a critique of the government with a critique of separate spheres and its attendant devaluing of female intelligence. Offering a parodic version of a woman who cannot understand government because it is out of her sphere, Ruiz de Burton uses Lavvy to disrupt dominant narratives of state, revealing the violence on which state-building is based. As in the use of Lola to disrupt narratives of race and to reveal the repressed truth of miscegenation, gender serves as the fulcrum of this critique.

The War Between the States and Manifest Destiny

Establishing that New England is a region of the nation rather than equivalent to it, and establishing that the government does not adequately represent the nation, *Who Would Have Thought It?* participates in a U.S. national discourse that fueled not only the Civil War but also the Reconstruction politics that followed it. At the same time, inflecting this discourse with race and gender, Ruiz de Burton shows that the Civil War, as a sectional conflict, is connected to the policy of Manifest Destiny and westward expansion. Her novel thus overlays an East/West geographic axis with a North/South axis, bringing into focus the multiplicity of U.S. regions and relations among them. Although Ruiz de Burton specifically puts New England as a region in relation to the West through the introduction of Lola into the Norval family, her discussion of regions, finally, implicates not just all the regions that constitute America but Mexico as well. For if Lola can be said to bring the West into relation with New England, she also brings Mexico into relation with both. Against the foil of New England's provincialism the novel insists that the region be conceived of as only a part of the nation, one of many parts, all of which are simultaneously in relation to each other and to the "foreign" by means of the government. Consequently, the novel also demands that the reader locate the United States in relation to what José Martí was to call "our America" rather than in isolation.

Part of the novel is set in Mexico, where Isaac Sprig (Lavvy and Mrs. Norval's brother), having come across the manuscript account of the dying Doña Theresa Medina, goes in search of her husband and father. This section gives Ruiz de Burton a chance to defend upper-class Mexicans (and by analogy, the Californios) through repeated examples of their gentility, learning, wealth, and class privilege.[36] It also, however, allows her to underscore the connections between Mexico and the United States, locating the nation in an international context and connecting government and regions. Mexico's role in bringing together various discourses is perhaps clearest in the passage following Don Luis and Don Felipe's reading of Doña Theresa's manuscript. Using the language of sentimental romance, the narrator describes their agony at her "fate," then goes on to muse over the role of government in the individual's life:

If Mexico were well governed, if her frontiers were well protected, the fate of Doña Theresa would have been next to an impossibility. When it is a well-known fact that savages will devastate towns that are not well guarded, is there any excuse for a government that will neglect to provide sufficient protection? Does a plea of economy counterbalance an appeal for life? How fearful is the responsibility of lawgivers and law executors!

Thinking of this, the mind is led to the thought that—with some exceptions of course—a nation can, with a good government, avoid the majority of those misfortunes which we now call '*unavoidable* human sorrows.' If we were to trace our troubles to their veritable source, we would often reach, more or less directly, their origin in *our lawgivers*. Not only the dwellers of the frontiers, not only the victims of lawsuits, not only—But I am no political philosopher. I am wandering away from my humble path. (201, emphasis in original)

By representing the Medinas as the civilized citizens who are victimized by the "savage" Indians, this passage aligns the Mexicans with Americans against the Other of the Indian, thus making it possible to read this as a piece of advice, a cautionary tale told by Mexico to America. The passage implies that the United States frontiers implicitly need protection from the "savages"—i.e., the Indians—not the Mexicans, and that it is the government's job to protect its citizens against such "savages." At the same time, however, Mexico's need to protect its "frontiers" must also refer to the U.S. takeover of 1848, implicitly aligning "American" with "Indian" in this passage: both as "savage" enemies of Mexico. In this light one can read Ruiz de Burton's depiction of the Mexican government's neglect of its frontier citizens as a comment both on the United States's conquest of Mexico transnationally and on the U.S. government's neglect of women and of the Californios within national borders. Pointing to "lawgivers and law executors"—certainly the source of the Californios' problems—Ruiz de Burton connects internal regional problems as well as transnational colonial expansion with governmental mismanagement, but she breaks off her meditation in the interests of consistency of genre. Falling back on a disingenuous and gendered generic plea—"I am no political philosopher. I am wandering away from my humble path"—she defers to the conventions of the "historical romance" to return to her characters and leave behind her political musings.[37] In *The Squatter and the Don* she will allow the "political philosopher" as well as the historian more of an explicit voice, but ultimately both it and *Who Would Have Thought It?* are testimony to the fact that political philosophy and historical romance are indeed not separate spheres: Ruiz de Burton uses the genre of the historical romance politically, critiquing Manifest Destiny and expansionism, then querying issues of region, nation, race, and gender alongside and within a courtship plot in order ultimately to remap the nation.

Ethnicity, Region, and Racial Discourses of the "American"

Rosaura Sánchez and Beatrice Pita, in their introduction to *The Squatter and the Don*, insightfully call the novel a "counter-history of the subaltern." Certainly, the novel, shifting from *Who Would Have Thought It?*'s East Coast subject matter to a Southern California focus, offers an account of the historical process of the appropriation of formerly Mexican land in the aftermath of annexation. In addition to providing this revisionist history, the novel also offers a sustained critique of U.S. imperialism. Thus, Ruiz de Burton's project is not simply to demonstrate the violence of the nation-building imperialism of Manifest Destiny and its use of Mexican-American identity and land, it is also to reposition California and the Californios within that imperialist project.

Homi K. Bhabha contends that "once the liminality of the nation-space is established, and its 'difference' is turned from the boundary 'outside' to its finitude 'within,' the threat of cultural difference is no longer a problem of 'other' people. It becomes a question of the otherness of the people-as-one" (301). Amy Kaplan, meanwhile, discussing a critical shift from the concept of "frontier" to "borderlands" in American Studies, argues that the "borderlands link the study of ethnicity and immigration inextricably to the study of international relations and empire. At these borders, foreign relations do not take place outside the boundaries of America, but instead constitute American nationality. The borderlands thus transform the traditional notion of the frontier from the primitive margins of civilization to a decentered cosmopolitanism" (17). Nearly four decades after the Treaty of Guadalupe-Hidalgo, concern over the political borderlands of the United States had indeed shifted from external frontiers to internal differences, and the Californios as cultural Other were firmly located within the nation. The question by this point was what part of that internal "people-as-one" would the Californios be. Shifting from a focus on the Mexican Lola to the Californio Mercedes and her family, Ruiz de Burton, in her second novel, offers an answer to this question, critiquing the internal workings of American empire building while simultaneously claiming a place for the Californios as part of the "people-as-one" by turning Californios into Californians.

The Squatter and the Don attempts to locate the Californios as part of the nation by simultaneously reworking the concept of *American* and the concept of Californio via a focus on race, land, and gender. Ruiz de Burton offers a complicated formation that emphasizes class and racial affiliations at the expense of ethnic and religious differences, disavowing the "Don's" status as colonized to emphasize his place as colonizer and using region and gender within a domestic/romance plot as vehicles of Californio-Anglo unification. Negotiating between the figure of the *indio* and that of the *American*, Ruiz de Burton's narrative "remembers" a European bloodline for the Californios while forgetting a mestizo heritage,[38] and through this action is ultimately able to demand the acceptance of the Californio by dominant American culture. But this is not a call for assimilation—for the Californio Other to adopt the culture of Anglo-America and abandon a Mexican heritage. In telling a story that locates Californios as a part of the nation, Ruiz de Burton refashions not merely the Californios but also the American nation, realigning geographic axes of the American cultural imagination and complicating discourses of race and ethnicity by deploying the category of the *Indian*, by introducing the category of the Californio, and by gendering both of them.

Part of this doubled strategy of critique and reformulation of American national identity entails linking white ethnic difference to regional difference, a transformation that yields high payoffs, since in the novel the regional will become a synecdoche for the national. Ruiz de Burton's representing the Dons as Californios rather than Mexicans thus does more than simply follow historical precedent: it also positions them as an internal, regional part of the (white imperialist) nation rather than an external threat to it. The California/Mexico geographical frontier having been established, Ruiz de Burton turns her attentions to internal American frontiers, where California's status as a region and as a part of the myth of the Southwest/West-wild-frontier allows it to serve as what Lauren Berlant has called a "place of national mediation" (395) and as a space where the "threat" of ethnic and religious difference can be displaced onto racial difference so that ethnic difference can become a safe cultural manifestation of regional diversity. A limited space for ethnic diversity within the nation opens up, a diversity that Ruiz de Burton figures as a strength, a positive element of American culture.[39] Hence, Californio slides into Californian, which then slides into American. As a result, "difference" can become not racial and/or foreign, but internal to the United States and familiar: just another variant of the happy American melting-pot image. Ruiz de Burton thus attempts to neutralize the threat of Californio "difference" by representing the Californios as descendants of a European elite—ethnically interesting but not racially different—in a rhetorical move that recognizes the power of race as a determining identity discourse in American culture at this historical moment. Although at this moment ethnicity is clearly a less dangerous location for difference than race, ultimately, as I will argue, what *The Squatter and the Don* reveals is that even ethnic difference is tolerable only when embodied by the figure of the woman. The national "problem" of political and cultural conflicts can here, as Doris Sommer demonstrates elsewhere, only be resolved through the romance plot.

The Squatter and the Don puts these transformations under way by means of a double plot structure, juxtaposing the primary domestic romance plot—the courtship of the Anglo hero Clarence Darrell and the Californio heroine Mercedes Alamar—with a public political plot involving the fading fortunes of Don Mariano Alamar, Mercedes's father. Ruiz de Burton's representative Californio landowner, the Don is slowly losing his lands to endless appeals of the Land Act as well as to Anglo squatters, but he hopes for eventual justice from the United States government.[40] The novel's romance plot serves as the arena for the working out of these political problems: the narrative block to lovers Clarence Darrell and Mercedes Alamar grows out of the fact that Darrell is the son of William Darrell, who appears to be one of the Anglo squatters on the Don's land.[41] The happy resolution of this courtship (as well as of the subsidiary ones among various of the Darrell and Alamar children) depends upon both families' recognition of the other's status as both American and genteel, cultured as both the *indios* and the squatters are not. It is this happy resolution of the domestic plot—not, significantly, a resolution of the political plot—that offers a refigured American national identity that includes the Californios.

Preparatory to identifying the Californios as part of the U.S., the novel emphasizes the distance between Californio and *indio*, projecting onto the *indio* all the qualities that Anglo-American racial discourse assigned to the Californios. Here Ruiz de Burton must be seen as responding to the

U.S. racist casting of Mexico as what Congressman Columbus Delano described in 1847 as a "sad compound of Spanish, English, Indian, and negro blood . . . resulting . . . in the production of a slothful, indolent, ignorant race of beings" (quoted in Horsman 240). The Dons are not "greasers" or "lazy Indians," *The Squatter and the Don* insists, but privileged European colonizers just like the "Americans." This rehearsal of the Californio claim to Spanish blood echoes that of the Californio *testimonios*, where, Rosaura Sánchez argues, such a claim functions "as an attempt to appear on the same racial plane with the Yankee invaders, as if national origin and race could be wielded as a strategic discourse to combat racist representations of the conquered Californios as half-civilized Indians" (59). Ruiz de Burton thus uses the Californios' "pure" Spanish blood to distance them from the U.S. rhetoric of, as Representative Edward C. Cabell put it, "the black, white, red, mongrel, miserable population of Mexico—the Mexicans, Indians, Mulattoes, Mestizos, Chinos, Zambos, Quinteros" (quoted in Horsman 242). At the same time, this "blood" functions both as an explanation of and as a synonym for Californio class privilege, a metaphor for displaced discussions of class, economic status, ethnicity, and political allegiances. Ruiz de Burton manipulates a claim of essentialized "blood" identity to override ethnic difference and to naturalize class status. Hence, as John M. González points out, "Ruiz de Burton contests not the process of incorporation of California's economy and culture into the national core as such, but rather the social position accorded to the Californios within that capitalist order" (31).

This class status is set up against the foil of *indio* laborer status: Elvira Alamar's servant is a "squaw" (198), whereas Elvira's father, Don Mariano, notes that one doesn't do the *"vaqueroing"* oneself; one hires "an Indian boy" to do it (94). This distancing of *indio* from the ideals of American economic prosperity is furthered by the novel's erasure of any *indio* claim to land. The novel suggests that the squatters should take the "government land" instead of the Dons' lands (67, 76), thereby ascribing land rights to the Californios but not to the California Indians.[42] This landless servant class is also represented as trouble-making and linguistically foreign, and the Indians' use of their colonizer's language serves ironically to displace any Spanish speaking by the Californios themselves. The Don's *vaqueros* encourage the conflict between William Darrell and the Alamars, shouting in Spanish and provoking Victoriano Alamar to respond in kind, in one of the very few instances where the Californios speak any Spanish at all in this novel (249–50).[43] The association of Indian, servant, and non-English speaker suggests that the *indios* are Other to dominant fictions of American identity on the grounds of both race and class and are foreign even in their (adopted second) language. The effect of this association is to underscore the conflation of race and class (*indio* = poor) then to mark this particular conflation as foreign. This cluster of associations emerges again in the one direct representation of an Indian that the novel provides. When Victoriano Mariano, one of the Don's sons, arrives home and orders a servant to look after his horse, the narrator offers this description:

"*Yes patroncito*, I'll do it right away," said the lazy Indian, who first had to stretch himself and yawn several times, then hunt up tobacco and cigarette paper, and smoke his cigarette. This done he, having had a heavy supper, shuffled lazily to the front of the house, as Clarence was driving down the hill for the second time, and Doña Josefa and Victoriano returning from Mrs. Mechlin, came in through the garden side gate. (278)

Clarence, Victoriano, and Doña Josefa's bustling activity aligns the Californios and Anglos in opposition to the "shuffling" Indian, an opposition underscored by Ruiz de Burton's repetitive use of "lazy."[44] The *indios'* poverty, lack of property, and "laziness" are thus figured as both the result of their race (non-whiteness, in the terms of this dichotomy) and the explanation of why they can never qualify as true Americans.

This vignette both Others the *indios* and defines the Californios in terms of dominant images of American "character," here marked as industrious and energetic. This is typical of *The Squatter and the Don*: ethnic "difference" in the male characters is sutured over by the showcasing of the male Californios, embodied by the Don, as good American citizens, refined and educated, a narrative enactment of the strategy employed by Californios as they attempted to save their land rights in the aftermath of the Treaty of Guadalupe-Hidalgo. In 1859, for instance, fifty Californios, led by former governor of California Pio Pico, submitted a petition to the United States Congress protesting their plight. In this petition Pico ostentatiously lauds the democratic principles of America, then deploys them ironically against the United States in his description of the Californios, who, he asserts,

immediately assumed the position of American citizens that was offered them, and since then have conducted themselves with zeal and faithfulness and with no less loyalty than those whose great fortune it was to be born under the flag of the North American republic—believing, thus, that all their rights were insured in the treaty, which declares that *their property shall be inviolably protected and insured*; seeing the realization of the promises made to them by United States officials; trusting and hoping to participate in the prosperity and happiness of the great nation of which they now had come to be an integral part. (quoted in Weber 196, emphasis in original)

Zeal, loyalty to the United States, trust in the American government, faith that it is indeed designed to promote prosperity and happiness: what could be more American than this? The rhetorical effect as well as the content of this statement reappear in what might be read as the Don's paraphrase of Pico when the Don says, concisely, that "the majority of my best friends are Americans. . . . Their sentiments, their ways of thinking suit me" (177).

But this statement also covertly critiques the rhetorical distance placed by Anglo-American culture between itself and the Californios. For in pointing out that his "best friends" are American, the Don makes it clear that, however many traits he shares with them, he himself is not seen as an American. The demand that the Californios be read as part of the nation is in the end untenable. The novel cannot resolve this public, political problem purely by means of a deployment of the public racial discourse. Therefore, even as Ruiz de Burton insists on the Californio's difference from the *indio* and similarity to the Anglo American, she concurrently reaffirms precisely the opposite: the Californios' similarity to the *indio* and difference from the Anglo American. The structural alignment of Californio and Anglo at the expense of the *indio* collapses under the weight of its own internal logic. The term Californio itself marks this collapse, for along with its effort to replace ethnic identity with regional identity, it also links the Californios to the irreparably Othered *indios* through its claim to the status of authentic, original inhabitant of the now-colonized land.[45] Ruiz de Burton implicitly acknowledges that the Californios occupy the position of the *indios* and are being eliminated like them when she has Don Mariano evoke the fate of the Mission Indians by saying, "I am sure I am to be legislated into a *rancheria*, as there is no poor-house in San Diego to put me into" (164).[46] He later aligns the Dons and the *indios* again as indigenous populations destroyed by foreign conquest, remarking, "I'm afraid there is no help for us *native Californians. We must sadly fade and pass away.* The weak and the helpless are always trampled in the throng . . . to legislate us into poverty is to legislate us into our graves. *Their* [Anglo] *very contact is deadly to us*" (177, emphasis added). The Californio here is killed metaphorically by the disease of contact with the Anglos, as the *indios* had literally been.

Similarly, although the narrative attempts to differentiate the Californios and the *indios* by defending the Spanish/Mexican treatment of the Indians even as it critiques the same treatment when it is practiced on the Californios by the Anglo Americans, this opposition too collapses. The Don claims that the Spanish/Mexican landowners did the Indians a favor by taking their land from them then making them work it for Spanish/Mexican profit, arguing that by employing the Indians, the Dons made the "savages" "less wild" (176). But in the very same speech, Don Mariano protests the American squatters' taking of the Dons' lands, in a language that links Don and Indian once again, even while ostensibly distinguishing between them:

The cry was raised that our land grants were too large; that a few *lazy, thriftless, ignorant natives*, holding such large tracts of land, would be a hindrance to the prosperity of the State, because such *lazy* people would never cultivate their lands, and were even too *sluggish* to sell them. . . . It was so easy to upbraid, to deride, to despise the *conquered race!* Then to despoil them, to make them beggars, seemed to be, if not absolutely righteous, certainly highly justifiable. Any one not acquainted with the real facts might have supposed that there was no more land to be had in California but that which belonged to the *natives*. Everybody seemed to have forgotten that for each acre that was owned by them, there were thousands vacant belonging *to the Government* and which any one can have at one dollar and twenty-five cents per acre. No, they didn't want Government land. The settlers want the lands of the *lazy, the thriftless Spaniards*. Such *good-for-nothing, helpless wretches* are not fit to own such lordly tracts of land. (175, emphasis added)

Rehearsing U.S. rationalizations for taking Californio land, the Don is using "natives" here to mean Californios, but the other "natives" hovering in the national margins, summonsed by this imagery, are, of course, the *indios*. The slippage between the two becomes more dramatic given the terms in which the Don characterizes the "natives": his rendition of American accounts of the "natives" uses the very terms ("lazy," "thriftless," "helpless," etc.) to describe the Californios that both he himself and the Americans use to describe the *indios*. This conflation of Californio and *indio* mirrors an Anglo-American historical process established by Ruiz de Burton's day. It also produces an imperative within the novel to disavow both the historical fact of Californio and *indio* mestizo lineage and the American political usage of that fact.[47] In 1853, well after the annexation of California, Senator John Clayton articulated the tension between the U.S. desire for more Mexican territory and the fear of the Mexican population that it would bring, stating, "Yes! Aztecs, Creoles, Half-breeds, Quadroon, Samboes, and I know not what else—'ring-streaked and speckled'—all will come in, and instead of our governing them, they, by their votes, will govern *us*" (quoted in Horsman 246). Ruiz de Burton's distancing of the Californios from the *indios* operates as a challenge to this depiction of Mexicans but asserts the Dons as fit citizens only by reinforcing U.S. racist representations of Indians. Ironically, then, her ineffective disavowal of Californio-*indio* commonalities simultaneously acknowledges a history of shared bloodlines and colonized status but prevents Ruiz de Burton from politically deploying that history in the larger interests of a demand for justice for all victims of U.S. imperial expansion.

Gendered Patriots

Ultimately, Ruiz de Burton cannot successfully use the public discourse to simultaneously launch a critique of U.S. imperialism and support a demand for Californio inclusion in the national imaginary. As a result, in part because of the difficulties of forging a national identity in the face of this complicated history and faced with the need to both deny and acknowledge the Dons' position as disempowered colonial subjects, Ruiz de Burton marshals gender as a way of imagining the possibility of a universalized category of the "American": she turns to the domestic and romance plot for the solution of her narrative problems. As it turns out, in *The Squatter and the Don* both the colonial status and the ethnicity of the Californios have meanings that are contingent upon how they are gendered and contingent upon which particular sexed body carries them. Because of gender's salience in this equation, it becomes possible in the end to imagine national unity only through the figure of the woman. Ethnicity's very definition is inflected by gender: in the private sphere it is "female"—quaint or even exotically erotic—and so is non-threatening. But in the public sphere ethnicity conflicts with the terms of masculinity and as such stands as a barrier to American identity. In a similar way, just as being female, if accompanied by class privilege, diffuses the threat of being ethnically marked, being female lines up with the already culturally overdetermined gender of the colonized subject while masculinity never can. Imbricated in a culture structured on the one hand by the sex/gender system and on the other by capitalist colonial economic relations, Ruiz de Burton mobilizes a very specific use of gender—embodied in women—as the guarantor of Americanness: one naturalized cultural category helps universalize another, in part because both become regionally inflected. Figuring her female characters as agents of region, morality, religion, and class, Ruiz de Burton uses the novel's women as the intermediaries between the Dons and the Anglos, a function marked by the novel's proposal that ultimately the Californios' status as "American" must be achieved in the domestic sphere: through intermarriage. National unity, the novel suggests, cannot be created in the public sphere; it can only emerge out of the "female" private sphere.[48] She thus takes a common nineteenth-century American narrative strategy (woman as conveyer of purity, morality, spirituality, and, conversely, exhibitor of the family's class status) and uses it to write in one of the very categories of people (and specifically, women) that contemporary notions of Americanness left out.

The Californio men cannot be used to this end because of the specific way their masculinity inflects the meaning of their ethnicity. For in men, the novel implies, non-Anglo ethnicity is always potentially a threat simply because it is embodied by the sex which has more cultural power to begin with and so is more potentially able to disrupt the dominant system. Specifically as men, the Californio men might conceivably have legal or economic rights and are thus inherently a greater threat to American imperial expansion than Californio women.[49] That ethnic "difference" is threatening in men is made clear in the novel's treatment of Gabriel Alamar, one of the Don's sons. Gabriel is married to Lizzie Mechlin, a daughter of the upper-class Anglo Mechlin family. The Mechlins are friends and neighbors of the Alamars and are Ruiz de Burton's model of the "good" class-privileged Anglos. When Gabriel loses his respectable position in a San Francisco bank (because he has been at home in San Diego, loyally helping his beleaguered parents), he cannot find work and eventually turns to learning a trade, a "step down" that upsets his wife.[50] Gabriel defends his actions as gentlemanly, noting that they are based on the desire to protect and support his wife and children and that they involve honest work. However, when stripped of class privilege, Gabriel's position radically changes and not just in terms of class status. Ruiz de Burton puts the observation of this change in the voice of Gabriel's wife Lizzie, who in a long meditation notes,

Years before, when she was Lizzie Mechlin, she had moved in what was called San Francisco's *best* society. Her family, being of the very highest in New York, was courted and caressed in exaggerated degree on their arrival in California. . . . When Gabriel came to his position in the bank, she was again warmly received by all her society friends. But this cordiality soon vanished . . . she and Gabriel returned from San Diego to San Francisco to find that he had lost his place at the bank . . . her fashionable friends disappeared. Nay, they avoided her as if she had been guilty of some disgraceful act. The fact that Gabriel was a *native Spaniard*, she saw plainly, militated against them. If he had been rich, his nationality could have been forgiven, but no one will willingly tolerate a *poor native Californian.* (351, emphasis in original)

This passage is worth quoting at some length because it so clearly articulates the ways in which class, ethnicity, and gender overlap and interconnect. As an economically privileged white woman, Lizzie marries a man whose ethnicity ("nationality") can be overlooked because of his class privilege and hers. But when he loses this privilege, society realizes that she had committed the "disgraceful act" of marrying a *"native Spaniard."* In the eyes of nativist America his ethnicity can no longer be neutralized by his class status and so is revealed as too disruptive of the system to be "tolerated." Gabriel's fall in class status combines with and provokes a new awareness of his ethnic "difference": he is now recognized by good society as a *"poor native,"* a combination that renders him a threat and an outcast.

If ethnicity here makes it impossible for Gabriel to qualify as an *American* man, the status of the Dons as colonized and, moreover, as not particularly committed to capitalism makes it impossible for them to qualify as American *men.* What Ruiz de Burton makes visible in *The Squatter and the Don* is the extent to which gender as a discourse is employed by the colonial machinery. The colonized male is rhetorically emasculated: as colonized subjects the Dons here occupy a feminized cultural space, coded as powerless, in contrast to the colonizer, who, through his link to power, is figured as masculine.[51] Don Mariano's grounding in a pre-capitalist system, as well as his position as disempowered and colonized, feminizes him: his powerlessness in the face of the squatters certainly emasculates him. Even the squatters, whom the novel explicitly represents as the Don's economic, social, and moral inferiors, recognize that they have a certain power over their superior, as the following conversation between two squatters shows:

"Those greasers ain't half crushed yet. We have to tame them like they do their mustangs, or shoot them, as we shoot their cattle," said Mathews.

"Oh, no. No such violent means are necessary. All we have to do is to take their lands, and finish their cattle," said Hughes, sneeringly. . . . (73)

While Mathews metaphorically reduces the Californios to animals in order to justify the settlers' exploitative actions,[52] Hughes realizes that the American legal system, coupled with the program of beliefs known as Manifest Destiny, offers an easier way for American men to conquer this particular "virgin land." The Dons and their lands are imaged as there to be taken, and if historically the Dons could not be simply rendered rhetorically invisible in the narrative of American "progress" across the "wild" frontier (as the Native Americans were), they could, this passage demonstrates, ultimately at least be feminized to the point where they, like women, had practically no legal rights.[53]

Ruiz de Burton underscores here how the gendering of colonial relations makes it impossible for the Dons, as colonized, to fully occupy the space of American masculinity. The novel also reveals the ways Anglo-American coding of the Dons as not proper capitalists further emasculates them.[54] Historically, Anglo Americans read the Californios as inadequate capitalists. Douglas Monroy points out that the Anglo intruders considered the Californios both indolent and non-productive: not market-oriented as good capitalist American bread-winners would be (165–66). The rancho lifestyle was not focused on individual accumulation of wealth. Anglos, using American capitalist tenets as a standard of judgment, often viewed the male Californios as lazy, lacking in "energy and self-regulation" (168). "Real" men, according to this American ideology, worked, battled in the market place, and left the leisurely enjoyment of life to "their" women.

Ruiz de Burton's representation of the Dons locates them outside of this capitalist model of male productivity, positioning them instead in a nostalgic realm of rancho leisure and generosity, where name and breeding meant more than money, and earning a living was something done by the *indios* for the Dons. The narrator criticizes the San Francisco "best society," for instance, for falling prey to capitalism's values and lowering its standards, commenting that "the weight of gold carried the day. Down came the jealously guarded gates; the very portals succumbed and crumbled under that heavy pressure. Farewell, exclusiveness! Henceforth, money shall be the sole requisite upon which to base social claims. High culture, talents, good antecedents, accomplishments, all were now the veriest trash. Money and nothing but money, became the order of the day" (315). Voicing the position of the pre-industrial landed aristocrat, Ruiz de Burton recognizes the dominance of this cash-based economy; however, she represents it not as progress but as a fall into crass market values. Her depiction of the Dons as the landed gentry (a depiction that counters the Anglo-American version of lazy and slothful Dons with a vision of open-handed, gracious, and generous Dons) has several effects. On the one hand, this representation identifies the Dons as not fitting into the role of American competitive capitalist man and thus feminizes the Dons and makes them unable to carry the weight of establishing the Californios as Americans. It further distances them from American identity because by evoking (even if to dispute) the American view of Californios as "lazy," the novel's representation of the Dons once again aligns them with the Othered *indios*.[55]

On the other hand, however, as the critique of money as the sole standard of value indicates, Ruiz de Burton views the rancho system's values as superior to those of capitalism and suggests that if the Californio man must inevitably adapt to the U.S. system, the system itself and its definition of manhood also need revision. Ruiz de Burton goes beyond merely representing a gap between Californio and Anglo-American models of masculinity; she offers a new model of American manhood that draws on the Californio model, suggesting that the American man of the future will and should be more like the Don. Interestingly, one of the traits that marks Don Mariano as feminized in an Anglo-American system is his refined sense of moral justice, because moral sensitivity was, of course, assigned to the female sphere.[56] But if this trait makes the Don less of a "man" to the squatters, it is a trait shared by Clarence Darrell, Ruiz de Burton's model American man. In a long monologue Clarence attacks the post–Treaty of Guadalupe-Hidalgo treatment of the "native Californians" as "stains on our national honor" and an "American shame" (103). He goes on, when the Don congratulates him for being an honorable man and one who shares the Don's own opinions, to blush and reply, "you are very kind, and that you, who are so generous, should be made to suffer as you have, it is, I assure you . . . revolting to me (as an American and a civilized being)" (103). In scenes like this Clarence serves as the antidote to Ruiz de Burton's version of conventional Anglo-American masculinity, represented by the crass, dishonest, immoral squatters. This model needs to be reformed in order to live up to the American ideal, and that reformation, Ruiz de Burton suggests through the figure of the blushing Clarence, would be best effected by American men adopting some of the "feminized" traits of Californio men.[57]

Ultimately, Ruiz de Burton suggests both that the American man is not living up to the American ideal and that the ideal itself needs to be revised. Simultaneously, by depicting Don Mariano as an old-fashioned Don willing to modernize and to learn to become a profit-making capitalist, Ruiz de Burton implies that the Californio man could and would adopt some American capitalist values and hence adapt to some extent to the American man's vocation. Manuel M. Martín Rodríguez goes so far as to read the Alamars as "eager to transform their way of life from a ranch economy to the industrial capitalism brought by the new conquerors," if only to protect their social status (43). In any case, it is clear that the novel's representative hope for America's future cannot be either the Anglo man or the Californio man or even a simple combination of the two, since neither in this narrative is quite the proper American. This, then, is where the figure of the woman enters.

Woman as the Bridge

Ruiz de Burton looks to the domestic sphere and to the category of American womanhood in order to imagine a solution to her narrative's conflicts and to locate the Californios within American national identity. As in *Who Would Have Thought It?*, Ruiz de Burton accomplishes this by first exposing the ideal of True Womanhood as a fiction. It is not, the novel contends, a universal unmarked category but rather an always racially, religiously, regionally, and class-inflected model. This act of revision is crucial to the process of opening up a space for Californio women, for in relation to a model that itself is marked, the Californio women's ethnicity is just one among many possible inflections. With their colonized status only reinforcing their femininity and their ethnicity established as not a threat, the Californio women can then figure as easily as the Anglo women as the heart of the domestic sphere and as the good mothers, daughters, and wives of their men. But like Pauline Hopkins, Ruiz de Burton goes beyond demonstrating that the ideal of American womanhood is an inflected and hence open category; she offers a revised model of womanhood through the figure of the Mother. Through this strategy she aligns Anglo and Californio women and portrays Mercedes Alamar as the ideal American wife and mother of future generations.

Mary Darrell, the mother of the novel's representative "good" Anglo settler family, is the narrative vehicle by which Ruiz de Burton deconstructs the supposedly unmarked category of American femininity, making part of Mary's representative status the specific regional, ethnic, and religious inflection of her character. By producing an ideal who is of French descent, Catholic, and specifically not a New Englander (as her husband is) but rather a native of the "Southern"-identified Washington, D.C., who has been transplanted to the West, Ruiz de Burton makes visible by contrast the specifically New England, Anglo, Protestant bourgeois coding of the ideal.[58] Hence, far from simply adopting a bourgeois American notion of womanhood and then patterning her heroines after it, Ruiz de Burton identifies the category of idealized womanhood for what it is and then goes on to read it as open to her Californio heroines.

As in her first novel the function of religion is particularly significant here, for by making Mary Darrell a Catholic, Ruiz de Burton not only brings into focus the fact that models of American womanhood are implicitly inflected as Protestant, she also establishes religion as a link between Mary and the Californios, particularly the Californio women.[59] That the Dons are Catholic and that the Californio women are the specific agents of both the practice and transmission of Catholic religious values (we learn of Don Mariano's exemplary daughter Mercedes, for instance, that "in all the sad tribulations of her mind, her heart turned to her Redeemer and the Blessed Virgin Mary" [263]) is hardly surprising. Less culturally predictable, however, is the fact that the representative Anglo settler family, the Darrells, is also Catholic and Catholic specifically because of Mary.

Ruiz de Burton makes much of Mary's religion, particularly in the novel's opening, where she details the history of the Darrells' courtship, identifying the two main obstacles to the marriage as William Darrell's temper and his Protestantism. The guarantee of the transmission of Mary's Catholicism to her family is figured as the most important condition of her agreeing to marry William Darrell: in order to marry Mary, William promises Mary's priest "not to coerce or influence his wife to change her religion, and that should their union be blessed with children, they should be baptized and brought up Catholics" (62).[60] Catholicism here becomes the site of another link between the Dons and the Anglos and a link specifically forged and embodied by Doña Josefa and Mary Darrell. For the Californio and Anglo women share not just a common religion but also a common maternal function: the transmission of this religion to their children.[61] Religion is represented in *The Squatter and the Don* as a cultural system carried down through generations by the mother, who ensures its continuing presence in the future. Timothy Brennan notes that nationalism is analogous to religion in providing a sense of mission and self-identity (59); what better way, then, to suggest a commonality of national identity than through a commonality of religious identity? Furthermore, by viewing this analogy through the lens of gender, it becomes clear that if the mother is responsible for instilling religion in her children, then analogously she is also the transmitter of national identity, and therefore the domestic realm must be read as constitutive of the national. In *The Squatter and the Don*, certainly, under the sign of the maternal, both Anglo and Californio women construct national identity through the family unit, a unit that is not only Catholic but is also the product of a kind of religiously or culturally "mixed" marriage. Such a marriage is a condition of origin that will also prove to be the model of the ideal American family envisioned by the novel's resolution.

The novel repeatedly locates the Californio women within the family, so that as mothers and daughters they fit comfortably into dominant American ideals of femininity. Like the proper American lady, represented here by the Anglo women who are excluded from the public, political sphere, prevented not only from attending a meeting of the squatter "heads of families" (89), but even from attending the banquet given in honor of politician/railroad lobbyist Tom Scott's visit to San Diego (122), the "Spanish girls" are contained in the private sphere, given, as Elvira Alamar says, "all the freedom that is good for us" (203). Within that private sphere the Californio women, like the Anglo women, transmit familial/national American values. Doña Josefa, for instance, perfectly occupies the space of the good bourgeois mother, teaching her daughters to be "ladies" in all senses of the word. Mercedes's "inbred self-respect, a lady's sense of decorum" is set forth as typical of "Spanish girls" and attributed to their being kept "strictly guarded" in the family (203). We are told that "Spanish mothers will never let a daughter go out of the maternal sight until they are married" (138). Mercedes's brother-in-law comments that "Spanish girls are trained to strict filial obedience, and it is a good thing when not carried too far" (139). The narrator later explains Mercedes's dignity and propriety as "the effect of Doña Josefa's doctrines, which she had carefully inculcated into the minds of her daughters" (240). The mother here both reproduces her moral and social values in her daughters and makes sure that they live according to them. It is Doña Josefa, for instance, who must be convinced that her daughter's suitor Clarence is not a squatter, and it is Doña Josefa who retracts her approval of the marriage after Clarence's father behaves dishonorably.

The daughters meanwhile serve both as vehicles of religion and moral values and as exemplars of beauty and grace, in keeping with the most conventional American lady. Clarence Darrell, the novel's romantic hero, falls in love at first sight with Mercedes in a wholesome American way, struck by her beautiful eyes. She and her sister both attract attention during their visit to New York, causing bystanders to remark upon their beauty and hapless young men to fall desperately, hopelessly in love. Mercedes's structural status in the novel as female object is emphasized by Ruiz de Burton's locating the scene in which Clarence offers to buy the Don's land immediately after the scene in which Clarence first sees and falls in love with Mercedes. Her position as object to be traded between men is suggested in its narrative displacement to the trading of land be-

tween those same men and also signals the displacement of public conflicts (over land) into the private realm (of romance).

The Dons' daughters further fulfill the duties of the proper American
lady by displaying and jealously protecting their family's social and class
positioning. When William Darrell calls Californios "inferior people," for
instance, Mrs. Darrell corrects him by pointing to the women, retorting,
"*inferior*? What are you talking about? It is enough to see one of those
Alamar ladies to learn that they are inferior to nobody" (222, emphasis in
original), whereas the Don identifies the Darrells' inherent gentility by asserting, "I shall be pleased to have Mercedes and her mamma and sisters
all call [on the Darrells], for I think Clarence's mother must be a lady"
(117). And the Dons' daughters not only embody their family's class privilege, they defend it in the face of possible threats: Carlotta and Rosario,
Mercedes's older sisters, object to the romance between Clarence Darrell
and their sister on the (mistaken) grounds that he is nothing but a squatter. Carlotta exclaims with righteous indignation, "The idea of an Alamar
marrying a squatter! For squatters they are, though we must dance with
them . . . I am shocked at Papa's partiality," and Rosario adds, "Yes, with
all due respect to Papa, I fear I will not be reconciled to the idea of Mercedes being a daughter-in-law of old Darrell." To this the narrator adds
pointedly, "And thus felt and thus reasoned these proud ladies *in those
days*. For although the shadows of black clouds were falling all around,
they had not observed them, or suspected their proximity; they held their
heads proudly" (125, emphasis in original). Even Clarence himself recognizes that it is the women of the Alamar family who suspect he is not
good enough to marry into their family: he tells the Don, "I did not fear
unkindness or rejection from *you*, but from Doña Josefa and the young
ladies I did" (127).

These depictions of the Alamar ladies suggest two reasons for Ruiz de
Burton's use of the figure of woman to link Californio culture with Anglo
culture. One reason that these women—whether upper-class Californio
or Anglo—occupy such an important structural position in *The Squatter
and the Don* is that they offer a metaphor of the Californio position as
at once colonizer and colonized. Both are "colonized" in their position as
women, but at the same time, the Californio women figure as colonizers
on the basis of their class privilege, as the Anglo women do on the basis
of their racial privilege.[62] Hence, these women embody the mediation of
conflicting identities and offer an example of a livable resolution to Ruiz
de Burton's narrative problem. The other reason that women prove so
useful to Ruiz de Burton is that dominant stereotypes allow Californio

women more access than they allow men to the category of "American."
Ruiz de Burton depicts Anglo-American culture as more willing to see
Californio women than men as American: the feminized status of the colonized is more acceptable in women. Given the overriding similarity of
moral codes, the novel implies, the Californio women's cultural/ethnic
difference from Anglo women can be easily overlooked or relegated to the
private sphere, so that as decorative features of the bourgeois home, the
Californio women might fulfill the role of the American lady and mother.

Ruiz de Burton, however, is not simply arguing that the Californio
women fit the ideals of American femininity. Instead, through her representation of the figure of the Mother, Ruiz de Burton relocates the American woman in relation to both the family and the nation, producing a
new cultural imperative for her plot. The novel grants the mother
tremendous authority, locating her in the private sphere but using her
moral authority to justify her occasional entrance into the public sphere.
In this Ruiz de Burton employs a strategy increasingly common to late-
nineteenth-century American women, but significantly, she goes beyond
simply staking a claim for women in public. Rather, she uses the claim of
the mother's moral superiority to refigure the American woman's relation
to national identity, arguing through the figure of Mary Darrell that only
the mother can truly embody the essence of America. Put another way,
one might argue that if Clarence Darrell is the novel's model American
hero and hope for the future, it is because he takes after his mother, not
his father: it is his mother who is not just the moral agent, but also, ultimately, the model capitalist and patriot.

From its opening the novel identifies Mary as the voice of moral reason
in opposition to her husband William. Whereas William supports squatters' rights to Californio land, believing that "Congress has the right to
declare *all* California open to pre-emption, and all American citizens free
to choose any land not already patented" (102), Mary Darrell, like Don
Mariano, recognizes the injustice of the squatters' actions. As her husband is about to stake a claim to part of Don Mariano's land, she tells
him, "I beg of you, do not go on a Mexican grant unless you buy the land
from the owner. This I beg of you specially, and must *insist upon it* . . . if
you again go into a Mexican grant, William, I shall not follow you there
willingly. Do not expect it of me; I shall only go if you compel me" (57,
emphasis in original). It is she who directs Clarence to buy his father's
claim secretly from Don Mariano in order to establish the Darrells as settlers rather than squatters, an action Clarence performs in his mother's
name but without telling his father. And indeed, when William Darrell

does discover the purchase, Clarence explains his behavior by means of his mother, telling his father, "All I thought was, that as you seem to love my mother, you would prefer to give her the kind of home that she desires. I thought that when you came to know all, you would approve of my having obeyed my mother's wishes" (266). This rhetoric, the justification of economic action on moral/emotional grounds, echoes both Mary's own explanation of the purchase and, in larger terms, her position in the novel.

At a meeting of the squatters Mary explains her motives for instructing Clarence to buy the land. Although it is a meeting of men only, she silences the astonished squatters by entering their circle and speaking before them, bodily enacting her entrance into the public/political sphere in a way that suggests to the squatters, as the narrator dryly comments, "some Banquo spectre or other terrible ghostly apparition" (254). She issues a long statement, part of which reads as follows:

I told my son, Clarence Darrell, that if he did not pay for the land which his father had located, I would never, *never* come to live upon it. Moreover, I told my son not to mention the fact of having paid for the land, because his father would think we were interfering in the business, and I did not wish him to know that the land was paid for until the question of the Don's title was settled. . . . And now, gentlemen, let me add this . . . I say, those laws which authorize you to locate homesteads upon lands claimed as Mexican grants, those laws are wrong, and good, just, moral citizens should not be guided by them . . . I love my country, as every true-hearted American woman should, but, with shame and sorrow, I acknowledge that we have treated the conquered Spaniards most cruelly, and our law-givers have been most unjust to them. (255, emphasis in original)

This speech establishes the terms of Mary's authority. Her words here, like her conversation with her husband at the novel's opening, clearly show that she is knowledgeable about and comfortable in the "male" public sphere of politics and economics. She advises her husband, directs her son, and exercises her power economically. At the same time, however, she exerts this power by drawing on her *maternal* authority. Her repetition of "I told my son" has an almost incantatory force and underscores the fact that her status as mother is the source of her moral power. If she is entering the public sphere by interfering in her husband's "realm," then, she does so while remaining within the limits of domestic ideology. She acts via her male child, and she acts inspired by love and moral righteousness. Middle-class, Anglo, and Catholic, Mary Darrell stands as a specifically inflected female American mouthpiece for truth and justice, and in her defense of Californio land rights she becomes, ironically, the model American patriot, standing up, as her son does, for her country's "lofty . . . beautiful ideal" (102).[63] Further, her defense of individual property rights identifies her as the virtuous capitalist, working to get ahead but not by exploiting her fellow citizens. Patriotism in the public sphere is here represented as a combination of the moral sense of the Dons and the capitalist acumen of the Anglo men: a combination that the novel presents as only possible in a woman.

In this revised version of American womanhood the political conflict of the novel is addressed in the private sphere, as Mary Darrell uses her maternal authority to intervene in the public conflicts between the squatters and the Dons. But ultimately, even the domestic cannot function to cure the political problems driving the narrative: the novel may reconcile the Darrells and the Alamars, but it cannot effect a reconciliation between the United States government and the Californios. A dual "happy ending" can only be possible as an envisioned future, so that the best the novel can offer is a happy ending to the domestic plot, which might be read as an allegorical happy ending to the political plot. This, I would suggest, is the weight carried by the marriage of the Anglo son, Clarence Darrell, to the Californio daughter, Mercedes Alamar, a marriage that recasts colonial domination as reciprocal interdependence and produces a new family unit to stand as emblematic of both American national identity and the Californio place within it.

Turning Californios into Californians

The Anglo mother Mary may provide a revised version of the American woman,[64] but ultimately, Ruiz de Burton envisions national unity through the figure of the Californio daughter and the metaphor of her intermarriage and the family she will mother. Intermarriage becomes the answer, productive of a truly unified national identity based on an intermingling of various "pure" European bloods and available only in the next generation. Ruiz de Burton pursues this strategy determinedly. By the end of the novel, most of the main characters are married or engaged: Mercedes Alamar and Clarence Darrell are paired as are their siblings Alice Darrell and Victoriano Alamar. Meanwhile, two of the Anglo Mechlins have married two of the Alamars, a double wedding occurring early in the novel that produces two "Hispano-American" babies by the novel's end.

That the children of the mixed marriage represent the answer to problems of American national identity is important for several reasons. By defining the marriages' mixing in religious, ethnic, or regional terms, Ruiz de Burton is able to sidestep tensions around racial difference, employing the racial discourse of late-nineteenth-century America but using it to elide the "race problem." That is, Ruiz de Burton avoids having to confront a discussion of the controversial concepts of "miscegenation" or *mestizaje* by insisting that the Californios are of "pure" Spanish blood and by defining their "difference" in other terms. Simultaneously, on a plot level, using intermarriage as a strategy of unity pays off for Ruiz de Burton by providing a happy resolution to the various romance plots and by uniting various groups and families. On a structural level, moreover, it serves to link the Californios and the Anglos once again, since both the Anglo model of American womanhood—Mary Darrell—and the Californio model—Mercedes Alamar—end up in metaphorically "mixed" marriages, whether religiously or ethnically so. This link further serves to establish the Californios as part of the U.S., because it unwittingly reveals that the historical disavowal of mixed blood practiced by the Californios is at the heart of U.S. culture as well. America tells a national tale of unity and homogeneity that forgets the endless construction of that myth out of racial, ethnic, national, religious, and regional diversity. In both cases a disavowed mixing produces the family and also the nation, underscoring the complex origins of both the Californios *and* the "Americans."[65] In these terms one might read Mary and William Darrell as emblematic of the nineteenth-century American culture, which overtly prohibited (literal and often even figural) "miscegenation" but which was also inextricably rooted in it. In *The Squatter and the Don* the Darrells' heterosexual love results in a kind of religious "miscegenation" that thus produces a religiously "mestizo" American population. Hence, the daughter's (Mercedes's) generation does not begin the tradition of "mixed" marriage. The mother's generation has already produced an "America" that is just as much a product of "mixed blood" as the Californio despite the fact that both claim to be "pure" (Catholics/Spaniards).[66]

Ultimately, neither the Anglo nor the Californio mother alone can represent this American "new mestiza,"[67] this vision of national unity. It is the daughters' generation that is charged with this imperative—specifically, the Californio daughters' generation. This generational formula is partly the result of Ruiz de Burton's inability to "solve" the Californios' problems in the present tense, but it is also a response to the question of difference itself and to the hierarchies of gender implicit in that difference. In attempting to write the Californios into American culture, the novel cannot and does not try to do so by erasing all difference; rather, it acknowledges difference on some level, diffusing its threat, and incorporating it. Even as the novel disavows and elides questions of racial difference, it implies that Mary Darrell is not different "enough" to embody the safely incorporated diversity of American identity. On the other hand, Doña Josepha cannot fill that role either, in part because her ethnic difference is not contained by marriage to an Anglo American, and in part, the novel implies, because she remains located in the signorial world of the Californio past rather than in the capitalist world of the American future. In contrast to the economically minded Mary, women like Doña Josefa would need to brush up on their capitalism in order to stake a claim to America's future: they would need to learn, for instance, to evaluate Clarence as much in terms of his business enterprises and achievements as in terms of his family name and dignity. In the end it is only Mercedes who embodies the "just-right" degree of difference. She is enough like dominant American cultural ideals of femininity to fit in while simultaneously being enough unlike them—in her ethnic difference—to represent the difference that America needs to acknowledge, diffuse, and turn into a celebrated diversity. She functions safely as this figure precisely because of her gender and the domestic containment it produces. Because she is a proper American lady, Mercedes can be written into a gender hierarchy of the home; she is submissive to her Anglo-American husband Clarence, and her ethnic difference has been turned into a domestic accent.[68] Put another way, the culturally sanctioned gender role she plays determines the status of her ethnicity. Intermarriage only works in one direction here.[69]

A very curious scene midway through the novel illustrates this point. George Mechlin, his new wife Elvira (née Alamar), Elvira's sister Mercedes, and Clarence Darrell are on a steamship en route to San Francisco, when it finally becomes clear to the thwarted lovers that Mercedes's mother only disapproves of Clarence's suit because she thinks he is a squatter and the son of a squatter. She does not yet know that he had secretly purchased the land his family has settled, a revelation that Mercedes and the others realize will win Alamar family approval of Clarence and the marriage. George then begins to tease his new sister-in-law, saying,

"What a pity. . . . It isn't half so romantic to love a plain gentleman as to love a brigand, or, at least, a squatter. . . . Exit tramp! Enter gentleman! I believe pussy is regretting she lost her squatter. Isn't that so, pussy? . . . Are you regretting that, after all, you cannot sacrifice to love your patrician pride by marrying a land-shark, thus proving you are a heroine. . . . I think our romance is spoiled. It would have been so fine—like a dime novel—to have carried you off bodily by order of infuriated, cruel parents, and on arriving at New York marry you, at the point of a loaded revolver, to a bald-headed millionaire! Your midnight shrieks would have made the blood of the passers-by curdle! Then Clarence would have rushed in and stabbed the millionaire, and you, falling across his prostrate body, said 'Tramp or not, I am thine!' . . . Whereas now," George went on, "the unpoetical fact comes out that Darrell is a decent sort of a fellow, and there is no reason why a proper girl shouldn't have him for her husband, and our romance is stripped of its thrilling features, as the hero will not steal, even when Congress tells him to. And that is the *denouement*, with the addition only that I am hungry. What have you got to eat in those two little baskets Tano brought on board, and which smell so nice?" (141–42 emphasis in original)

José Saldívar reads this scene as a sort of strategic pandering on Ruiz de Burton's part to what he calls "the mawkish dime novel popular in the United States"; further, he perceptively observes that such narrative form might provide Ruiz de Burton a broader audience for her political critique than a less popular narrative form might have (175). But if Ruiz de Burton's narrative form makes her novel more "American," more familiar to an American reading public, this scene also specifically places not just the novel but its heroine squarely in the center of the canonical American novel tradition. Issuing a standard nineteenth-century critique of novels as sensational and melodramatic—reducing, in effect, the American novel to a badly written dime novel—Ruiz de Burton speaks through the voice of George to defend by implication her own novel's status as both realistic and American. As part of this she has George define his sister-in-law's plot as also both realistic and American. Clarence is a gentleman rather than a brigand, and Mercedes, George explains, is no melodramatic heroine but rather just another "proper girl": a nice American girl-next-door who just happens to be of "pure" Spanish blood. The scene thus defends both novelistic and racial hierarchies at once.

What is most peculiar about this scene, however, is that immediately after it goes to great lengths to establish Mercedes as a virtuous American girl and not a melodramatic heroine, it turns into one of the only scenes in the novel in which the Alamars are explicitly ethnically marked by the narrative itself. For George's hunger leads to a picnic, the consumption of a lunch packed by Doña Josefa that the narrative describes in some detail. The lunch includes "boned turkey, '*a la española*,' stuffed with mashed almonds and '*ajonjolí*,' . . . a '*tortita de aceituna*,' with sweet marjoram" and "*empanaditas de pollo*" (142, 143). In a novel that represents its Californio characters as speaking English and, in fact, rarely even mentions Spanish or the speaking of it, except by the *vaqueros*, this lunch description stands out. What it signals is that Ruiz de Burton's narrative can celebrate ethnic "difference" only in terms of its heroine, only in the domestic sphere, and only once its heroine's status as "American" has been forcefully defended. The "problem" of the Alamars' ethnicity is resolved by and contained in the domestic sphere, becoming a piquant accent to the story of the American heroine. Mercedes can look forward to an American future of serving her husband "ethnic" food, retaining the specificity of her cultural history but in a secondary role, a role made possible by her gender.[70] This then is the context for the novel's refigured American national identity, as the mixed blood family promised by the union of Clarence Darrell and Mercedes Alamar becomes the new representation of a national past turning into a national future.

The American that Ruiz de Burton creates, both in *The Squatter and the Don* and in *Who Would Have Thought It?*, ultimately functions as a national palimpsest, a story written over a story written over a story, each containing both erasures and fragments of the story before, each adding something new. Drawing on imperialist topoi of land and race, Ruiz de Burton rewrites her story on the body of the woman, recasting both region and ethnicity through her heroines, a strategy to which I will now turn in the work of Kate Chopin. Hortense Spillers describes a version of a palimpsest as a screen that "carries traces of preceding moments that alter the contemporaneous rendition, making the latter both an 'originality' and an 'affiliated,' or the initiation of a new chain of signifying as well as an instance of significations already in intervened motion" ("Who Cuts" 15). Intervening into the motion of a Californio colonialist past as well as a United States imperialist expansionist present, Ruiz de Burton's fiction attempts what Genaro Padilla calls one of the "generative principles" of Chicano literary production, "the reconciliation of vexing contradictions" (310), as she both critiques U.S. imperialism and imagines an America based on, but rescripting, these United States.

5 Kate Chopin and (Stretching) the Limits of Local Color Fiction

> Realism is nothing more and nothing less than the truthful treatment of material . . . let fiction cease to lie about life; let it portray men and women as they are . . . let it show the different interests in their true proportions . . . let it not put on fine literary airs; let it speak the dialect, the language, that most Americans know—the language of unaffected people everywhere.
> —William Dean Howells, *Criticism and Fiction* (1891)

Local Color, Southern Femininity, and the Politics of Canonization

In May of 1899, a month after Kate Chopin (1851–1904) published *The Awakening* and at the time when its negative reviews had begun to appear, Chopin responded to her critics:

Having a group of people at my disposal, I thought it might be entertaining (to myself) to throw them together and see what would happen. I never dreamed of Mrs. Pontellier making such a mess of things and working out her own damnation as she did. If I had had the slightest intimation of such a thing I would have excluded her from the company. But when I found out what she was up to, the play was half over and it was then too late. (quoted in Toth 344)[1]

Such a disclaimer is as disingenuous as it is ironic, but even if Chopin knew full well that Edna Pontellier was going to make "a mess" of her life in exploring her self and her erotic desires, one might argue that she could not have anticipated the critical abuse that this most famous of her works was to receive, since she had, in fact, previously published material which, although every bit as outrageous, had not been attacked by the press. On the other hand, given that Chopin was, as Emily Toth has shown, a savvy businesswoman who knew the currents of the publishing industry, she might have expected the negative critical response to *The Awakening*, since it was in this novel that Chopin finally abandoned the cover of Local Color fiction to depict an upper-class white woman's discovery of her subjectivity and the role sexuality played in that subjectivity.

Unlike Ruiz de Burton, Chopin is now an accepted member of the American literary canon, largely on the basis of *The Awakening*. Her membership in this club, however, is fairly recent: in contrast to Jewett, say, who has always been allowed a space (if a diminutive one), Chopin was largely ignored for the first half of the century, then recovered first by the work of Per Seyersted and later, more forcefully, by feminist literary critics of the 1970s and 80s.[2] These critics celebrated *The Awakening* for its depiction of its upper-class, white female heroine's erotic desire and for its refusal of motherhood as an all-consuming identity category; by now *The Awakening* is a text likely to appear in any recent discussion of literary treatments of the female body and female sexuality, not to mention many American literature survey courses. But while feminist literary critics succeeded in bringing Chopin into the canon, the grounds on which they did so, ironically, more faithfully reflect issues central to second-wave (largely white, bourgeois) feminism than to Chopin's work as a whole. As a result her canonical status, I would argue, really only applies to *The Awakening*. Her earlier work—her first novel, *At Fault* (1890), her two collections of short stories, *Bayou Folk* (1894) and *A Night in Acadie* (1897), and numerous short stories published in national magazines— remains underread and is often seen as simply the apprenticeship leading up to the more "universal" text of *The Awakening*. But this narrative misrepresents Chopin and her work, for *The Awakening* is neither fully representative, nor is it the culmination, of Chopin's fiction as a whole. While her short fiction does display an interest in female erotic and maternal desire, it does so in explicitly regionally, racially, and ethnically marked ways. It directly engages—challenging, complicating, and replicating—dominant notions of Southern womanhood in order to offer not a transcendent vision of an emerging female identity (such as Edna Pontellier's) but rather multiple representations of locally grounded Louisiana Creole and Cajun women (among others), representations that both reflect and disrupt Chopin's own positioning as a "local color writer" in a national discourse of American letters.

The discrepancy between the critical reception of *The Awakening* and the critical reception of Chopin's short stories (in her own day, and, less directly, in ours) locates her work at the center of turn-of-the-century debates over regionalism both as an American literary form and as a part of the broader cultural discourse on national identity. Perhaps more than any other author under discussion here, Chopin consciously entered these debates through both her essays and her fiction; consequently, her work provides an illustrative instance both of the way regionalism, as Richard Brodhead points out, "was so structured as to extend opportunity above all to groups traditionally distanced from literary lives" and of the way it "made places for authors but made them *in a certain position*. By virtue of its historical situation, when writers came into authorship through this genre they were placed in inevitable relation with the field of forces that structured its social place" (116, 137). In Chopin's positioning as (not) a Local Color writer, the complexities of her relation to regionalism begin to emerge, both in terms of the ways critics—then and now—understood and defined her work and in terms of her resistance to being positioned by this "field of forces." This resistance can be seen in Chopin's efforts to locate herself by exploiting regionalism as a literary category while simultaneously insisting, on the level of plot, on an American culture made up of internally fractured and marked regions.[3] That is, although Chopin had publicly positioned herself as a writer in relation to both Local Color and Realism, disclaiming the former and celebrating the latter, in her early work she concurrently exploited Local Color, using it to subvert the terms of middle-class models of womanhood, dismantling a monolithic image of America and American True Womanhood by representing various "American" women whose identities are marked by a variety of ethnic, racial, regional, religious, and class identifications. Her work and its reception thus illustrate the force of expectation in the reception of Local Color fiction and speak to the genre's power to contain and diffuse the power of women's writing. This same body of work, however, also shows how those same expectations and categorical assumptions can be used against a genre by a self-conscious writer, and how they can be used to produce a body of work that reflects American racial, regional, and ethnic relations through a gendered lens.

The literary context of Chopin's self-positioning might best be exemplified by recourse to William Dean Howells. As editor first of the *Atlantic Monthly* and later of *Harpers'*, Howells was, of course, one of the most important editors in postbellum America: for roughly twenty-five years he championed Realism and in the process helped both to define its American form and to label that form as particularly American. In his enormously influential work, *Criticism and Fiction*, Howells defines Realism as implying a mimetic fidelity to "life," but a fidelity that he demands be "proportional." He both calls for mimesis and dictates its contents, arguing that what he calls an American literary "tradition of decency" is "truer to life" than a French "tradition of indecency" and that "the study of erotic shivers and fervors," for instance, is not true realism because it is not proportional to life (72). Finally, Howells dictates the very form of this "proportional" and "decent" Realism, calling for the use of dialect and the continued development of the short story form, a form he saw as a particularly American genre (64). A content that chronicles American life is thus, for Howells, happily wedded to a particularly American form.

Howells's argument is worth tracing because it throws into relief the generic hierarchies that subsequently emerged from it. As Howells charts American literature, Local Color is not merely related to Realism, it represents its apogee. By the end of the century, however, this hierarchy had been inverted, so that Local Color had become a minor subgenre of the privileged Realism. This hierarchy is still enacted by contemporary literary critics such as James Cox, for instance, who calls regionalism "a small-scale representation of the larger reality of national literature" (767). The shift in the valence of regionalism/Local Color occurred as a hierarchy of gendered and geographic literary value emerged in antebellum America. That Local Color became a marginalized literary form on the basis of (racially inflected) gender and that as a marginalized form it has been used to contain and dismiss women writers is by now fairly clear. Although both men and women wrote Local Color fiction, white women make up the majority of Local Color writers, and the authors most celebrated as exemplary Local Color writers then and now have been white women: Chopin, Sarah Orne Jewett, Mary Wilkins Freeman, Mary Noailles Murfree, Mary Austin, and Grace King, to name only a few. As a literary category, this "woman's" subgenre has been represented as a diminished version of canonical Realism: though both attempt to represent lived reality with an attention to detail and common life, Local Color has been dismissed as a quaint, backward-looking, and diminutive form (often short stories) written by women writing on a small scale, a form dismissed as nostalgic and concerned with loss and the rural. Canonical Realism and its heir, Naturalism, in contrast, have been valued for centering on the urban industrialized present/future.[4] This contrast has often been represented in terms of form as an opposition between the short story and the novel.

Informed by these nineteenth- and twentieth-century gender hierarchies, Local Color is also deeply imbricated in broader national discourses of region and race. Centered in Boston and New York, the postbellum publishing industry (conveniently bodied forth by Howells) contributed to the ideological work of national reconciliation while also confirming the Northeast as America's literary center, in keeping with the

North's position as victor of the Civil War. Amy Kaplan, in "Nation, Region, and Empire" goes so far as to read the Civil War as *the* structuring paradigm for American literature from the war until the turn of the century, calling national reunification "the cultural project that would inform a diversity of American fiction for the following three decades" (240). While this claim needs to be complicated in the case of Western fiction like Ruiz de Burton's, it is certainly tenable for Southern fiction. The Northeast (New England/New York) claim to the cultural primacy of center (de facto defining all other areas as outlying regions) produced a dichotomy that, in the case of the postbellum South, took on other meanings as well: North/South became urban/rural, future/past, masculine/feminine, and victor/vanquished.[5] Thus, Northern publishers publishing "regional" writers both displayed the North's cultural monopoly and celebrated the complexity of America without any fear of the bitter sectarianism of the Civil War, demonstrating that the South as region had become entertaining rather than threatening. As Helen Taylor has noted, by "the late 1870s the northern magazines were very keen to foster a fresh sense of nationalism, and the major publications adopted a policy of reconciliation that meant deliberately seeking copy from regions hitherto little known or courted for their literary output" (18–19). Simultaneously, this regional discourse intersects with the racial discourse of the period, since part of Local Color's ideological work of postbellum reconciliation, of course, was to play down racial dissent by offering happy portraits of Southern racial harmony at a time when virulent racism was evident everywhere from the rise of lynching to the NWSA's white suffragists' abandonment of African-American women. To this end, as Taylor points out, "the invention through a dialect of a tamed, quaint black folk-hero contributed in large measure to popular complacency about the condition of southern blacks in postbellum America" (20). If Southern Local Color fiction was in the process of being marginalized within literary canons, then, it remained at the center of struggles over representations of national identity.

This marginalizing of the South both in broader cultural terms and in the more narrow terms of its fiction speaks to Chopin's position as a "Southern" writer,[6] for on the graph of specifically Southern Local Color fiction, gender and geography run on more than parallel lines; their lines intersect in ways that confirm nineteenth-century Southern literature's status as "minor." Twentieth-century literary history's vision of Local Color fiction as a "female" genre has its analogy in a more generalized feminization of Southern fiction and culture. Anne Goodwyn Jones has shown that the ideal of the Southern Lady, the white, privileged, regional complement to the American Ideal of True Womanhood, operated in nineteenth-century America as the figure for the South itself, embodying "the values by which southerners have defined the region's character through Civil War and Reconstruction, New South and Modernism" (8).[7] Add to this the fact that the South was emasculated both literally and figuratively by the Civil War: in literal terms, as Taylor notes, by 1890 "there were around sixty thousand Confederate widows in the South; in every state women outnumbered men in all age groups" (6); in figurative terms the South became the powerless, passive captive by its loss. Southern Local Color, then, provided the literary enactment of a larger cultural alignment between the South and femininity, an alignment metaphorized in the postwar fictional plots that showed a war-torn nation reunited by the marriage of the Southern belle to the Northern hero. Through Local Color the South acquired its literary status as one of "America"'s (read the North's) Others: the exotic and often eroticized stranger onto whom was displaced the qualities of violence, passion, and a not-quite-civilized rural world of the past.

Postwar Southern letters in the form of Local Color fiction was thus written out of "real men's" literature, aligned with the losers and the women, providing a space for fiction that was popular but rarely taken seriously. That Southern Local Color fiction came to be gendered female is hardly surprising given the accumulated links between the South and images of femininity, but Chopin's Southern Local Color fiction has a far more important, though less evident, link to gender. Cecilia Tichi argues that "the [American] new-woman writers . . . rejected the camouflage of domesticity but gained acceptance, many of them, under another rubric—regionalism" (597). But what in Tichi sounds coincidental was, in fact, no accident at all: Chopin was quite aware of the politics of Local Color—both the benefits and costs of being associated with it—and so chose to identify with Realism as a political strategy of self-authorization in the face of the threat of marginalization. At the same time, however, Chopin used both the conventions and the marginalized status of Local Color fiction as a cover: as a marginalized form it allowed Chopin to experiment with representations of American womanhood, rejecting a kind of Northeastern Puritan tradition of non-representation of female sexuality and following Realism's move toward mimesis so as to dismantle models of True Womanhood as well as those of the Southern Lady. In a complex set of multiple positionings, Chopin, the upper-class, white, St. Louis–born, widowed mother of six children, translated her knowledge of Creole and Cajun culture into nationally published fiction. And just as regionalism didn't exclude the exotic but rather translated it into something quaint and safe, Chopin herself, like her subject matter, was regional enough to be taken by Northern audiences as an authentic voice while central enough (by virtue of her race and class positioning and her schooling in high culture) to be perceived as a safe translator by her audience. Within her early work Chopin is constantly in conversation with the conventions of Local Color fiction, both challenging its gender norms and often reinscribing its racial and ethnic stereotypes as she attempts to push at Realism's representational limits. Offering heroines who disrupted a monolithic representation of American womanhood in the multiplicity of their ethnic, racial, class, religious, and regional positioning, Chopin complicates dominant definitions of both what gets to count as Southern and what gets to count as American.

Celebrating Realism, Deploying Local Color

Chopin was clearly aware of the hierarchy of genres operating in American literature, and in her essays and critical writing she carefully positioned herself accordingly in relation to Realism and regionalism, as well as to European letters. Of French and Irish family, Kate O'Flaherty Chopin was raised within her mother's extended French family and was widely read in French literature, a national/cultural association that proved influential, as I will discuss, in her marriage and also in the worlds she would portray in her stories. In terms of her literary alignments, this background was influential in that it grounded her in a tradition of French, as well as American, literature.[8] The only literary influence she ever acknowledged as an adult was Maupassant, traces of whose form and content both can be seen in her short stories. Although she did not like Zola ("his constructive methods," she complained in a review called "Emile Zola's 'Lourdes'," are too "glaringly revealed" [697]), she praised Maupassant in an 1896 essay entitled "Confidences," for being realistic in form:

I read his stories and marvelled at them. Here was life, not fiction; for where were the plots, the old fashioned mechanism and stage trappings in that vague, un-thinking way I had fancied were essential to the art of story making. Here was a man who had escaped from tradition and authority, who had entered into himself and looked out upon life through his own being and with his own eyes; and who, in a direct and simple way, told us what he saw. When a man does this, he gives us the best that he can; something valuable for it is genuine and spontaneous. (700–701)

For Chopin, Maupassant's value lies in his fiction's proximity to "life" and its distance from "tradition," "authority," and "old fashioned" narrative machinery. In contrast, in "As You Like It," an 1897 essay on *Jude the Obscure*, she condemns Hardy's novel as humorless, unconvincing, and not lifelike, complaining that its "brutality is an obvious and unhappy imitation of the great French realism" (714), implying that it is the unskilled handling of "brutality," not the brutality itself, that is objectionable. She concludes that the novel "is detestably bad; it is unpardonably dull; and immoral, chiefly because it is not true" (714). Unlike many of her contemporaries, Chopin objects to what she sees as a nonmimetic content (its lack of "truth" or adequately "real" realism) rather than an immoral one.

In her stories Chopin also ridiculed generic plots that fell back on conventions at the cost of Realism. In "Miss Witherwell's Mistake" (1889, 1891),[9] for instance, Chopin rehearses the comic plot of the eventual uniting of thwarted lovers, but in doing so she also parodies it, making the "old fashioned mechanism and stage trappings" the butt of her joke. Miss Witherwell's niece Mildred, sent to her aunt to recover from the love her parents have forbidden, fictionalizes her own plight to her aunt, representing it as "a little story" that she is writing. Mildred, under the cover of this fiction, asks her writer aunt's advice on how to resolve the action, claiming that she is stalled at the point where the crossed lovers, deeply in love, have been brought together again by fate. When Miss Witherwell explains that the hero "must now perform some act to ingratiate himself with the obdurate parent," and recommends having him save the father from a train crash or shipwreck or "avert a business catastrophe," Mildred objects:

"No, no, aunt! I can't force situations. You'll find I'm extremely realistic. The only point for consideration is, to marry or not to marry; that is the question."
    Miss Witherwell looked at her niece, aghast. "The poison of the realistic school has certainly tainted and withered your fancy in the bud, my dear, if you hesitate a moment. Marry them, most certainly, or let them die." (65)

Mildred's realism—she secretly marries her suitor then brings him home and reconciles the family to him—is one of life imitating an art that is really a disguised version of life, a narrative move that suggests Chopin's support of "the realistic school," as opposed to the "mistake" of Miss Witherwell's school of romantic and rhetorical excess.

Chopin's championing of Realism takes the form not only of an attack on conventional narrative "machinery," but also of an attack on regionalism, which she characterizes as naïve and unrealistic. And while her defense of Realism includes European fiction (indeed, often citing French literature as the model), her critique of regionalism is specifically focused on American letters. In an extraordinary piece she wrote for the *Critic* after attending her first literary conference, the 1894 annual meeting of the Western Association of Writers, for instance, Chopin equates regionalism with an American provincialism of the worst kind, despite her opening disclaimer:

Provincialism in the best sense of the word stamps the character of this association of writers, who gather chiefly from the State of Indiana and meet annually at Spring Fountain Park. It is an ideally beautiful spot, a veritable garden of Eden in which the disturbing fruit of the tree of knowledge still hangs unplucked. The cry of the dying century has not reached this body of workers, or else it has not yet been comprehended. There is no doubt in their souls, no unrest: apparently an abiding faith in God as he manifests himself through the sectional church, and an overmastering love of their soil and institutions. (691)

Her snideness here is striking, as is her disapproval of what she clearly views as a naïve and narrow-minded approach to life and literature. She notes that these writers show "a clinging to past and conventional standards," then goes on to proclaim that there is "a very, very big world lying not wholly in northern Indiana, nor does it lie at the antipodes, either. It is human existence in its subtle, complex, true meaning, stripped of the veil with which ethical and conventional standards have draped it" (691). Rejecting the regional as limited and censored by "ethical and conventional standards" and, like Miss Witherwell, as "too often sentimental" (691), she aligns herself with the Realists, an alignment that clearly implies for her a freedom of representational choice as well as a move toward narrative authority and away from the marginalized status of the regional.

In the same year Chopin more directly acknowledged the geographical politics of American regionalism. In an article entitled "'Crumbling Idols' by Hamlin Garland" she responds to Garland's critique of the East as a literary center by viewing his attitude as one "to be deplored." She goes on to comment,

The fact remains that Chicago is not yet a literary center, nor is St. Louis (!), nor San Francisco, nor Denver, nor any of those towns in whose behalf he drops into prophesy. There can come no good of abusing Boston and New York. On the contrary, as "literary centers" they have rendered incalculable service to the reading world by bringing to light whatever there has been produced of force and originality in the West and South since the war. (694)

As a native of St. Louis who lived in and wrote about Louisiana and was published by Northern publishers for a largely Northern audience, Chopin clearly had experience of the regionally inflected power structures that organized the publishing world. Her response to Garland reflects this; it is no accident that as a regional woman writer Chopin chooses here to represent Northern publishing of Western and Southern fiction as an "incalculable service" to the public rather than as an act of appropriation or postwar reconciliation. This sort of response was typical of Chopin, indicating a caginess toward the industry that she was to exhibit throughout her career and that suggests a region's strategic response to a center's condescension.

However, if Chopin defended publishing powers and aligned herself with Realism, ridiculing both provincial writers and generic plots as limited and partial, and calling instead for a mimetic depiction of life, she also exploited the "provincial" form of Local Color fiction to get published. Consider, for instance, her choice of *Bayou Folk* as the title of her first collection of short stories. And certainly, notwithstanding whatever allegiances Chopin herself claimed, critics had identified her with Local Color as early as 1890 in reviews of her first novel, *At Fault*. The *St. Louis Republic* called *At Fault* "a clever romance of Louisiana life" (quoted in Toth 190); the *New Orleans Daily Picayune* identified it as a "life of a handsome Creole widow" (quoted in Toth 192); and a St. Louis magazine called *Fashion and Fancy* linked Chopin to "that bright galaxy of Southern and Western writers who hold today the foremost rank of America's authors" (quoted in Toth 192). But if these Southern reviews celebrated Chopin as a Local Color author and promoted her depiction of their region, national reviews of *Bayou Folk* shifted the tenor of that label, establishing Chopin as an important Local Color writer but making it clear that Local Color was Realism's poor country cousin. The *Review of Reviews* called *Bayou Folk* "realistic" and "direct" and identified the influence of Maupassant (quoted in Toth 625), but reviews such as *The New York Times*'s and *The Critic*'s, among others, not only identified Chopin's work as Local Color but also helped to delineate the genre more clearly for their audience. Taking great pains to set the scene, these reviews explain the "exotic" bayou to the reader as if Louisiana were a foreign country. The *Times* review, entitled "Living Tales from Acadian Life," goes on to establish the inhabitants as anachronistic "Frenchmen of the seventeenth century" who are "barbarians softened by Catholicism . . . showing a pagan primitiveness" (23). For all this, however, the reviewer smugly claims that theirs is "a world easily understood, because it is not in the least affected" (23).[10] Louisiana thus in one sweep becomes a regional Other and inferior to New York while also representing the non-"American" national and religious identity of the French Catholic. As in reviews of Sui Sin Far's representations of Chinese-American communities of the West Coast, a national/ethnic Other is conflated with a regional Other. The regional hierarchy being established here is obvious, but reviewers like *The Critic*'s also conflate this with a genre hierarchy. Calling *Bayou Folk* an "unpretentious, unheralded little book," the reviewer remarks upon the book's "queer *patois* people" and then characterizes both the stories and their contents as diminutive, calling them

simple tales, whose very simplicity increases their verisimilitude and makes in some cases a powerful impression on the imagination. She takes Middle-Upper Louisiana . . . as the scene of her little dramas and reproduces for us, often very realistically and pathetically, the oddities in life and character which she has observed there. In her sheaf of twenty-three sketches some are like rude cartoons whose very rudeness brings out a more vivid effect. . . . These are admirable little bits. (300)

While the reviewer recognizes and praises Chopin's "photographic realism," such praise operates as a throwaway line in the face of the reviewer's patronizing categorization of both the region and the stories as "little bits." Toth shows that "*charming* was a recurring word in later reviews of *Bayou Folk*" (226): it is a word that aptly indicates a general attitude toward Kate Chopin's short stories, a word gender-coded female and implying a patronizing praise of a marginalized form.[11]

In addition to establishing Chopin as the author of charming female Southern stories, these reviews also make clear that the exotic nature of her fiction is located not simply in a representation of Southern life, but of a specific form of Southern life and a form specified in ethnic rather than simply geographical terms. That is, although Chopin created a wide variety of heroines—urban, rural, Northern, Southern, African-American, Anglo-American, Native American—she rarely wrote about and was almost never understood as writing about a generic Southerner. In fact, critics generally understood her to be representing Creole or Cajun heroines and cultures, with all the ethnic and racial complexity carried by these terms in the context of nineteenth-century Louisiana. As a term, *Cajun* is derived from *Acadian*, a reference to this population's origin in Nova Scotia's Acadian population. In the mid-eighteenth century this population dispersed, with a part of it settling in Louisiana's bayou country. Ethnically French, the settlers brought French language and culture to rural Louisiana. Although they were a complicated and multiply-classed society, by the end of the nineteenth century they had come to be viewed by outsiders, as Carl Brasseaux puts it, "as a monolithic group of honest but ignorant and desperately poor fishermen and trappers, clinging tenaciously to an ancient way of life in the isolation of Louisiana's swamps and coastal marshes" (3).[12] Because they maintained linguistic, religious (Catholicism), and other cultural markers of their French heritage, Cajuns were also seen as un-American. Significantly, they were criticized by both Northerners and other Southerners in terms that replicated the broader stereotypes about the South in the postwar period: Brasseaux notes the terms of the complaints as "laziness, lack of ambition, ignorance, backwardness, and an unrelenting refusal to assimilate" (103). By Chopin's day, then, Cajuns were seen as white ethnics who were regionally specific, always inferior, always of French descent, and always of lower-class standing.

Moreover, by the postbellum period, outsiders often conflated Cajuns with Creoles, a term complicated enough in its own right. Albert Rhodes, in an 1873 article titled "The Louisiana Creoles," for instance, calls the Cajuns "a small portion of the Creole population" and asserts that they are "the least intelligent of the Creole population, and occupy small patches of land along bayous and the coast, which are just sufficient in extent to satisfy the wants of their simple lives" (254). In fact, the two groups are, in derivation and later identification, distinct. As I discuss in Chapter 2, the Louisiana usage of "Creole," while originally signifying the first-generation, American-born offspring of European parents, swiftly became a complicated and contested term. Not originally racially inflected, by the 1830s "Creole" was, as Virginia Domínguez notes, taken to mean a descendent of French settlers although not necessarily white (121). In the postbellum period, however, in part because Louisiana shifted from its original French tripartite legal categorization of race to an American binary system, racial lines became more at issue and two competing definitions came into circulation. As Domínguez explains it, for white Creoles, "Creole" came to mean white "blood" only, of French or Spanish descent, and generally of class privilege, while "Cajun" meant the white descendant of the Acadians; for Creoles of color, however, "Creole" came to mean of racially mixed blood, not necessarily of French or Spanish descent, while "Cajun" meant of Acadian ancestry but not necessarily white (149, 150). Moreover, in addition to these two groups and sometimes overlapping with them, the Louisiana population contained the descendants of what had been known in the antebellum period as the *gens de couleur libre* (free people of color) as well as in some areas a population known as Redbones, defined by Marcia Gaudet as "people of part-Indian ancestry" (45). Michael Omi and Howard Winant remind us that "the categories employed to differentiate among human groups along racial lines reveal themselves, upon serious consideration, to be at best imprecise, and at worst completely arbitrary" (55); both in the Louisiana of Chopin's day and in her work, these long-complicated categories were deeply intertwined with categories of ethnicity and class and were often contingent on an urban/rural dichotomy that identified New Orleans's "founding families" as Creole while locating Cajuns as specifically rural, sometimes accompanied by Creoles of color.

Chopin's stories reflect this complicated landscape and also reflect her own complicated positioning in relation both to these margins and to cultural centers. Like many of the writers we now view as regionalists, Chopin was not really an "authentic" voice of the communities she depicted—either Cajun or Creole Louisiana—although she had ties to both of them.[13] She was, first of all, not from Louisiana at all, but from St. Louis, Missouri, a city that although in a free state had had many supporters of the Confederacy during the Civil War, including Chopin's own upper-middle-class slave-owning family. As "the gateway to the West" St. Louis was seen variously as a Western city and as a Northern city, a blurring Chopin reflects in *At Fault* in her positioning of the protagonist David Hosmer. The narrator reports that Thérèse Lafirme, the Creole widow heroine, "had guessed he was no Southerner," but just what he is proves harder to identify (744). When he meets Thérèse, Hosmer "introduced himself vaguely as from the West; then perceiving the need of being more specific as from St. Louis" (744), but the flexibility of St. Louis's regional affiliation becomes clear when, in response to the fact that none of the servants on the Lafirme plantation will work for Hosmer's sister Melicent, Thérèse explains that "the negroes were very averse to working for Northern people whose speech, manners, and attitude toward themselves were unfamiliar" (753). Whether viewed as Northern or Western, St. Louis was definitely not Southern.[14]

At the same time, however, Chopin, while the daughter of an Irish immigrant father, was also French on her mother's side and was raised largely in that context, so that she was both Catholic and bilingual.[15] As a result, when she married into the French Creole family of Oscar Chopin she was geographically an outsider but not entirely culturally foreign to his world. After spending the first nine years of their married life in New Orleans, Kate and Oscar Chopin moved with their young family to Oscar Chopin's family plantation in Cloutierville, Natchitoches Parish, Louisiana, where they lived for five years until Oscar Chopin died in 1882. Kate Chopin remained there until 1884, when she returned to St. Louis to live for the rest of her life. Chopin thus might be said to have been neither quite an insider nor an outsider to Louisiana culture. As Roxana Robinson so aptly states, Chopin was "an outsider with inside information" (xi), linked to Louisiana Creole and Cajun culture by language, religion, marriage, and nearly fifteen years residence; separated by a St. Louis origin and upbringing.

Situating Chopin's work in this context allows us to realign both the work and Chopin's attitude toward it. Taking as a starting point that the valence of Local Color was never neutral and that Chopin was well aware of this, one can read her stories as responses to this politics of marginalization. They are manipulations of the very form meant to contain them, a strategy exemplified by "A Gentleman of the Bayou Têche," a story from Chopin's 1894 collection, Bayou Folk. In the story Mr. Sublet, an artist visiting the Bayou Têche plantation of his friend, sees the Cajun Evariste and wants to draw his picture, for Evariste is, the narrator notes, "rather a picturesque subject in his way, and a tempting one to an artist looking for bits of 'local color' along the Têche" (319). Sublet pays the man two dollars in advance, but when Evariste's daughter, Martinette, tells her neighbor, "Aunt Dicey," the news, the woman interprets the artist's intentions as indicative of patronizing appropriation, claiming that the artist will label the picture "Dis heah is one dem low-down 'Cajuns o' Bayeh Têche!" (320). Hearing this, Martinette convinces her father that to allow his picture to be drawn would be humiliating and then goes in his place to return the money. As she does, her father rescues Sublet's child from a boating accident, a rescue that prompts the artist again to want to draw Evariste and label him "a hero of Bayou Têche," a label that only further embarrasses Evariste. Finally, in the story's resolution Evariste himself names his portrait, calling for it to be titled, "Dis is one picture of Mista Evariste Anatole Bonamour, a gent'man of de Bayou Têche" (324). Through the battle over the picture's caption, Chopin delineates the artist's appropriation of "local color" and the patronizing condescension at the root of it. Read as a metaphor for the North's consumption of Southern Local Color fiction, it becomes a pointedly political tale that reveals that a romantic objectification of the Cajun (or the Cajun as stereotype of the Southerner in general) strips him of his dignity, his power to name himself, and even, Chopin implies, some of his humanity.

When Sublet first approaches Evariste with his request, Evariste agrees and promises to make himself "fine" for the event. But as Evariste recounts to his daughter Martinette, Sublet "say', 'No, no,' like he ent please'. He want' me like I come out de swamp. So much betta if my pant'loon' an' coat is tore, he say, an' color' like de mud" (319–20). Mud-covered and emerging from the swamp, Evariste embodies Sublet's vision of the stereotypical Cajun: more animal than human. But while Evariste is puzzled by this, it takes Aunt Dicey to explain the "eccentric wishes on the part of the strange gentleman" (320) as a covert insult. She does so by means of a story she tells Martinette, the story of how the artist's child tries to photograph Aunt Dicey as she stands at her ironing board:

> "Dat li'le imp he come a hoppin' in heah yistiddy wid a kine o' box on'neaf his arm. He say' 'Good mo'nin', madam. Will you be so kine an' stan' jus like you is dah at yo' i'onin', an' lef me take yo' picture?' I 'lowed I gwine make a picture outen him wid dis heah flati'on, ef he don' cl'ar hisse'f quick. An' he say he baig my pardon fo' his intrudement. All dat kine o' talk to a ole nigga 'oman! Dat plainly sho' he don' know his place."
>
> "W'at you want 'im to say, Aunt Dice?" asked Martinette, with an effort to conceal her distress.
>
> "I wants 'im to come in heah an' say: 'Howdy, Aunt Dicey! will you be so kine and go put on yo' noo calker dress an' yo' bonnit w'at you w'ars to meetin', an' stan' 'side f'om dat i'onin'-boa'd w'ilse I gwine take yo photygraph.' Dat de way fo' a boy to talk w'at had good raisin'." (321)

The boy's request offends Aunt Dicey for two reasons. She is offended first by the kind of representation the boy wants to record: his image of her, which reduces her to a laborer (and might be read as echoing images of house slaves at work). Against this she posits her own image of herself, presented in her best clothes, representing Sunday leisure. The belittling of Aunt Dicey implicit in the boy's image is echoed in the form of his request, where his formal and polite language is read by Aunt Dicey as a disrespectful ridiculing of her. Her comment that the boy does not know his place suggests this, contravening the common usage of knowing one's place, where the phrase carries the connotation of lower status: that is, it is usually people aspiring "above" their place who are accused of not knowing it. While Aunt Dicey's statement might imply this meaning because of the boy's inferior position relative to an adult, in fact, this white boy's "place," because of race and gender hierarchies, is above hers as a black woman, a hierarchy that leads Aunt Dicey to suspect she is being ridiculed. This incident stands as a metaphor of the story as a whole, fore-grounding as it does the question of who controls representation and whose purposes it serves.

In the end, the story hinges not on whether a given representation is positive or negative: Evariste is as distressed at the possibility of being labeled a hero as a "low-down 'Cajun." Rather, the issue here focuses on who controls the representation. Calling attention to this, Chopin inverts a more conventional plot (a father protecting his daughter's honor) by having Martinette defend her father's dignity, and gives the power of naming to the subject of the portrait. In addition, she gives the power of interpretation, ultimately, to Aunt Dicey, a pointed reminder that the charming and exotic Other both recognizes and resents his/her appropriation. In doing so Chopin offers a critique of the outsider's (Sublet's/the North's) appropriation of the South and the accompanying demand that the South embody Northern stereotypes of backward poverty—the swamp man, the ironing woman. Significantly, this particular plot—especially the incident between Aunt Dicey and Sublet's son—underscores the analogies and intersections among racial, regional, and gender hierarchies. In doing so it simultaneously insists on a recognition of the multiple levels of Louisiana culture that these hierarchies produce, from the plantation owner, to the racially unmarked Cajun, to the African American. Chopin can thus here be read as reappropriating Local Color for her own ends, contesting the image of the South, specifically the Cajuns, as exotic, quaint primitives, and locating them instead in a complex social system composed of various class, race, and gender stratifications.[16]

At the same time, however, Chopin might be read as offering an ironic self comment on the position of the Local Color artist: was she, a non-Cajun writing bayou stories in local dialect, any less guilty of appropriation than her character Sublet? Chopin clearly benefited from being seen as an inside chronicler of Louisiana life; certainly, many people read her as just another quaint Local Color writer playing into generic stereotypes and thus saw her early work as part of that "charming" Local Color tradition (and so saw *The Awakening* as a shocking break from it).[17] But this reading does not do justice to the complexity of Chopin's early work. While her depictions of race and gender relations in a class-stratified Louisiana are often deeply or irreparably flawed by the use of racist discourse (to some extent substantiating accusations that Local Color offers quaint, charming images of a primitive people), Chopin also frequently offers more radical interventions into dominant national discourses of region and gender, sometimes deploying both reactionary and progressive discourses in the same story.

If her early work escaped the censure attached to *The Awakening*, I would argue that it did so specifically because of the cover of Local Color and the strategies of displacement it afforded Chopin. Critics and readers didn't see Chopin's stories as shocking partly because of their form and the force of expectation: Local Color, as a genre, was seen as quaint and conservative of old values, not suggestive of complicated or new ones. Additionally, however, Chopin's choice of heroines in her short stories also diffused a potentially hostile response to her stories. In choosing for the most part to depict the "exotic" heroines of Local Color fiction—characters who were Cajuns, African Americans, or poor Creoles—rather than simply focusing on white upper-class Anglo Americans (or even, at a stretch, upper-class, white Creoles), Chopin was choosing characters who were already, in the terms of dominant cultural and literary codes, not eligible for the white, middle-class category of the True Womanhood. Moreover, Chopin not only chose to focus on such characters, she also frequently employed a conventionally racist discourse to represent them. Hence, while Chopin was able in her fiction to disrupt certain dominant norms of femininity, she often did so only at the cost of offering images that reinscribed others and thus would have reassured her largely white audience.

Within the context of Local Color fiction, then, one might read Chopin, as Judith Fetterley and Marjorie Pryse do, as a sympathetic insider chronicling Louisiana life, or as just another Sublet: an outsider artist looking for a bit of local color to put into stories about Cajuns, free people of color, New Orleans Creoles, and Cane River Creoles. Alternatively, one might abandon this dichotomy altogether to consider the fact that Chopin also wrote stories featuring Missouri farms and Northern heroines, as well as stories set in St. Louis, and that in most of her fiction, regardless of its setting, her heroines are ethnically, racially, religiously, and class marked, frequently Other, not only to some amorphous Northern readership but, within the world of the fiction, to each other as well. Paradoxically, Chopin's short fiction ultimately broadens certain representations of American identity at the same time as it often replicates easy stereotypes of Southern Local Color fiction. Moreover, these representations are not simply the products of the immature writer who would grow up to write *The Awakening* as the masterpiece of her late career. Rather, her representations of regional identities are intricately bound up with her representation of female identity (and often, specifically, female desire) in ways that allow us to see *The Awakening* as thematically overlapping with Chopin's early fiction though in some ways quite distinct from it.

Fetterley and Pryse, in their introductory comments on Chopin in

American Women Regionalists 1850–1910, suggest a link between these two concerns by arguing that "regionalist fiction opened up possibilities [for Chopin] that were not publishable—the 'region' of women's sexuality" (411), a link that I have suggested that Chopin made by using Local Color as a strategic cover. In this sense the marginalized form serves as a vehicle for a discussion of female sexuality; the protection afforded by marginalization allows the author to push the envelope of what can be represented in fiction. At the same time, however, just as the regional enabled Chopin's representations of female sexuality, her representations of female sexuality serve as the vehicle for an articulation of regional and national identity. In the remainder of this chapter I will examine the ways gender and regionalism intersect in Chopin's short stories, focusing this broad examination on the ways Chopin's reworking of two central components of American Womanhood—passion(lessness) and maternity—recast these often essentialized areas as still important but always in conversation with other equally important identity categories of ethnicity, region, and race. Drawing on the narrative values of Realism, Chopin offered unusually explicit representations of female desire under the cover of Local Color fiction, but her attempts to open a narrative space for the representation of a new sort of heroine ultimately foundered on the racist and sexist discourses underpinning Local Color fiction.

Passionate True White Womanhood

Working within the dominant culture's terms, Chopin's fiction frequently contests the notion of the proper (white) American woman as passionless. She does this in stories that frame white female erotic desire in terms of class while concurrently marking it as regionally inflected.[18] That these stories are also structured in racialized/ethnic terms is often less explicitly marked in the texts, but such structuring is nonetheless central to them, for a combination of racial and ethnic marking becomes the necessary ground for Chopin's representation of white erotic desire. I will look here at only two such stories, "A Shameful Affair" (1891, 1893) and "A Night in Acadie" (1896, 1897), as a way of exploring various of Chopin's versions of white womanhood inflected by erotic desire.

In Mildred Orme, the protagonist of "A Shameful Affair," Chopin ironically embodies the Northeast as cultural center of the U.S.: Mildred is a white and privileged New England woman whose snobbery is intellectual as well as class-based. Her story interweaves class and gender identities and locates desire on the ground of exoticized ethnicity.[19] The "affair" in question involves Mildred and a nameless worker on the German Missouri farm where Mildred has chosen to vacation. Mildred's patronizing yet clearly erotic interest in the farmhand leads her to seek him out in a confrontation that results in a sudden, passionate embrace and kiss. The nature of Mildred's response—a shamed panic—operates as the core of the story, revealing a class-determined erotic desire as a component part of white female identity.

That Chopin locates this story on the Kraummer farm is not incidental, for this specifically German site, in combination with Mildred's class privilege and extreme class-consciousness (both of which Chopin satirizes), positions Mildred in the space of the patronizing outside observer of local color. Mildred sits on the porch of the farmhouse, reading Ibsen or Browning and watching, for her amusement, the work of the farm going on around her. Rhetorically erasing the actual work of the farm, Mildred views it as simply a backdrop for herself, describing herself, as the narrator reports, as "Mildred Orme, who really ought to have been with the rest of the family at Narragansett—who had come to seek in this retired spot the repose that would enable her to follow exalted lines of thought" (133). The story emphasizes that Mildred's is not a curiosity based simply on rural or class difference but also on the ethnic "difference" of the farm; Chopin includes conversations between Mildred and Mrs. Kraummer that underscore both Mrs. Kraummer as Other and Mildred as outsider, as, for instance, when Mildred asks Mrs. Kraummer about her farmhands:

> "Who are these men, Mrs. Kraummer, that work for you? Where do you pick them up?"
> "Oh, ve picks 'em up everyvere. Some is neighbors, some is tramps, and so."
> "And that broad-shouldered young fellow—is he a neighbor?. . . . "
> "Gott, no! You might yust as well say he vas a tramp. Aber he works like a steam ingine." (132)

The use of dialect for Mrs. Kraummer's speech marks her as the "exotic other," her local color ethnic rather than regional or racial. And it is precisely in this space of the Other that Mildred first experiences desire, in a scene that also underscores her status as outside observer. The narrator tells us that Mildred never looked at the workers because "farmhands are not so very nice to look at, and she was nothing of an anthropologist" (131), then goes on to offer the following:

But once when the half dozen men came along, a paper which she had laid carelessly upon the railing was blown across their path. One of them picked it up, and when he had mounted the steps restored it to her. He was young, and brown, of course, as the sun had made him. He had nice blue eyes. His fair hair was di-shevelled. His shoulders were broad and square and his limbs strong and clean. A not unpicturesque figure in the rough attire that bared his throat to view and gave perfect freedom to his every motion. (131)

Mildred's position, as the leisured and privileged outsider observing the "not unpicturesque" local worker, recalls that of Sublet as he goes look-ing for "bits of 'local color' along the Têche" (319). It also recalls Richard Brodhead's claim that "the late nineteenth-century American elite, self-defined through its care for high art, was also identified by its other distinctive leisure practices . . . particularly its arts of leisure travel" as well as its "habit of mental acquisitiveness" (125, 133), but the privi-leged tourist's voyeuristic acquisitiveness here is specifically marked as erotic, charged with a desire the story suggests is only accessible to the proper lady in the context of an ethnically and class-marked margin. From her seat of repose Mildred plans to offer the laboring farmhand a "condescending little smile" (132) and is offended when he refuses to drive her to church. Played out in gendered terms—the man's refusal to perform social courtesies for the woman—this snub operates as a class-based insult as well. As a woman whose family summers in the moneyed classes' seaside resort of Narragansett, and who clearly has literary pre-tensions, Mildred may summer with the "farmhands" but only as the lady who expects to be served.

The depictions of Mildred's direct interactions with the man are simi-larly structured by a combination of class and gender codes in which she casts him as the lower-class Other. In a scene where Mildred engineers a confrontation with him, the narrative establishes her motives grounded both in erotic desire and in a desire to reassert class superiority. While she speaks "politely and with kindly dignity, which she supposed would de-fine her position toward him" (133), the narrator points out that at the same time Mildred's hat has "slipped disreputably to one side" (133) and her eyes "gleamed for an instant unconscious things into his own" (134). Her response to his embrace and kiss is equally shaped by her class posi-tioning, her immediate reaction purely conventional shame, articulated in conventional middle-class language: "her chaste lips had been rifled of their innocence" (134). The shame of violation later gives way, however, to the shame of an admission of a pleasure forbidden to the proper lady, as she admits that his kiss was the "most delicious thing she had known in her twenty years of life" (135). Class, both in terms of the power hier-archies it establishes and in terms of the behavior and interpretations it dictates, permeates this erotic encounter.

In a rapid denouement Mildred learns that the man is not an ordinary farmhand but rather one Fred Evelyn, a man of her own class, a "crank" who "likes to live more lives than one kind" (135) and so is spending the summer living life as a farmhand in his own particular version of the privileged tourist in search of local color. But the revelation of this identity is followed by a more salient plot twist, as Mildred realizes that the class status of her object of desire, ultimately, is not the problem: her shame lies more in her own desire than in his class background. Even the knowledge of his class status cannot "take somewhat of the sting from the shame that tortured her" (135). Ultimately, the story suggests that whether Mildred desires an eccentric gentleman or a sexually aggressive lower-class stereotype is irrelevant in the face of her transgression of middle-class female ideals in desiring at all.[20] Chopin's representation of the unmarked American lady, the white, class-privileged New England "passionless" woman, thus foregrounds class as the structuring determinant of that woman's (lack of) desire. Moreover, while the story works to call into question the passionlessness of its proper lady, it does so only by drawing on the inverse of that model, which links desire to the cultural Other. That is, to ascribe erotic desire to Mildred, the story must borrow it, as it were, from the space of the exotic Local Color setting that is marked as class and ethnically Other. The story thus calls into question one stereotypical representation only by reinforcing another.

In contrast to this representation of the Northern white lady, Zaïda Trodon, the protagonist of "A Night in Acadie," provides a portrait of a white Cajun woman, a country girl from Avoyelles Parish, the setting of most of Chopin's Cajun stories.[21] The story's plot traces Zaïda's secret plan to marry one André Pascal, as seen through the point of view of her new suitor, Telèsphore Baquette. Unlike Mildred, Zaïda is explicitly ethnically marked, both by her name and her language—a mixture of English and Cajun French—as well as by her affect. That is, Chopin attributes Zaïda's independence, spirit, and sensuality to her Cajun identity, using this ethnic/regional tag to define the character as a special category of American Womanhood—"American" but not precisely embodying the values of the proper lady. In other words, Chopin simultaneously rehearses conventional images of Cajun/French character and insists on the regional specificity and distinctiveness of that character. Telèsphore's initial encounter with the young woman on a train establishes this: "he wondered if she would speak to him. He feared she might have mistaken him for a Western drummer, in which event he knew that she would not; for the women of the country caution their daughters against speaking to strangers on the trains. But the girl was not one to mistake an Acadian farmer for a Western traveling man. She was not born in Avoyelles parish for nothing" (486). Zaïda here embodies the dominant culture's conventional female traits of modesty and discretion in public, but at the same time she emerges as Cajun specifically because of her quick-witted discernment and her ability to identify those of her own community. This community further serves to dismantle a homogenized version of regional others and to replace that with a version of multiple regions that are in relation to each other rather than in relation to the center. Although Acadian community would function for a Northern readership as implicitly set against the North and as easily conflatable with or representative of the South as a whole, Chopin explicitly sets it here against the wildness of the "West" (a space generalized here but marked more specifically in many of Chopin's stories by Texas). This narrative move insists on the differentiation of various regions and puts Avoyelles Parish in relation to, say, Sabine Parish (to the west, near Texas) or Nachitoches Parish (to the north), marking this intraregional differentiation through the characterization of Acadian women, specifically Zaïda.

The protagonist's character is revealed through her conceiving and enacting a plan to marry the lover forbidden her by her family: she slips out of a Cajun ball at midnight and, accompanied by the hapless Telèsphore, drives through a dark countryside to meet her lover, whom she then rejects because he turns up late and drunk. Zaïda's power and agency in choosing the object of her desire are coded by the narrative as Cajun and as positive, but they remain grounded in the body, a conventional source of female power, and grounded in the specifically ethnically marked body. As a result, like Mildred Orme's, Zaïda's desire ultimately reinforces racist, dominant cultural alignments of racially/ethnically Othered women with the sensual and the erotic even as it claims that same erotic for the white (ethnic) woman. The clearest instance of this is the fact that the narrator signals the heroine's combination of self-assurance and sensuality by noting that she "carried herself boldly and stepped out freely and easily, like a negress. There was an absence of reserve in her manner; yet there was no lack of womanliness. She had the air of a young person accustomed to decide for herself and for those about her" (487). Martha Cutter argues that this description associates freedom with blackness (20); I would more directly point out that "negress" here functions as a racist shorthand, evoking, through its alignment with "boldly," "freely" and "easily," the stereotype of the eroticized African-American woman. Michele A. Birnbaum, in a perceptive study of the role of race in *The Awak-*

ening, contends that Edna "first discovers the erotic frontiers of the self by exploiting the less visible constructions of sexual difference associated with the blacks, quadroons, and Acadians in the novel" and that she "employs as well their tropological potential, their associations with the marginal, and ultimately, with the erotic" (321, 324): Chopin's representation of Zaïda, I would suggest, performs the same movement. Ironically, then, at the very moment when Chopin posits an alternative to the model of proper white femininity that denies female sensuality or desire, she falls back on the inverse of this image: the stereotype that assigns all sensuality and desire to African-American womanhood. Although it is clear that this description is meant to function as positive, just as Zaïda's courage and spirit function as positive within the context of the story as a whole, as Birnbaum points out, "white women's desire for sexual expression . . . may lead to a sympathetic admiration nevertheless predicated upon racialist notions of sexuality" (332). Simply put, Chopin here stakes a claim to white female erotic desire only by way of reinscribing a racist eroticizing of black women.

The ending of the story, however, complicates this set of alignments somewhat. In the original version of the story, as Toth points out, after Zaïda watches Telèsphore and André fight, "the original Zaïda, her will as strong as ever, had demanded that Telèsphore marry her on the spot" (283), a demand that leaves Zaïda with her desires unpunished and with control over her life. (Control, of course, is here limited: in the original ending Zaïda remains within the structure of the heterosexual marriage, where control translates to the choice of a husband.) But this ending was unacceptable to *Century*'s editor Richard Watson Gilder, to whom Chopin submitted the story, so she produced a revised ending that, significantly, reworked her heroine into a far more conventional "good" American girl. In this version Zaïda's experience with her drunken fiancee André serves as a cautionary lesson, so that, as Chopin wrote to Gilder, "the girl's character [is] softened and tempered by her rude experience" (quoted in Toth 283). The story then follows a more conventional plot line, as an overly exuberant girl is taught to dampen her spirits, to become passive and to rely on men for her rescue and direction. By the story's close the revised Zaïda is described as submissive, and the narrator notes that her "will, which had been overmastering and aggressive, seemed to have grown numb under the disturbing spell of the past few hours" (498). Numbness gives way to a proper female passivity, so that in the story's closing lines, when Telèsphore announces that he is taking her home, "she was like a little child and followed whither he led in all confidence" (499).

However, because desire and agency in this story function as part of the definition of the Cajun woman, when Chopin writes them out, the protagonist becomes unconvincing: by the story's end Zaïda reads less like a Cajun girl than like an imitation of a Northern-magazine-story, white heroine dressed unconvincingly in Cajun trappings.[22] Roxana Robinson contends that Chopin's Cajun women are wilder, more dramatic, and less conventional than her Creole women (xiii), and that within the collection of stories Robinson edits, "social status is inversely related to female power: Chopin's black women are more powerful than the whites, and Cajun women more powerful than Creoles" (xx). While this is not true in terms of social, economic, or class power, in terms of emotional and erotic force and/or agency, it is certainly true of Chopin's Cajun and Creole women at least. (The argument is more complicated with respect to Chopin's African-American female characters.) Rather than linking female power to social status, however, I would reformulate Robinson's claim to read "female erotic power is inversely related to ethnic/regional status": that is, the degree of erotic agency and power Chopin grants her female Creole and Cajun characters is directly related to their ethnic/regional identities. In inverse proportion to their proximity to the category of unmarked but implicitly Northern, class-privileged, white womanhood, this power thus replicates conventional racialized thinking of the period, locating erotic desire in the Othered woman and offering the white ethnic woman access to this desire via her status as ethnic. The category Cajun thus does double labor in Zaïda's story: it signals white and also ethnic, the latter a category that can slide from safe, entertaining difference to cultural Other. And just as Chopin played this doubled valence as it applied to Local Color fiction, she plays it here as well, for one might read the rewriting of Zaïda as a process of moving from one aspect of Cajun to the other: the original version of the story emphasizes traits that Chopin ascribes to Zaïda's ethnicity, while the final version with its revised ending emphasizes traits associated with whiteness as the category of conventional femininity. Thus, when Chopin rewrote Zaïda as less powerful and more conventional—closer to dominant norms of white femininity—she also made her, in the logic of the story, less ethnic and more "white." Because Chopin left the character's regional and ethnic marking intact, however, she ended up with a heroine who is internally inconsistent on the plot level and yet still unqualified for True Womanhood. Ultimately, what both Zaïda's and Mildred Orme's stories show, then, is that both the dominant American ideals of femininity and Chopin's challenge to them are compromised by the terms of the racial discourse out of which they emerge and are defined not simply by behavior and race, but also by regional identity, class, and ethnicity.

Versions of a Regional Maternal

Just as representations of female agency and erotic desire in Chopin's short fiction emerge from a complicated matrix of racial, gender, and ethnic discourses and so intervene in both radical and reactionary ways in dominant discourse on women, Chopin's representations of the maternal both draw on and discredit conventional universalized models of motherhood. While using certain elements of the maternal to link her Southern heroines to Northern ideals, Chopin simultaneously uses the category as a means of differentiating among various Southern heroines and among various enactments of the maternal. In doing so she disrupts monolithic representations of Southern womanhood by disrupting the absolute meaning of maternity and emphasizing the wide variety of forms motherhood can take. In Chopin's stories the space of the maternal takes on wildly varying meanings according to who occupies it where and when. There is here no idealized type for the American mother or even the Southern mother; instead, there are *mothers*: a range of identities that make it impossible, ultimately, to essentialize maternity. One result of this recasting of the maternal is that white, class-privileged motherhood is no longer celebrated as innate and natural but rather revealed to be socially constructed within a discourse of power, contextual, and contingent on other aspects of female identity—race, region, and class, primarily. A second result of this deessentializing of the maternal is that Chopin's stories foreground and to some extent challenge the strategies by which slavery attempted to strip enslaved black women of access to the category of the maternal. Taken as a group, the stories that focus on maternity make visible the fact that motherhood, like erotic desire, is neither "natural" nor unmarked but rather ultimately determined by factors such as region, race, ethnicity, and class. In what follows I will attempt to trace the ways and places in which these discourses interrupt each other, tracking the intersection of a racist and reactionary racial discourse with more progressive gender and regional discourses, as well as the degree to which a focus on ethnicity allows Chopin to sidestep a direct confrontation with race.

In "La Belle Zoraïde" (1893, 1894) the representation of maternity is specifically inflected by race and racial discourse's relations to a maternal that might arguably be seen as regional, that is, Southern. The story focuses on slavery's structuring impact on the maternity and erotic desire of both the African-American and the white Creole women in the story, establishing that the maternal is a highly contingent rather than natural category.[23] As my discussion of Hopkins in Chapter 3 indicates, maternity and erotic desire were, of course, already imbricated in a racial discourse by Chopin's day. The category of the Southern lady constituted her as always chaste and white, but moreover the category also always demanded that her sexual excess be projected onto her racial Other, the African-American woman. At the same time, maternal instinct was attributed to the Southern lady but denied to all Others, particularly the enslaved (and even at times the free) African-American woman. Thus, maternal and erotic desire functioned as mutually exclusive. As Anna Shannon Elfenbein cogently notes in her article on *The Awakening*, "for much of Chopin's audience the troublesome issue of female desire was resolved through a racist conception of passion and purity according to which passion was projected onto 'dark' women while purity was reserved exclusively for 'white' women" (304). In setting "La Belle Zoraïde" in the antebellum South, Chopin participates in this American cultural discourse, which occurred at the crossroads of racial, regional, and gender discourses. While such a story contributes to postwar regional reconciliation by offering images of racial conflict safely located in the antebellum past, it simultaneously complicates the terms of the racialized discourse on femininity, revealing it as regionally inflected and never fixed.

The story reworks the plot of the slave woman parted from her lover by her "owner":[24] Zoraïde is the beautiful and privileged mulatto slave of Madame Delarivière. She is well-treated until she defies Madame by falling in love with the handsome black slave Mézor rather than the mulatto M. Ambroise, whom Madame has chosen for her. When Zoraïde becomes pregnant by Mézor, Madame, first angry and then pained, has him sold by his "owner," her own suitor, then lies to Zoraïde at the child's birth, telling her that the child is dead. Zoraïde grows demented in response, so much so that when Madame finally returns the child to her in an attempt to cure the madness, Zoraïde does not recognize the child and clings instead to the bundle of rags she has substituted for her baby. Hence, she dies an old, mad, unmarried woman, known as "Zoraïde La Folle" instead of "La Belle Zoraïde." Her story is presented within a frame in which Manna-Loulou ministers to her mistress Madame Delisle, ministerings that include the telling of the bedtime story of La Belle Zoraïde. The frame story insists that Zoraïde's story is fact, for Madame Delisle, Chopin notes, "would hear none but those [stories] which were true"

(304). Set in the antebellum south, Zoraïde's tale thus works in tandem with the frame tale to produce the story's effect.

Zoraïde's history, as told by Manna-Loulou, emphasizes slavery's impact on both female erotic desire and maternal "instinct." Because she is a slave, Zoraïde is not attributed the maternal "instinct" that is culturally assigned to white women, and her "owner" views neither Zoraïde's desire nor her reproductive potential as her own; both are, rather, commodities belonging to her "owner." Manna-Loulou's version of Zoraïde's story, however, offers a counternarrative to this one. Manna-Loulou represents Zoraïde as bearing an erotic desire that is linked to romantic love, racially inflected, and self-directed. She also attributes to Zoraïde a form of maternal "instinct" that is in keeping with idealized models of white womanhood but is forcibly redirected by slavery. These competing versions of the enslaved African-American woman's relation to erotic and maternal desire stand alongside the story's representation of Madame Delarivière, who, as an upper-class white woman, is assumed to have maternal "instinct"—enacting it metaphorically with her non-offspring, the enslaved young woman—and to lack overt erotic desire. Manna-Loulou's narrative also counters this particular, racially inflected version of womanhood, revealing that the white slaveholding woman's maternal sense is simply another form of ownership, and her passionlessness is accompanied by the knowledge of her erotic power. Chopin's choice of an enslaved woman as narrator thus provides a space for a complicating of both black and white racialized narratives of American womanhood, although ultimately this counterdiscourse is contained both by the fate of Zoraïde (madness) and by Chopin's safely locating the story in the antebellum past.

Racial location structures the face of maternity and desire in the Creole white woman, Madame Delarivière. In a combination of class and racialized gender expectations—a combination of a sort of *noblesse oblige* and maternal "instinct"—she initially poses as a surrogate mother for Zoraïde. As the "privileged" slave, Zoraïde is raised in comfort by her mistress, who is also her godmother; her "fingers," Manna-Loulou recounts, "had never done rougher work than sewing a fine muslin seam" (304). But while Zoraïde's "mother" makes plans to have Zoraïde married in the prestigious New Orleans Cathedral and promises to provide her with a fine wedding gown and *corbeille*, the maternal role is merely a fiction, a cover for what is in fact a relationship grounded in power and economics: Madame's power over Zoraïde comes not from a "natural" mother-child bond but from a legal master-slave bond. When Zoraïde refuses to marry the man Madame has chosen for her, Madame drops the fiction of maternal love and exposes her power as a white woman and slaveholder. Trading on her own position as desirable white woman and revealing it as an economic/social location, she induces Mézor's owner, who is in love with her, to sell Mézor (Manna-Loulou explains that Mézor's owner "had long wanted to marry Madame Delarivière, and he would willingly have walked on all fours at noon through the Place d'Armes if she wanted him to. Naturally he lost no time in disposing of le beau Mézor" [306]). She then manipulates Zoraïde for her own convenience by lying, telling Zoraïde that her newly born child is dead. This is the action of the irritated slave owner, not the concerned mother: Manna-Loulou explains that "Madame had hoped, in thus depriving Zoraïde of her child, to have her young waiting-maid again at her side free, happy, and beautiful as of old" (306). This comment at once divests Madame of her maternal role and locates her as part of the racist dominant culture that denies the enslaved woman an affectional bond to her child. Continuing to think of the offspring of a slave mother as chattel rather than child, Madame cannot understand why Zoraïde becomes "demented" at the loss of her child; mystifying the cause of this dementia, Madame thinks of it as "this terrible affliction that had befallen her dear Zoraïde" (307). Manna-Loulou's tracking of Madame's coercion and controlling of Zoraïde's sexuality— her denial of both Zoraïde's choice of erotic object and her status as mother—makes it obvious that Madame Delarivière's behavior mirrors the actions of white male slaveowners toward their female slaves rather than those of a mother toward her child.[25] Manna-Loulou's narrative thus exposes this white woman's maternal instinct as neither instinctual nor even real. At the same time, this narrative reworks dominant images of white female passionlessness, acknowledging white female erotic power but detaching it from the innate or bodily realm and relocating it as a social power relation.

In contrast, Manna-Loulou's narrative attributes to Zoraïde a kind of innate maternal love while also claiming erotic desire for her. Zoraïde's love for Mézor offers the first instance of this particular racial counternarrative, both in Zoraïde's object choice and in her story's complicated relation to stereotypes of African-American female desire. The description of Zoraïde falling in love, for instance, locates this love within a discourse of race:

Zoraïde had seen le beau Mézor dance the Bamboula in Congo Square. That was a sight to hold one rooted to the ground. Mézor was as straight as a cypress-tree and as proud looking as a king. His body, bare to the waist, was like a column of ebony and it glistened like oil.

Poor Zoraïde's heart grew sick in her bosom with love for le beau Mézor from the moment she saw the fierce gleam of his eye, lighted by the inspiring strains of the Bamboula, and beheld the stately movements of his splendid body swaying and quivering through the figures of the dance. (304)

This description represents Zoraïde's love as both erotic and romantic and as specifically racially inflected: Zoraïde loves the "ebony" Mézor, whose body here signifies pride, grace, and stately power. This power is directly linked to his race; significantly, Zoraïde first sees Mézor dancing in Congo Square, a New Orleans gathering place where slaves celebrated their traditional cultural identities through dance and ritual. In contrast to and underscoring this point, Manna-Loulou describes Monsieur Ambroise, the man Zoraïde's owner wants her to marry, as a "little mulatto, with his shining whiskers like a white man's and his small eyes, that were cruel and false as a snake's" (304). As Elfenbein points out in *Women on the Color Line*, the fact that the object of Zoraïde's desire is the blacker of the two men itself inverts a conventional fictional representation of a hierarchy of racial value.[26] Yet the fact that Chopin ascribes erotic desire to Zoraïde and that she focuses in the passage above on the eroticized body of the black man also opens the possibility that Chopin is simply rehearsing stereotypes of the hypereroticized African American or of a primitivized "savage" who is closer to natural rhythms. Although these stereotypes lurk in the margins of this story, I would argue that the representation of Zoraïde's desire complicates, if not disrupts, that racialized discourse in several ways: by involving "true love"; by aiming that love at the African man; and by being self-directed—Zoraïde actively chooses Mézor over Ambroise.

Through Zoraïde, Chopin explicitly marks race as determining the cultural meaning of romantic or erotic agency: race is the structuring axis of the slave system, and because Zoraïde is a mulatta slave rather than a white lady, she does not have ownership of her own desire. At the same time, however, the story charts Zoraïde's resistance to this equation, as when, after confessing her love of Mézor, she rhetorically asks Madame if she is white and answers her own question: "'I am not white,' persisted Zoraïde, respectfully and gently. 'Doctor Langlé gives me his slave to marry, but he would not give me his son. Then, since I am not white, let me have from out of my own race the one whom my heart has chosen'" (305). This momentary rhetorical doubt over Zoraïde's race (like the uncertainty over whether the heroine of "Désirée's Baby" is a white aristocrat or a tragic mulatto) produces a moment in which Chopin subversively uses one woman to represent the possibility of both the black woman's and the white woman's desire. Ultimately, however, regardless of the privileges her owner might bestow on her, Zoraïde recognizes that in occupying the place of "mulatto slave" she by definition has only limited rights and has access to privilege only at the discretion of a white patron. In an act that is doubly transgressive, however, Zoraïde opts for autonomous choice, a choice within her "own race," telling Madame, "I have chosen a husband, but it is not M'sieur Ambroise; it is le beau Mézor that I want and no other" (305).

Just as Chopin represents Zoraïde's desire as both constrained by and in resistance to slavery, the enslaved woman's occupation of the space of the maternal here takes on meaning both through its erasure within slavery and through Zoraïde's ironic deployment of it at the story's end. Zoraïde's rejection of her child once Madame relents and brings the little girl back to Zoraïde, her "sullen suspicion," and her reading of the strategy as "a plot to deprive her of" her rag bundle surrogate child—all these signal Zoraïde's awareness that Madame would control and redirect Zoraïde's maternal desire just as she has attempted to do with Zoraïde's erotic desire (307). Further, through the rag bundle fantasy child, Zoraïde not only reclaims the maternal, she also evades a forced marriage to M. Ambroise. In a key moment near the end of the story, we learn that despite the "death" of the child and Zoraïde's paralyzing grief in the face of it, M. Ambroise continues to want to marry Zoraïde, information Manna-Loulou glosses by noting, "and she seemed to consent, or rather submit, to the approaching marriage as though nothing mattered any longer in this world" (306–7). But immediately after this, Manna-Loulou presents Zoraïde in her dementia, sitting with "a look of strange and vacuous happiness" next to the rag baby (307). This juxtaposition, along with Manna-Loulou's comment that Zoraïde was known ever afterward as "Zoraïde la folle, whom no one ever wanted to marry—not even M'sieur Ambroise" (307), points to several conclusions at once. It first stakes a claim to an innate maternal on behalf of Zoraïde, suggesting that the African-American woman has, just as the white woman is assumed to have, a mother's love that she cannot be forced to surrender. Secondly, this scenario forces the recognition that slavery has reformed and deformed the maternal for the enslaved woman, as represented here by Zoraïde's being forced to rechannel her maternal love from her child to the surrogate rag doll child. Finally, Manna-Loulou's telling of the story suggests an ironic or canny deployment of the maternal on Zoraïde's part, a claiming of a "demented" version of it in order not only to defend her right to the maternal but also to defend her right to erotic agency against the controlling of her desire through a forced marriage to M. Ambroise. By linking these two rights, this claim also challenges dominant notions of erotic and maternal desire as mutually exclusive.

As a foil to this image of the slave woman nursing a fantasy child, the story framing Zoraïde's presents another form of a rechanneled maternal allowed to black women under slavery: the role of surrogate mother to the white child. The opening of the story establishes Manna-Loulou's relation to Madame Delisle as one of intimacy structured by a racial power hierarchy, for Manna-Loulou is presented as a "Mammy" figure to her infantilized white owner. At the opening of the story Manna-Loulou, "herself black as night," has already, we are told, bathed and kissed her mistress's feet, and she has "brushed her mistress's beautiful hair, that was as soft and shining as satin, and was the color of Madame's wedding ring" (303). The alignment of whiteness with economic privilege signaled by the gold of Madame's hair and ring stands in contrast to the "black" Manna-Loulou's position of servitude, as she actively waits on the passive, infantilized Madame, "who lay in her sumptuous mahogany bed, waiting to be fanned and put to sleep to the sound of one of Manna-Loulou's stories" (303). This image of white power over the faithful black slave demonstrates Chopin's rehearsal of nostalgic racism, gesturing toward post–Civil War fantasies on the part of the white South to the prewar slave order.

However, this image might also be read as one of passive white dependence on black agency, a reading that is mirrored on a certain narrative level. For while Manna-Loulou is the servant, she also has control of the narrative, which grants her a kind of authority, particularly when compared with Madame Delisle's obvious misinterpretation of the tale, her listening to "the sound of one of Manna-Loulou's stories" rather than understanding the meaning of it. Manna-Loulou's interpretive authority gets enacted initially over the issue of Zoraïde's desire, as Manna-Loulou locates Zoraïde's actions within a plot of "true love": the comic plot of the two lovers overcoming obstacles in order to be together. Following this, once Chopin has opened the story with the introduction of Manna-Loulou and Madame Delisle, these characters interrupt Zoraïde's story only once before their reappearance at the story's close. Significantly, Manna-Loulou interrupts just after Zoraïde asks to choose her own husband. In an important and complicated passage, Manna-Loulou tells Madame Delisle,

"However, you may well believe that Madame would not hear to that. Zoraïde was forbidden to speak to Mézor, and Mézor was cautioned against seeing

Zoraïde again. But you know how the negroes are, Ma'zelle Titite," added Manna-Loulou, smiling a little sadly, "There is no mistress, no master, no king nor priest who can hinder them from loving when they will. And these two found ways and means." (305)

Elfenbein reads this interjection as Manna-Loulou's implication that "whites envy [black] passion forbidden them and would control it or appropriate it if they could (132):[27] one might also read this as Manna-Loulou's support of the "negroes"' resistance to white authority's attempt to coerce their desire, as well as her recognition (signaled by her sad smile) of the costs of such resistance. At the same time, however, extra-textually, of course, Manna-Loulou's interpretive authority is still in the hands of the white woman writer, and so this passage must also be read reinscribing the stereotype of "natural" African-American female erotic desire uncontrollable by church or state. Moreover, this alignment of Zoraïde and sexuality is echoed in the terms of Manna-Loulou's relationship to Madame: Birnbaum rightly argues that women of color tend to serve as "sexual coaches" for white women in Chopin's work, that "the experienced women is always of a lower racial or ethnic status than her novitiate; if the heroine is white Creole, her mentor may be Acadian; if she is Acadian, her guide may be 'black' ." She points to Manna-Loulou as an example of this (327).

Yet Manna-Loulou's understanding of Zoraïde's story also offers a foil to Madame Delisle's self-protective and equally racist misreading of it. That is, both Manna-Loulou's and Madame Delisle's versions of Zoraïde's story are written in the terms of the dominant racial discourse, and although Chopin ultimately critiques Madame's version, she does so only by means of the version to which Manna-Loulou gives voice. At the story's close Madame Delisle comments, " . . . Ah, the poor little one, Man Loulou, the poor little one! better had she died!" (307). By shifting the focus of the story from Zoraïde to her child, Madame Delisle reveals that she has missed the point entirely, but such a misreading works in her favor. For by turning Zoraïde's story into the story of a poor orphaned baby, Madame Delisle erases Zoraïde, sidesteps the issue of a white woman's power over a slave woman's life, and thus avoids identifying with Madame Delarivière. Ironically, however, this comment also aligns Madame Delisle with Madame Delarivière in that it positions Madame Delisle in the same space of false maternal solicitude that Zoraïde's "owner" occupies. The narrative itself further produces this identification by the imposition of one last narrative level to frame the frame.

After recounting Manna-Loulou and Madame Delisle's final conversation, the story closes by re-presenting it in Creole patois, prefaced by the statement that "this is the way Madame Delisle and Manna-Loulou really talked to each other" (308). Recalling Converse's claim to be translating her characters' French, this narrative strategy is a model of efficiency, operating both without and within the story to structure an understanding of that story. Exterior to the narrative, the patois positions the story as a deferential yet exotic Local Color tale. Comforting to a Northern reader, this strategy produces maternity as an issue in the South and in the past, an issue familiar to the Northern reader yet rendered safe by distance. At the same time, however, this strategy also insists on a recognition of regional difference: the patois forces an understanding of the story and its representation of the maternal as regionally specific because of the conditions of slavery, while that same patois distances the non-patois speaking reader from an identification with the story's characters. It is, after all, on the reader's behalf that Chopin has ostensibly served as translator, rendering the story in English. At the same time, however, the patois breaks down the monolithic image of the "South," showing that even within the South there are a variety of regions and, moreover, that even within a given region, there are a variety of both identifications and splits. That is, internal to the story the patois links both Manna-Loulou and Madame Delisle to Zoraïde and her mistress (who, the reader might assume, would also speak patois), thus indicting Madame Delisle for her refusal to identify with Madame Delarivière's structural position of power. The use of patois also represents a regional identification across racial and class lines between Manna-Loulou and Madame Delisle, indicating both their difference from the reader and their similarity to each other. The patois, then, both differentiates among and links the characters, underscoring the regional and racial specificity of this version of maternity within the larger context of white-black power hierarchies in the postbellum South. As it does in both Pauline Hopkins's and Sui Sin Far's works, motherhood emerges here as not "natural" to white women; as not alien to Othered women; as not necessarily a source of joy; and as not mutually exclusive of erotic desire. What it does emerge as is contingent, visibly reworked by slavery and race, and no less determined by the less explicitly violent factors of regional and class location.

As in "La Belle Zoraïde," the impact of racial positioning on the maternal is also at stake in "Désirée's Baby" (1892, 1893), but "Désirée's Baby" also foregrounds class status (as influenced by race) as a determinant of the maternal. Where Zoraïde's final deployment of a fantasy maternal saves her from a coerced marriage, Désirée's accession to the place of the maternal destroys her marriage, reassigns her racial status, and indicates just how fragile and contingent both racially and class-privileged identities are. As Pauline Hopkins would go on to do in a more optimistic vein, Chopin in this story reworks the "tragic mulatto" plot to foreground the doubled powerlessness of a "black" woman while also commenting on the dangerous force of the maternal.[28] Désirée, found as an abandoned child by the Valmondés at their plantation gate, provides Madame Valmondé with the opportunity of figurative motherhood: Madame believes that Désirée "had been sent to her by a beneficent Providence to be the child of her affection, seeing that she was without child of the flesh" (240). Once grown, Désirée marries the proud and wealthy Armand Aubigny but finds her idyllic life destroyed by the birth of her son, who is visibly of mixed "blood." Aubigny casts off his wife, who disappears into the bayou rather than heeding her mother's plea to "come home to Valmondé; back to your mother who loves you. Come with your child" (243). The story ends by establishing that Aubigny himself is the offspring of a white man and a mulatto mother, but Désirée's parentage is never clearly established.

As Anna Shannon Elfenbein has so skillfully demonstrated in *Women on the Color Line*, the "white" man's is the only real position of power here: even as the apotheosis of white womanhood, Désirée, as her name implies, has only a tenuous power, one that is dependent on her being desired (127) and, I would add, on an always unstable myth of purity of blood.[29] Even maternity serves only to reveal just how tenuous even the privileged white Southern woman's power is: both Désirée's desirability and her blood's "purity" are called into question by the birth of her son. "Désirée's Baby"'s thematizing of issues of "blood" and maternity echoes antebellum narratives (Stowe's *Uncle Tom's Cabin* or Harriet Jacobs's *Incidents in the Life of a Slave Girl*, for example), which protested against slavery on the basis of its disruption of a "natural" mother-child bond. Motherhood in these texts is depicted as far more dangerous for the slave woman than for the free woman, both because the slave woman's child was not legally her own and because it was often born of white man's rape.[30] Chopin frames the issue slightly differently; maternity in intersection with race in "Désirée's Baby" becomes the site of danger for both mother and child both because Désirée's becoming a mother puts her into the space of the "black" woman, figuratively if not literally enslaved, and because her becoming a mother shows just how uncertain racial identity can be. Maternity, that is, here destabilizes not only the child's but also the mother's racial identity: it is the birth of the son that calls Désirée's racial "purity" into question. Nevertheless, the danger here is posited as a threat only to the privileged white woman, revealing racial logic that here as elsewhere limits Chopin's achievement; as Ellen Peel points out, the story "directs sympathy less toward black characters than toward characters on the margin between black and white," and it "invites sympathy for Désirée partly on the sexist grounds that feminine women are weak and on the racist grounds that white members of the master class do not deserve to be treated like slaves" (64, 66).[31] Hence, while "Désirée's Baby," like "La Belle Zoraïde," denaturalizes an idealized version of the maternal in which maternity is the highest fulfillment of a woman's life (for Désirée, maternity proves to be not her fulfillment but her ruin), it does not challenge the conventional hierarchies of the racial discourse out of which it emerges.

Further, the image of unconditional maternal love in this story is white, embodied in the figure of Madame Valmondé. But in contrast to Armand Aubigny's love, a love that is dependent on racial "purity," Désirée's adoptive mother's love is not only loyal, it is also independent, in two senses, of fictions of "blood." Whereas Désirée's mother's love is not dependent on Désirée's having "white" blood, it is also independent of literal mother-child bloodlines: that Désirée is "the child of her affection" rather than "the child of the flesh" has no impact on Madame Valmondé's love. Chopin thus implicitly retains dominant racial hierarchies while she links maternity to questions of shifting racial identity and prizes it apart from essentialized claims of blood ties, locating it in the realm of social power relations rather than in an apolitical, universalized bodily space.

"Athénaïse" (1895, 1896) similarly foregrounds the maternal as a sphere of social power, linking it, as does "La Belle Zoraïde," to erotic desire, and coding it, as does "Désirée's Baby," as determined by class and race. Unlike in "Désirée's Baby," however, where the maternal reveals the tenuousness of even the privileged white Southern lady's class positioning, in "Athénaïse"'s story of the white Creole woman, the protagonist's move into the space of the maternal both produces her erotic desire and secures her class position. The story traces a fairly conventional plot: the move of the unhappy newlyweds to a state of marital accord as a result of the wife's discovery of her pregnancy, a discovery that produces a sense of family unity and, less predictably, the wife's erotic response to her husband. Through focusing most of the story on Athénaïse's unhappiness in and rebellion against her marriage, Chopin offers a critique of that institution that anticipates that of *The Awakening*, but by giving "Athénaïse" the particular happy, if abrupt, ending that she does, Chopin not only mitigates the threat of her critique, but also implicates maternity in the construction of female erotic desire and depicts maternity as the site of the solidifying of class and racial privilege.

The story opens with Athénaïse's fleeing from her marital home and husband Cazeau to return to her family, then charts her eventual return to the place of wife. It concurrently traces her move from child to woman, innocent to self-conscious (including an awareness of her own erotic desire) adult. Near the opening of the story the narrator notes that "people often said that Athénaïse would know her own mind some day, which was equivalent to saying that she was at present unacquainted with it" (433). By the narrative's close, however, this narrator notes that "no one could have said now that she did not know her own mind" (452). Knowing her own mind, it turns out, means locating herself in the social/economic/racial context of the Creole planter world, a process that occurs through Athénaïse's realization that she is pregnant and her consequent recognition of erotic desire for her husband.

Initially, Athénaïse is represented as unhappy despite the social and economic benefits her marriage brings her, and the story suggests that she has traded her sense of autonomy, privacy, and independence for the class comfort and protection her husband embodies. Cazeau comes from a white, privileged, slave-owning family, so that marriage to him signals for Athénaïse a move up from the social position of her family, who are "running" the "old Gotrain place" for an absentee owner (428). But Athénaïse is unhappy, offering complaints that form a critique of marriage as an institution that confines and limits women. Employing the image of wife as slave, Chopin draws on a problematic parallel frequently evoked in nineteenth-century white women's texts and simultaneously marks her story as specifically Southern: Cazeau, bringing Athénaïse back from her parents' home, is reminded of his father's driving a captured runaway slave home. But indicating his status as ultimately a good husband, when Athénaïse runs away a second time, he decides that although he has the legal right to do so, he will not again "compel her to return to the shelter of his roof, compel her cold and unwilling submission to his love and passionate transports" (438), and so he waits instead for her voluntary return.

As this reference to the wife's "unwilling submission" to her husband implies, what Cazeau recognizes as Athénaïse's "growing aversion" (427) and her brother Monteclin calls her "constitutional disinclination for marriage" (431) is based on physical distaste as much as psychological confinement. For Cazeau, by Athénaïse's own admission, has never mistreated her: his "chief offense seemed to be that he loved her" (434), a love, clearly, that is meant to be understood as physical as well as emotional. Speculating about an acquaintance's romantic history, for instance, Athénaïse, we are told, "could not fancy him loving any one passionately, rudely, offensively, as Cazeau loved her. Once she was so naïve as to ask him outright if he had ever been in love, and he assured her promptly that he had not. She thought it an admirable trait in his character, and esteemed him greatly therefor" (449), while she assesses her marriage by stating,

"No, I don't hate him," she returned reflectively; adding with a sudden impulse, "It's jus' being married that I detes' and despise. I hate being Mrs. Cazeau, an' would want to be Athénaïse Miché again. I can't stan' to live with a man; to have him always there; his coats an' pantaloons hanging in my room; his ugly bare feet—washing them in my tub, befo' my very eyes, ugh!" She shuddered with recollections, and resumed, with a sigh that was almost a sob: "Mon Dieu, mon Dieu! Sister Marie Angélique knew w'at she was saying; she knew me better than myse'f w'en she said God had sent me a vocation an' I was turning deaf ears. W'en I think of a blessed life in the convent, at peace! Oh, w'at was I dreaming of!" and then the tears came. (431)

That Athénaïse's complaint against marriage is grounded in Cazeau's physical presence in her room (especially when read against the contrast of the "blessed convent") suggests that part of the process traced by the story—the process of Athénaïse "knowing her own mind"—involves Athénaïse's coming to terms with the physical, heterosexual relationship implicit in marriage, a shift here figured not simply as the passive acceptance of her husband's desires but also as a recognition of her own: Athénaïse moves from feeling repugnance at her husband, synecdochically represented by his feet, to a moment of desire for him; at the story's end the narrator notes that as Cazeau "clasped her in his arms, he felt the yielding of her whole body against him. He felt her lips for the first time respond to the passion of his own" (454).

This potentially radical claim to erotic desire on the part of the white lady is made further disruptive by Chopin's identifying it with maternal desire. For it is on learning that she is pregnant that Athénaïse first thinks of Cazeau with a newfound sense of desire:

One mood quickly followed another, in this new turmoil of her senses . . . Cazeau must know. As she thought of him, the first purely sensuous tremor of her life swept over her. She half whispered his name, and the sound of it brought red blotches into her cheeks. She spoke it over and over, as if it were some new, sweet sound born out of darkness and confusion, and reaching her for the first time. She was impatient to be with him. Her whole passionate nature was aroused as if by a miracle. (451)

But in fact the language of the story represents this transformation not as an inexplicable "miracle," but specifically as the result of pregnancy and the new knowledge and maturity it implies. Chopin first employs the abstract language of the passage above in describing Athénaïse's response not to Cazeau, but to the news of her pregnancy itself, which is figured as a fall into knowledge as well as a sensuous experience in its own right. The narrator comments that in the conversation where Athénaïse learns she is pregnant, the "extent of her ignorance and the depth of her subsequent enlightenment were bewildering," and describes her as "stunned" and "still" in response, as "her whole being was steeped in a wave of ecstasy" (451). Interestingly, after Athénaïse's realization of both her pregnancy and her desire for her husband, the narrator describes her as "silent and embarrassed as Eve after losing her ignorance" (453). That Chopin retreats to metaphoric and abstract language to describe the topics of pregnancy and erotic desire is not especially surprising given the literary codes of her day, but the fact that she uses the same sort of language to describe the two is significant, for the effect of this shared rhetoric is to link erotic desire/knowledge with the maternal, a link rarely made in Chopin's day.

The disruptiveness of this representation of the erotic and maternal and of their conjunction, however, is ultimately compromised by the story. The claim to essentialized erotic desire is mitigated in part through that desire's being legitimated by being aimed at a husband and in part through Athénaïse's status as Creole; as the use of dialect in her speech signals, Athénaïse, like Chopin's Cajun women, is ethnically marked and so more easily conflatable by a white audience with the eroticized female Other. Further, the fact that it is her "quadroon" landlady Sylvie— whom, we are told, "was very wise" while Athénaïse "was very ignorant" (451)—who reveals Athénaïse's pregnancy to her both supports Birnbaum's claim that Chopin's women of color do the work of "teaching" white women about their sexuality and helps to further code the erotic as the province of the racially/ethnically marked woman.

This intersection of racial and gender discourses is further complicated by the introduction of a discourse of class: the story dilutes the Othering effects of Athénaïse's alignment with erotic/maternal desire by framing that desire in an economic context as well, a context that partly determines the desire and simultaneously locates Athénaïse in the space of the privileged white lady. The connection between economic desire and erotic desire is raised early in the story, when the unhappy Athénaïse tries to explain why she married Cazeau. The narrator comments:

Why indeed? It was difficult now for her to understand why, unless because she supposed it was customary for girls to marry when the right opportunity came. Cazeau, she knew, would make life more comfortable for her; and again, she had liked him, and had even been rather flustered when he pressed her hands and kissed them, and kissed her lips and cheeks and eyes, when she accepted him. (430)

Athénaïse responds dually, being physically "flustered" and economically reassured. The story's conclusion reiterates this yoking of determinants. While hiding in New Orleans, Athénaïse cannot find a means of support "with the exception of two little girls who had promised to take piano lessons at a price that would be embarrassing to mention" (451); but the return to Cazeau made possible by her discovery of her pregnancy and her erotic desire implies an insertion into not only the position of the maternal, but also that of the white plantation mistress; like the conclusion of Zaïda's story, the ending of "Athénaïse" emphasizes that she occupies the cultural space of class and racial privilege. Following the description above of Athénaïse's passionate reunion with Cazeau, the story closes by grounding this passion in local circumstance:

The country night was dark and warm and still, save for the distant notes of an accordion which some one was playing in a cabin away off. A little negro baby was crying somewhere. As Athénaïse withdrew from her husband's embrace, the sound arrested her.

"Listen, Cazeau! How Juliette's baby is crying! Pauvre ti chou, I wonder w'at is the matter with it?" (454)

The story's end thus conflates Athénaïse's erotic desire with her identification with the maternal and a concurrent *noblesse oblige* that signals her status as the white lady who stands, like Madame Delarivière, in the position of pseudo-mother toward her "dependents." As the use of dialect in Athénaïse's comment suggests, however, this story allows its heroine ethnic specificity as well as the status of white and class-privileged; or perhaps Chopin can afford to allow Athénaïse her ethnicity *because* of that privileged racial and class status. Athénaïse's identification with the cultural place held by the maternal ultimately secures her racial and class locations, locations that shore up each other and enable her erotic desire. Michael Omi and Howard Winant remind us that "racial dynamics must be understood as determinants of class relationships and indeed class identities, not as mere consequences of these relationships" (34): "Athénaïse" demonstrates the intertwined, determining effects of both racial and class discourses on femininity.

The use of the maternal as the vehicle for the enactment of regionally specific, class-privileged, white female identity occurs as well in "A Matter of Prejudice" (1893, 1895), a story that, like "Athénaïse," focuses on Creole womanhood but in this case on its urban version: the upper-class New Orleans Creole woman. The maternal here serves to foreground white ethnic difference within New Orleans culture while providing the means for family reunification in the face of the ethnic prejudice that has divided it. As Florence Converse does with her portrait of the Dumarais family, Chopin, in Madame Carambeau, depicts the old-guard French Creole privileged class of New Orleans:

Old Madame Carambeau was a woman of many prejudices—so many, in fact, that it would be difficult to name them all. She detested dogs, cats, organ-grinders, white servants and children's noises. She despised Americans, Germans and all people of a different faith from her own. Anything not French had, in her opinion, little right to existence.

She had not spoken to her son Henri for ten years because he had married an American from Prytania street. (282)[32]

The story traces the transformation of Madame Carambeau's "prejudice"—a combination of elitism, racism, nativism, and assorted other biases—into a willingness to accept her son and his family, a transformation that occurs through an "American" child's triggering of Madame's maternal feeling. A skilled nurse, Madame Carambeau transcends her prejudice in the exercise of this talent; the narrator notes dryly that Madame "would have treated an organ-grinder with tender consideration if one had presented himself in the character of an invalid" (283), so that when faced with a small, sick "American" child, she nurses her back to health.

Similar to Florence Converse's representation of Roma Campion, Chopin's depiction of Madame Carambeau and her interaction with the child provides the opportunity to display some of New Orleans's ethnic/cultural diversity to a Northern readership. At the same time, Chopin traces the impact of Madame Carambeau's maternal feeling on her ethnic prejudices. The child does not understand French, and "prattle[s]" in what the narrator describes as "that language which madame thought hideous" (284), an identifying tag that leads Madame to identify the little girl as "American" and to complain that "Americans" do not deserve children because they are unable to care for them properly. Predictably, however, the child is "a sweet child, gentle and affectionate" (285), and so undermines Madame's biases:

Madame . . . had never before nursed so objectionable a character as an American child. But . . . after the little one went away, she could think of nothing really objectionable against her except the accident of her birth, which was, after all, her misfortune; and her ignorance of the French language, which was not her fault.

But the touch of the caressing baby arms; the pressure of the soft little body in the night; the tones of the voice, and the feeling of the hot lips when the child kissed her, believing herself to be with her mother, were impressions that had sunk through the crust of madame's prejudice and reached her heart. (285)

As a result of this experience Madame crosses into the Garden district, the "American" quarter of the city, to visit her son, his wife, and her granddaughter, who turns out to be the little "American" girl she has nursed. The story ends with an image of family reconciliation that might also stand as a metaphor for the unification of diverse white ethnic American traditions: Madame Carambeau says of her granddaughter, "her grandmother will teach her French; and she will teach her grandmother English" (288). This happy image of a polyglot American family achieved through maternal love reflects a nativist national rhetoric of white ethnic assimilation, a sort of "melting pot" version of U.S. society. At the same time, Chopin uses this implicitly racist model to participate in American discourses of region and gender. For this plot device also allows Chopin to have the maternal, as it were, both ways: Madame Carambeau's nursing of what turns out to be her own granddaughter can be read as the innate enactment of maternal love and recognition of kinship, or it might be read as the embodiment of a French Creole sense of *noblesse oblige*, a regionally and class-specific form of social power relations that resists a homogenizing national pressure to identify "American" as Northern and Anglo.

Ultimately, understanding Chopin's representations of both erotic and maternal desire as contingent can help us reassess her work and its importance. Viewing femininity not as the central focus of Chopin's fiction—as critics of *The Awakening* have been wont to do—but rather as a site of the convergence of a number of different vectors enables a fuller appreciation of both the complexity and the importance of her early work. Using Local Color as a cover to write about female identity and sexuality, Chopin also exploited the form and many of its racist conventions to publish. Simultaneously, she used female identity and sexuality to write about regional identity and, implicitly, national identity. Taking the short stories as a group, it becomes clear that Chopin both challenged and rehearsed regional stereotypes in her representations of Southern women. Implicitly dismantling certain norms of white American femininity by revealing their regional, class, and religious inflections, Chopin's short fiction offers female characters who are specifically not New Englanders, also not generic Southerners, generally not Protestants, and not even unmarked Anglo-Americans, but who, instead, are explicitly racially, ethnically, regionally, religiously, and class marked, and who rewrite narratives of female purity and passionlessness. At the same time, however, these revisions of white femininity are grounded in the rehearsal of racist alignments of women of color and eroticism. As a result, while Chopin's use of realist literary strategies in her depiction of regionally marked heroines does allow for more narrative space for the representation of white female erotic desire and (at points) both black and white maternal desire, her manipulation of Local Color leads her to draw on a racist discourse of sexuality in her search for a language and form to represent such desires. Ultimately trapped within the literary conventions that she in some ways set out to overthrow, Chopin demonstrates the limits of any literary endeavor grounded in the racial, regional, and sexual discourses of her day.

6 Transnational Geographies of Race

"EURASIAN" COMMUNITIES AND THE NATION IN 'MRS. SPRING FRAGRANCE'

> At the centre, the nation narrates itself as *the* nation: at the borders, it must recognize that there are other nations on which it cannot but depend.
> —Geoffrey Bennington, "Postal Politics and the Institution of the Nation"

> Throughout the twentieth century, the figure of the Asian immigrant has served as a "screen," a phantasmatic site, on which the nation projects a series of condensed, complicated anxieties regarding external and internal threats to the mutable coherence of the national body: the invading multitude, the lascivious seductress, the servile yet treacherous domestic, the automaton whose inhuman efficiency will supersede American ingenuity.
> —Lisa Lowe, *Immigrant Acts: On Asian American Cultural Politics*

Orientalism and Its Gaps: Available Discourses for the Voice of the Eurasian

Daughter of an English father and a Chinese mother, Sui Sin Far (1865–1914) begins her 1909 autobiographical essay, "Leaves from the Mental Portfolio of an Eurasian," with a memory of hearing her nursemaid tell another nursemaid that the child's mother is Chinese, a revelation that causes the other woman to exclaim and stare. The child rushes home and tells her mother, then the narrator recounts, "My mother does not understand, and when the nurse declares to her, 'Little Miss Sui is a story-teller,' my mother slaps me" (218).[1] The incident prefigures the adult Sui Sin Far's relation to her world and trade: the dual connotations of "story-teller"—as creative force or as liar—signaling both the writer she was to become and the hostility incurred by one who spoke out on behalf of the Chinese during a particularly sinophobic period of North American history. In a body of work composed of short stories, journalism, and autobiographical essays, Sui Sin Far took as her subject the condition of the Chinese—broadly interpreted—in North America, providing the American and Canadian reading public with both a portrait of Chinese-American and Chinese-Canadian communities and a portrait, carefully and rhetorically constructed, of herself.[2] Her insistent attention to border locations within American and Canadian culture, to insiders, to outsiders, and to borderland inhabitants, throws into high relief not simply the lines that limn these categories but also the ways in which these lines are drawn and by whom. Sui Sin Far's work foregrounds the role of the Chinese immigrant in the production of both literal and metaphorical national borders, namely, the U.S. national borders produced in part by the Chinese Exclusion Acts and the metaphorical borderlands emerging through the constitution of Chinese-American identities and communities. As work by various scholars has established, over the course of "the last century and half, the American *citizen* has been defined over against the Asian *immigrant*, legally, economically, and culturally" (Lowe 4): in representations of Chinese-American communities and the characters who constitute them, Sui Sin Far reveals and challenges the ways the American cultural imagination depends, as Geoffrey Bennington puts it above, on the "other nation," embodied by the figure of the Chinese, in order to naturalize national binary oppositions such as citizen/immigrant, American/foreigner, insider/outsider, and white/Chinese.[3] But while her work denaturalizes these universalizing categories, it simultaneously recognizes their cultural force, their real and powerful material ramifications. Thus, she both recognizes the impact of, and at the same time challenges, the late-nineteenth/early-twentieth-century American cultural narrative wherein blood determines both personal identity and cultural location. Sui Sin Far emphasizes through her portraits of Chinese Americans and Eurasians the interconnected juridical, economic, and social aspects of American definitions of race, and she highlights the ways that a biologizing narrative of "blood" masks these interconnections in the service of an unjust social order.

Half English, half Chinese, born Edith Eaton in England in 1867, Sui Sin Far moved with her family to the United States briefly as a small child, then returned to England, then moved to Montreal at age seven or eight. In her adult years she lived in both Canada and the United States, migrating from Montreal to Seattle to San Francisco to Los Angeles to Boston before dying in Montreal in 1914.[4] Identifying as a Eurasian and a woman who traversed not just racial borders but also geographic ones, then, Sui Sin Far obviously had a personal stake in issues of individual, racial, community, and even national identity formation, but this personal stake also reflects the larger cultural debates of her day, particularly those focused on the question of the relationship of Chinese-American communities to the United States as a whole.[5]

As an immigrant population, the Chinese began arriving in significant numbers in the U.S. beginning in the 1850s, and are distinctive in that they entered via the West Coast and were originally an overwhelmingly male population. Although they, like many other immigrants, were in part drawn by the lure of the Gold Rush, the reasons for their emigration were specific to China as well. As Sucheng Chan reminds us, "in the 1850s and early 1860s, while gold pulled Chinese to California, the political, social, and economic turmoil caused by the two Opium Wars, the T'aip'ing Rebellion, the Red Turbans uprisings, and the Punti-Hakka feuds pushed Cantonese out of their homeland" (37). But while the original wave of Chinese immigrants mostly worked mining claims, by the mid 1860s they had been driven out of the mines by white prospectors, and the increasing numbers of immigrants arriving in the 1860s and 70s turned to both agriculture and industrial labor, providing ninety percent of the workforce for the building of the transcontinental railroad. Bought over via the credit-ticket system fostered by American capitalists, these workers were needed to meet growing labor demands in the West and were viewed by employers as "temporary and mobile," as Ronald Takaki points out: employers "wanted a labor force of single men, a mobile work force ready to move to the next construction site or the next harvest" (*Strangers* 39). Very few Chinese women were present, most of whom, as Lucie Cheng Hirata has discussed, worked as prostitutes in "a highly organized institution" spanning the Pacific (226).

Sui Sin Far's stories address various racially and ethnically marked border locations through her heroines.[6] Some of these heroines have mixed Chinese and Anglo parentage that calls into question supposedly discrete "racial" categories. Other heroines, Chinese-born immigrants now settled in American Chinatowns, blur discrete national/cultural boundaries. Cumulatively, these characters and their communities provide Sui Sin Far's critique of an American narrative of national identity grounded in a monolithic racial purity. Race is indeed a structuring element of American life in Sui Sin Far's work but not race as the reductive, biologizing discourse that locates the Chinese as the national/racial Other to the "American." Rather, Sui Sin Far uses race in the sense described by sociologists Michael Omi and Howard Winant as "an unstable and 'decentered' complex of social meanings constantly being transformed by political struggle . . . *race is a concept which signifies and symbolizes social conflicts and interests by referring to different types of human bodies*" (55, emphasis in original). In addition to performing this broad debiologizing of race, Sui Sin Far focuses on the specific forms of "social conflicts" that Chinese-American "human bodies" were deployed to resolve in American culture, as well as on the resistant forms of community created by her Chinese-American characters. Put another way, given a historical context in which, as Lisa Lowe argues, the racial meaning ascribed to "Asian American" has been defined "in terms of institutionalized, legal definitions of race and national origin" (10), Sui Sin Far's representations, focusing specifically on the Chinese-American portion of the category "Asian American," problematize the legal, economic, and cultural Othering of the Chinese in America by pushing at categorical absolutes until they collapse. Working within a cultural discourse that depended on discrete categories formed of binary oppositions, Sui Sin Far scrambles the terms of dominant American discourses of race and gender; consequently, both her work and its critical reception afford us insight into the construction and deconstruction of boundaries of various sorts—racial, sexual, regional, national, and literary. First, her work deconstructs racial binaries through her use of the third term of "Eurasian" identity and a consequent underscoring of "whiteness" as a culturally constructed rather than a "natural" category. Second, her work produces a blurring of lines performed by critics who slide from reading her work as "ethnic" fiction to reading it as regional. Third, her writing tracks the shifting ethnic and regional "identity" or configuration of the California of Sui Sin Far's day and provides a vision of Chinese-American community as a kind of process involving a shifting and internally heterogeneous group that calls into question national fictions of pure identity.[7] Fourth, her life and work both display a significant traversal of geopolitical borders. Fifth, she challenges heteronormativity through her representations of homoerotic desire. In these ways the work of Sui Sin Far brings together and complicates the various vectors of American identity categories and their literary representation under discussion in this book, and so offers a fitting place to end this study.

Although the Chinese were a much needed economic presence in the United States, legally and culturally, they quickly came to occupy the position of outsider. As Amy Ling notes, "Anti-Chinese sentiment had been high nearly from the beginning of Chinese immigration, as demonstrated in a series of statutes and resolutions passed at the city and state levels, particularly in California, where most Chinese immigrants landed and remained" (*Between* 23).[8] The Foreign Miner's Tax of 1852 is an early example of California's anti-Chinese legislation; although it was originally passed in 1850 and aimed primarily at Mexicans and South Americans, after 1852 it was enforced, as Stanford Lyman notes, "almost exclusively against the Chinese" (163). Meanwhile, the 1854 California Supreme Court *People v. Hall* decision put the Chinese in the same legal category as American Indians, disqualifying their legal testimony against whites and, more importantly, defining them as "nonwhite" and so ineligible for citizenship.[9] While the 1886 Supreme Court decision *Yick Wo v. Hopkins* established "that the Constitution protects all individuals inside the United States, including aliens, from invidious discrimination at state hands," as legal scholar Hiroshi Motomura points out, "later cases made clear that this principle would apply only outside the immigration context" ("Curious Evolution" 1626).

However, the immigration context became crucially important because racialized anti-Chinese bias occurred in a period of broad cultural unrest. As Ronald Takaki puts it, the "closing decade of the nineteenth century witnessed America in crisis: the frontier had come to an end, migration of peoples from Asia and Europe broadened ethnic diversity and provoked the rise of nativism, class conflicts intensified, and at the same time the economy became stagnant" (*Iron Cages* 292). One response to this crisis was a national scapegoating of the Chinese that was played out on the terrain of racialized immigration regulations. These regulations culminated in a series of anti-immigration acts, beginning with the 1882 Chinese Exclusion Act, an act suspending nearly all immigration for a period of ten years. The act was extended for another ten years by the 1892 Geary Act, then extended indefinitely in 1904, to remain on the books until 1943. Hence, while expanding labor needs drew great numbers of Chinese men to America in the second half of the nineteenth century, legislation increasingly barred women or additional men from entering. As a result there were comparatively few women in the Chinese-American community, leading to the image by the late nineteenth century of the Chinese as a "bachelor" society.[10]

Hiroshi Motomura articulates "the fundamental questions that immigration law poses" as "who are 'we' as a community, and what do we demand of those who want to join?" ("Immigration Law" 546). In the period during which Sui Sin Far published—the late 1880s to shortly before her death in 1914—the United States answered these questions largely through the figure of the Chinese immigrant. While the narrative of immigrant assimilation dictated that the immigrant must be, as Stow Persons describes it, "absorbed into the population . . . made to approximate an ideal American type" (42), by being categorically defined as nonwhite the Chinese immigrant was both legally ineligible for citizenship and culturally figured as eternally Other, "a race," as Amy Ling puts it, "generally perceived as alien and unassimilable" ("Reading" 69). From unwritten laws relegating Chinese to small specific "Chinatowns" in all the major American cities to the legal prohibition of marriage between "whites" and "Mongolians" passed in 1880, to the Exclusion legislation, dominant American culture made it clear that the Chinese immigrant (whether or not she or he wanted to) would not be permitted to assimilate into mainstream white culture. Rather, defined as sojourners, a term that Sucheng Chan reminds us "excludes them [Chinese immigrants] categorically from American immigration history" (xx), Chinese immigrants guaranteed the limits of the nation, the point where the American "us" became "them."

The contradictions that "place Asians 'within' the U.S. nation-state, its workplaces, and its markets, yet linguistically, culturally, and racially marked Asians as 'foreign' and 'outside' the national polity" (Lowe 8) have been replicated spatially in the creation of urban "Chinatowns." A form of urban ghetto, "Chinatowns" developed as the Chinese were pushed out of the labor market and relegated to the lowest levels of work. They reflect, as Robert Blauner argues, "the basic contradiction of racial systems, which bring nonwhites into a society to appropriate their land or labor and not to associate with whites as free and equal citizens" (32). As separate commercial enclaves, however, they also "served as an economic basis for ethnic solidarity, and their business and cultural separateness in turn reinforced both their image and condition as 'strangers'" (Takaki *Strangers* 13–14). Chinese Americans were thus caught in an ideological double bind in which they were forbidden entry via assimilation into "mainstream" America. At the same time, while dominant culture fostered the growth of Chinese community in spatial terms by more or less forcing the Chinese into Chinatowns, it simultaneously also prevented or at least retarded the development of separate Chinese-American families by controlling immigration, particularly of Chinese women. Chinatowns thus become, as Lisa Lowe reminds us, "at once the deviant space ghettoized by the dominant configurations of social space and the resistant locality that signifies the internalization of 'others' within the national space" (122). Not surprisingly, then, questions of community and national identity and place were at stake in very material ways for Chinese in late-nineteenth-century and early-twentieth-century America, and in ways unique to the Chinese as an immigrant group.[11]

The position of Eurasians like Sui Sin Far, who in her autobiographical essay calls herself a "halfbreed" (228), was arguably even more complicated and shifting, located as it was on the borders of both Anglo and Chinese America. Sui Sin Far reflects this complex sense of place, for not only does her work focus mainly on life in various borderlands, she also persistently located herself in multiple margins—racial, ethnic, and national—a location she clearly saw as providing her with a kind of trickster mobility and consequently the ability to critique culturally fixed binary oppositions.[12] In contrast to this thematizing of border and multiple locations, however, critics in Sui Sin Far's own day felt compelled to fix a location for her and her work, an effort that recasts the writer's work in order to conform to the binary structures of identity that this work challenges. For these critics the "problem" of how to categorize the literary form (and, relatedly, the value) of Sui Sin Far's work is solved by an easy recourse to her racial identity. As I will argue, this discourse was used to marginalize both Sui Sin Far and her work in her own day, neutralizing the force of her social critique. Contemporary feminist critics who are engaged in a serious attempt to restore Sui Sin Far's literary status and to listen to the multiple and complicated voices issuing from her texts have understood both her identity and its relation to her work in more complicated terms, terms that recognize the complex racial formations in circulation around this writer and her work.

Fixing Identities: Critical Responses to Sui Sin Far and Her Work

Reviews of Mrs. Spring Fragrance set the original terms of the discussion of literary location in rhetoric that implicitly reduces Sui Sin Far's literary place to her racial/ethnic identity, a link made ultimately by way of regionalism. Alternately taking seriously and dismissing the stories, many reviewers read the collection as political protest fiction or realism, aimed at educating white audiences about the mistreatment of Chinese in America. The Independent review, for instance, states that the "conflict between occidental and oriental ideals and the hardships of the American immigration laws furnish the theme for most of the tales and the reader is not only interested but has his mind widened by becoming acquainted with novel points of view" (388). The *New York Times*'s review also labels the stories as descriptions of hitherto unrepresented worlds but codes this somewhat differently, calling the book "a new note in American fiction," a portrait "for readers of the white race [of] the lives, feelings, sentiments of the Americanized Chinese of the Pacific Coast, of those who have intermarried with them and of the children who have sprung from such unions" (405).

This comment implies educational value but also begins to bleed into the rhetoric of the voyeuristic observer of the exotic peoples, a valence even more clearly represented in the advertisement of the book located directly below its review in the *New York Times*. The ad displays the book's title and author in the form of hand-lettered calligraphy accompanied by Chinese characters, images that appear on the book itself and clearly point to the orientalizing tone of the ad.[13] The copy furthers this tone:

> Quaint, lovable characters are the Chinese who appear in these unusual and exquisite stories of our Western Coast—stories that will open an entirely new world to many readers.
>
> Our understanding and sympathy are awakened by the joys and sorrows of Little Me, Pau Tsu, Tie Co, and the Prize China Baby, while their misdeeds and misfortunes become of absorbing interest. Altogether they make as desirable reading as the title suggests. (405).

This orientalizing vision of the lovable and "quaint" Chinese offers the East Coast, white audience an entertaining glimpse into a nonthreatening, exotic world where social and political content have disappeared: the Chinese become little more than a "desirable" object of consumption; Mrs. Spring Fragrance herself becomes, as the *Boston Globe* review calls her, simply "that delicious Americanized person."

The terms of this "exoticism," though, are complicated. They are first linked to Sui Sin Far's own identity: the *New York Times* review gestures toward this by referring to "the unusual knowledge she undoubtedly has of her theme" (405).[14] More directly, the *Montreal Daily Witness* makes a point of identifying Sui Sin Far as "a Canadian Chinese, or half Chinese, woman" then goes on to insist on her close relationship to the communities she chronicles while simultaneously explicitly marking her parentage: she is a woman "whose sympathies range her on the side of the Chinese mother rather than of the British father" (quoted in White-Parks's *Sui Sin Far/Edith Eaton* 48).[15] Hence, these reviews imply, the stories are exotic because of the racial/ethnic "difference" they represent, a difference replicated and authorized by their author's "difference." At the same time, however, as the ad's reference to the "Western Coast" and the *New York Times*'s reference to the "Pacific Coast" suggest, racial or ethnic "difference" here is conflated with regional "difference": these stories offer the (Northeast) center a view of the (Western) margins, just as Ruiz de Burton's fiction does. This conflation, significantly, is echoed in generic terms. That is, the rhetoric used here to describe representations of Chinese-American and Chinese-Canadian life is precisely the rhetoric used elsewhere at the time to describe representations of regional life or local color: witness *The Independent*'s description of the stories as "dainty" (388); the *Montreal Daily Witness* review's characterization of the collection as "one of the charming gift books of the season" (quoted in White-Parks's *Sui Sin Far/Edith Eaton* 48); and the *Boston Globe*'s recommendation of the book to "any person with half a day to spare." Kate Chopin's bayou stories, recall, were described by reviewers as quaint and charming depictions of "primitive" Louisiana folk. This coupling of racial/ethnic difference with regional exoticism and a subsequent dismissal of both in gendered terms—diminutive "feminine" modifiers—appears even in Sui Sin Far's publishers' representations of her. In the November 1909 "With the Publishers" column of *The Westerner*, for instance, the editor calls Sui Sin Far "one of the cleverest writers on the Pacific coast," then goes on to print a letter from her, in which she herself links her regional and racial affiliations, writing,

There may be a certain literary prestige in having one's work accepted by the Eastern critics; but my stories and articles in "The Westerner," "Out West," and "Post-Intelligencer" accomplish more the object of my life, which is not so much to put a Chinese name into American literature, as to break down prejudice, and to cause the American heart to soften and the American mind to broaden towards the Chinese people now living in America—the humble, kindly, moral, unassuming Chinese people of America.

This statement suggests that Sui Sin Far was aware not only of regional categorizations in American fiction, nor simply of the Eastern audience's position as consumers of regional fiction. She also understood that audience's tendency to associate the regional area of the West, and California especially, with the Chinese while simultaneously understanding ethnically marked fiction as generically regional.[16]

What these rhetorical constructions suggest is threefold. First, the critics assessed Sui Sin Far's work by drawing on the available literary and cultural categories, and those categories dictated that her work (like everyone else's) be defined in relation to certain sets of binary oppositions. This occurred despite the fact that the content of her work pushes to col-

lapse or at least to complicate dualistic models. Second, certain representations of ethnic or racial identity come to function structurally within literary canon formation as a form of American regionalism, i.e., a marginalized and diminutive literary form.[17] Third, as a result of this equation,
both forms get written out of the category of "serious" American fiction,
their political content elided. Xiao-Huang Yin points to this effect, arguing that "prior to her [Sui Sin Far] 'Chinamen' were chiefly used as a rich
source of local color to reinforce the exotic effects of various kinds of tall
tales" (56). Local "color," as applied to Sui Sin Far's representation of the
"Chinamen," thus might be read as condensing the regional, the national,
the ethnic, and the racial Other, all of whom are located at the periph-
eries, serving to entertain and reinforce the boundaries of the center. The
literary locating of Sui Sin Far's work in her own day thus exoticizes her
fiction and dilutes its political force by casting her as an ethnic regionalist. It also oversimplifies her work's content and form, reducing a hetero-
logic voice to a monologic one in order to fit it into pre-existing literary
and national/regional/racial categories.

More recently, Sui Sin Far's work has come under reassessment, a reassessment that not only recognizes but indeed underscores the political
nature of her writing.[18] Perhaps as a result of this focus, contemporary
critics have explored Sui Sin Far's relationship as a Eurasian to Chinese-
American and Chinese-Canadian communities, reading both these communities and the identities that constitute them less as innate and more as
grounded in process. Argued in terms of cultural practices or process
rather than in terms of some essentialized understanding of "blood," this
notion of identity reflects Stuart Hall's formulation of identity as "a 'production', which is never complete, always in process, and always constituted within, not outside, representation" (222).[19] This formulation allows for a more subtle and complex relationship between identity and
community, and it underscores the role of representation in this relationship: Hall goes on to note that he envisions representation as "able to
constitute us as new kinds of subjects, and thereby enable us to discover
places from which to speak" (936–37).

Contemporary feminist critics emphasize this sense of process both in
Sui Sin Far's identity and relationship to Chinese-American community,
and in her representations of these. In an early discussion, for instance,
Amy Ling emphasizes Sui Sin Far's distance from the Chinese community,
commenting, "how foreign Chinese was to Sui Sin Far is demonstrated in
her referring to herself as Miss Far in her autobiographical essay. In Chinese, the family name comes first; thus she should have been Miss Sui"

("Writers" 414), while later in her introduction to Part One of Mrs. *Spring Fragrance and Other Writings* she points out "that Sui Sin Far was indeed an outsider to Chinatown and unfamiliar with the Chinese language," citing as an example of this the appearance in the author's "Chinese Laundry Checking" of a laundry receipt in which the Chinese characters are printed upside down (12).[20] In her groundbreaking study, *Between Worlds: Women Writers of Chinese Ancestry*, however, Ling tracks Sui Sin Far's increasing knowledge of and relation to that community, locating her ultimately "between worlds" and reads Sui Sin Far's personal location as at least partly determining of the fiction she produced. She argues that Sui Sin Far's and her sister's use of pseudonyms served "not so much to cloak their English patronym but to assert and expose their Asian ancestry. Both pseudonyms were the means to imply and thus acquire an ethnic authenticity to support writing careers based in large part on ethnic themes" (21). In a process that replicates in some ways the logic of the "one drop" theory of blood,[21] ancestry of any degree here produces identity, which informs literary content. Lisa Lowe calls for a consideration of "'Asian American cultural practices' that produce identity," arguing that these processes "are never complete and are always constituted in relation to historical and material differences" (64). Ling's reading points to the historical and material forces that produced a child schooled in the British culture of her father and kept from the Chinese culture of her mother, as well as the forces that enabled the young woman that child became to reclaim a connection to Chinese America through her writing.

Annette White-Parks, too, in her introduction to Part Two of Mrs. *Spring Fragrance and Other Writings*, tracks a shift in Sui's positioning from that of a "sympathetic outsider" to the Chinese-American community, a woman who in 1896 was still seen as an "English woman" (171), to that of "a Eurasian, an insider to the experiences she relates" by 1909 (173).[22] Interestingly, White-Parks uses Sui Sin Far's own broad definition of Chinese-American communities; that is, Sui Sin Far's "mixed blood" functions not to disqualify her from Chinese-American identity status but rather to entitle her to claim it. White-Parks, for instance, asserts that Sui Sin Far's articles from 1909 forward "illustrate Sui Sin Far's increasing identification with the Chinese American community; these writings are the first in which she explicitly identifies herself as a Eurasian and speaks with an insider's voice" (173); rhetorically, Eurasian here counts as Chinese American.[23] At the same time, however, White-Parks allows for the sort of multiple and shifting identity locations that Sui Sin Far herself promulgated. In her impressively painstaking and detailed biography of Sui

Sin Far, White-Parks at times, as above, seems to naturalize "the Eurasian" as a subset of "the Chinese in North America," while at other moments she reads "the Chinese in North America" and "the Eurasian" as separate categories, arguing that Sui Sin Far is representative of both (1). At still other times she more specifically locates Sui Sin Far as representative of only the Eurasian, although in contact with the Chinese-American. This is apparent when she describes Sui Sin Far's *Westerner* pieces as showing that in the late work of her career, "as a narrator Sui Sin Far was careful to position herself on the borderland, in the 'third person' stance she termed 'Eurasian,' rather than to claim full status as a Chinese American 'insider'" (163). The ultimate effect of this sense of shifting process is White-Parks's quite persuasive argument that Sui Sin Far used her borderland position—her identity as Eurasian—as a sort of enabling trickster location.

Contrast this with S. E. Solberg's description of Sui Sin Far as "an individual without racial, national, or group claims" (36), an interpretation that reads her borderland positioning as fixing her identity and shutting her out of any location, rather than giving her access to multiple ones. Like the original reviewers of *Mrs. Spring Fragrance*, then, Solberg links this biographical positioning to both the content of Sui Sin Far's work and its formal qualities, claiming,

She was not a regionalist nor nationalist. If anything, she was an internationalist. . . . She is not naturalist or local colorist, and her essays at humor . . . can hardly be looked upon as falling in the Mr. Dooley or Mark Twain 'native American' style. She was trapped by experience and inclination into working with a sub-genre of American prose: what, for lack of a better term, we might call Chinatown Tales. Such classification by subject matter (Chinatown, or more broadly, the Chinese in America) breaks down an established literary form, the novel, into sub-genres defined by content, not form or stylistic skill. (32)

Unlike Ling or White-Parks, Solberg unproblematically reads Sui Sin Far's biography as determining her work's content ("She was trapped by experience and inclination"), then—like the early reviews of her fiction—collapses content and generic form. Presuming a fixity to both the author's personal locations and her work's generic location, Solberg sets up an analogy between the two, the use of "regionalist" both suggesting the literary category and, when used in relation to "nationalist" and "internationalist," implying the author's personal identification with and championing of an area. Just as Sui Sin Far's personal positioning here leaves her fixed outside the American border on the dominant map of national identity, her writing also falls into the interstices of American literature, categorized as a marginal form that confirms a literary center just as the national outsider confirms the insider. Significantly, this move also collapses genre and content, defining the fiction's subject matter ("the Chinese in America") as a form of American regionalism: content here replaces form as the determining factor of a genre.[24] Solberg argues, indeed, that literature about the Chinese was "an essentially formless field" (32); that is, a category to be described not in terms of its formal elements but only in terms of its subject matter. This description has roughly the same effect as the early reviews of Sui Sin Far's work; it employs a rhetoric that establishes writing about an Othered American community as a form of (ethnic or racial) regionalism, depoliticized, fixed, exoticized, and outside the privileged categories of American fiction.

Elizabeth Ammons, in *Conflicting Stories*, offers a more contemporary discussion of form's relation to subject matter, providing a sophisticated and nuanced reading that, rather than replicating earlier marginalizing of both this form and content, reevaluates both. She points out that because Sui Sin Far did not write in the privileged literary form of her day—the novel—critics have challenged the value of her work (116). But rather than read her as a failed novelist, Ammons suggests that we read Sui Sin Far as successful in the attempt to do something other than write a novel, then links her choice of form to this "other" effort. Arguing that Sui Sin Far's effort was to portray a community, she notes that the novel form, a form closely linked to the rise of the bourgeois individual, would not be the ideal form for Sui Sin Far, concluding that shorter narratives would work better. In an illuminating comparison, Ammons links Sui Sin Far to Sarah Orne Jewett, arguing that "like Jewett before her . . . she manipulated to her advantage the tradition of regional and sketch fiction that she inherited primarily from women to offer not a long narrative about one individual but a multifaceted, collective narrative about a group of people and a network of issues" (118).[25] Ammons thus pays attention to biographical location but reads it as inflecting rather than determining Sui Sin Far's choice of subject matter and form, as neither authorizing nor overdetermining Sui Sin Far's words.

Lisa Lowe offers further insight into the connections between identity and representation, arguing that the Asian-American immigrant subject cannot be represented in the novel's narrative of development, a narrative that produces "national or cultural uniformity" (51). Instead, she sees a "'performativity' of immigration" at work in the formal choices of Asian-American writers that leads to an "aesthetics of disidentification and the practices of resignification that the 'outsider-within' condition of Asian in

America enables" (33). This approach usefully illuminates Sui Sin Far's work. The analogy between Sui Sin Far's structural positioning as marginal to dominant white culture and her work's literary marginalization from canonical American fiction is illustrative here. That Sui Sin Far is, on the basis of her race, read as a marginalized American subject both parallels and enables a literary marginalizing of her work on the basis of its "racial/ethnic" content, indicating just how salient a force ethnicity/race continues to be.[26]

In fact, however, her deconstruction of a strictly biologized version of racial identity and her representation of shifting and multiple processes of community and individual identity formation provides a powerful critique of the binary oppositions used to contain her and her work. In throwing these categories of identity into disarray, Sui Sin Far does not create a utopic new site or subject of American identity, but the categorical chaos her work produces performs important labor necessary to this project.

Representative Sui Sin Far

Sui Sin Far herself, in both her autobiographical essay and elsewhere, specifically addresses the question of her own cultural positioning and that of Eurasians like herself, a thematizing of the issue that certainly partially accounts for the degree to which it has become a salient feature in critical assessments of her work. Ammons argues, and I would agree, that the fact "that Sui Sin Far invented herself—created her own voice— out of such deep silencing and systematic racist repression was one of the triumphs of American literature at the turn of the century" (105). Rather than focusing on the depth of that silencing and racism, a topic well-charted by others, I would like to focus on Sui Sin Far's invention of herself, not so much in the sense that Ammons suggests—the coming to voice—but rather in the sense of the actual invention of a persona through representation. Unlike most of Sui Sin Far's critics, I would like to approach her autobiographical essays not simply as transparent accounts of facts of her life, but rather as sites, no less than her fiction, of the invention of a character, a representation: Sui Sin Far as both a rhetorical construction and a representative voice.[27] For like Hopkins, Ruiz de Burton, and Converse, she constructs a protagonist in her essays who stands as representative: but the question in terms of Sui Sin Far is, representative of what?

Stuart Hall asserts that cultural identity "is a matter of 'becoming' as well as of 'being.' It belongs to the future as much as the past" (225); this emphasis on process is suggested in Sui Sin Far's self-construction most literally by tracking her use of her pseudonym. Sui Sin Far's self-naming moved from her early bylines—from 1888 onward—which identified her as "Edith Eaton" or "E.E." to her work in the 1890s through around 1905, which she signs in various ways: "Sui Sin Fah," "Edith Eaton," "Sui Sin Far," "Sui Seen Far," and "Edith Eaton (Sui Sin Far)." By the publication of her important late autobiographical essays in 1909, however, Sui Sin Far was naming herself "Sui Sin Far" (in "Leaves") and "Sui Sin Far/Edith Eaton" (in her sketches published in the *Westerner*), while the 1912 *Mrs. Spring Fragrance* is attributed to "Sui Sin Far."[28] This variety of names serves as a literal record of Sui Sin Far's shifting affiliation with Canadian, Chinese, and Eurasian identities. As Ling and White-Parks have pointed out, Sui Sin Far changes alignments in a trajectory which moves generally from a self-identification as Canadian to Eurasian. In "A Plea for the Chinese," for instance, a defense of the Chinese in Canada published in 1896 in the *Montreal Daily Star*, she locates herself with statements such as "the Chinese who come to *our* shores are not 'scum'" (195 emphasis added). But by the time she writes her autobiographical "Leaves from the Mental Portfolio of an Eurasian," however, she identifies herself as a Eurasian. This trajectory turns out not to be simple at all, for it throws into question the meaning of Eurasian: is it a national identification (and so in opposition to "Canadian") or a description of racial/ethnic positioning (and so potentially a subset of "Canadian")?

The answer for Sui Sin Far appears to be both: over and over in her writing she blurs the lines between national, ethnic, and racial identity by means of a self-conscious rhetorical construction of a self who relentlessly crosses and collapses borders, offering itself as representative of several conflated and confounded categories at once. What is striking about Sui Sin Far's statements on the subject of her individual, racial, regional, and national identities is not only the degree to which she refuses to locate herself on one side or another of a number of different dichotomies, but also the degree to which she refuses the dichotomies altogether, insisting instead on blurring lines, collapsing categories, and using various different identity categories as interchangeable or as substitutions for each other. Sui Sin Far's persona thus both embodies a challenge to categories and borders, and it provides a figure through which her work can interrogate these categories, reworking marginal categories' relations to each other and to the "center."

Firstly, Sui Sin Far—in both her writing and her life—consistently dis-

rupts dominant cultural constructions of nation and individual identification with a single nation, offering instead a transnational view of herself
and North America. Living all over both Canada and the United States,
Sui Sin Far cannot adequately be described as either "Canadian" or
"American." She is never simply one or the other, both because the details
of her biography defy this national categorization and because as cultural
Other she represents a complicated Other internal to each of these national identities—Chinese-Canadian or Chinese-American. Representing
the Chinese in America, for instance, Sui Sin Far represents what her contemporaries viewed as an internal national Other: historically, recall, Chinese immigrants had been viewed as unassimilable sojourners—citizens
of another nation temporarily living in the United States but ultimately
returning to China, never destined to become "American." Sui Sin Far
speaks to this view of the Chinese as a nation within a nation in America
in her portrait of San Francisco's Chinatown community in "A Chinese Is-
mael," specifically through the story's treatment of the Chinese Six Companies' role in community life.[29]

Historically at the top of a pyramid of internal regulatory bodies in
Chinatown and made up of district associations deriving from China, the
Chinese Six Companies was "the most important association representing the Chinese community to the larger society;" it "challenged the dis-
criminatory laws and protested against anti-Chinese harassment and violence" (Takaki, *Strangers* 113). It also functioned within the Chinese
American community, where it "helped settle interdistrict conflicts and
provided educational and health services to the community" (Takaki,
Strangers 113). The importance of the Chinese Six Companies sprang in
part from the exclusion of the Chinese from American jurisprudence: as
Tomás Almaguer puts it, "lacking any meaningful recourse to state and
local government, the Chinese Six Companies frequently functioned as a
quasi-government for the Chinese community" (157). Sui Sin Far's representation of the Chinese Six Companies foregrounds their status as a sort
of Chinese governmental body that is internal to the United States and
fills the void left by the fact that the Chinese had little recourse to American due process of law. Hence, rather than read this story, as James
Doyle does, as a "melodrama . . . related to the Chinese inability to adapt
to the West" (52), I would suggest we read it as precisely about a Chinese-
American adaptation and resistance to their marginalization within U.S.
jurisprudence and culture.

When the story's Lum Choy goes to the Chinese Six Companies asking
for help in recovering a runaway slave-girl, Ku-Yum, the council tells

him, "Lum Choy has suffered grievous wrongs, and we must do all in our power to assist him in bringing his wronger to justice; but the purchase of slave-girls, which is just and right in our own country, is not lawful in America. Therefore, the task of recovering Ku Yum cannot be undertaken by the Six Companies. It must be intrusted to the hands of private parties and conducted secretly" (48). This passage suggests that the Chinese Six Companies represents a sort of Chinese regulatory body at work within the United States, implying the coexistence of two national juridical systems. But by having the Chinese Six Companies advise Lum Choy on an alternate means of attaining justice (the return of his slave via the work of "private parties"), the story leaves ambiguous the status of a Chinese-American legal system. That is, while the story establishes that an American citizen has no claim to a slave within the American legal system, by offering Lum Choy a means of getting what he wants, the Chinese Six Companies implicitly recognizes his exclusion from this system. Moreover, by sanctioning the Chinese legal system's view of the matter, it implicitly recognizes it as no less valid than the American view. Hence, the story represents the two nations, through the metonymy of their legal systems, as overlapping, the fiction of national boundaries interrupted and replaced by a less categorically pure and discrete image of nations. By foregrounding Lum Choy's need for an alternative space to air his grievance, the story exemplifies Lowe's claim that "Chinatown society has reconfigured spatial discipline and has rearticulated the ethnic ghetto as a resistant, recalcitrant 'historical' space" (121).

But Sui Sin Far's depictions of Chinese life on this continent not only challenge a notion of internal singular national coherence, they also collapse external ideological borders between nations by showing Canada and the United States as similarly structured by racism. In "A Plea for the Chinaman," her 1896 letter to the *Montreal Daily Star*, for instance, Sui Sin Far protests a proposed tax on Chinese immigrating into Canada but immediately renders the national border between Canada and the United States arbitrary in this matter by citing evidence from both Montreal and New York Chinese communities and by criticizing both "America and British America"'s treatment of the Chinese immigrant (198).[30] This conflation of America and Canada is repeated in "Sui Sin Far, the Half Chinese Writer," where the narrator slides from one to the other as if differences between the two are insignificant in global terms. In a section titled "Arrival in America" the narrator states, "when I was 6 years old my father brought us to America. . . . We settled in Montreal, Can, and hard times befell" (289). Looking across the Atlantic from England, distinctions between the United States and Canada are subsumed under the sign of North America.

But while Sui Sin Far's work emphasizes the arbitrariness of national borders, it simultaneously throws the purity of the category of nation itself into question, overlaying notions of nation with those of race and ethnicity, exposing the reliance of myths of "America" on naturalized racial and ethnic markings. Through representations of the category "Chinese" Sui Sin Far accomplishes this both by blurring the lines between categories and by refusing the finality of any given categorical assignment. In "A Plea for the Chinaman," for instance, she first states that she has known "Chinamen in all characters," both good and bad, and draws from this the conclusion that "Nations are made up of all sorts" (192). Later in the same article, however, she codes "Chinese" as a racial rather than a national tag, in observations such as "some complain that they object to the Chinese because they will not settle here, nor associate with other races" (197). National, cultural, and racial categories here collapse upon each other. Similarly, in her meditation on her own positioning in "Leaves from the Mental Portfolio of an Eurasian," she reflects upon the effects of having an English father and a Chinese mother. At one moment she identifies Chinese as a race, commenting, "I have come from a race on my mother's side which is said to be the most stolid and insensible to feeling of all races" (221). But sentences later she states,

I am only ten years old. And all the while the question of *nationality* perplexes my little brain. Why are we what we are? I and my brothers and sisters. Why did God make us to be hooted and stared at? Papa is English, mamma is Chinese. Why couldn't we have been either one thing or the other? Why is my mother's *race* despised? I look into the faces of my father and mother. Is she not every bit as dear and good as he? Why? Why? . . .

I do not confide in my father and mother. They would not understand. How could they? He is English, she is Chinese. I am different to both of them—a stranger, tho their own child. (222, emphasis added)

A great deal is accomplished in this seemingly transparent representation of Sui Sin Far's childhood confusion. Race and nation are here used interchangeably, but the resulting category is neither singular or pure but rather mixed and complicated. In contrast to Florence Converse's model, both race and nation emerge here as mixed, multiple, heterogeneous, and interdependent, so that race and nation cannot be fully disentangled from the other or tidily divided into neat dichotomies.

Concurrently with this challenging of lines between categories, the passage collapses the binary oppositions upon which the American discourse of race is based. Recounting instances that illustrate the power of the "one drop" ideology—that is, the belief that having "mixed" blood locates her in the category of the Other—Sui Sin Far complicates that notion both by linking race and nation and by marking the "mixed" child as a third term to both racial and national dichotomies. The binary oppositions represented by her father and mother—English/Chinese, white/Chinese—are revealed as inadequate, unable to account for the third term of the Eurasian.

Sui Sin Far frequently uses the figure of the mixed-race child and generally uses the figure, as above, to call into question the underlying premises of American racial discourse. A passage in "Half-Chinese Children" offers a particularly focused example of this. In the context of a discussion of the marital options of mixed-race boys and girls (one in which the narrator claims that boys often marry white women while the girls' husbands, chosen by their fathers, are usually Chinese), the narrator comments, "in some families, one daughter is married to a Chinaman, another to an American. It gives food for thought—the fact, that a couple of centuries from now, the great grand children of the woman who married an American will be Americans and nothing else, whilst the descendants of her sister, who married a Chinaman and probably followed her husband to his own country will be Chinamen, pure and simple" (189). Once again displaying the American conflation of "American" with "white," the passage foregrounds the way dominant American discourse constructs nationality through a naturalized racial status. At the same time, the passage explicitly challenges the notion of the Chinese as the "alien" and unassimilable race, offering instead a vision of a future American population made up of mixed-race peoples. Whether we are to understand these peoples as one in which racial difference has been absorbed and erased or one in which it is the idea of racial purity that has disappeared is unclear, although the use of "pure and simple" makes this passage read as more than a little ironic in tone as well as self-consciously oppositional in content.

Annette White-Parks comments that "Sui Sin Far's condition was a duality (trilogy?) inherent at birth, given the split that society conceived between European and Asian ('West' and 'East'), the regions of her two parents" (240). The formulation "duality (trilogy?)" seems particularly suggestive, implying both the dominant American constructions of the world (the "West"/the "Orient"), of nationality (American/not American), and of race (white/other), and, at the same time, implying their inadequacy. More specifically, this formulation suggests not only the third term that

Sui Sin Far insists on recognizing but also the way in which it is made to stand for all Others, all categories not on the American/Western/white side of the binary opposition's bar. I have argued that Sui Sin Far's work deconstructs the binary; equally importantly, it also deconstructs this trilogy both by insisting on a recognition of difference and multiplicity within communities and identities and by refusing to locate her in one racial/ethnic category (much as she refuses to locate herself in one national category). Thus, if Sui Sin Far reflects dominant racial discourse in claiming at points to occupy the space of the Chinese in North America, she also insists on speaking as a Eurasian, an identity category she sees as linked to, but not interchangeable with, that of the Chinese.[31]

Indeed, Sui Sin Far explicitly multiply codes her own nationality/ethnicity/race, claiming as hers both "Chinese" and "Eurasian" (though, interestingly, never "English") and depicting herself as representative of both. Hence, like Converse in her representation of Enid, Sui Sin Far proffers the image of the martyr dying for the good of the people, evoking the image of Joan of Arc: "I dream dreams of being great and noble. . . . I glory in the idea of dying at the stake and a great genie arising from the flames and declaring to those who have scorned us: 'Behold, how great and glorious and noble are the Chinese people!'" (222). To this image of the representative servant of the Chinese people she adds the image of the representative servant of Eurasians, observing, "I believe that some day a great part of the world will be Eurasian. I cheer myself with the thought that I am but a pioneer. A pioneer should glory in suffering," a comment that, in its use of the pioneer image, also implicitly figures her as a representative American (224).

Moreover, this image's reliance on the future tense points to the way American identity is forged at the intersection of transnational capitalism, nationality, and race. Pursuing the idea of internal colonialism as a model for U.S. race relations, Robert Blauner draws comparisons between U.S. people of color and third-world nations, arguing that they share conditions of "economic underdevelopment, a heritage of colonialism and neo-colonialism, and a lack of real political autonomy and power" (72). He concludes that "the fate of colonized Americans is tied up with that of the colonial and former colonial peoples of the world" (72). While his model has its limits,[32] its invocation of colonialism explicitly links race to global economic and geographic relations: relations that might today be understood as the workings of transnational capitalism. That the position of the Chinese in America was understood in these terms during the nineteenth century is suggested by Ronald Takaki, who points out that in "the white imagination, the Chinese were located in the future. Unlike blacks and Indians, they were 'coming' to America; moreover, they were directly identified with America as a modern industrial society, and their presence as an 'industrial army of Asiatic laborers' was exacerbating the conflict between white labor and capital" (222). We might read Sui Sin Far as recasting this image of the Chinese as the menace of the future, the racial Other and foreign threat to domestic labor. In its place she offers an image of herself as Eurasian pioneer, a representative of the American future emerging from a breakdown of binaries of nation and race.

One result of this blurring of boundaries both within and between the categories of nationality, race, and ethnicity is an implicit challenge to the one-drop logic of racial categorization. Linking race, ethnicity, and nationality makes the category less essentialized, allowing for more of a sense of process and individual self-construction/location. Discussing Sui Sin Far's work, S. E. Solberg argues along these lines that "the most impressive aspect of the writing is the conviction that environment is more important that heredity, that race is an accident, and, when, as with the Eurasian, there is a question of choice, the individual has the power to make that choice" (35). But while Sui Sin Far does challenge the determinism of the one-drop school, she also consistently refutes the myth— here voiced by Solberg—of American bourgeois individualism, of free choice and self-determinism; if Sui Sin Far represents race as a social, not a strictly biological category, it remains a category that must always be understood in terms of its relation to centers of power. For Sui Sin Far's work emphasizes that nationality/race/ethnicity—identity categories in general—are never simply self-chosen but are also—even primarily—culturally assigned and always assigned in ways that work to naturalize and protect the dominant order. As Virginia Domínguez puts it in a discussion of racial identity, "the individual exercise of choice takes place within sociohistorical environments that deem only certain kinds of choices possible" (9). Moreover, the degree to which an individual has "choice" depends on her/his proximity to the center. Hence, because Sui Sin Far was born Edith Eaton and "looked" English (i.e., had some connection to centers of power), she paradoxically had the privilege to identify as Chinese-Canadian/American. The dominant culture allowed her claim to the "margins" more willingly than it would have allowed the reverse claim: there was less danger (both for her and to the structural systems of power) in the half-Chinese, half-English woman claiming to be Chinese than passing as white. Sui Sin Far's work, particularly in its emphasis on borders, consistently demonstrates that mobility—cultural and ethnic mobility as well as literal, physical mobility—is always dependent on and is a form of power.[33] Rather than showing us, in Solberg's terms, that race is an arbitrary "accident," Sui Sin Far's work reveals the individual always already interpolated into a much broader ideological system that shapes, although it does not fully determine, the individual's identity.[34]

In both "A Plea for the Chinaman" and "Leaves," for instance, Sui Sin Far makes an ostensible plea for the importance of the individual over the national, racial, or ethnic, a plea that appears to contradict her self-positioning as martyr for her people but ultimately relocates the individual in relation to these broader categories. In the former article she states, "what does it matter whether a man be a Chinaman, an Irishman, an Englishman or an American. Individuality is more than nationality. 'A man's a man for all that.' Let us admire a clever Chinaman more than a stupid Englishman, and a bright Englishman more than a dull Chinaman" (196). On a more specifically personal level, she closes her autobiographical essay with the claim, "After all I have no nationality and am not anxious to claim any. Individuality is more than nationality. 'You are you and I am I,' says Confucius" (230). Both these statements complicate their apparent valorizing of individual autonomy and self-determination. In the first statement the comparison between the "Chinaman" and the "Englishman" signals the autobiographical voice, for these are, of course, the terms of Sui Sin Far's parentage. But this national dichotomy is undermined by the list of nationalities that precedes it. Not only does the list offer multiple national categories, it can also be read in both racial and ethnic terms. That is, this list can be read as setting up a dichotomous racial contrast between Chinese and white. At the same time, of course, the list can be read ethnically to delineate not simply Chinese as an ethnicity but also the so-often unmarked categories of "white ethnicity": English, Irish, Scottish (in the reference to the Robert Burns poem) and, arguably (at least in the eyes of the dominant culture), "American." Similarly, Sui Sin Far's claim in her autobiography that she has no nationality but only an individual identity is immediately undercut by her reference to Confucius, which links her at the very least to a specific cultural/religious tradition. In both these cases Sui Sin Far's final point—ostensibly that nationality pales in the face of individual identity—turns out to be that nationality is comprised of and often naturalizes racial and ethnic identities. She thus offers an implicit critique of the American ideology of bourgeois individualism, of the Emersonian self-made man, by pointing out the larger structural determinants that help enable some and prevent others from acceding to that position.

Sui Sin Far goes on to complicate still further these questions of the relation between individual and national identity and the effects of centers
of power on how and by whom one's national, racial, and ethnic identity
is constructed. She does this by introducing geographical space, a material, American embodiment of margin/center, into the issue. Like Chopin
she strategically deploys regionalism, using the term in multiple ways that
ultimately link it to national identity. Just as reviewers of *Mrs. Spring Fragrance* identified it as not just portraits of the "Chinese" but also portraits of the "West" (and, analogously, identified it with both "ethnic"
and "race" literature as well as regional literature), Sui Sin Far deploys
the term "west" in a way that plays off of multiple meanings, both regional and transnational. In her autobiographical essay she refers to
friends in "the West," meaning the west coast of Canada, but then goes
on to comment, "So I roam backward and forward across the continent.
When I am East, my heart is West. When I am West, my heart is East. Before long I hope to be in China. As my life began in my father's country it
may end in my mother's" (230). What begins as an explicit reference to
regions of North America—Eastern vs. Western Canada—segues into a
reference to China, so that Sui Sin Far's claim that her heart is East might
be read as locating it either in Eastern Canada or in China, North America's notion of "the East." She employs this same device from the opposite perspective in "The Story of a Forty-niner," part of her newspaper series "The Chinese in America, Part III," where the Chinese laborer describes moving from China to California by saying, "I had better food
and more than I had ever had in my life, and the sunshine and freshness
of this western country transformed me both physically and mentally"
(245). Here "western country" condenses two meanings into one: Sui Sin
Far plays both on the notion of California as the regional "West" in the
eyes of America, and America's notion of itself as "the West" in global
terms in relation to China, perspectives that circle the globe in opposite
directions to meet in California gold country.[35]

This locating of California in a transnational context performs a yoking, overlapping, and blurring of categories of region and nation that
might stand as emblematic of Sui Sin Far's work. It also brings me back
to the issues of mobility, "chosen" racial/ethnic identity, and passing, specifically in relation to border crossing. That much of Sui Sin Far's fiction
focuses on border crossing and border communities (in all senses) is in
one sense only fitting, since she spent a good deal of her life crossing the
national border between Canada and the United States. As an image this
crossing condenses the various foci of my reading of Sui Sin Far's work.

The extreme limitations on Chinese immigration produced by the Chinese Exclusion Act of 1882 and its various extensions suggest that Sui Sin Far would have literally passed over national boundaries by passing as a white Englishwoman. Or as Annette White-Parks puts it, "that Sui Sin Far was able to manage border crossings without, as far as we know, any difficulty suggests her English name and appearance conferred an invisible Chinese status, one that she was forced to exploit whenever she crossed national borders" (101). The irony of this situation for a woman who dreamt of dying at the stake for the Chinese people was surely not lost on Sui Sin Far, but rather, I would argue, informs her vision. Her ability to cross this border, her mobility, results from her link to the centers of power; the racial privilege resulting from her "white" appearance allows her to cross literal borders as well as the more figurative borders of the Chinese-American community. At the same time, the need to "pass" underscores the very real and material power of cultural categories such as race. For if disclosed, her Chinese "blood" could have prevented Sui Sin Far's crossing national borders. Ironically, this situation, in demonstrating the cultural weight of appearance, demonstrates both the fictionality of "race"—that it is not traceable to biological origins or reliably legible on the body—and the material ramifications that fiction has. These multiple levels of meaning echo those found in Sui Sin Far's collapsing of borders in her fiction. She collapses borders in her life and work—an act she performs involuntarily simply by being of "mixed" blood, and at the same time is enabled to perform by virtue of her access to the center (her "whiteness")—while simultaneously emphasizing the extent to which such categorical borders position individuals, determining identity and cultural location.

White-Parks characterizes Sui Sin Far's work as having an "ambivalent stance" that reflects an ambiguous identity, "wrought from the division between the colonizer and the colonized in the North America in which she was working" (3). Such a formulation calls to mind the position of Ruiz de Burton, whose fiction, as I have argued, quite clearly reflects the tension inherent in a position of a people who have been both colonizer and colonized and indeed thematizes that issue directly. But where Ruiz de Burton's fiction attends to the question of what place the Californios will have in the nation (offering an argument for locating them as structurally central/privileged), Sui Sin Far's fiction and journalism is less intent on locating the Chinese-American community within centers of power. Unlike Ruiz de Burton writing of the Californios, Sui Sin Far could not, of course, on the basis of "blood," have represented either

Eurasians or the Chinese in America as part of Anglo centers of power.[36] Moreover, she was clearly less interested in America as a nation than in America in relation to other nations—Canada and China in particular. In any case, where Ruiz de Burton's fiction strains to erase racial difference and transform questions of race into those of class, Sui Sin Far's work (perhaps in part because of its author's tenuous legal position of racial privilege) focuses more explicitly on race, reflecting the knowledge that racial identity is both contingent and determining of social location and, at the same time, overlaps with and is inflected by ethnicity, gender, and nationality on a grid of identity.

Gendered Production of the Ethnic

Multiple and heterogeneous in their representations, both Sui Sin Far's journalism and stories depict Chinese-American communities made up of Chinese immigrants, first-generation American-born Chinese, marriages between Anglos and Chinese, "mixed bloods," Eurasian immigrants, and others, representations that resist the social determinism of an evolutionary discourse that would determine identity by "blood" and would insist on "purity" of both race and nation. Instead, her work represents Chinese-American identity and community as processes—in part individually chosen and in part culturally determined—specifically enacted through the gender and sexuality of her fiction's female characters. Lowe suggests that Chinese-American "culture—the ways in which it is imagined, practiced, and continued—is worked out as much 'horizontally' among communities as it is transmitted 'vertically' in unchanging forms from one generation to the next" (64). In Sui Sin Far's work cultural and individual identity takes its form through this active and often public horizontal process.

Gender roles both signal and help produce this location/identity, enabling or preventing, for instance, a heroine's movement across cultural borders and helping to shape the choices these heroines face.[37] More surprisingly, an individual's relation to community is also signaled and partly produced through a racially inflected sexuality: many of Sui Sin Far's stories focus on a Chinese-American woman's body, in a way that overlays its sex on its race to position the heroine. This strategy complicates the sources of individual and community identity, opening up the category of Chinese American to include "mixed bloods" like Sui Sin Far herself while indirectly responding to gendered stereotypes of Chinese women.

The body specifically functions here as the site of both maternal and erotic female desire, linking these desires in complicated ways to racial identity. This in turn figures women as crucial agents in the construction and transmission of culture. Here Sui Sin Far can be heard talking back to stereotypes of Chinese women specifically and of the Bachelor Society model of Chinese community in general. Dominant representations figured all Chinese women as prostitutes, a view that informed both the passage and enactment of the 1875 Page Law, for example, which attempted to prevent the immigration of "immoral Chinese women" (Peffer 28). George Peffer points out that the American consuls who enforced the law "suspected all but the wives of merchants and diplomats of prostitution" (42), a view shared by many Americans. In reality, as Lucie Cheng Hirata and Ruthanne Lum McCunn among others have shown, prostitution peaked in the 1870s, and thereafter while the number of women in Chinese-American communities remained low in the nineteenth century, those women present did indeed play a significant role in shaping their communities. Additionally, the numbers of Chinese women grew in the twentieth century, particularly after the 1906 San Francisco earthquake and fire made it possible for men to bring in their wives: Takaki notes a huge influx of Chinese women between 1907 and 1924 (*Strangers* 235) and reminds us that twentieth-century Chinatowns "were no longer way stations to service single-male workers in transit to the gold fields, farms, and railroads. While they remained a place of refuge for a bachelor society, Chinatowns became residential communities for families, Chinese economic enclaves, and tourist centers" (245).[38] Functioning both as workers and as transmitters of culture, women thus played an important role in Chinese community formation: in her depictions of women's relations to men, to their communities, and amongst themselves, I will argue, Sui Sin Far articulates this important role and locates it in relation to the various discourses of race, gender, ethnicity, and nationality of her day.[39]

Over and over in her fiction Sui Sin Far uses gender markers to signal a woman's cultural positioning; clothing and public behavior, for instance, become the indicators of a woman's adoption of dominant American values or, conversely, her defense of traditional Chinese values. The eponymous heroine of "Mrs. Spring Fragrance," the first story in Sui Sin Far's collection, for instance, is described by the narrator in that story as "even more 'Americanized'" than her merchant husband (17), a description attested to by Mrs. Spring Fragrance herself by the evidence of her clothing. "The Inferior Woman" (the second story of *Mrs. Spring Fragrance* and one that carries over the central characters of the first) contains the following observation: "'When I first came to America,' returned Mrs. Spring Fragrance, 'my husband desired me to wear the American dress. I protested and declared that never would I so appear. But one day he brought home a gown fit for a fairy, and ever since then I have worn and adored the American dress'" (30).[40] Similarly, clothing signals the conflict between maintenance of traditional values and assimilation in "The Americanizing of Pau Tsu," where her husband's gift of a "dress of filmy lace" meant to enable his Pau Tsu to "dress like an American woman when we go out or receive" (88) conflicts with his wife's desire to continue wearing "her peach and plum colored robes . . . a bit of Eastern coloring" (85). This same conflict is expressed in the domestic space of this story, for while the husband provides a home for his wife that is "furnished in American style" (85), she, by virtue of screens, fans, carvings, and other ornaments, "transform[s] the American flat into an Oriental bower," including "a little chapel" for the worship of her gods and ancestors (86). That Pau Tsu's private space is the site of her assertion of Chinese custom and that the dresses worn by both her and Mrs. Spring Fragrance are publicly visible and readable underscores the public and collaborative nature of the process of Americanization: this is a process enacted both by the individual and by the community's reading of her or him.

Conventional rules of interaction between the sexes also serve in these stories to help locate a character's relation to various communities: Sui Sin Far formulates interaction between men and women in American culture as less formal than that in Chinese culture, then represents Chinese-American culture and specifically gender practices as made up of a combination of both. In "Mrs. Spring Fragrance" Mr. Spring Fragrance voices what is consistently Sui Sin Far's representation of American relations between the sexes. In America, he says, "a man may speak to a woman, and a woman listen, without any thought of evil" (22); that Mrs. Spring Fragrance "speaks" to men who are not her husband serves as another indicator both of her "Americanization"—her location within the Chinese-American community rather than her original (pre-immigration) Chinese community—and of the ways in which the Chinese-American community itself has adapted to America by incorporating certain mainstream American customs and values while retaining certain Chinese ones. In contrast to Mr. Spring Fragance's description of America, China is described by the narrator of "The Wisdom of the New" as "a land where friendship between a man and woman is almost unknown" (46). Sui Sin Far offers a similar contrast between American and Chinese marriage customs and similarly represents Chinese-American communities as containing both. Mr. Spring Fragrance again becomes Sui Sin Far's spokesperson, asserting of America that "love . . . comes before the wedding in this country" (23) and noting that "in China, it is different" (24), a difference represented in "Children of Peace," a story from the "Tales of Chinese Children" section of *Mrs. Spring Fragrance*, where two young Chinese lovers marry for love without their parents' knowledge. When the marriage is revealed, the heroine, Pau Tsu, receives a letter from her parents asking "are you not ashamed to confess that you love a youth who is not yet your husband? Such disgraceful boldness will surely bring upon your head the punishment you deserve" (129). But Sui Sin Far disrupts this gendered national binary opposition in her representations of the multiple different forms of marriage occurring in the Chinese-American community she creates. The Spring Fragrances themselves offer a good example of the blurred lines between arranged and chosen marriage: "he had fallen in love with her picture before *ever* he had seen her, just as she had fallen in love with his! And when the marriage veil was lifted and each beheld the other for the first time in the flesh, there had been no disillusion—no lessening of the respect and admiration, which those who had brought about the marriage had inspired in each young heart" (25). Hence, this marriage embodies both the trope of American companionate marriage and the Chinese model of filial obedience to an arranged marriage. Peggy Pascoe asserts that, "in part because of the actions of mission-educated immigrant women, the gender system that came to characterize Chinese-American communities would be distinct from both the traditional Chinese system immigrants had brought to the United States and the Victorian system they encountered there" (171–72); Sui Sin Far's representation of a distinct and hybrid Chinese-American cultural practice of gender here and elsewhere offers a fictional example of this claim.

In biographical assessments both Amy Ling and Annette White-Parks rhetorically and more literally link Sui Sin Far's race to her gender and, implicitly, her sexuality. In *Between Worlds* Amy Ling notes that Sui Sin Far never married and refers to her description of herself in "Leaves" as a "very serious and sober-minded spinster" then goes on to argue that "that she boldly embraced this pejorative term was comparable to her insistence on asserting her Chinese identity. In both cases, she rejected the negative connotation and employed both terms with pride" (29).[41] Representing gender and race/ethnicity as distinct but analogous categories, Ling here sets up an analogy between two positions of marginality that Sui Sin Far occupied in a culture that privileged both whiteness and heterosexual family life. A few pages later, however, Ling implicitly rejects this analogy in her assessment of "Leaves," which, she argues, "touches only briefly on sexuality" and "focuses almost exclusively on ethnicity" (35), a comment that prizes apart the two categories more or less entirely. White-Parks similarly locates Sui Sin Far's marital status and her ethnicity/race in relation to each other, arguing that Sui Sin Far's "decision not to marry, her stand as a defender of Chinese North American populations, and her leave taking from Montreal were all steps in the labyrinth through which she would probe the ambiguities of her identity" (31). She later links these categories more explicitly, contending that the "question of race assumed additional importance in the lives of Sui Sin Far and her sisters by influencing their marriage choices; her dual parentage is no doubt one root of Sui Sin Far's choice not to wed and have children" (39). She also cites Sui Sin Far's representation of the mixed heritage of Sweet Sin, the protagonist in a story of the same name, as "at the core of Sui Sin Far's own rejection of marriage" (90). That White-Parks feels compelled to "explain" Sui Sin Far's unmarried state at all indicates both the degree to which heterosexuality continues to be the unmarked, universalized "norm" in North American culture and the extent to which gender roles (participation in the institution of family via the role of wife) continue to be grounded in the assumption of heterosexuality. Rather than reading gender and sexuality as parallel or analogous categories to those of race and ethnicity, I would like to turn to Sui Sin Far's fiction to demonstrate what I see as her interweaving of these categories and, more specifically, her use of both gender and sexuality (in terms both of desire in general and desire's object in particular) as markers of the female body and signifiers of that body's location in relation to Chinese-American communities.

"Its Wavering Image," from *Mrs. Spring Fragrance*, offers a particularly focused representation of these issues, using the protagonist's desire as the site where her racial identity and her relation to Chinese-American community is determined. A story in which the mixed-race Pan is betrayed by the white journalist Mark Carson, who makes her fall in love with him in order to use her as a story source, "Its Wavering Image" foregrounds Pan's parentage from the start, opening with "Pan was a half white, half Chinese girl" (61). Her white mother dead, Pan has been raised by her Chinese father in Chinatown, feeling "natural and at home" with "her father's people" but "strange and constrained" with her mother's (61). The narrative thus represents Pan as part of and different from the Chinese-American community in which she lives. This happy innocence—this construction of the community in terms of both/and rather than either/or—is ended by the advent of the white journalist, who awakens in Pan her erotic desire and simultaneously refigures her as marginal to her Chinese-American community. After causing Pan to fall in love with him, Mark Carson tells her first that she does not belong in Chinatown because she is "white," and then, when she protests, tells her that "You have got to decide what you will be—Chinese or white. . . . You cannot be both" (63). Although, in fact, the narrative has represented Pan as living quite happily as "both" up to Carson's arrival, his view of the world as a binary opposition comes to take precedence both for Pan and for the narrative as a whole. While she refuses to respond to Carson's demand that she "decide what [she] will be," she admits her love for him, an admission signaled by her shedding tears. Carson claims that her tears (and, implicitly, the love for the white man they signal) "prove" that she is white (64)—that is, that both the object of her desire and the fact that she experiences desire at all constitute "proof" of her whiteness.[42] His labeling of her also allows him to label her "alien" to the very community whose private ceremonies and beliefs she has shown him and which he has then exposed in his article (63). Locating her outside the Chinatown community, he rhetorically asks himself, "why should a white woman care about such things? Her true self was above it all. Had he not taught her *that* during the weeks in which they had seen so much of one another?" (65, emphasis in original). But, in fact, what he has taught her is to recognize both her own desire and the threat that this desire—and the "white" self it is here conflated with—will render her marginal to her home and community.

However, Sui Sin Far refuses to follow the conventional plotline of the doomed mixed-blood woman. The narrative suggests instead that it is Pan's imminent choice of "whiteness" in the form of a romantic attachment to Carson—a man aligned with the white world and attached to the Chinese community only through exploitative voyeurism—that is driving her plot toward misery. Rather than figuring Pan's half white/half Chinese status as predetermining tragedy, the narrative figures it as offering her a choice: a choice here between a loving, long-familiar community and an untrue suitor.[43] What makes this more than simply the story of a girl's narrow escape from a fall, however, is the narrative's alignment, on the one hand, of erotic desire with dominant Anglo-American identity and, on the other, of maternal desire with Chinese identity.

Although Pan ultimately casts off Carson, both she and the narrative itself structure her response in his binary oppositional terms, a narrative move that illustrates my claim that Sui Sin Far simultaneously reads binary oppositions as fiction and recognizes their powerful cultural effects.

Pan signals her rejection of Carson by changing from "American dress" to "the Chinese costume," asserting, "I am a Chinese woman" (66), a shift that accompanies her shift from claiming erotic desire to claiming maternal desire, and that is represented in the juxtapositioning of the story's final two scenes. In the first, Carson responds to Pan's claim of Chinese identity with "you cannot say that now, Pan. You are a white woman—white. Did your kiss not promise me that?" Pan responds, "a white woman! . . . I would not be a white woman for all the world. *You* are a white man. And what is a promise to a white man!" (66). This interchange is immediately followed by a description of Pan's illness after Carson's betrayal. A toddler comes to visit, prompting a new set of tears from Pan. The child's mother tells Pan, "Thou wilt bear a child thyself some day, and all the bitterness of this will pass away," a prediction followed by the narrator's observation "And Pan, being a Chinese woman, was comforted" (66). The story's two representations of Pan's tears figure as somatic indicators of her shifting alignments. The first set of tears suggests the erotic desire that the narrative aligns with white Anglo-American womanhood; the second signals Pan's maternal desire, which here locates her as part of the Chinese community.[44] Thus, it is the gendered and raced body that figures Pan's location in relation to the Chinese community. This reworking of bodily meaning foregrounds the cultural rather than the racial aspect of that community, and thus renders it open to Pan. It simultaneously operates as a narrative rebuttal of a discourse that read Chinese women as prostitutes—nonmaternal, highly sexualized figures—responding, like Hopkins and indeed all women of color, to a discourse that would fix the meaning of the woman of color's body.

American Families; "American" Masculinities

Pan's story exemplifies the ways in which Sui Sin Far's gender-shaped constructions of identity enables her to "talk back" to the turn-of-the-century racial discourse of "blood" that fueled discussions of American national identity. This defining of communities by reworking both their internal and external borders at the point where gender intersects with race and ethnicity occurs elsewhere in Sui Sin Far's work as well. *Mrs. Spring Fragrance*'s "The Story of One White Woman Who Married a Chinese" and its companion story "Her Chinese Husband: Sequel to the Story of the White Woman Who Married a Chinese" provide the first-person account of the white female narrator's first marriage to an "American," James Carson, and her second marriage to "Liu Kanghi, a Chinese" (66), setting up a contrast that enables the stories' focus on the issue of difference. But while racial and ethnic difference are certainly central to both stories, it is sexual difference and its social encoding in gender difference that are the explicit issues at play in the stories. Condensing race, ethnicity, and nationality, the narrator refers to her first husband as "an American," by which she also means white, but it is, ultimately, her marriage to Liu Kanghi that embodies the ideal American middle-class family unit, complete with conventional roles for husband and wife.

Although the narrator Minnie represents the problem in need of explanation as an issue of race/nationality ("Why did I marry Liu Kanghi, a Chinese?" [66]), she consistently represents the salient difference between her two husbands as one of gender, as represented by their relationship to the narrator. She is a white, working-class woman, a stenographer, who longs to embody conventional ideals of American femininity. She explains that a "home of my own filled my heart with joy. It was a pleasure to me to wait upon James, cook him nice little dinners and suppers, read to him little pieces from the papers and magazines, and sing and play to him my little songs and melodies" (67). Later she observes, "I am a narrow-minded woman. All I care for is for my husband to love me and be kind to me, for life to be pleasant and easy, and to be able to help a wee bit the poor and sick around me" (68). Spokesperson for sexual difference as sexual hierarchy and separate spheres, the narrator responds to Carson's vision of women as comrades of men with the observation that "much as I admired a column of men keeping step together, yet men and women thus ranked would, to my mind, be a very unbeautiful and disorderly spectacle" (67). After the birth of her child, she goes back to work as a stenographer to please her husband but pines for her baby and hates life in the public sphere, longing for her husband to join "the majority of men [who] had no wish to drag their wives into all their business perplexities, and found more comfort in a woman who was unlike rather than like themselves" (68). Her "American" husband, however, does not share this American dream: Sui Sin Far represents Carson as a self-serving Socialist who wants his wife to work outside the home (to help him "develop himself" [68] and write his book on socialism) and to share his political views.

The woman who embodies Carson's ideal serves as a foil to the narrator, providing an image of the un-American woman whose deviancy is marked not by her racial difference but by her resistance to conventional gender roles. Miss Moran, a bookkeeper with whom Carson writes his book, is described as "broad-shouldered, masculine-featured" and completely non-maternal, reacting to a sick child by commenting that "there is no necessity for its being sick. . . . There must be an error somewhere" (69). When Carson makes a pass at her, she knocks him down, an act that confirms her alignment with masculinity but, interestingly, also explicitly marks her as not to blame for his attempted infidelity. White-Parks argues that Sui Sin Far occupied "a border position on feminist issues" (167) while Ammons contends "One White Woman" demonstrates Sui Sin Far's "criticism of white middle-class feminism, portraying it as a culturally and class-based ideology that is arrogant and authoritarian in its ethnocentricity" (115): readings that the portrait of Miss Moran both does and does not confirm. While Moran replicates dominant stereotypes of the unsexed public woman, insensitive and able to repel Carson's advances while remaining "cool and collected" (71), Sui Sin Far is also careful to exonerate her from charges of betraying other women. Moran rebuffs Carson as soon as he propositions her, before either is aware that his wife has overheard the exchange, and while she does not understand the position of Carson's wife, it is the gender roles to which they aspire more than racial or ethnic difference that divides them. Hence, although racially "American," both Carson and Moran emerge here as distinctly radical and divergent from conventional American political and gender norms, not simply in their "advanced" Socialist political beliefs but more specifically in the gender roles in which these beliefs are made manifest.[45]

Against this foil Sui Sin Far offers the portrait of a conventionally normative American marriage, ironically represented by the narrator's marriage to Liu Kanghi. For it is only with Liu Kanghi that the narrator can achieve her American domestic dream; only he values and enables her desire for a conventional marriage based on a naturalized vision of gender difference. Analogous to Ruiz de Burton's portrait of the Californios, Sui Sin Far's depiction of Liu Kanghi represents him as embodying normative American gender ideals—here ideals of the family man—providing a conservative nuclear family life for Minnie, the narrator. He also stands simultaneously as the representative Chinese man; he is referred to as "just an ordinary Chinaman," a comment that, taken in context, suggests both a middle-class status and a status as representative man (79). Hence, the representative "Chinaman" becomes the idealized embodiment of the middle-class American husband and father, and becomes more the bedrock of the "American family" and the gender hierarchy on which it is based than the "American" man himself. From his initial appearance in the story, Liu Kanghi is shown to be a protector of women: he rescues the narrator and her child when they are wandering destitute, provides them shelter with a Chinese family, his cousins, then provides Minnie with a fittingly private and "feminine" employment: he pays her to do embroidering for his shop, work she can do while staying at home with her child.

That "One White Woman" and "Her Chinese Husband" are about American norms of masculinity, and masculinity specifically defined in relation to femininity, is underscored repeatedly as the narrator recounts her failed attempts to live the active/passive, male/female dichotomy with her first husband and her success at this with her second. Of Liu she states: "I followed him, obeyed him, trusted him from the very first. It never occurred to me to ask myself what manner of man was succoring me. I only knew that he was a man, and that I was being cared for as no one had ever cared for me since my father died" (72) then later adds "my Chinese husband has his faults . . . but he is always a man, and has never sought to take away from me the privilege of being but a woman. I can lean upon and trust in him. I feel him behind me, protecting and caring for me, and that, to an ordinary woman like myself, means more than anything else" (77). In contrast to this, she tells Carson, "You were unwilling to protect and care for the woman who was your wife or the little child you caused to come into this world; but he succored and saved the stranger woman, treated her as a woman, with reverence and respect; gave her child a home, and made them both independent, not only of others but of himself" (77).

Although masculinity is defined here in terms of the husband as figurative father of the wife, Sui Sin Far invokes literal fatherhood as well in her portrait, contrasting Carson's indifference to his child—"he did not ask for the child" (71) the narrator comments in recounting their divorce—with Liu Kanghi's loving and engaged attention not only to the son he and the narrator have, but also to his nieces and nephews and to the narrator's child from her marriage to Carson.[46] Sui Sin Far explicitly links the role of "good father" to that of Chinese-American masculinity in the ending of "Her Chinese Husband," where Liu Kanghi's murder is contextualized within a portrait of his happy domestic relations. The last image the narrator has of her husband alive is one in which her two children follow him to their gate as he leaves in the morning, each child asking to be brought a red ball. In the final lines of the story the narrator then recounts that "when they brought my Chinese husband home there were two red balls in his pocket. Such was Liu Kanghi—a man" (83), a rhetorical juxtapositioning that aligns concerned paternal love with idealized masculinity. In terms of the role of father/husband/protector, then, Liu performs American masculinity far more effectively than does Carson.

In this representation, however, gender difference—represented by Carson and Liu's differing styles of performing their gender—not only serves as the displacement of racial difference, gender itself is inevitably inflected by race and participates in the racial discourse of Sui Sin Far's day. For the depiction of Liu must be read as a refutation of the image of the bachelor Chinese sojourner: he is a dedicated family man, represented amidst a family and community rather than alone. Moreover, this image can also be seen as in conversation with the American stereotype of the emasculated Chinese man: Liu Kanghi is strong and determined, even to the point of being overbearing. In "Her Chinese Husband," for instance, he is described as "imperious by nature" and Sui Sin Far shows him telling his wife what to wear and reproaching her for expressing "certain opinions" (80). But this naturalized gender hierarchy intersects and conflicts with racial hierarchies: the narrator comments that her "white blood rose" (80) at her husband's reprimands. The narrative's complicated conflation of racial and gender hierarchies and simultaneous displacement of tension from the former to the latter emerges explicitly in the following passage from "Her Chinese Husband":

> There was also on Liu Kanghi's side an acute consciousness that, though belonging to him as his wife, yet in a sense I was not his, but of the dominant race, which claimed, even while it professed to despise me. This consciousness betrayed itself in words and ways which filled me with a passion of pain and humiliation. "Kanghi," I would sharply say, for I had to cloak my tenderness, "do not talk to me like that. You *are* my superior. . . . I would not love you if you were not."
>
> But in spite of all I could do or say, it was there between us: that strange, invisible—what? Was it the barrier of race—that consciousness? (81)

This passage simultaneously asserts a naturalized hierarchy of man and wife—she "belong[s] to him as his wife"—and overlays this with a racial hierarchy that challenges it, calling to mind Omi and Winant's observation that "racial minorities['] . . . distinctiveness from the white majority is often not appreciably altered by adoption of the norms and values of the white majority" (21). The wife's response to this dilemma is to defend her husband's superiority in terms that are, significantly, not specified. While the "barrier of race" implicitly continues to privilege the wife, the rhetoric of the passage simultaneously reinscribes the positioning of wife as object by its setting up of a conflict of "claims" to the wife between husband and "the dominant race," a conflict that uses the language of a property dispute.

Further, this passage raises another issue disputed by Sui Sin Far's critics and at stake in her representation of gender roles: passion and its relation to both conventional masculinity and conventional femininity. The tension over racial hierarchies produces in the narrator "a passion of pain and humiliation," a response that is as close as Sui Sin Far ever gets to representing any erotic desire in the narrator for her Chinese husband. While Sui Sin Far repeatedly represents Minnie's marriage to Liu Kanghi as based in mutual love, respect, and care, linked to the production of family and parental devotion of both father and mother, she does not characterize it as based in erotic desire. In contrast to this, she represents Minnie's marriage to Carson as grounded in erotic desire but lacking in love and paternal commitment and preventing Minnie from fulfilling her maternal desires:

James Carson had been much more of an ardent lover than ever had been Liu Kanghi. Indeed it was his passion, real or feigned, which had carried me off my feet. When wooing he had constantly reproached me with being cold, unfeeling, a marble statue, and so forth; and I . . . would wonder how it was I appeared so when I felt so differently. For I had given James Carson my first love. Upon him my life had been concentrated as it has never been concentrated upon any other. Yet—! (78–79)

Carson is characterized as stereotypically masculine in his passion, passion figured as active and erotic, as above, and as violent, as when he threatens his wife or when Sui Sin Far kills him off by "death of apoplexy while exercising at a public gymnasium" (77). There is here a multiple coding of masculinity as erotically attractive, violent, and non-intellectual, a coding repeated elsewhere in Sui Sin Far's writing and ambiguously valued. In "A Plea for the Chinaman," for instance, she reinterprets the stereotype of the Chinese as "docile and easily managed" (194) as "quiet dignity" (194) and asserts that the

Chinese are taught to treat the rude with silent contempt. A Chinaman does not knock a man down or stab him for the sake of an insult. He will stand and reason, but unless forced, though not by any means a coward, he will not fight. In China a man who unreasonably insults another has public opinion against him, whilst he who bears and despises the insult is respected. (195)

Which side of this cultural dichotomy of masculinity she valorizes is clear when she goes on to add that "in future we in this country [Canada] may attain to the high degree of civilization which the Chinese have reached, but for the present we are far away behind them in that respect" (195). Her use of the term "civilization" here signals that this representation of

Chinese masculinity is in conversation with late Victorian images of masculinity: in her depiction of white men Sui Sin Far draws on a dominant Euro-American stereotype of men as savage and sexual, then represents Chinese masculinity as superior to and more evolved than this norm.

More ambiguous, however, is her representation of the erotic desirability of the Chinese man to (implicitly heterosexual, non-Chinese) women. In a peculiar aside, Sui Sin Far claims in that same article that

I believe the chief reason for the prejudice against the Chinese, I may call it the real and only solid reason for all the dislike shown to the Chinese people is that they are not considered good looking by white men; that is, they are not good looking according to a Canadian or American standard for looks. This reason may be laughed at and considered womanish, but it is not a woman's reason, it is a man's. Women do not care half as much for personal appearance as do men. (197)

A similar moment appears in "Leaves," where she writes,

I also meet other Chinese men who compare favorably with the white men of my acquaintance in mind and heart qualities. Some of them are quite handsome. They have not as finely cut noses and as well developed chins as the white men, but they have smoother skins and their expression is more serene; their hands are better shaped and their voices softer.

Some little Chinese women whom I interview are very anxious to know whether I would marry a Chinaman. I do not answer No. (223)

She does not answer "Yes" either: Sui Sin Far's ambiguous representations here of Chinese masculinity certainly valorize what she represents as a characteristic intelligence and sensitivity, but she sets up and then sidesteps the question of their physical attractiveness. What seems salient here to me is not the question of whether or not Sui Sin Far found and/or represented Chinese men attractive (an issue some critics have used this passage to examine), but rather what is at stake in her pursuit of this issue at all. These passages all serve to foreground the stereotyping of the Chinese by virtue of their appearance, an issue that serves once again to remind us that racial identity is usually assigned and judged by culture rather than being self-chosen or defined. They also serve to remind us that masculinity as a cultural category is both historically and culturally contingent and so in flux in a hybrid transnational community.[47]

As Sui Sin Far's use of Carson as a name for both the "American" husband in "One White Woman" and "Her Chinese Husband" and for the white journalist in "Its Wavering Image" suggests, "Her Chinese Husband" shares that story's racialized dichotomy of erotic passion and maternal or here, more broadly, familial, desire. This representation, like the stories' representations of masculinity, offers multiple and complicated levels of meaning, for it is in conversation with several competing discourses of race and sexuality of Sui Sin Far's day. Focusing on the Chinese husband, Xiao-Huang Yin argues that Sui Sin Far here replicates dominant American stereotypes of the weak, emasculated, and de-eroticized Chinese man, claiming that "the lack of passion and masculinity of Chinese men contrasts sharply with the ruddy and stalwart image of American men and the rough elegance possessed by them" (79). He goes on to argue that Minnie views Liu as the ideal husband "not because he is attractive as a masculine or romantic figure, but because he is reliable and can provide her with a sense of security" (79).[48] Elizabeth Ammons reads this representation in a more positive light, commenting that "sexual passion, frequently the pretext for the sexual domination and exploitation of women in hierarchical heterosexual society, does not constitute the center of their relationship. Instead, at the heart of their bond is a genuine emotional compatibility and rapport" (115). In fact, both these readings are accurate and while seemingly at odds can be understood within the context of Sui Sin Far's intervention into both racial and gender discourses of her day via her racialized division of erotic and maternal/family desire.

In her representations of "American" and "Chinese" masculinity Sui Sin Far can be seen not only to be countering the bachelor society image of the Chinese male immigrant but also to be in conversation with various other competing stereotypes of Chinese masculinity. While at various points her portrait of Liu Kanghi might be seen as either challenging or replicating the stereotype of the emasculated Chinese man, her representation simultaneously is in conversation with stereotypes of Chinese men as vicious and violently treacherous. *Overland Monthly*, one of Sui Sin Far's main publishers, provides a context here: in its November 1899 issue, four months after Sui Sin Far's "A Chinese Ishmael" appeared in its July issue, a poem appeared called "Ah Foy Yam."[49] The poem describes a cook in a Western "cook-house," a man whose face, the poem asserts, "looks like a human's" only when "he's thinkin' bout his fambly back in Chiny." Described as a "pig-tailed heathen," and "satanical," Ah Foy Yam appears suspicious to the miners to whom he serves food:

> Mongolians is taught, they say, to answer back perlite:
> Ah Foy Yam is no exception. His cussin's a delight.
>> But his sleeves is big and spacious—plenty spacious fer a knife,
>> And his skinny hands look sometimes awful thirsty fer a life.

While the overall effect of the poem is to critique the miners' point of view rather than to support it, the articulation of this point of view replicates the image, widespread in dominant American culture, of the untrustworthy and deadly Chinese sojourner.

More specifically, Sui Sin Far's representation of Liu's marriage to Minnie can also be read as a rebuttal of the early stereotype of the Chinese man not just as aggressor but as sexual aggressor. Tomás Almaguer reminds us that Chinese men were "perceived as a threat to the moral well-being of the white population, and most especially to white women. As an overwhelmingly male immigrant population, Chinese men were initially seen as menacing sexual 'perverts' that preyed upon innocent white women" (160). One might read Sui Sin Far's de-eroticizing of Liu and Minnie's relationship as a strategy for diffusing the potential danger of representing an interracial couple by offering an image wherein, if the Chinese man gets the Anglo-American girl, he does so only to honor and protect her, not to ravish her. In the representation of Liu Kanghi, then, Sui Sin Far can be seen to be responding to the multiple and contradictory stereotypes in circulation around Chinese masculinity. In response both to these stereotypes and to that of the passionate but brutish white Socialist Carson, Sui Sin Far's representation offers an honorable and civilized Liu Kanghi, a man whose non-violent character and his bourgeois class status marks him simultaneously as a non-stereotypical Chinese-American and as more in keeping with Anglo-American ideals. Chinese-American masculinity thus emerges in this representation as ideal in both the private sphere of the family and the public sphere of the United States market economy, a racialized subject whose gender mediates his relationship to national identity.

Sui Sin Far's deployment of maternal and erotic desire in her representations of her heroines is similarly imbricated in surrounding cultural discourses. Linking Chinese womanhood in "Its Wavering Image" to the maternal, and linking erotic desire to heterosexual whiteness in this story as well as in "One White Woman" and "Her Chinese Husband," Sui Sin Far, like both Ruiz de Burton and Hopkins, directly challenges the racial and class inflections of the ideology of American True Womanhood, where the white middle-class woman occupied the space of the maternal and was defined as non-sexual, while Othered women—women of color and working-class women, primarily—carried the burden of the True Woman's displaced sexuality. In both stories the conventionally Othered woman—the "Chinese" part of Pan and the working-class Minnie—occupy the space of the maternal, while their erotic desire is figured as resulting only from their being misled by white men. Elsewhere Sui Sin Far works on a transnational level in her critique of such sexual politics, implicitly linking North American and British imperial expansion to these systems of gendered racism. In her account, in "Leaves," of her time working in Jamaica, for instance, Sui Sin Far recounts becoming the sexual prey of a "big, blond" naval officer. While this man's name and nationality are never specified, his race and connection to imperialist machinery are clear and evoke the larger historical context of Western military production and exploitation of Asian prostitution. She explicitly links this man's pursuit of her to racist assumptions, noting that "when it begins to be whispered about the place that I am not all white, some of the 'sporty' people seek my acquaintance" then quoting him directly as saying "I came just because I had an idea that you might like to know me. I would like to know you. You look like such a nice little body. Say, wouldn't you like to go for a sail this lovely night? I will tell you all about the sweet little Chinese girls I met when we were at Hong Kong. They're not so shy!" (226). Both by directly attributing words to this officer and by refusing to comment on his proposition (this passage is followed by a break in the narrative), this "nice little body" allows the blond man to indict himself, revealing the extent to which the assignment of racial categories inflects the construction of gender.[50] In this light, analogous to Hopkins's representation of African-American femininity as virtuous True Womanhood, Sui Sin Far's peeling apart of erotic desire and Chinese womanhood might be read as narrative resistance to the image of the Chinese woman as prostitute.

We might read Sui Sin Far's aligning of protagonists such as "Its Wavering Image"'s Pan with the image of the devoted American mother, rather than Other to that mother, in a similar light. Yet her representation of the maternal is complicated, for if it is coded as Chinese and paradoxically truly American, it rarely appears in Sui Sin Far's fiction as happily embodied. Pan may yearn to be a mother and find comfort in that image, but her story does not position her as one by its close. Other stories offer Chinese immigrant mothers whose version of maternal love leads to death, as in "The Wisdom of the New" or "The Prize Chinese Baby," or to the loss of a child to American assimilation, as in "In the Land of the Free." One of the only happy mothers in *Mrs. Spring Fragrance*, in fact, is Minnie, the white woman. All of this suggests that, if Sui Sin Far posits Chinese women as innately maternal, her fiction simultaneously represents that essentialized character as culturally contingent, its forms determined by cultural—national, ethnic, and racial—location and proximity to centers of power.

It is significant that it is the white woman who can be the happy mother and can marry into the Chinese community, choosing the position of being both marginal to and part of that community, feeling at home amongst Liu and his family but feeling "strange and lonely" when she moves outside of Chinatown (75). Again, racial privilege allows for some choice, for some agency in one's location in relation to community. Sui Sin Far's discussion of Minnie's two children—her "white" daughter from her marriage to Carson and her "half-breed" (82) son from her marriage to Liu Kanghi—underscores this claim that, insofar as choosing one's community is possible, it is a privilege only granted to those already (racially) privileged. Minnie's marriage to Liu Kanghi makes her daughter a part of the Chinese-American community: he tells Minnie, "your child shall be as my own" (75) and she notes, "I watched with complacency my child grow amongst the little Chinese children" (74). The child's relationship to Chinese-American community is enabled by her racial identity and the power it carries. In contrast, however, the narrator worries about her son, using a rhetoric to position him that echoes that of the speaker of "Leaves" when she discusses her own location.[51] Minnie states that as the boy "stands between his father and myself, like yet unlike us both, so will he stand in after years between his father's and his mother's people. And if there is no kindliness nor understanding between them, what will my boy's fate be?" (77). Here society locates the child outside of both sides of a racial binary, as well as outside both Anglo- and Chinese-American communities, rather than in the both/and position of the white child, a difference in positioning clearly determined by each child's racial identity. But in a rhetorical move also echoing her positioning of herself in "Leaves," Sui Sin Far refuses the finality of this social determinism in a striking comment on this son's birth: the child, the narrator notes, "was born with a veil over his face. 'A prophet!' cried the old mulatto Jewess who nursed me. 'A prophet has come into the world'" (82). This moment is memorable in part because it is one of the few appearances in Sui Sin Far's work of a character who is racially/ethnically marked as other than white/Anglo or Chinese or some combination of the two. That Sui Sin Far defines this child as a prophet (recalling her representation of herself as a Joan of Arc) is less surprising than that she puts this pronouncement in the mouth of a "mulatto Jewess." But perhaps this figure, explicitly embodying both a refutation of fictions of "purity" of blood as well as an acknowledgment of the diversity of religious and cultural populations of the United States, is the perfect mouthpiece for a prediction of a future where borders collapse and consequently both margins and centers of American culture are reworked.[52]

Transgressive Desire: Border Crossing, Cross-Dressing, and Same-Sex Desire

Sui Sin Far's representation of transgressive love in the form of Minnie and Liu Kanghi's interracial marriage is not her only depiction of transgressive desire overwritten by nationality and race. In this final section I will turn to one other such depiction of desire operating outside its prescribed boundaries: homosocial desire, both between women directly and, more figuratively, between a man and a woman passing as a man. I have chosen to examine this cluster of issues from a focus on desire, but here, perhaps more than in any other place in Sui Sin Far's work, the intersecting and overlapping of issues makes prizing apart the issues impossible and choosing a starting focus relatively arbitrary. In "The Chinese Lily," "The Smuggling of Tie Co," "Tian Shan's Kindred Spirit" (all from the "Mrs. Spring Fragrance" section of Mrs. Spring Fragrance), and "The Heart's Desire" (from the "Tales of Chinese Children" section of the book), homosocial desire recasts conventionally defined relationships and identities, undermining categories of absolute difference by offering pairs of heroines who are simultaneously the "same" and "different," and by offering individual heroines who are simultaneously both and neither men and women.

Sui Sin Far offers two representations of female homosocial desire, the most direct of which occurs in "The Chinese Lily," a story that recounts the relationship between Sin Far and Mermei, a Chinese woman who lives in Chinatown among other Chinese women but who, the narrator notes, "was not as they were" (101). While this difference is overtly attributed to the fact that "she was a cripple" (101), it also can be read as a marker of her distance from the heterosexual female norm. Mermei lives alone and sees no one but her devoted brother, Lin John, until one night when he is late in his visit. Out her window Mermei sees "six young girls of about her own age, dressed gaily as if to attend a wedding" (102), and the narrator notes that "the sight of those joyous girls caused sad reflections" (102). The reader is left to speculate on the nature of these reflections, but immediately following this moment and the tears it produces, the narrative introduces Sin Far, "the most beautiful young girl that Mermei had ever seen" (102), a "young girl" who drives Mermei's tears away.[53] The narrative juxtapositioning implies that Sin Far is the solution to Mermei's lack of either a wedding or female community. The two women open their "little hearts" to each other, with Mermei commenting that "one can't talk to a man, even if he is a brother, as one can to one the same as oneself" (103). Predictably, Lin John falls in love with Sin Far, a conventional narrative move that produces unconventional narrative results of displaced and triangulated desire. One might read Lin John's desire as the enactment of Mermei's desire; given that Mermei represents Sin Far as "the same as" herself, one might read this figuratively as either narcissistic or incestuous love. The denouement of the story forces Lin John to choose between rescuing his sister or Sin Far from a burning building; Sin Far sacrifices herself out of love, but love for whom?

Sui Sin Far's second representation of homosocial desire also provides for multiple readings. A fairy tale, "The Heart's Desire," tells the story of Li Chung O'Yam, a sad and lonely princess whose attendants try to please her by providing her with a father, mother, and brother, but with no success. The girl then seeks out her own desire, sending out a note that reaches a little girl named Ku Yum, a poor child who is "hugging a cat to keep her warm and sucking her finger to prevent her from being hungry" (151). As White-Parks points out, Ku Yum is not a name but a description of "a miserable person or someone in need of help" (xvii); this strategic choice fits into Sui Sin Far's foregrounding of class difference in the story. When Ku Yum arrives, O'Yam turns out to meet her, dressed in her finest and surrounded by her dolls and cats. Ku Yum, described as wearing a "blue cotton blouse" and carrying a "peg doll" and her cat, "looked at O'Yam, at her radiant apparel, at her cats and her dolls" and exclaims, "'How beautifully you are robed! In the same colors as I. And behold, your dolls and your cats, are they not much like mine?'" (151).[54] O'Yam agrees and announces to her people that she has found her "heart's desire—a little sister" (151). The story ends with a conventional fairy-tale happily-ever-after. But while this story on its surface reads as the story of a girl's search for a sister, its reworking of fairy-tale form recodes the desire in circulation here by structurally locating Ku Yum in the place of the prince, conventionally a princess's object of desire and provider of her narrative closure. As Amy Ling points out in *Between Worlds*, the conventional nature of this ending is interrupted by the fact that the "princess does not ride off to live happily ever after with a handsome prince, but finds her 'heart's desire' and life-long happiness in a relationship with 'another like herself'" (47). Like "A Chinese Lily," then, this story privileges sameness and community formed by it, figuring O'Yam and Ku Yum as doubles. At the same time, both stories complicate this representation of sameness (same sex characters bonding) by adding to it a representation of difference. That is, Mermei and Sin Far, like O'Yam and Ku Yum, are the same sex, but the first pair includes difference in terms of both the characters' physical ableness and the different worlds they inhabit, Mermei living solely in the private space and Sin Far, more mobile, occupying both public and private spheres. O'Yam and Ku Yum's sameness is complicated by class difference, a difference the story highlights throughout and plays upon in Ku Yum's name.

Calling it "pure speculation on my part," Ling suggests that these two stories "are suggestive of a lesbian sensibility" (48),[55] a suggestion that White-Parks takes issue with, calling "The Heart's Desire" "a story of female bonding" (213). It clearly is this, but White-Parks's position might more accurately have been articulated as "a story of female bonding *only*," because she goes on to respond to Ling's suggestion by stating, "the intimate bonding of Sui Sin Far's women, which occurs in many stories, is not sexual but essentially psychological and spiritual, a bonding envisioned by the author as springing from women's common experience—as mothers, victims of the patriarchal system, preservers of culture—and with roots in both sides of her heritage."[56] While I would certainly agree that Sui Sin Far's representations of female-female relationships offer portraits of "psychological and spiritual" bonding, they also allow for readings in excess of this: they are not explicit representations of lesbianism—note Ling's careful claim of a "lesbian sensibility" rather than overt lesbian representation—but they clearly provide narrative space for unspoken and displaced female desires. Here is another example not only of how Sui Sin Far's work crosses and breaks down boundaries—blurring the lines between heterosexual and homosexual desire—but also of the ways critics reinforce those boundaries: to read even the hint of homosocial desire in these texts provokes (as in Jewett criticism) the desire to locate the texts on one or the other side of yet another binary opposition, in one clear category. On a larger and, to use Ling's word, more speculative level, claiming homosocial (even without going so far as so claim lesbian) desire in these texts also challenges a common tradition of the elision of women of color from homosocial/lesbian representation: the representation of homosocial desire here appears—as obviously it is—not merely as the province of the white lesbian.

The issue of homosocial desire circulates on a more figurative level in stories such as "The Smuggling of Tie Co" and "Tian Shan's Kindred Spirit," through the device of passing women. "Passing" in this context means gender passing—Tie Co and Fin Fan, the heroines of these two stories, cross-dress and pass as men. "Passing" here also simultaneously implies passing across national borders, because both these stories involve Chinese "men" illegally crossing from Canada into the United States. Sui Sin Far thus plays with two forms of passing: the first, a national border crossing that implies moving from one literal space to another, and the second, a cross-dressing that metaphorically places its performer in two gender spaces at the same time and, paradoxically, not quite in either one. These two forms of passing are intertwined in the stories, in that both heroines cross the national border by crossing the figurative border of sex, and both do so out of love for a man.

As scholars have shown, historical circumstances resulting from the intersection of U.S. racist discourse on the one hand and the economic forces driving labor needs on the other helped construct the late-nineteenth-century U.S. border, defining quite literally who could or could not legally cross that border, as well as more metaphorically, of course, who could or could not qualify for "American" identity. This historical nexus produced not just the border, however, but also the consequent need on the part of certain peoples to "pass" in order to cross that border. As I have discussed, Sui Sin Far herself clearly deployed her Anglo birth name—Edith Eaton—and her Anglo features to pass as a white Englishwoman in order to cross from Canada into the U.S.; others of Chinese descent, such as her own sister, Winnifred Eaton, passed as Japanese instead. Lisa Lowe suggests that we view immigration as "the *locus* for the encounter of the national border and its 'outsides' as the site of both the law and the 'crossing of the borders' that is its negative critique" (35). These two stories offer representations both of the power of that law and of the ways it uses the figure of the illegal Chinese immigrant to produce that very national border itself. At the same time, both stories suggest that homosocial desire also helps to secure the border.

"Tian Shan's Kindred Spirit" begins as a conventional comic plot: Tian Shan and Fin Fan, Chinese workers in Canada, are in love, but their love is blocked by the fact that Tian Shan, trafficking in illegal border crossings, is impoverished. He leaves his lover for a year to earn money in the United States, but when he returns to claim his bride he wounds another suitor in a fight and so must flee from the law. The plot is resolved finally when Tian Shan is caught by the border police, and Fin Fan learns that he is to be deported to China. It is here that Sui Sin Far's comic form swerves, for the event which should separate the lovers forever becomes the means of their reunion, one impending border crossing inspiring two calculated crossings. Fin Fan reacts with hope to the news of Tian Shin's impending deportation: the narrator tells us that "fresh air and light had come into her soul. Her eyes sparkled. In the closet behind her hung a suit of her father's clothes. Fin Fan was a tall and well-developed young woman" (124). Cross-dressed, Fin Fan crosses the border and allows herself to be caught so as to be deported with Tian Shan. The story closes in the jail cell, where Tian Shan has ignored the boy now incarcerated with him, until the boy approaches. When Tian Shan asks the boy what he wants, the boy responds, "to go to China with you and to be your wife," a statement that unveils Fin Fan to Tian Shan (125). Thus, the story ends in a conventional comic plot fashion: boy gets girl in the end. Yet, the reworking of structure of this plot, like that of "The Heart's Desire," opens a space for homosocial desire in the brief moment when it appears that boy-gets-boy. Safely contained in the reinscription of heterosexuality on the level of plot, homosocial desire nevertheless simultaneously stands as a disruption to that reinscription, a moment of possibility, of alternate plots waiting to be written. Does the homosocial provide a space for challenges not only to heteronormativity but also to the national border? Is there some way in which the destabilization of the nuclear family implied by the homosexual couple here and in "The Heart's Desire" also destabilizes the nation-state that is built on that family unit? Sui Sin Far's use of gender passing and the homosocial desire it enables can certainly be read as carrying these implications: the homosocial couple at the story's close is in the process of being deported from North America to China. Neither their racial identity nor their homosocial desire can be incorporated into "American" identity; both serve instead to guarantee the limits of that national category. At the same time, however, this couple has been revealed—to the reader at least—as heterosexual, a revelation that calls into question the ultimate disruptiveness of their desire.

This disruption functions even more explicitly in "The Smuggling of Tie Co," in which the narrative presents Tie Co as a boy in love with Jack Fabian, a man who lives by "contrabanding Chinese from Canada into the United States" (104). Although Tie Co is clearly represented as in love with Fabian, it is only at the story's end that we learn, at the same time that Fabian does, that Tie Co is actually a woman passing as a man. Hence, until its final moments this story stands as an explicit representation of homosexual love. In the story's opening Tie Co is depicted as a hard-working laundry man in Canada. Despite the fact that he has a steady job, Tie Co, the "nice looking Chinaman" (107), hires Fabian to take him across the border, an act the narrative represents as motivated not by any desire on Tie Co's part to cross, but rather by the desire to help Fabian, whose business is slow. The interrelated nature of Tie Co's various border crossings emerges in a conversation with Fabian during their journey:

"Haven't you got a nice little wife at home?" he [Fabian] continued. "I hear you people marry very young."

"No, I no wife," asserted his companion with a choky little laugh. "I never have no wife."

"Nonsense," joked Fabian. "Why, Tie Co, think how nice it would be to have a little woman cook your rice and to love you."

"I not have wife," repeated Tie Co seriously. "I not like woman, I like man."

"You confirmed old bachelor!" ejaculated Fabian.

"I like you," said Tie Co, his boyish voice sounding clear and sweet in the wet woods. "I like you so much that I want go to New York, so you make fifty dollars. I no flend in New York." (107)

While Tie Co's statement that "I not like woman, I like man" carries an overtly homosexual/social meaning due to its juxtapositioning with "I not have wife," that meaning is immediately muted by Fabian's interpretation of Tie Co as a bachelor. Yet while Fabian's statement recontains the subversive content of this statement, the passage as a whole leaves it in play, in part because recontainment never equals erasure and in part because Fabian's statement opens up a new reading of the "bachelor society." [57] At the story's close Tie Co throws himself into a river to prevent Fabian's being caught by border police with an illegal alien: this ending simultaneously punishes Tie Co's apparent homosexual desire by death—a conventional narrative closure to homosexual desire—and rescripts that desire as heterosexual desire: his body is found to be that of a woman. In the end, then, both of Sui Sin Far's stories of cross-dressing allow for multiple meanings and room for marginalized desires. Here, the negotiation of borders both performs and produces American identity: the illicit crossing of geopolitical borders resists a national/racial Othering of the Chinese body, read by the United States as irremediably unassimilable and racially "foreign." At the same time, the public margins of the nation both allow for and immediately recuperate homosocial desire, as the heroines publicly perform a taboo desire that the stories ultimately rewrite as heterosexual, a revision that becomes a public performance of the naturalized version of the American erotic. The erotics of the border remain safely there contained. For ultimately, in these two stories, the heroines' crossing of a national border demands the temporary crossing of both gender lines and naturalized codes of sexual orientation—and even so, fails. That the plot of homosexual love ends in death and even the plot of heterosexual love ends in deportation signals Sui Sin Far's critique of the constraints of dominant "American" identity and of the kinds of violence entailed in the production of that identity. Sui Sin Far here focuses on those who cannot come to count as "American," foregrounding their status as ineligible for the American dream. Put another way, what she allows us to see is that the production of American identity and borders depends upon a very real and material disruption of families as well as the deportation and death of people like her characters.

While it is interesting that the only overt representations of homosocial desire that Sui Sin Far presents are of men (or, more precisely, of passing men and men), her work as a whole suggests a broader understanding of the way passing can constitute an act of resistance to both racial and sexual oppression. For Tie Co's passing as a boy and his emigration to Canada from China to work in a laundry as a boy offers us a fictional narrative of the historical phenomenon of the working-class women who, regardless of sexual orientation, passed as men in order to gain safety, mobility, and economic opportunity. On the level of plot, then, passing operates as a form of protection. On the narrative level the cloaking of homosocial desire in overtly heterosexual plots serves as another form of protective passing, passing that here allows for the possibility of the voicing of Othered, marginalized desires. Both these uses of passing are also at work, of course, in Sui Sin Far's accounts elsewhere of racial passing.

In the two stories I have discussed, gender passing replaces racial passing as the vehicle for the Chinese heroine's crossing the U.S. border. In fact, Sui Sin Far never in her fiction directly represents racial passing as a strategy for the Chinese who seek to cross the national border. This omission is curious, particularly given her own experiences crossing the U.S./Canadian border. In her journalism and essays, however, Sui Sin Far does directly discuss racial passing and protest the racist border policies of both the U.S. and Canada. In articles such as her 1890 "In the Land of the Free" and "The Ching Song Episode," she satirizes the selective immigration tax being levied on Chinese entering Canada and New York, while in her 1896 "A Plea for the Chinaman" Sui Sin Far protests the Canadian government's proposal to raise Chinese head taxes to an exorbitant five hundred dollars. Perhaps Sui Sin Far felt constrained by the form of fiction, which works, as Lowe points out, to subsume "differences—of gender, race, nationality, or sexuality . . . through the individual's identification with a universalized form" (52–53). Perhaps journalism and essays offered her more space for the voicing of dissonance. Certainly, these forms' association with the public and "factual" would have allowed Sui Sin Far to locate her explorations of large structural problems like racism in the broader public sphere, rather than subjecting her, as fiction would, to a pressure to individualize and privatize such problems. Whatever her reasons, however, in her journalism and essays Sui Sin Far directly confronts racial passing in ways she is unable to do in fiction.

Sui Sin Far turns from the racism and economics of immigration politics to the racial passing that results from these politics in her 1909 autobiographical essay "Leaves from the Mental Portfolio of an Eurasian." Here she chronicles what amounts to a "coming out" experience she has in the Midwest, an experience wherein she self-identifies as Chinese. Her narration of this event reveals the complexities of producing oneself as white while also suggesting certain structural similarities in this context between this process and the process of passing for straight. The narrator is attending a dinner party where the guests assume she is white and make repeated racist comments about the Chinese. Her employer opens the conversation by questioning whether the Chinese have souls and commenting, "I cannot reconcile myself to the thought that the Chinese are humans like ourselves," while the narrator's landlady states, "I wouldn't have one in my house" (224). The narrator describes her dilemma in the following terms:

A miserable, cowardly feeling keeps me silent. I am in a Middle West town. If I declare what I am, every person in the place will hear about it the next day. The population is in the main made up of working folks with strong prejudices against my mother's countrymen. The prospect before me is not an enviable one—if I speak. I no longer have the ambition to die at the stake for the sake of demonstrating the greatness and nobleness of the Chinese people. (224)

Passing for white here serves as a form of protection, allowing the narrator social and physical safety, mobility, and acceptance. Coming out in this context is dangerous: the scene's resolution underscores this danger but also underscores the complexity of the narrator's racial passing in terms that suggest connections to sexual passing. For after the employer asks "What makes Miss Far so quiet?," the narrative produces the confessional moment, the moment of revelation of the secret, in which the narrator proclaims her Chinese identity. Although her employer apologizes immediately for what he calls his prejudice and appears to have learned from the event, the narrator closes the story with the comment, "I do not remain much longer in the little town" (225). That Sui Sin Far has the employer call the narrator "Miss Far" (rather than Miss Eaton) raises two questions: first, is the narrator actively or passively passing for white?; second, how successful is that passing? The incident as a whole forces us to examine both the stakes and the costs of the narrator's original production of herself as white and her subsequent revelation of herself as Chinese in a context where the way her body is read has material ramifications for the health and safety of that body.

Later in "Leaves" Sui Sin Far's account of "a half Chinese, half white girl" (227) who is passing as Mexican in California clearly illustrates the slippery and complex production of racial hierarchies in California at the time.[58] The narrator describes the girl's mobility—"born in the East, and at the age of eighteen came West" (227)—and her passing to avoid "abuse of the Chinese" (227). However, the story of this particular passing woman illustrates, in addition, racial passing's intersection with and ability to provide a cover for a form of marginalized desire: here, interracial desire. Living in fear of discovery, the girl "comes out" as Eurasian only after falling in love with a white man and only after her "fearless American girl friend" forces her to do so.[59] The white "American" girl, we are told,

realizing that the truth sooner or later must be told, and better soon than late, advises the Eurasian to confide in the young man, assuring her that he loves her well enough not to allow her nationality to stand, a bar sinister, between them. But the Eurasian prefers to keep her secret, and only reveals it to the man who is to be her husband when driven to bay by the American girl, who declares that if the half-breed will not tell the truth she will. (228)

This passage is remarkable for several reasons. Reflecting the racialization of "nationality," it also illustrates the force of the social taboo on interracial love and the reasons why a "halfbreed" might choose to pass; that is, her desire for physical safety against the "abuse of the Chinese" and her desire to protect a marginalized interracial desire under the cover of a protected heterosexual one. At the same time, the passage also reflects another, less explicit, desire: that of the "American" girl. While the narrator never explains or even comments on the "American" girl's investment in the "halfbreed"'s disclosure, the force of that investment is clear in the language of the description. The passing girl is "compelled" to reveal her secret by the "American" girl; she is "driven to bay" by her. One might read this scenario as one of triangulated desire, but whether the American girl's desire is aimed at the "halfbreed" or her husband-to-be is unclear. In any case, the scene closes in a typically multivalenced fashion: the man accepts the woman's "Chinese blood," but, the narrator notes, "neither he nor she deems it necessary to inform his 'folks'" (228). Passing serves as a vehicle here, as throughout Sui Sin Far's work, to link the production of racial identity, erotic desire, and national borders. Who gets to count as "American" depends on who gets to count as Chinese (as well as, in this final example, Mexican). Transgressive desire here produces metaphorical borders no less than the Chinese Exclusion Act helped produce the literal U.S. border, as Sui Sin Far uses the figure of passing to signal the complicated and shifting grounds of inclusion and exclusion on which "American" identity is produced.

Sui Sin Far's discussion of "Chinese blood" here and throughout her work provides us not only with an account of Chinese-American and Chinese-Canadian communities at the turn of the century but also with a sardonic intervention into the American nineteenth-century discourse of blood. Refuting fictions of purity of blood even while delineating the devastating material effects of those fictions, Sui Sin Far offers representations of identity and community that collapse clear borders and singular categories, overlaying, blurring, and mixing these categories instead. Xiao-Huang Yin argues that Sui Sin Far believes that Chinese and American cultures cannot be mixed "because American culture values individualism, free competition, and personal success, whereas Chinese tradition emphasizes conformity, egalitarianism, and the importance of community" (65). In fact, by refusing to represent herself or her mixed blood characters as tragic victims, and by chronicling the multiple and diverse relationships within Chinese-American and Chinese-Canadian communities and between them and dominant Anglo-American communities, Sui Sin Far traces a mixing of cultures already long underway in American culture. She thus locates Chinese-American identity as solidly a part of that culture, both as a literal internal immigrant presence and as a figurative marker of the limits of national identity. As a result her version of Chinese-American community is intimately and complicatedly connected to "American" national identity rather than marginal or Other to it: a gender-shaped sense of cultural identity reworks the locations and relations of center and margins, locating the borderlands as simultaneously marginal and central to American life. Indeed, these borderlands can even be read as emblematic of that national identity, for ultimately what Sui Sin Far's fiction shows us is that "American" does not necessarily imply the invisible prefix "Anglo" but is rather a national identity constituted by multiple internal borders constantly in the process of being transformed, reworked, and invented.

Notes

INTRODUCTION

1. "America"'s usage as synonymous to "the United States" is of course evidence of the success of Manifest Destiny at least rhetorically. I will frequently enclose the word in quotation marks to underscore the constructed and contested nature of the concept.

2. Crucial to both a postbellum project of reimagining internal U.S. racial relations and the transnational project of imperial expansion, race functioned then as now as one of the structuring axes of American identity. One effect of the discourse of race was that whiteness—a discursive category naturalized as an allegedly biologically based racial category which was (and still is) often confused or conflated with ethnic categories—became an implicit condition of national identity. As a kind of cultural metaphor, whiteness, then, not surprisingly came to carry a tremendous burden of cultural meaning. Ruth Frankenberg points out in *White Women, Race Matters: The Social Construction of Whiteness* that "'white' is as much as anything else an economic and political category maintained over time by a changing set of exclusionary practices, both legislative and customary" (11–12). See her introduction to *White Women, Race Matters: The Social Construction of Whiteness.* Minneapolis: University of Minnesota Press, 1993. 1–22.

3. I have chosen to focus on these writers as particularly suggestive of these issues, but many other women writers of this period also engage in similar projects. Work remains to be done, for instance, on these issues in the work of writers such as Mary Austin, Alice S. Callahan, Alice Dunbar-Nelson, Helen Hunt Jackson, Mary Noailles Murfree, and Zitkala-Sä, among others.

CHAPTER 1: (RE)DRAWING BOUNDARIES

1. The dates of the early editors of the magazine are as follows: James Russell Lowell, 1857–61; James T. Fields, 1861–71; William Dean Howells, 1871–81; Thomas Bailey Aldrich, 1881–1890; and Horace Scudder, 1890–98. Jewett came to prominence under Fields but published with all the subsequent editors as well. For more on this context see Donovan's *New England Local Color Literature*, Bell, and Brodhead.

2. The ad hominum attack in this argument is curious and so prominent as to undermine the effectiveness of the claims; Wood asserts, for instance, that these writers often had a "neurotic fixation" on their parents (14). That her dismissal of this body of fiction is based both on region and gender is clear throughout the ar-

ticle, even in casual comments, as when she argues that the women of interest to Local Color writers are "those stranded in the nearly manless backwater of northern New England and the rural South" (17–8) or, even more extremely, when she dismisses the country village (specifically as represented by Mary Noailles Murfree, but arguably as represented more generally in Local Color fiction) as "a kind of concentration camp filled with the feminine relics of the past" (19).

3. This is not to say, of course, that this model has completely disappeared. As recently as 1988 Eric J. Sundquist, in "Realism and Regionalism," defined Local Color as "a literature of memory" (508) and argued that in Jewett's and Mary Wilkins Freeman's work (the work he sees as the most important of the New England Local Color writing) "memory is often lodged in the vestiges of a world of female domesticity . . . a ghost world of spinsters, widows, and bereft sea captains" (509).

4. Bell makes a similar point, comparing Elizabeth Ammons to Warner Berthoff and concluding that the two "agree, albeit with different emphases and agendas, that the culture of women exists somehow outside the competitive culture of men" (73).

5. In my analysis of *The Country of the Pointed Firs* I use the Norton edition, which follows the form of the original 1896 edition, then adds, in a second section, the four additional Dunnet Landing stories along with several unrelated stories. Unlike Willa Cather's reordering of the stories in her 1925 edition of the text, this arrangement follows Jewett's original plan for the text, but also allows the reader to assess the related Dunnet Landing stories as well. My reading of Jewett centers on the stories of the original edition but will also, at points, touch upon the four other Dunnet Landing stories ("A Dunnet Shepherdess," The Foreigner," "The Queen's Twin," and "William's Wedding"). These four stories, while structurally different from the 1896 edition stories, are thematically similar and frequently offer useful counterpoints to the larger text.

6. Implicit in this rejection of the American Romance, of course, is a simultaneous refusal to read as "dull" the limited spaces and plots that the American Romance offered women.

7. Not surprisingly, given *The Country of the Pointed Firs*'s thematizing of issues of connection and separation, Ammons is not the only critic to find Object Relations theories illuminating in relation to Jewett and hence not the only critic to replicate a set of essentializing claims about gender. See also Jean Rohloff's "'A Quicker Signal': Women and Language in Sarah Orne Jewett's *The Country of the Pointed Firs*," *South Atlantic Review* 55:2 (May 1990): 33–46. I would also note, however, that Ammons's more recent work on Jewett not only moves away from this position but critiques it. As should be clear, I find her later work extremely helpful and am indebted to it.

8. Although it has many problems when applied to questions of contemporary twentieth-century "lesbian" identity and community formation, Adrienne Rich's notion of a "lesbian continuum" might be usefully applied to this idea of

nineteenth-century female community. Rich defines a lesbian continuum as "a range—through each woman's life and throughout history—of woman-identified experience . . . including the sharing of a rich inner life, the bonding against male tyranny, the giving and receiving of practical and political support" (156–57). While this notion erases a twentieth-century distinction between erotic and/or physical relationships and relationships lacking this element, in a nineteenth-century context in which this distinction was not drawn in the same way, an expanded version of Rich's description seems appropriate. See her "Compulsory Heterosexuality and Lesbian Existence," *The Signs Reader: Women, Gender and Scholarship*, Elizabeth Abel and Emily K. Abel, eds. (Chicago: University of Chicago Press, 1983): 139–168, repr. from *Signs* 5:4 (Summer 1980): 631–60.

9. See Smith-Rosenberg for a discussion of leaders of the women's colleges and settlement house movement who were involved in Boston marriages. Helen Horowitz provides a fascinating history of the women's colleges in which so many of these women lived and worked. For a discussion of the Boston marriage's representation in nineteenth-century fiction, see Lillian Faderman, especially Part Two, Section A, Chapter 4.

10. I discuss the pathologizing and eroticizing of this relationship by sexologists and the medical industry in Chapter 2.

11. The past decade has seen a huge growth in both scholarly and biographical work on Jewett; detailed information on her life is thus now available. Many of the biographical details I give here I have taken from Sarah Way Sherman's excellent *Sarah Orne Jewett: An American Persephone* and from Paula Blanchard's *Sarah Orne Jewett: Her World and Her Work*.

12. James's image of Jewett as the "new centre" of Fields's life is resonant in several ways. On the one hand it implies that Jewett replaced James T. Fields, suggesting a sun/moon image for a husband/wife relationship in which the wife's life is "centered" around her husband's. This image does at least recognize the importance of Jewett in Fields's life, but it reflects a conventional heterosexual tendency to figure homosexual and/or homosocial relations in heterosexual terms. Moreover, by constructing the relationship as a hierarchy of two individuals, it misrepresents the flexible nature of Fields and Jewett's relationship. My reading of the Boston marriage as the core of a centric formal structure in *The Country of the Pointed Firs* is at odds with James's formulation as well, since I read the *relationship* constituted by the two women as the core.

13. Howe explains that "Father laid a restraining editorial hand across her enthusiasm, particularly 'regarding the nicknames . . . four-fifths of them—I think—should go for the mere sake of the impression we want the book to make on readers who have no personal association with Miss Jewett . . . I doubt . . . whether you will like to have all sorts of people reading them wrong'" (84).

14. While Roman is quite right to point out the anachronism in calling a nineteenth-century relationship lesbian, her text suggests additional reasons for her defending against this term. In her discussion of the Fields-Jewett relation-

ship she feels compelled to offer a number of reasons for Fields's interest in Jewett, including many of the most standard homophobic responses. Thus, she suggests that Fields was lonely after the death of her husband, that it was too difficult for independent women to find happy relationships with men, and even that there were not enough men to go around in the post–Civil War period (see her discussion 105–6 and passim). The point here is not that these observations are necessarily wrong, but that they serve to deflect and elide other equally plausible explanations.

15. This is analogous to the critical response to Sui Sin Far's identity, which I will discuss in Chapter 6. Both these drives indicate, among other things, the degree to which we have inherited both the nineteenth-century desire to categorize and its confidence that all experience can be neatly defined.

16. Sherman offers biographical support of this when she points out that James T. Fields remembered knowing Annie Fields as a small child. Sherman goes on to observe of Annie Fields's shift from her relation with Fields to her relation with Jewett, "earlier Annie Fields had come to her husband as an 'adoptive daughter;' now she would begin by playing the parental role" (79).

17. Sherman also notes that "although the Fields/Jewett relationship may not have been exclusive, there can be no doubt about its primacy in each's life. And there can be no doubt about its passion" (82).

18. As I will demonstrate, this vision of the Boston marriage offers freedom, flexibility, and inclusivity to its members, but at the cost of a certain form of exclusivity: not everyone, that is, can be admitted to the Boston marriage or, consequently, the community Jewett models on it. This simultaneous inclusiveness/exclusiveness of the Boston marriage also renders it an apt model for Jewett's model of region and nation.

19. That is, although it was James T. Fields who was the publisher/editor, prior to his death Annie Fields did some of the actual editorial work and most of the networking work, establishing and maintaining ties with the authors and often facilitating their publication. See Donovan's *New England Local Color Literature* and Brodhead for more on this context.

20. The term "women's culture" emerges from cultural feminist work—represented in Jewett criticism by such critics as Josephine Donovan—that posits an essentialized and distinct culture of women grounded in gender and viewing femininity as being maternal, nurturing, and empathetic, characteristics that are seen as both innate and positive. This twentieth-century feminist branch thus shares certain fundamental beliefs with the nineteenth-century proponents of separate spheres, who believed in a distinct and innate female (private) sphere. Both models' reliance on gender as an ahistorical unifier, of course, has been critiqued as eliding other important differences among women. I use the term "women's culture" here to signify the late-nineteenth-century circle of women in which Jewett moved, but wish to underscore that this circle itself was open only to certain types of women.

21. See Ammons and Zagarell, among others, for the mother-daughter reading; see Brodhead for the landlady-tenant reading.

22. Two other critics have begun the work of reconceptualizing Jewett from a nonheterosexist perspective. Josephine Donovan reads Jewett's *A Country Doctor* as a more or less explicit response to the sexologists, arguing that the novel "may have been one of the earliest feminist repudiations of Krafft-Ebing and other theorists who saw women's choice of masculine vocations as unnatural, indeed pathological" ("Nan Prince" 23). While Donovan addresses the issue of gender roles, her discussion implicitly raises the issue of sexuality, since the sexologists conflated the non-gender normative behavior of independent women with "inverted" sexual object choice. Hence, for the sexologists, the decision of the protagonist of *A Country Doctor* to become a doctor would have cast suspicion on her heterosexuality. Donovan's contextualizing of *A Country Doctor* in relation to the sexologists is persuasive. As will become clear, however, her approach more closely resembles my work on Florence Converse's *Diana Victrix* than my treatment of the Boston marriage in *The Country of the Pointed Firs*. More explicitly, Judith Fetterley reads *Deephaven* as a lesbian text. I do agree with Fetterley's claim that "*Deephaven* articulates the attraction of sameness" (176) and that the summer stay in the village of Deephaven of the two young women "provides the occasion for trying out a perspective from which one might view the marginal as central and the central as marginal" (173). While I would not use the term *lesbian* in reference to this or any nineteenth-century text (in part because the word itself is an anachronism and in part because the identity category it denotes—at once eroticized and pathologized—did not exist in such clear terms in the nineteenth century), one might read the heroines' relationship as a muted form of Boston marriage. Although *Deephaven* as a whole is not *structured* by the Boston marriage, on the plot level it offers a coded representation of one in what might be seen as Jewett's early effort at such a representation.

While I do not see *The Country of the Pointed Firs* as explicitly in conversation with the sexologists, but rather articulating an older model of romantic friendship, and while I would not call it a lesbian text for the reasons I give above, I would place my reading in the context of these two critics' work, as we share an interest in representations of female-female relations in Jewett's work. Further, Fetterley's formulation of a perspective that reverses margin and center resonates—both in terms of gender relations and regional locales—in *The Country of the Pointed Firs*.

23. Richard Brodhead's reading of this passage as indicative of tourist culture and the class privilege of the narrator is persuasive. I will take up his argument in more detail below, but would here like to acknowledge the coexistence of the tourist's desire for appropriable haven with the lover's desire for the beloved.

24. That women writers would draw on a maternal model in order to represent female-female desire at the turn of the century is easily understood given that this was a model that was already available, was socially sanctioned, and pro-

vided for a level of physical closeness between women. One might contextualize this model historically, in terms of the first generation of college women, a generation of women who rejected their mothers' domestic position yet created alternate maternal relationships with other women. Smith-Rosenberg, in a discussion of American New Women of this period, argues that "significantly, while rejecting the patriarchal family and their mothers' domestic lives, the first generation of New Women did not repudiate the traditional world of female love or the concept of the female family. It was the male-dominated, not the female-guided, family that restricted women's full development, they insisted. Educated women could develop alternative, single-sex familial institutions which would foster women's autonomy and creative productivity" (254–255). Further, these same women went on to draw on a cultural discourse of maternity to justify their own entrances into the public sphere. Metaphorically transforming themselves into the mothers of "fallen women" and the urban poor (among others), as well as figuring themselves as the guardians of fallen man's morals, these women often rejected literal motherhood while embracing metaphoric motherhood.

25. One might also read this passage as depicting that form of flirting in which one rehearses past loves/lovers in order to represent oneself as desiring and desirous to a prospective or current lover.

26. The narrator steps into the structural position of mother elsewhere in the text as well, as when Mrs. Todd invites the narrator to come to her family reunion by asserting, "Oh certain, dear . . . Oh no, I never thought o' any one else for comp'ny, if it's convenient for you, long's mother ain't come" (84). The merging or interchangeability of mother and husband is also suggested elsewhere, as in the opening of "The Foreigner," as Marjorie Pryse implies in describing the narrator's and Mrs. Todd's sitting through a sea storm and worrying about Mrs. Blackett. Pryse observes, "the two women might be the wives of seagoing men from the days when Dunnet Landing was an active port, except that neither woman is worried about a man. Both join in worrying about 'mother' out on Green Island" (91). See her "Women 'at Sea': Feminist Realism in Sarah Orne Jewett's 'The Foreigner,'" in Critical Essays on Sarah Orne Jewett, ed. Gwen L. Nagel (Boston: G. K. Hall, 1984): 89–98.

27. Hobbs's reading of "Martha's Lady" ultimately reinforces the binary oppositions that I argue Jewett is confounding, for while she does read the relationship of the story's two female protagonists as simultaneously spiritual and passionate, she feels compelled to define the limits of what that passion might contain. That is, while she goes so far as to claim it includes "amorousness," she concludes that the relationship "is undoubtedly passionate, but not necessarily erotic" (26), and interprets Jewett's calling for the reader's ability to read between the lines of the story by stating "rather than calling for her audience to read a physical relationship 'between the lines,' Jewett is probably again stressing the depth of Martha's love" (27). As I argued earlier, the problem with this reading is not that it is wrong (i.e., I would agree that Martha's love does not necessarily

have to be read as erotic, and I would also agree—indeed insist—that Jewett is emphasizing Martha's depth of love) but rather that it insists on constructing mutually exclusive binary oppositions for the reading of complicated relations. That Hobbs simply ignores the class difference in the two protagonists only exacerbates this problem.

28. This follows the narrative's thematization of the erotic object as lost: witness Joanna's lost love, Elijah's dead wife, and Mrs. Todd's lost lover and dead husband.

29. Support for the argument that William is not the object of the narrator's desire but rather a displaced location for it might be found in the fact that the narrator recounts at great length and with evident approval both William's courting of another woman, Esther, (in the narrative proper) and his marrying her (in "William's Wedding").

30. Sherman goes on to suggest that indeed the narrator and Mrs. Todd are mates as they walk home hand in hand after William's wedding, although she does not go on to develop this point. As I hope to have made clear, hers is a nuanced and persuasive reading of this issue.

31. Interestingly, Jewett uses this term in *A Country Doctor* in reference to a mismatched couple: a villager explains their marriage's failure by noting that "they wa'n't mates. He'd had a different fetchin' up, and he *was* different," a comment which suggests that a heterosexual marriage alone does not make a pair mates or, put another way, that "mate" signifies in excess of "spouse." See *A Country Doctor* (New York: Penguin, 1986; repr of 1877), 22.

32. This thematization of childhood as a source of joy recalls Jewett's comment, when she was forty-eight years old, "Today is my birthday and I am . . . always nine years old." *Letters of Sarah Orne Jewett*, ed. Annie Fields (Boston: Houghton Mifflin, 1911): 125.

33. This reading also helps to account for the so-called "plotlessness" of this text, the fact that no one character or plot is either foregrounded or totally forgotten in this constantly shifting and elastic world. This counter-canonical "plotlessness" of the text also, of course, helps work against a fixity of roles for the narrator and Mrs. Todd by resisting a forced choice of one among a group of received narrative locations for a female character.

34. Paradoxically, then, the narrative distances Mrs. Todd from her mother both by identifying her with William (as his double in his separate status) and by separating from him (in his status as double of Mrs. Blackett). This thematic use of William is paralleled on the narrative level. For the twenty-one chapters that compose *The Country of the Pointed Firs* proper are accompanied by four other stories that are located in the world of Dunnet Landing. Two of these four ("A Dunnet Shepherdess" and "William's Wedding") center upon William's status as external to a female world. The first tale concerns his courting, the second his marrying: a plot that makes him, as Mrs. Todd notes, more "like a man" (281) than ever before. It is in these two stories, also, that most of the displacement of

a supercharged energy from the narrator-Mrs. Todd relationship to the narrator-William relationship is to be found. While the other two stories ("The Foreigner" and "The Queen's Twin") focus specifically on female bonding and the strength and comfort women gain from it, the stories dealing with William thus work to highlight both his status as separate from this world and the ways in which this status provides the female characters a means of connection.

35. This move is reminiscent of New Women's rejection of the domestic sphere and concurrent appropriation of maternal imagery to justify their public careers.

36. Through the mediation of her career as herbalist, Mrs. Todd thus stands as a model of a woman who has negotiated a dual desire for a connection to the community and a concurrent sense of individual identity and power. In this way she is analogous to *A Country Doctor*'s protagonist, Nan Prince, although Nan chooses to follow her male guardian's example to become a doctor, thus leaving the private, domestic sphere that Mrs. Todd can be said to inhabit for the public sphere, a sphere still gendered male.

37. Captain Littlepage is the sole exception to this model, but he, of course, is a parody and his tale serves to isolate him from his community rather than to link him to it: because of his belief in the tale he is considered mad or at least eccentric. His tale neither educates nor fully entertains its listeners and as such serves as a model of a failed oral tradition, a tradition Jewett genders male.

38. Jewett makes a claim for stories as a means of community formation—here specifically a rural community—in *A Country Doctor* as well, where she asserts, "The repetitions of the best stories are signal events, for ordinary circumstances do not inspire them. Affairs must rise to a certain level before a narration of some great crisis is suggested, and exactly as a city audience is well contented with hearing the plays of Shakespeare over and over again, so each man and woman of experience is permitted to deploy their well-known but always interesting stories upon the rustic stage" (13).

39. This treatment of writing offers an interesting comparison to Florence Converse's more explicit representation of Enid furnishing the subject matter for Sylvia's book (discussed in Chapter 2). It also calls to mind Jewett's own periods of separation from Annie Fields, during which Jewett did most of her writing.

40. That Jewett puts this important comment in the voice of Littlepage, a character whose embodiment of the American Romance is generally ridiculed by both characters and narrative, suggests that Jewett's narrative can identify the limits of the usefulness of the romance form for the nation while also recognizing the benefits it offered.

41. Jewett has her narrator reiterate this conviction that seafaring broadens the perspective: the narrator remarks upon "a look of anticipation and joy, a far-off look that sought the horizon; one often sees it in seafaring families, inherited by girls and boys alike from men who spend their lives at sea, and are always watching for distant sails or the first loom of the land. At sea there is nothing to

be seen close by, and this has its counterpart in a sailor's character, in the large and brave and patient traits that are developed, the hopeful pleasantness that one loves so in a seafarer" (48).

42. The frame of this story, which I will not discuss at length here, concerns the narrator's relationship with Mrs. Todd. For more on the frame story, see Pryse's "Women at Sea."

43. The *Oxford English Dictionary*, for instance, defines tolerance as the "disposition or ability to accept without protest or adopt a liberal attitude toward the opinion or acts of others."

44. Like many of her white and privileged contemporaries, Jewett believed in racial hierarchy. As Sandra Zagarell notes, Jewett articulates the dominant racist discourse of her day throughout her fiction and most obviously in her 1887 history *The Story of the Normans*, where she represents the Normans as an advanced, aristocratic elite. See her *The Story of the Normans* (New York: Putnam's, 1887). Bishop's treatment replicates to a large extent the unexamined racism found in Jewett's work. It was, however, until very recently, the only study of race in Jewett. Recently and fortunately, more work has appeared; see, in particular, Zagarell and Gillman. As should be evident, my thinking on this issue has been informed by their work.

45. Compare this to Jewett's description in *The Story of the Normans*: "England the colonizer, England the country of intellectual and social progress, England the fosterer of ideas and chivalrous humanity, is Norman England, and the Saxon influence has oftener held her back in dogged satisfaction and stubbornness than urged her forward to higher levels" (356).

46. Jewett's use of hereditary theory as an explanatory model is perhaps strongest in *A Country Doctor*, where, in a move akin to that of Converse in *Diana Victrix*, she uses it to explain and justify her heroine Nan's departure from conventional gender norms. In a typical passage, for instance, she writes, "she had a power which made her able to use and unite the best traits of her ancestors, the strong capabilities which had been unbalanced or allowed to run to waste in others. It might be said that the materials for a fine specimen of humanity accumulate through several generations, until a child appears who is the heir of all the family wit and attractiveness and common sense, just as one person may inherit the worldly wealth of his ancestry" (52). Later her guardian Dr. Leslie links this inheritance specifically to Nan's "unfitness" to marry, stating, "Nan's feeling toward her boy playmates is exactly the same as toward the girls she knows . . . the law of her nature is that she must live alone and work alone" (103).

47. The narrator repeats this implicit celebration of conquest along with an assumption of "taste" as an inherited trait, stating, "I began to respect the Bowdens for their inheritance of good taste and skill and a certain pleasing gift of formality . . . their ancestors may have sat in the great hall of some old French house in the Middle Ages, when battles and sieges and processions and feasts were familiar things" (105).

This attitude is echoed in Jewett's autobiographical essay "Looking Back on Girlhood" where, for instance, she comments that "in my home the greater part of the minor furnishings had come over in the ships from Bristol and Havre. My grandfather seemed to be a citizen of the whole geography" (5). See "Looking Back of Girlhood," *The Uncollected Short Stories of Sarah Orne Jewett*, ed. Richard Cary (Waterville: Colby College Press, 1971): 3–7. That Jewett, descendent of wealthy ship owners, would support imperialist expansion is not entirely surprising, for as this quotation makes clear, the privilege underpinning her position—and that of the Boston marriage—resulted from such expansion.

48. That the outsider here is a woman underscores that while community/the family is constituted by women, it is simultaneously exclusive, not open to all women.

CHAPTER 2: "BUT SOME TIMES . . . I DON'T MARRY,—EVEN IN BOOKS"

1. For a detailed discussion of the construction of heterosexuality, see Jonathan Ned Katz's *The Invention of Heterosexuality* (New York: Dutton, 1995).

2. The Boston marriage is related to another model of female-female relationship that developed in both Britain and America when young women entered colleges and universities beginning in the 1870s and when girls increasingly began attending boarding schools: a kind of crush of a younger student for an older student or teacher within the all-female world of the school. These crushes, called by various names including "raves" and "smashes," differ from Boston marriages in part in that they were described by their participants specifically in the language of heterosexual romantic love rather than a more generalized familial or spiritual love. Nancy Sahli, in her account of smashes in American women's colleges, for instance, quotes Alice Stone Blackwell's description of smashes as "an extraordinary habit which they [the "girls"] have of falling violently in love with each other, and suffering all the pangs of unrequited attachment, desperate jealously &c &c , with as much energy as if one of them were a man" (22). Smashes also can be differentiated from Boston marriages, as Horowitz points out, in part on generational grounds: while the students were indulging in smashes, their professors were at home living in Boston marriages (191–92). Martha Vicinus, in her discussion of English boarding-school girls' friendships, notes that "although a religious vocabulary effectively masked personal desires, a woman who loved another girl or woman always spoke of this love in terms that replicated heterosexual love" (602). These friendships, Vicinus concludes, offered the young women "a combination of practical information, moral advice, and personal affection" (611), and might be seen as romantic attachments that functioned as surrogate familial relationships. See Vicinus's "Distance and Desire: English Boarding-School Friendships," *Signs* 9:4 (Summer, 1984): 600–22; see also her *Independent Women: Work and Community for Single Women, 1850–1920* (Chicago: University of Chicago Press, 1985).

3. My discussion here, I would underscore, applies only to the discourse surrounding female inversion and homosexuality. Discourses—medical, legal, and others—surrounding male homosexuality in this period and others were in important ways quite distinct from those of female homosexuality. For a discussion of male homosexuality in the period, see Jeffrey Weeks, *Coming Out: Homosexual Politics in Britain from the Nineteenth Century to the Present* (London: Quartet Books, 1977); see also *Hidden From History: Reclaiming the Gay and Lesbian Past*, eds. Martin Bauml Duberman, Martha Vicinus, and George Chauncey (New York: New American Library, 1989); see also Jonathan Ned Katz's *Gay American History: Lesbians and Gay Men in the U.S.A.* (New York: Crowell, 1976) and his *Gay/Lesbian Almanac: A New Documentary* (New York: Harper & Row, 1983). For a discussion of the varying impact of the sexologists on gay male and female identity formation and/or rights movements, see Sheila Jeffreys, *The Spinster and Her Enemies: Feminism and Sexuality, 1880–1930* (London: Pandora Press, 1985), especially Chapter 6. Finally, for a collection of essays and a comprehensive bibliography of gay/lesbian studies, see *The Lesbian and Gay Studies Reader*, eds. Henry Abelove, Michèle Aina Barale, and David M. Halperin (New York: Routledge, 1993).

4. These categories were overlapping but not identical, as Chauncey establishes.

5. See, for instance, Smith-Rosenberg's chapter, "The New Woman as Androgyne . . . " in *Disorderly Conduct*; Sahli; and Chauncey.

6. For a compelling discussion of the ways the medical, legal, and popular discourses on homosexuality were intertwined in this period, see Duggan.

7. The full-blown fictional representation of this does not appear until the twentieth century, most famously, of course, in the tortured figure of Stephen Gordon, the aristocratic, Krafft-Ebing–reading heroine of Radclyffe Hall's *The Well of Loneliness* (1928) and her lover Mary. Less easily definable representations begin appearing in British and American women's fiction largely in the 1890s, in novels such as Edith Johnson's *A Sunless Heart* (London: Ward, Lock & Bowden, 1894), Mary Cholmondeley's *Red Pottage* (New York: Virago Press, 1985; repr. of 1899), or Gertrude Dix's *The Image Breakers* (London: W. Heinemann, 1900). See Jeannette Foster's *Sex Variant Women in Literature* (Baltimore: Diana Press, 1975; repr of 1956 original) for a more detailed account of this. For an atypical representation (in that it appears in a novel by a British anti–New Woman female author), see E. Lynn Linton's *The Rebel of the Family* (New York: Harper & Bros., 1880).

8. For more on twentieth-century discussions of butch-femme, see, for instance, Sue-Ellen Case, "Toward a Butch-Femme Aesthetic," *The Lesbian and Gay Studies Reader*: 294–304, repr. of *Discourse: Journal for Theoretical Studies in Media and Culture* 11.1 (Fall–Winter 1988–89): 55–73; Amber Hollibaugh and Cherrie Moraga, "What We're Rollin Around in Bed With: Sexual Silences in Feminism," *Powers of Desire: The Politics of Sexuality*, ed. Ann Snitow, Christine Stansell, and Sharon Thompson (New York: Monthly Review, 1985): 394–405;

Joan Nestle, "Butch-Femme Relationships: Sexual Courage in the 1950's," *A Restricted Country* (Ithaca: Firebrand Books, 1987): 100–109; and Esther Newton's "The Mythic Mannish Lesbian: Radclyffe Hall and the New Woman."

9. Put another way, sexologists envisioned the congenital invert as a woman who (like a "normal" heterosexual man) had a male identification and a female erotic object choice, while the passive invert had a female identification and a varying object choice, varying in that the passive invert was thought by the sexologists to be capable of taking both the female object choice of the congenital invert and the "normal" male object choice (if she could be exposed to a more "healthy" heterosexual environment). Additionally, her object choice might be seen as variable in that she loved the "masculine soul" housed in the female body.

10. Sue-Ellen Case also makes this point, arguing that "the butch-femme couple inhabit the subject position together—'you can't have one without the other,' as the song says. The two roles never appear as . . . discrete" (295). See her "Toward a Butch-Femme Aesthetic."

11. Scudder, in her autobiography *On Journey*, published in 1937, notes that "in 1919, Florence Converse and her mother came to make one family with us [Scudder and her mother]. Miss Converse had for years shared my life in all ways except in living under the same roof. Now that joy was given us, and we have never been separated since" (275). An index to the unconventional mix of domesticity and radical politics that fueled their lives might be found in the grace that Scudder cites the two as using: "We have food: others have none: / God bless the Revolution!" (302). Very little information is available on Converse; on Scudder the autobiography provides some background while Theresa Corcoran's *Vida Dutton Scudder* (Boston: Twayne Publishing, 1982) features Converse remarkably rarely but does at least offer some sense of the social milieu of the couple's world. On the two women's relationship see Nan Bauer Maglin, "Vida to Florence: 'Comrade and Companion'," *Frontiers* 6.3 (1979): 13–20.

12. As I discuss in Chapter 1, Fields was one of the most important publishers of his day, both through his publishing house and through his editorship of *Atlantic Monthly* (from 1861–71). He was at the center of a literary circle that was highly influential in shaping the direction of American fiction in the second half of the nineteenth century. Annie Fields, a writer and editor in her own right, was what Josephine Donovan calls "the emotional center" of a large group of women writers, many of whom she was influential in having published by her husband. She also, not incidentally, was, recall, from the time of her husband's death in 1881, herself a member of a Boston marriage with Sarah Orne Jewett. Converse, writing throughout this period and working as assistant editor of *Atlantic Monthly* from 1908 to 1930, would certainly have had contact with this circle of women. For more on this circle see Josephine Donovan's *New England Local Color Literature: A Woman's Tradition* (New York: Frederick Ungar, 1983); see also Fryer.

13. In this, I disagree strongly with Tess Cosslett, who in her *Woman to Woman: Female Friendships in Victorian Fiction* (Brighton: The Harvester Press,

1988) contends that female friendships "nearly always operate to assimilate one or both of the women into marriage" (3) and that the "main alternative to the male-female ending is thus the woman-alone ending" (138). She also sees New Woman novels as essentially conservative and individualistic (14), a position I read as not in concordance with the evidence of the novels themselves.

14. The differences in cultural and political power between France and Mexico and in their respective relationships to the United States are mirrored in the fact that while speaking French is a sign of culture and sophistication for Converse's characters, and a skill to be displayed, as I will discuss in Chapter 4, in Ruiz de Burton's fiction the Californios' use of Spanish is played down, scarcely represented at all, and is a liability within American culture.

15. This set of associations is widespread at the time. As early as 1873, for instance, Albert Rhodes asserts that the Creole "still lingers in the past, dallying with the flowers of love and sentiment, while the American hurries forward with unhappy haste to pluck the thorns of ambition and pelf" (253).

16. Converse's ability to represent each region's complaints about the other may be the result of her own regional positioning: although she spent her adult life in New England, she was, according to Theresa Corcoran (*Vida Dutton Scudder* [Boston: Twayne, 1982]), originally from New Orleans.

17. In keeping with this, when Jacques goes looking for a "capitalist" (43) to finance and go into partnership with him, he finds his man in the New Yorker Curtis Baird.

18. This coding of the North/New England's language/accent as central, as a national norm, is replicated by the narrator on other levels throughout the novel and, like the novel's rehearsal of stereotypes of the South as romantic, quaint, and somewhat behind the industrial times, identifies the narrative point of view as Northern. So that while Converse goes on substantially to rework the possibilities for women inherent in New England values, she simultaneously contributes to a Postbellum dominant discourse that worked to naturalize the North as dominant over the South. The most explicit/egregious example of this Northern dismissal of the South comes from the New Yorker Curtis Baird, who employs the fairly widespread rhetorical practice of coding the South as primitive, charming, childlike, and simple. He says, for instance, that "the Southern people . . . are as pleased as a parcel of children when you praise them. . . . It is delightful! . . . Here they are, throwing themselves into this preposterous carnival make-believe with the abandon of children at a dancing-school festival. You wouldn't find a Northern city capable of tossing dignity to the winds, and kicking up its civic and social heels in this jolly fashion. It takes imagination to do this sort of thing, and that's what this people has as a people. It is the Southern temperament, I suppose" (155). While the narrator does treat Baird with a certain amount of irony, making fun of his affected drawl, for instance, she is in the main sympathetic to him, making it difficult to locate precisely an authorial point of view in this statement.

19. That Southern writers like Kate Chopin, Grace King, and (the more

confusingly-regionally identified) Alice Dunbar-Nelson would recognize and trade on this cultural capital is not, perhaps, surprising; to find it surfacing in the New Englander Converse's work might suggest both a lingering loyalty in Converse to her native city and a measure of how pervasive an image it was in the late-nineteenth-century cultural imagination.

20. I discuss Roma Campion in greater detail below; here I would simply point out that, like Jacques, her identity is contextual and signals two distinct uses of "American" in the novel. That is, she is "American" in the context of New Orleans, which sets up French/American as an internal opposition of that city. She is not, however, "American" in the novel's other use of the term: in the context of the nation Converse images "American" to mean, ultimately, "Northern."

21. The widespread nature of this association, too, is suggested by Albert Rhodes's claim that New Orleans's "race of Creoles has lost the virility of its prime, and is sinking into old age" (256).

22. Jocelin's father is dead, his mother is represented as weak and ineffectual, and his sister is so old-fashioned in her desires that the narrative writes her into an early death. Jacques Dumarais is connected to this family (the Castaignes) only through his father's marriage to Jocelin's mother; in the terms of the salient discourse, he is not related to them "by blood."

23. While Jocelin's deviance is explained specifically as the result of his ancestors' behavior, the origins of inverts' "deviance" are less clearly accounted for by the sexologists, but they are certainly seen as the same combination of cultural and biological inheritance. The sexologists often linked inversion to the dissipation of ancestors but also rhetorically linked it to prostitution and drugs, just as Converse attributes Jocelin's decay to his ancestors but also situates his disintegration in the slums, where Jacques finds him living amidst prostitutes and taking opium.

24. This plot line is similar in many ways to the line Radclyffe Hall was to take in *The Well of Loneliness* some thirty years later, but in 1897 the narrative of deviance that was to have become the preeminent narrative by 1928 was still only one of several competing explanations of same-sex desire, so that while Hall makes this the central plotline in her novel, it is in *Diana Victrix* merely a subplot and not even one focused explicitly on sexual inversion. And while Converse's novel exhibits a faith in Darwinian science, she tells the story of social evolution so that it has, as I will show, an ending that writes into prominence, rather than writing out, the Boston marriage and the women who form it.

25. The complicated and multiple definitions and usage of *creole/Creole* in a specifically New Orleans context has long historical precedent and continues to this day. I discuss this issue further in my reading of Kate Chopin; for more details see Brasseaux, Domínguez, Elfenbein, and Taylor.

26. Eva Saks draws a perceptive and useful analogy in her discussion of the nineteenth-century American association of miscegenation with incest, pointing out that the "taboo of too different (amalgamation/miscegenation) is interchangeable with the taboo of too similar (incest), since both crimes rely on a pair of bodies which are mutually constitutive of each other's deviance, a pair of bodies in

which each body is the signifier of the deviance of the other. Neither body can represent the norm, because each is figured as deviance from an other. (This complex of anxiety and taboo also evokes the jurisprudence of sodomy, another area of the law in which a pair of bodies constitutes deviance upon conjunction. Because they are too similar to each other, and too different from the 'norm,' the bodies of sodomy are legally Other. 'Miscegenation was once treated as a crime similar to sodomy,' notes one dissent in *Bowers v. Hardwick* [U.S. 1986])" (53–54). Hence, in both interracial couples and lesbian or gay male couples, the bodies are constituted as a pair, in relation to the other, and it is the relation—their very likeness or unlikeness to each other—that makes them deviant. It is this reading of likeness that Converse's rhetoric challenges.

27. For more details on the historical incident, as well as the ongoing hostility toward Italian immigrants, see Higham. It is worth noting that the lynching of Italians continued—in the North and the South—well into the twentieth century. Higham cites lynchings in Illinois occurring in 1914 as well as the beating of Italians and the burning of their homes as late as 1920 (184; 264).

28. Italians figured as a particularly prominent immigrant group in Boston in Converse's day. Scudder's autobiography devotes a significant section to a discussion of her work with the Italian immigrant neighborhoods, and notes a "racial" tension between Irish Catholic and Italian Catholics in Boston factories (263).

29. Converse takes an ambivalent but affectionate tone toward New Orleans, a city the novel represents as charming and cultured but degenerate. That is, against the foil of the Puritan North, which figures as the type for American culture, New Orleans, through its link to France, is figured as having a distinct culture (unlike the South in general). But New Orleans, because of its diluted status, cannot serve as a model for the nation; the best the novel can imagine for it is a slow shift into Northern/national values.

30. Not coincidentally, it is in the North that Jocelin first realizes that he cannot compete in the musical world, and it is also in the North that he falls by the wayside and cements his failure.

31. Henry Abelove suggests a psychoanalytic link between American capitalist production and homophobia. In his deft and sophisticated reading of Freud he points out that Freud believed Americans to be "extraordinarily overrepressed," a condition Freud linked to capitalism and saw as productive of American homophobia. Abelove argues, "Why were Americans such nonentities sexually? Because they sublimated their sexual energy so completely. As for their despicable moralism, that was the rationale for the sublimation. And was the goal of American sublimation the production of art, science, law, architecture, music, literature? No: the goal was cash, acquisition, accumulation. All the energy that was not loosed sexually was going toward making money and toward very little else" (387). See Henry Abelove, "Freud, Male Homosexuality, and the Americans," *The Lesbian and Gay Studies Reader*: 381–93.

32. Scudder uses the term "friend" in a similarly complicated way, in reference first to Clara French, the woman of whom Scudder said that "the dream of

her life and mine had been that we might work together" (113). French died shortly after Scudder joined the Wellesley faculty, an event Scudder marks in the autobiography by stating "from the day that the friend of my youth died, the door to what people call passion swung to in my heart" (113). She later refers to Converse as one of her ex-students who "has entered the inmost region [in her mind] in my power to open" and calls her "a friend who can share both jokes and prayers" (220; 223).

33. The reference to Jocelin's nose of course raises the specter of Freud to today's reader. Although I am not suggesting that Converse was here responding directly either to Freud or the sexologists, it is clear that both these discourses would have been available to the women of Converse's circle from the 1890s onward. Scudder, for example, commenting on the tendency of modern autobiography to talk about what she calls the "Sex Life," asserts casually that "Freud is of course largely responsible; and he has much to answer for" (211).

34. Sylvia's response to this, a guilty blushing over her implied love of Jocelin, makes bodily manifest her recognition that her relationship with Enid is more than simply a friendship; it is a relationship betrayed by what amounts to another romantic love.

35. The Greek Artemis and her Roman version Diana, of course, were figures of both strength and beauty and were specifically imaged as living in the wild, far from men. Pomeroy notes that Artemis was associated as well with the Amazons, and that the "Amazons worshipped Artemis and resembled her. Both goddess and Amazons wore short tunics, were archers, and avoided the company of males" (5). Pomeroy further explains that Artemis "never submitted to a monogamous marriage" but took various "consorts," and that this unmarried state was reinterpreted by later generations as a state of virginity (6).

36. For a study of another fictional response to the sexologists, see Josephine Donovan's analysis of Sarah Orne Jewett's *A Country Doctor*: "Nan Prince and the Golden Apples."

37. Originally considered a victim of her context (girls' schools, for instance) or of the predatory active invert, the passive invert was generally ignored by sexologists through the 1890s, only coming under discussion as a serious pervert in the early twentieth century. Interestingly, more recent lesbian discussions of the contemporary version of the active/passive dichotomy—the butch/femme couple—have also centered on the butch, continuing often to view the femme's lesbianism as somehow suspect or less "real" than the butch's. Correctives to this can be found in the work, among others, of Joan Nestle, Lesléa Newman, and Minnie Bruce Pratt. See especially Nestle's *A Restricted Country* (Ithaca: Firebrand Books, 1987), Newman's edited collection *The Femme Mystique* (Boston: Alyson Publications, 1995), and Pratt's *S/HE* (Ithaca: Firebrand Books, 1995).

38. She associates this with tasting "the fruit of the Tree of Knowledge," a reference that conventionally links heterosexual erotic desire not only with knowledge but also with sin.

39. That Enid shoulders this weight in the novel becomes particularly clear when she is viewed alongside Jeanne Dumarais, the embodiment of conventional Southern and New Orleanian femininity. Although Converse names the young woman after Jeanne d'Arc, suggesting a comparison, Jeanne is not only not a model of the future, she is not even able to survive into that future: Converse writes out the sweet but childish Jeanne, who dies an early, tragic death by fire.

40. This reconfiguration is reflected in Enid's use of what the businessman Jacques dismissively calls "sentimental principles" as underlying rules of Enid's socialism, a usage that blurs the lines of public and private and that reflects the version of Christian Socialism that Converse and Scudder lived by and worked for in their involvement in the settlement house movement.

41. For an extremely helpful overview of these issues' intersections in the American novel of Converse's period, see Amy Kaplan, "Nation, Region and Empire," *Columbia History of the American Novel*, ed. Emory Elliott (New York: Columbia University Press, 1991): 240–66.

42. James goes on to write, "at any rate, the subject is very national, very typical. I wished to write a very *American* tale, a tale very characteristic of our social conditions, and I asked myself what was the most salient and peculiar point in our social life. The answer was: the situation of women, the decline of the sentiment of sex, the agitation on their behalf" (20). Given the literary context of Converse's life and work, it seems probable that she would have been familiar with James's novel by the time she wrote *Diana Victrix*, but even without a direct link between the two, they suggest the broad circulation of ideas on Boston marriages and/or inversion.

CHAPTER 3: SLAVERY, SEXUALITY, AND GENRE

1. As the cultural repository of all of the white bourgeois lady's denied sexuality, the stereotype of the black woman was seen as the True Woman's direct opposite, her Other, thus disqualifying the black woman from occupying the space of virtuous Victorian lady. For a further discussion of stereotypes of black women as they appeared specifically in fiction, see Christian and Carby, *Reconstructing*. For discussions of the American version of this gender ideal and its ideological function, see Nancy F. Cott, *The Bonds of Womanhood: "Woman's Sphere" in New England, 1780–1835* (New Haven: Yale University Press, 1977) and Barbara Welter, "The Cult of True Womanhood: 1820–1850," *American Quarterly* 18 (Sept. 1966): 151–74.

2. *Colored American Magazine*'s 1901 biographical article entitled "Pauline Hopkins," which was probably written by Hopkins herself, explicitly addresses the different reaches of different genres, noting that Hopkins's "ambition is to become a writer of fiction, in which the wrongs of her race shall be so handled as to enlist the sympathy of all classes of citizens, in this way reaching those who never read history or biography" (219).

Hopkins served between 1900 and 1904 as editor of the women's department, literary editor, and, evidence suggests, unacknowledged editor-in-chief of *Colored American Magazine*. For details of Hopkins's involvement at *Colored American Magazine* see William Stanley Braithwaite, "Negro America's First Magazine," *Negro Digest* 6.2 (Dec. 1947): 21–26; Jane Campbell, "Pauline Elizabeth Hopkins," *Afro-American Writers Before the Harlem Renaissance*, Vol. 50 of *Dictionary of Literary Biography*, eds. Trudier Harris and Thadius M. Davis. (Detroit: Gale Research, 1984): 182–89; Carby "Introduction"; Abby Arthur Johnson and Ronald M. Johnson, *Propaganda and Aesthetics: The Literary Politics of Afro-American Magazines in the Twentieth Century* (Amherst, Mass: University of Massachusetts Press, 1979); Marilyn Lamping, "Pauline Elizabeth Hopkins," *American Women Writers: A Critical Reference Guide From Colonial Times to the Present*, Vol. 2, ed. Lina Mainiero (New York: Ungar, 1988): 325–27; Ann Allen Shockley, "Pauline Elizabeth Hopkins: A Biographical Excursion into Obscurity," *Phylon* 33 (Spring 1972): 22–26; see also the essays in *The Unruly Voice: Rediscovering Pauline Elizabeth Hopkins*, ed. John Cullen Gruesser (Urbana: University of Illinois Press, 1996).

3. At this point in her career, as should become evident through a reading of *Contending Forces*, Hopkins was still fairly optimistic and imagined the possibility of African-American community as part of a larger, democratic America. In her later magazine novels, she grew less and less hopeful, removing her heroines first to England for their happy ending and then to ancient Africa.

4. Harriet Jacobs makes an analogous political use of sentimental conventions, although she employs them within the slave narrative.

5. Baker sees a link between what he calls Hopkins's "white-faced minstrelsy" and what he more respectfully calls Booker T. Washington's "manipulations of minstrel discourse." Extending the metaphor in gendered terms, he goes on to dismiss nineteenth-century women writers such as Hopkins (writers he casually refers to as "daughters"), characterizing their use of minstrel discourse as the wearing of "makeup" while characterizing Washington's use of it as "mastery of form" (26).

6. For charges of assimilation in *Contending Forces*, see Robert A. Bone, *The Negro Novel in America* (New Haven: Yale University Press, 1958); Gwendolyn Brooks, Afterword [to *Contending Forces*] (Urbana: University of Illinois Press, 1996); Dickson D. Bruce, *Black American Writing From the Nadir: The Evolution of a Literary Tradition, 1877–1915* (Baton Rouge: Louisiana State University Press, 1989); Jane Campbell, *Mythic Black Fiction: The Transformation of History* (Knoxville: University of Tennessee Press, 1986); Arlene Elder, *The "Hindered Hand": Cultural Implications of Early African-American Fiction* (Westport, Conn.: Greenwood Press, 1978). Brooks's afterword to *Contending Forces* comes to mind here as an example of what I would read as a historically grounded misreading of Hopkins's text. That is, Brooks, speaking out of the historical context of 1978, charges Hopkins with "assimilationist urges" (437), as well as "a touching reliance on the dazzles and powers of anticipated integration" (434).

And while she grants that Hopkins "was understandably a daughter of her time" (436), she criticizes what she sees as Hopkins's lack of anger and cites Hopkins's use of a mulatto heroine as evidence that Hopkins "consistently proves herself a continuing slave, despite little bursts of righteous heat" (434). While Brooks's reading of Hopkins might be used to support an argument that Hopkins had internalized some of her culture's racism, Brooks's holding Hopkins to the standards and issues of Brooks's day rather than Hopkins's own time does a disservice to Hopkins's work. For charges of "nonrealism" or sentimentalism, see Bone; Hugh M. Gloster, *Negro Voices in American Fiction* (Chapel Hill: University of North Carolina Press, 1948); and Vernon Loggins, *The Negro Author: His Development in American to 1900* (Port Washington, New York: Kennikat Press, 1931).

7. Hazel V. Carby, in her Introduction to *The Magazine Novels of Pauline Hopkins*, and Claudia Tate, in *Domestic Allegories of Political Desire*, both discuss in some detail the composition of the audiences of black magazines at the turn of the century. While *Contending Forces* was not, of course, published serially in that magazine as Hopkins's other novels were, it seems reasonable to assume that her readership would have been similar to that of the magazine, particularly since the book was published by the magazine's publisher, the Colored Co-operative Publishing Company.

8. See also Jane P. Tompkins, *Sensational Designs: The Cultural Work of American Fiction, 1790–1860* (New York: Oxford University Press, 1985) and Judith Fetterley, Introduction, *Provisions: A Reader From 19th Century American Women*, ed. Judith Fetterley (Bloomington: Indiana University Press, 1985): 1–40.

9. The sentimental novel, of course, needs to be read as both radical and limited or generically constrained. As a genre, this "domestic fiction" was used by nineteenth-century American writers to lay claims to (among other things) female spheres and powers, a radical cultural intervention in terms of gender roles. At the same time, however, these spheres and powers were absolutely middle-class and so participated in the consolidation of middle-class cultural hegemony—hardly a radical undertaking. Thus, while it is important to collapse Yarborough's (and others') dichotomy between the sentimental novel and the political novel, it is also important to remember that "political" can mean many (and conflicting) things at once.

10. For extremely helpful readings of Hopkins's later "magazine fiction," see Ammons's *Conflicting Stories* and Tate's *Domestic Allegories*.

11. Gloster points out that in plantation fiction "the Mixed blood is portrayed as the embodiment of the worst qualities of both races and hence a menace to the dominant group. To these propagandists the mulatto woman is the debaser of the white aristocrat, while the mulatto man is the besmircher of white virginity" (12). Thomas Dixon and Thomas Page, two of the most important authors of the plantation school, thus conflated the racial with the sexual to figure black men and women as animalistic and inferior to the white man.

12. For an alternative reading of miscegenation, see Dearborn.

13. See Campbell, *Mythic*; Peterson; and Tate, "Pauline Hopkins," as well as her *Domestic Allegories*.

14. Shortly after this Mrs. Willis reiterates this claim stating, "We are not held responsible for compulsory sin, only for the sin that is pleasant to our thoughts and palatable to our appetites" (154–55).

15. This question of choice is one to which I will return, as it is central to my reading of Sappho's eventual "happy ending."

16. Similarly, much later in the novel, the narrator comments that "time and moral training among the white men of the South are the only cures for concubinage" (332), a moral training presumably in the hands of women.

17. The reference here to "the foreigner, all races" suggests that while she does not explicitly address the position of other outsiders to dominant American identity categories, Hopkins was not unaware either of their presence or of the analogies among the situations of various of these groups.

18. While Hopkins clearly portrays Southern racism as more overtly violent than the economic racism of the North, she certainly does chronicle Northern racism. The white racist Colonel Clapp, for instance, tells John Langley that he never hires African-American clerks, claiming, "I have had a number of your best men tried in clerical positions, and you always fail to compete favorably with an ordinary white clerk. You can't ask the people to pay for ignorant incompetents" (232).

19. Harriet Wilson makes this point in graphic detail in her 1859 account of the life of a "free" Northern black in *Our Nig; or, Sketches from the Life of a Free Black* (1859; repr. New York: Vintage, 1984).

20. Hopkins echoes this claim in her first magazine novel, *Hagar's Daughter*. A white character from the South (Kentucky) points out to Cuthbert Sumner, Hopkins's representative of New England white liberalism, "You know yourself, Mr. Sumner, that caste as found at the North is a terrible thing. It is killing the black man's hope there in every avenue; it is centered against his advancement. We in the South are flagrant in our abuse of the Negro but we do not descend to the pettiness that your section practices. We shut our eyes to many things in the South because of our near relationship to many of these despised people" (*Hagar's Daughter: A Story of Southern Caste Prejudice*, 1901; repr. in *The Magazine Novels of Pauline Hopkins*, ed. Hazel V. Carby (New York: Oxford University Press, 1988), 159–60).

21. Interestingly, perhaps in a gesture of recognition of her importance or of her age, Ophelia Davis is always referred to by the narrator either by her full name or by "Mrs. Davis" (although we receive no account of a husband): unlike Dora and Sappho she is never called simply by her first name, a usage I follow here.

22. The church scene too shows the complicated nature of race relations in late-nineteenth-century American life, as both Mrs. Robinson and Mrs. Davis get financial support in their rivalry from their employers.

23. There is, however, an emphasis on fashion and clothing in all of the novel's depictions of Mrs. Davis: Davis explains how she came by her silk dress and often describes or discusses her own and others' appearance.

24. Interestingly, Hopkins draws no distinctions of gender in her depictions of regional character: Hopkins attributes Langley's sensuality as well as his racism and lack of commitment to community to his Southern origins, blaming the man that he has become at the novel's end to "events of his childhood in the South" (335).

25. This body is, among other things, constructed as heterosexual. In a tradition stretching from Enlightenment dichotomies of mind/body as male/female to the woman as body under slavery, in which body implies object to be sexually exploited by the male slave owner, woman in western tradition is always embodied in relation to man. Female erotic desire directed toward another woman produces an entirely different constellation of relations among notions of mind, body, desire, and subjectivity so that, for instance, we cannot assume that a woman's desire for another woman would need to be displaced into moral service in order to render both women as subjects rather than objects. I take up this discussion in greater detail in my reading of Florence Converse's *Diana Victrix*.

26. Recall that Boston marriages, a phenomenon of late-nineteenth-century America, took their name from the popular perception that they flourished in Boston, although historical evidence suggests that they existed all over America.

27. As should be clear, I am in direct disagreement here with both Houston Baker's claim and his implicit value judgment in *Workings of the Spirit* that Sappho's name does not imply what he calls "anomalous sexual proclivities" but only "a classical mastery of the word" (24).

28. For a brief but effective discussion of Grace Montfort's symbolic rape, see Carby, *Reconstructing*, 132. For a reading of Hopkins's treatment of the slippage between legal and popular constructions of race in *Hagar's Daughter*, see Claire Pamplin's "'Race' and Identity in Pauline Hopkins's *Hagar's Daughter*," *Redefining the Political Novel: American Women Writers, 1797–1901*, ed. Sharon M. Harris (Knoxville: University of Tennessee Press, 1995), 169–83.

29. Although Baker never explains why he recodes enslaved women's rape as seduction, his words offer a veiled reference to Jane Gallop's *The Daughter's Seduction: Feminism and Psychoanalysis* (Ithaca: Cornell University Press, 1982).

30. It is crucial to remain aware both of Hopkins's radical use of the figure of the mother and of the ways in which dominant culture has both romanticized this figure and turned it against African-American women, attempting to recontain its radical potential. Contemporary uses of the stereotype of the powerful black matriarch conflate racial and gender attacks by casting the African-American matriarch as too powerful (i.e., masculine) and consequently casting the absent African-American patriarch as powerless (i.e., emasculated or feminized) so that the African-American woman simultaneously becomes a threat to both African-American and white culture. In the *Moynihan Report*, for instance, the strong mother is read as the stereotype of the superpowerful emasculating African-

American woman. For an extremely perceptive reading of the effects of the *Moynihan Report* on contemporary American constructions of African-American female subjectivity, see Spillers.

CHAPTER 4: MARÍA AMPARO RUIZ DE BURTON'S GEOGRAPHIES
OF RACE, REGIONS OF RELIGION

1. *Testimonios* are first-person accounts commenting on the larger social and political transformations of the period. The California *testimonios* were solicited by Hubert Howe Bancroft for his research project on the history of California.

2. David J. Weber points out that the average duration of a claim was seventeen years (156); the result was that eventually, in addition to losses through rejected claims, "at least 40% of the land owned under Mexican grants was sold, by the owners, to meet the costs and expenses involved in complying with the Act" (McWilliams 62).

3. Ruiz de Burton's own family, landowners in Southern California, lost a great deal of land through the combination of the Land Acts, squatters, and the railroad debacle. This loss continued into Ruiz de Burton's adult life; her letters to George Davidson contain frequent references to her court battles. She tells him in a letter of March 6, 1874, for instance, that

> the judge has allowed the Squatter Robinson to remain here in our property only because his lawyer said that the trial of the suit of ejectment might case [sic] him to have a relapse & become insane again. So that, as the man has been crazy and might be so again if exited we cannot have our property because if he is ejected he will be exited!
>
> What do you think of such justice?

See her Letter (March 6, 1874). George Davidson Correspondence. Bancroft Library, University of California, Berkeley. In August of 1882 she goes on to tell him that she hopes "to effect a compromise & stop litigation. . . . They see we have the advantage & chances of winning entirely on our side. But they can annoy us and keep us in litigation for a long time." See her Letter (August 16, 1882). George Davidson Correspondence. Bancroft Library, University of California, Berkeley.

4. While the discovery of gold brought Americans into Northern California from the 1850s onward, Southern California remained largely untouched by this wave of settlers so that through the 1870s Mexican ways of life remained intact in the South, and the Dons retained some power. It was only with the advent of the railroad that Anglo immigrants finally began to take over Southern California. The arrival of the Southern Pacific line in 1876 began this process, but it wasn't until 1886, with the appearance of the rival Santa Fe line, that the Dons' fall from power became inevitable.

5. As the northern frontier of the Spanish colony, California was sparsely populated under Spanish rule, originally colonized through settlement mainly by the

Spanish Missions. Founded between 1769 and 1823, these Missions were run by Franciscan priests and were intended to "civilize" the "savage" indigenous peoples, the "*indios*," and, of course, to convert them to Catholicism while exploiting their labor. The Mission system began the process that eventually wiped out nearly all of the California Indians, partly by exposing them to alcohol and diseases such as syphilis, and partly by stripping them of their cultures and living patterns. In 1796, when the Missions were first established in Southern California, the native American population was about 30,000, but by 1910 there were only around 1250 California *indios* remaining, a decrease that leads historian Carey McWilliams to conclude that "so far as the Indians were concerned, contact with the Missions meant death" (29). This system also established the *indio* as the exploited labor source, a position s/he continued to hold during the period of secularization (beginning in the early 1830s and completed by 1846). After Mexico became independent of Spain in 1821, a few land grants placed some Southern California land in secular hands, but it wasn't until what became known as the "rancho period"—1833 to 1846—that the government parceled out large portions of land in Southern California to upper-class Mexicans. These Mexicans, known as the *gente de razon*, continued the Mission tradition of "peon labor" and built a system of profitable ranchos on the backs of *indio* labor, a system that remained intact until the war with America (1846–48) and the subsequent breakup of the great landed estates. My redaction of California history draws on the work of McWilliams, Monroy, Pitt, and Weber.

6. Being neither mainland Spaniards nor American *indios*, the ruling class was forced to establish an identity between these poles. But whereas the *gente de razon* and their descendants might have been seen as "Spanish" in the eyes of the *indios*, increasingly both these ruling and ruled classes became *mestizo*—a mix of Spanish settlers, African slaves, and indigenous Native Americans. What truly differentiated the *gente de razon* from the *indios*, then, was not biological difference—since neither category had "pure" bloodlines—but rather caste or cultural difference—class privilege and, in the early days of settlement as least, religion and language.

7. Carey McWilliams argues that the social structures suggested by this metaphor are also analogous. Citing the work of Charles Dwight Williard, McWilliams offers the analogy that "the Indians were the slaves, the *gente de razon* were the plantation owners or 'whites,' and the Mexicans were the 'poor whites'" (52). He goes on to remind us that "the *gente de razon*, in addition to being conscious of their class and status, were extremely race-conscious. They looked down upon the Mexicans and Indians as a different breed of people— darker, illiterate, churlish, incapable of progress or understanding" (52); this is certainly a formulation echoed in white slaveowners' representations of the enslaved.

8. This rhetorical process was by no means confined to the nineteenth century: Neil Foley reports one Congressman Box describing Mexicans in 1928 as "dis-

eased of body, subnormal intellectually, and moral morons of the most hopeless type." See his *The White Scourge: Mexicans, Blacks, and Poor Whites in Texas Cotton Culture* (Berkeley: University of California Press, 1997), 54.

9. This also rehearses a Spanish claim to purity of blood as a way of disavowing a racially and culturally mixed heritage. As Roberto Fernández Retamar argues in his essay, "Against the Black Legend," "Spain's capital sin was the doctrine of 'purity of blood'" according to which Spain was occupied by, but warded off and eventually drove out, "Arab infidels" (63). Fernández Retamar points out that, in fact, "a much richer truth can be registered: Christians, Moors, and Jews, all equally Spanish, lived side by side for more than seven centuries, mutually and fruitfully influencing each other" (63–64). Hence, Ruiz de Burton must be seen here as using a nineteenth-century racial discourse to serve two purposes. She defends against what Roberto Fernández Retamar calls the historical "richer truth" that "European" doesn't necessarily describe a racially or ethnically single people, and furthermore she defends against the fact that, even within the discourse of her day, "Spanish blood," like the category of Californio she uses it to guarantee, was a hybrid category open to interpretation (63).

10. Although Ruiz de Burton has Dr. Norval, in his original account of Lola, specify that Doña Theresa Medina "was carried off by the Apache Indians and then sold to the Mohave Indians" (28), in all subsequent references tribal affiliations are entirely elided, with the effect of conflating and collapsing all Indians into "rascally Indians" (34). Against this homogenized backdrop of the Indian Other, the narrative emphasizes that Lola is Mexican: the Medina family has a countryseat outside of Mexico City and a town house in the city but her mother is captured while pregnant with Lola from their hacienda "in the northern part of Sonora" (194). Coming from a wealthy, cultured, educated, landed family, however, Lola can be read figuratively as occupying the space of the Californio in the novel as well, given that Ruiz de Burton is most interested in *Who Would Have Thought It?* in establishing the cultural capital of the Medina family in relation to an East Coast American culture, a cultural capital she was interested in establishing for the Californios as well.

11. Her narratives of West to East movement resemble those of certain Native Americans of the period. See, for instance, Zitkala-Sä's accounts of being taken from the West to Eastern Anglo schools in *American Indian Stories* (Lincoln: University of Nebraska Press, 1985; repr of 1921).

12. Mr. Hackwell comes in for much of Ruiz de Burton's most savage sarcasm and stands as the novel's main representative of external decorum and repression, which veils internal self-indulgence. First as minister and then as successful war hero, Hackwell appears to be a model of propriety, but the narrator presents to the reader a Hackwell who is corrupt from the novel's beginning, drinking in private, gossiping with his fellow minister, flirting with various women, seducing Mrs. Norval for her money (when it appears that Dr. Norval has been killed during an expedition to Africa), and ultimately plotting to force Lola to marry him against her will.

13. Ruiz de Burton explicitly links this discussion to the punitive politics of Reconstruction when at the end of the novel she has Julius Caesar Cackle, rising political star and representative of the most provincial, corrupt, and self-serving of American politicians, condemn Grant's generous and honorable treatment of the surrendering Lee. The narrator explains that Cackle wants Americans to forget "the soldierly courtesy, the gentlemanly consideration" of Grant, then comments that the "moderation and good sense shown then by General Grant were enthusiastically praised by the grateful South and held up in striking contrast with the spirit of vengeance and unforgiveness which unhappily at that time pervaded this country" (294–95). Although she distances this critique by locating it in the moment of the South's surrender, the "spirit of vengeance and unforgiveness" can certainly be seen as descriptive of Reconstruction politics in general.

14. For more on the complex and varying Native American cultures of the Southwest, see Monroy; see also Lisbeth Haas's *Conquest and Historical Identities in California* (Berkeley: University of California Press, 1995).

15. Here Ruiz de Burton is clearly in conversation with abolitionist discourses, invoking their language and their topos of the white child mistaken for black and sold into slavery to both revise them and call attention to their limits. Her representation of the "white" child who "looks" "black" might be read as an ironic inversion of a narrative such as William and Ellen Craft's, for instance. In the opening of their slave narrative, William states that

> slavery in America is not at all confined to persons of any particular complexion; there are a very large number of slaves as white as any one; but as the evidence of a slave is not admitted in court against a free white person, it is almost impossible for a white child, after having been kidnapped and sold into or reduced to slavery, in a part of the country where it is not known . . . ever to recover its freedom (2–3).

He then goes on to recount the story of a child who "had no trace of African descent in any feature" but was nonetheless sold into slavery, a story that serves to underscore the degree to which bodily color and legal racial identity are detachable concepts. Ruiz de Burton's Lola more closely resembles Craft's example of "a white boy who . . . was stolen from his home in Ohio, tanned and stained in such a way that he could not be distinguished from a person of color, and then sold as a slave in Virginia" (7): both these images suggest the inverse of Ellen Craft, "of African extraction" "passing" for white (2). See *Running a Thousand Miles for Freedom* (Salem: Ayer Co., 1991).

16. The racism of this anti-Indian position recurs through both of Ruiz de Burton's novels, suggesting that it reflects her personal views as well as a larger American racial geopolitics. See, for instance, her reference in a letter to Hubert Howe Bancroft to the "Santo Tomás Indians" as "barbarian" and "savage." See her Letter to Hubert Howe Bancroft (August 5, 1878). Savage Documents 2:121–23. Bancroft Library, University of California, Berkeley.

17. This passage, along with Mrs. Norval's comment, "I shall do *my duty as*

a Christian woman; but she cannot expect to grow up in idleness and be a burden to us" (23–24 emphasis in original) link the treatment of Lola to that of Topsy in Stowe's *Uncle Tom's Cabin.*

18. This process, as I will discuss, is central to *The Squatter and the Don.*

19. Similarly, the discussion of Lola's color as a skin "stain" (100), by drawing on a language of cleanliness/filth, gestures ironically toward Anglo-American stereotypes of "dirty Mexicans."

20. The blush here marks a form of bodily color which is both desirable and gendered: rather than marking Lola's race, it proves her femininity.

21. That is, unlike many novels of the Civil War and Reconstruction periods, this plot does not function to reunite the divided North and South or to offer a model of happy coexistence of black and white races in America. That it might well have done so is signaled by the symbolic weight of Lola's bodily color(s) as potential metaphor of United States racial and regional relations. Eva Saks points out that "the social body was conceived as doubly miscegenous: between 1850 and 1880, the South often portrayed itself as different from, yet conjoined with or imprisoned within, the United States" while at the same time "another recurrent theme is that the nation, in its socio-political identity, was becoming 'miscegenous.' Here the national body was explicitly conceived as a white body, while blacks were portrayed in a simile as the fraction of polluting blood within this body, an unassimilable *clot* in the national body and the white family" (64 emphasis in original). But while Lola's spots occupy a structural position similar to that of the "clot" in Saks's formulation, Ruiz de Burton's narrative turns the force of its reconciliatory romance to the transnational plot.

22. Lola's father is also portrayed as very white: "his hair was very light and his eyes were blue" (250).

23. Even the narrative convention of a moment of redemptive maternity, in which it seems that even Mrs. Norval can be humbled and cleansed by the influence of her wounded son, has only a temporary effect on Mrs. Norval. When Julian asks for a kiss, the narrator tells us, Mrs. Norval "almost recoiled, but she could not deny it. She gave him the kiss, and the pure touch of his lips was the heavenly charm which unsealed the fountain of her best feelings, her purest affections; and the tears which had not flowed for her lost husband rushed to her eyes now, and she fell on her knees weeping by her boy's bed" (136). The highly conventional rhetoric of redemptive maternity that Ruiz de Burton uses here only underscores Mrs. Norval's inadequacy as a mother, for even these best feelings evoked by her son are only temporary: the results last only as long as she watches "by the bedside of her son" (137).

24. Ruiz de Burton is, of course, in keeping here with the majority of dominant American writers. For detailed discussions of biblical and Puritan sources of American literature, see, for instance, Werner Sollors or see Sacvan Bercovich's *The Puritan Origins of the American Self* (New Haven: Yale University Press, 1975).

25. Ruiz de Burton eventually brings together both the criticism of Mrs. Norval and the defense of Catholic (read Mexican) motherhood in a conversation between Emma Hackwell and Lola regarding Mrs. Norval's arrangement of nurses for Hackwell and her son Julian:

> "Mrs. Norval is a noble woman,—the best Christian, best mother, best everything I ever did see; and what she does, she does actuated by the best and purest motives. She is perfectly unselfish, and she wished us to do what is best for us all."
>
> "Why, you make her almost the equal of the Virgin Mary!" exclaimed Lola, astounded.
>
> "I should think she was! Why shouldn't she be regarded as the equal of the Virgin Mary?" (138–39)

Lola labels this "blasphemy" but Emma's description is as fitting of Doña Theresa as it is inappropriate for Mrs. Norval, so that the effect of this interchange is not only to establish Mrs. Norval as disqualified from the role of ideal American mother, but also to establish Doña Theresa (and Catholic motherhood in general) as fitting that role.

As I will discuss, this representation of maternity is taken up in *The Squatter and The Don*, where Catholic motherhood, represented by Mary Darrell and Doña Josepha Alamar, again occupies a privileged position.

26. Franchot links anti-Mexican Catholicism in the 1840s to a New England anti-Irish sentiment, because the Irish famine had produced a huge wave of Irish Catholic immigration into the U.S., particularly New England (40 and passim). Ruiz de Burton's novel reflects this in a curious fashion through the figures of the Norval's two Irish servants—the cook and the chambermaid. The novel represents the two as bigoted and racist, describing the cook, for instance, as "a good Catholic" but showing the two servants as identifying on racial lines with the Norvals against Lola rather than identifying on religious lines with Lola. When Lola is sent on her first night in the Norval home to sleep with the servants, for instance, the cook tells Lola, "I am shure I don't want to slape with any of the likes of ye, naither. Niggers ain't my most particliest admirashun, I can tell ye, no more nor toads nor cateypillars" (30). While the sentiments of this statement echo those of Mrs. Norval and thus might be read as a satirical condemnation of the cook's racism by the narrator, the attempt at dialect and the representation of the two servants as dirty, living in foul air, suggests that the narrator is as eager to distance herself from these Catholics on the basis of class difference as the servants are to distance themselves from Lola on the basis of racial difference.

27. The novel's favored New England characters generally fail altogether to repress their feelings, a failure used by the narrator to signal not the characters' shortcomings as New Englanders but rather the flawed nature of the New England model itself. Julian Norval, for instance, expresses a boyhood crush on Emma Hackwell, an expression that marks him as atypical: his "impetuosity" is "alarming" to Emma, the narrator dryly notes, "being to her way of thinking un-

natural in a good New Englander, and not to be trusted by a sensible Yankee girl" (51). Julian, the narrator admits elsewhere, "boy though he was, had been the hardest to teach the self-restraint which Mrs. Norval thought the great desideratum in a well-organized family" (84) and in fact never learns that restraint. He professes first his boyhood infatuation with Emma and then his mature love of Lola. His aunt Lavvy's "pent-up caresses," meanwhile, are given to her pet canaries, a displacement the novel represents as at least a partial solution to the problem of repression, noting that "in the sunshine of Miss Lavvy's love the canaries thrived, as though in a genial atmosphere" (85). Her love of both Julian and Hackwell eventually gets expressed in her careful nursing of them, just as her love of her brother Isaac compels her to suffer various indignities at the hands of Congressmen as she battles bureaucracy trying to locate him in a confederate war camp.

28. I am grateful to Anne E. Goldman both for first identifying Popocatepetl for me and for many helpful conversations about Ruiz de Burton in general. Interestingly, this volcano offered an opportunity for metaphor to other writers in the U.S. as well: Jenny Franchot argues that W. H. Prescott, in his 1843 *The History of the Conquest of Mexico*, represents Mexico as a New World Italy in part through a metaphorization of the volcano. She quotes his description: the "long dark wreaths of vapor, rolling up from the hoary head of Popocatepetl, told that the destroying element was, indeed, at work in the bosom of the beautiful Valley" (44).

29. This is a risk for many women writing in this period. Their responses to the problem vary, but at least some take on the project more directly, as my discussions of Pauline Hopkins and Florence Converse show.

30. Ruiz de Burton's sarcasm and bitterness is apparent as her letter continues,

> I wrote to the Genl a few days ago about the allowance of 3 months extra pay granted by Congress for services in the Mex. War, and which the disbursing officers of the Treasury Dept. have obstinately refused to pay.
>
> They have faught [sic] against the poor disheartened beneficiaries for over 30 years, and now the matter went through the Court of Claims and is appealed to the Supreme Court and it is contended that the little pittance must be shaved down more than half!
>
> If Congress wishes, the agony might be stopped at any day, as the protest of the Controllers and Auditors of the Treasury is, that congress meant to say what it *didn't*. So if Congress will have the kindness to say to the Treasury gentlemen, that it does speak english, and it meant what it said, then we might get our pittance.

31. This parallel is suggested in the letter cited above. Just after Ruiz de Burton's request for help she goes on to comment on the fate of her own land battles as a Californio with the government, noting, "the court here has made such a sweeping decision in our case, that it has swept away my homestead and every acre of our land. The man has no more sense of justice or idea of honor than a sorrel mule. I feel desperate, as you may suppose."

32. This use of the individual's relation to the government to emblematize a group's relation (whether the group is defined by gender, nationality, ethnicity, or region) calls to mind Barbara Fields's assertion that it was "much more fundamental to the historic task of Reconstruction to define the proper relation of the Southern states to the national government, and of the citizen to the national government, than it was to supervise relations between the ex-slaves and the ex-masters" (164).

33. The relentless satire informing the novel, however, suggests that Ruiz de Burton is actually far more critical of and skeptical about the great nation of America than her narrative goals allow her to directly express. This sarcasm, however, does emerge in her tone throughout, as well as in narrative touches such as the characters' names: the New England ministers Hackwell and Hammerhead; the government man Mr. Blower; and especially the rising political family, the Cackles.

34. In contrast, Julian experiences a disillusionment similar to the narrator's when he battles the bureaucracy of the government, a battle in which he too appears as the honest individual suffering at the hands of an indifferent or corrupt government. Unlike Lavvy's, his complaints are eventually heard and redressed, a response not unconnected to the fact that he is a man.

35. It also points to Lavvy's alignment with the Californios, echoing as it does the pen name Ruiz de Burton used for publishing *The Squatter and the Don*: "C. Loyal," a name that Sánchez and Pita, in their introduction to *The Squatter and the Don*, point out signifies *Ciudadano Leal* (Loyal Citizen), "a common letter-closing practice used in official government correspondence in Mexico during the nineteenth-century" (11).

36. We are told, for instance, that Don Luis Medina (Doña Theresa's husband and Lola's father) reads English, German, Spanish, and French (195), and the novel tracks his conversation with his father-in-law Don Felipe over Mexican government, a discussion that exhibits his understanding of European precedents and American influences. Ruiz de Burton also gives detailed descriptions of the generous and lavish treatment Isaac receives in one of the Medina family's several homes from Don Luis Medina and Don Felipe.

37. Irony here masks a clear understanding of the ways that both gender and genre determine whose voice gets heard. Ruiz de Burton exhibits a similar understanding of the way nationality in combination with gender inflect the reception of a voice: in a letter to Hubert Howe Bancroft, referring to his attempts to collect Californio histories as part of his projected history of California, Ruiz de Burton writes, "So, we must not blame the disheartened Californians if they do not rise to the importance of appreciating your work, and you, without resentment for their unambitious indifference, which is the result of their misfortune, must speak kindly of them. You can afford it. And being an American you can say many things that the American people would perhaps not accept from a foreigner." See her Carta a Hubert Howe Bancroft (July 15, 1878), Savage Documents, 2: 121–23,

Bancroft Library, University of California, Berkeley. For more on the Californio relationship to Bancroft see Sánchez.

38. Ironically, she thus replicates the very rhetoric historically used against the Dons, merely shifting it onto the *indios*.

39. It is this positive valence that differentiates Ruiz de Burton's narrative from so many other nineteenth-century discussions of difference. The nativism of the period, for example, figured immigrant difference as a liability, an old-world legacy to be abandoned, like an accent, as soon as possible.

40. Additionally, Ruiz de Burton uses Don Mariano as a vehicle for a discussion of the "Big Four" railroad monopoly and the ruinous effect it had on the Southern California economy when it successfully redirected a national railroad line from its originally proposed terminus in San Diego to a San Francisco terminus. The Don and his fellow San Diego landowners wait through the course of the novel for the proposed railroad, pinning their hopes of economic revival on the railroad that never arrives. The first transcontinental line did indeed run into San Francisco, beginning in 1869, largely as a result of the machinations of the Big Four.

41. The use of domestic plots to resolve cultural/political tensions is common in this period in the fiction of African-American writers as well, as Claudia Tate demonstrates in *Domestic Allegories of Political Desire*. I discuss this in more depth in my reading of Pauline Hopkins, but it is worth remarking here that Ruiz de Burton employs many of the narrative strategies Tate describes, using a familiar sentimental narrative form to convey to her readers what might have been somewhat radical and upsetting political ideas.

42. In this, Ruiz de Burton replicates the United States's policy (as, for instance, in the Homestead Act of 1862) of referring to Native American lands as "public lands."

43. I will discuss the question of language in more detail later in this chapter but at this point would comment that ironically the valence of "Spanish blood" is not at all that of Spanish as a spoken language. While the fiction of Spanish blood implies racial similarity to Anglos, the use of Spanish language suggests a more threatening difference from Anglos (a "foreign" language). Twentieth-century disputes about the "official" language used in California public schools (English or Spanish) suggests that this conflict is still a salient one.

44. This binary replicates a similar use of industrious/lazy to categorize (white) Americans in opposition to the enslaved.

45. Paradoxically, this link does help legitimize the Californios as Americans but as what might be seen as the wrong kind of Americans for Ruiz de Burton's purposes. That is, while the Native Americans were invoked by some nineteenth-century writers as the "real" Americans, they were inevitably represented in a nostalgic light, as what Werner Sollors calls the "legitimating ancestors" (124): the constantly disappearing past on which America would build its future.

46. This echoes her comment to Bancroft in her letter of July 15, 1878, where she says of "Californians in general" that

the fact of it is, (and a very serious fact which you as a conscientious historian must not omit) that *"the natives"* with their loss of all their property & their prestige, they have also lost all ambition. Without their realizing the fact, or analyzing the cause, they languidly surrender to the effect, and without struggling, or even protesting, they allow themselves to be swept away to "oblivion" by the furious avalanche let loose upon them by the hand of the Anglo-American the pitiless Anglo-American!

47. In terms of the land issue, the notion of Californios not being fit to own land also echoes the treatment of Native Americans in general (as opposed to specifically the California tribes) within American legal discourse. As Priscilla Wald points out, within the American legal system, "the natural right to own property is a critical component of the definition of personhood" (63). Thus, Native American "lack of tribal concept of private ownership" (65) of land was not only used to discount their claims to land but was also used as evidence that they were not legal subjects. What Anglo Americans considered Californio sloppiness or impreciseness in measuring land holdings might be read as similarly functioning to disqualify their claim not only to good capitalist status but also to American subject status.

For an interesting discussion of what gets to count as "Indian," see James A. Clifton's "Alternate Identities and Cultural Frontiers," in *Being and Becoming Indian: Biographical Studies of North American Frontiers*, ed. James A. Clifton (Chicago: The Dorsey Press, 1989). I would like to thank Malea Powell for helping me to think through the tangled question of "Indianness."

48. This distinction is paralleled on the level of plots: like *Who Would Have Thought it?*, *The Squatter and the Don* offers happy endings for the marriage plots but cannot imagine a happy ending for the public, political problems of the Dons.

49. This threat is mitigated by the Dons' class privilege, of course, but given that one of the main impulses behind *The Squatter and the Don* is to protest the loss of Californio class privilege, it is clear that any protection afforded the Dons by class is weak and contingent.

50. It also, according to Gabriel, refutes accusations that "the Spanish" are "indolent, unwilling to work" (343). In so doing, the "Spanish" are once again both linked to and distanced from the *indio*: linked by class status but differentiated on the basis of the Spaniard's industriousness.

51. Examples and discussions of this phenomenon are rife; for discussion of how this plays out in the specific context of the American "settlement" of the West, see, for instance, Annette Kolodny's *The Land Before Her: Fantasy and Experience of the American Frontiers, 1830–1860* (Chapel Hill: University of North Carolina Press, 1984) and Jane Tompkins's *West of Everything: The Inner Life of Westerns* (New York: Oxford University Press, 1992).

52. This rhetorical maneuver is parallel, of course, to slave holders' efforts to construct the enslaved as "beasts" so as to rationalize inhuman treatment of the enslaved. This analogy can be extended through a consideration of the Texas

Rangers, who were originally formed to fight Indians in Texas but became well known for lynching Indians and Mexicans in Texas and throughout the Southwest. Douglas Weber notes that "the Rangers (*los rinches*) have been regarded by some Texas Mexicans as the region's Ku Klux Klan" (187).

53. America could then simultaneously take Californios' land but still preach an ideology of individual rights (not the least of which were property rights), since within this logic rights attached only to white American men and Californios were not quite white American men.

54. This was not a new process even in Ruiz de Burton's day; Roberto Fernández Retamar, quoting Julio Le Riverend, notes that "at bottom, the conquest and colonization of America in the sixteenth century is part of the 'rise and consolidation of capitalism.' Those crimes can therefore be imputed to the 'rise and consolidation of capitalism,' not to this or that nation" (59), an insight that clearly locates capitalism as the underlying motivation of colonial expansion, a motivation, one might add, that still governs the United States's relations (economic and otherwise) with Mexico.

55. This linking of non-productive, effeminate, and culturally Other was well established by Ruiz de Burton's day. As early as 1850 Anglos were dismissing California Native Americans as "too lazy and effeminate to make successful hunters" (quoted in Monroy 193).

56. It is important to qualify this claim by noting that Californio men are figured as more sensitive to political and moral injustices but only up to a point. The Don, for instance, never objects to the oppression of the *indios*.

57. Clarence's blush, like Lola's in *Who Would Have Thought It?*, signifies both a good form of bodily color and a feminine one.

58. That she does not point out the racial inflection of this category is itself significant and is of course linked to her investment in coding the Californios as white.

59. Manuel M. Rodríguez perceptively observes a punning linguistic encoding of this link, commenting that Mary Darrell's "maiden" name, Moreneau, "would be pronounced 'Moreno,' meaning 'brown' or 'dark-haired' in Spanish; her sympathies for the Californios are in this way symbolically conveyed by her name" (55).

60. His temper later becomes a major force in the action of the novel despite his pre-marriage vow to control it, but as should be clear here, I read his family's religion as no less salient a force in the action of the novel.

61. This paralleling of the Don's wife with the settler's wife also stands as a counter argument to dominant Anglo conflations of the Don with the "savage" and "heathen" *indios*, since both Mary and Doña Josefa are devout Catholics. Tomás Almaguer notes that historically in California Catholicism helped differentiate the Mexican-American population from the "heathen" Chinese and Indians in the eyes of Anglo America. Catholicism, he argues, "drew religious boundaries and ethnic bonds among Mexicans and other Catholic populations in the

area. As a consequence Catholicism provided a stabilizing basis for Mexicans' ethnic identity and facilitated their structural integration into Anglo society in a period of intense political and economic upheaval" (63).

62. This reading also helps to explain why the figure of the mother is so important in the novel: whether Californio or Anglo, as the site of reproduction, both of the individual child and of the broader cultural order, the mother also embodies both the colonizer and the colonized.

63. In this context her buying of the Don's land signifies not Anglo-American appropriation of Californio land but rather one American citizen's legitimate economic contract with another, a recognition of the Don's rights of ownership over his own land.

64. That she is the mother Mary, of course, further links Mary to Californio religious and cultural tradition and underscores her authority by evoking the Virgin Mary—whose status as the mother of god gives her close to goddess status within the Catholic Church—and the Virgin of Guadalupe.

65. Benedict Anderson offers an interesting perspective on this issue, claiming that "Male-male bondings in a Protestant society which from the start rigidly prohibited miscegenation are paralleled by male-female 'holy loves' in the nationalist fiction of Latin America, where Catholicism permitted the growth of a large mestizo population. (It is telling that English has had to borrow 'mestizo' from Spanish)" (203). Male-female heterosexual bonds (marriages) thus shore up nationalist plots and are accompanied in the Latin American fiction by a recognition of the mixed nature of the population.

66. Here Ruiz de Burton may be said to be rehearsing the Spanish colonial attitude toward the Other (as historically embodied in the California Indians) rather than the American attitude. As historians have noted, the two cultures treated the indigenous population in different ways. The Spanish and Mexicans saw the *indios* as inferior but viewed them as having souls worth saving and labor worth extracting. The *indios* were, at least in theory, granted the rights of citizens and were allowed, even encouraged, to intermarry with the lower classes of Mexicans. Anglo America, in contrast, categorized the Native peoples as "savages" who were not entitled to legal rights. The United States, as David Weber notes, "either exterminated them or segregated them on reservations" (20). One might term these two approaches as assimilation and eradication: as Carey McWilliams points out, the "Spanish policy was to regard the Indian as a potential economic asset, but, under American rule, he was regarded as a liability to be liquidated as rapidly as possible" (42). Viewed in relation to these poles, Ruiz de Burton can be seen to employ the "Spanish policy" in her efforts to redefine "American" as mestizo.

67. This term is taken from Gloria Anzaldúa's *Borderlands/La Frontera: The New Mestiza* (San Francisco: Spinsters/Aunt Lute Press, 1987).

68. This formulation follows a historical model: especially when backed by the claim of European blood, privileged Californio women like Mercedes were frequently considered beautiful by Anglo men. As exotic, erotic objects, they

could be and often were acquired like land from their fathers and absorbed through marriage into the Anglo world.

An Anglo-American representation of this can be found in "Doña Dolores," a story published in an 1899 issue of *Overland Monthly*. The story replays images of the exotic, erotic Californio woman. Called "Lola" and "Lolita," like the Ruiz de Burton heroine she resembles, Dolores marries one Dick Bellamy, who (in terms also reminiscent of those used to describe Lola Medina) "often spoke of his wife as his 'luckiest find'" (265). Despite the fact that she marries the "rich Americano" (264), Dolores has been raised by her dead grandmother Doña Ysabel, who tells her of the days before the "Gringos" in Southern California, tells her "story after story of the insult and injury that had been heaped upon them by the hated race, and the child listened, her little hands clinched and her eyes gleaming with rage. These two lives . . . nursed the wrath of a whole nation against an invader" (265). Although Dolores claims "I am an American myself now, and I love Dick's people" (271), she grows "passionate" when she remembers her grandmother and calls her daughter "Dolly" rather than her given name, Dolores, because the child is, she claims, "American all through, without one trace of her Spanish blood . . . a little American Dolly" (269). Hence, this representation rehearses the passionate Spanish-blooded woman who in her heart hates the Americans and ultimately cannot be incorporated into the nation but must kill herself instead. She is a clear contrast to both Mercedes Alamar as American lady and, not incidentally, to Don Alamar in his claim that some of his best friends are Americans. See Kathryn Jarboe's "Doña Dolores," *Overland Monthly* 34: 201 (Sept. 1899): 265–73.

69. For an example of how it cannot work in the other direction, consider the marriage of Gabriel Alamar and Lizzie Mechlin: her gender locates her as subordinate to him, so that when he falls economically and socially, she accompanies him. Because she is a woman, her privilege cannot protect him.

70. The precariousness of the novel's placement of the Californio helps explain both the novel's content and its form; that is, it helps account both for Ruiz de Burton's use of the figure of woman and for the novel's awkward shifts from fictional account to historical documentation of the Californios' oppression. It can also help explain the curious double ending of the novel, the fact that after Ruiz de Burton tidily ties up the threads of her romance plot in a chapter aptly titled "Reunited at Last," she adds what amounts to a second ending in a chapter called "Out With the Invader." This chapter steps completely outside of the narrative proper to launch an invective against the "Big Four," offering a catalogue of evidence of their plotting to control a railroad monopoly. Structurally, the chapter's existence serves as an admission that the domestic plot cannot fully resolve the public, political plot, except on an allegorical level. Thematically, the fact that Ruiz de Burton here displaces her pleas for justice for the Californios onto a cry for justice for the American people signals a shift from a regional canvas to a national one, and it brings us back to the status of the regional as synecdoche for the

nation. Californios slide into Californians and then into Americans. Once having accomplished this metonymic slide, the novel offers in its final paragraph an even more radical rewriting of the American narrative. Linking "Southern California" with "the entire Southern States"—both suffer from this monopoly as blight—Ruiz de Burton calls for a Redeemer "who will emancipate the white slaves of California" (372). Through this complicated image, not only does the Californio come—through its link to region—to signify American, and so the colonized here comes to signify colonizer, but at the same time, the colonized Californio collapses into the African-American enslaved. America is envisioned as a nation where, as in Californio history, the roles of colonizer and colonized are not always clearly distinct.

CHAPTER 5: KATE CHOPIN AND (STRETCHING) THE LIMITS
OF LOCAL COLOR FICTION

1. Publication information is taken from Emily Toth's recent biography (412). Toth's biography supersedes both Daniel S. Rankin's *Kate Chopin and Her Creole Stories* (Philadelphia: University of Pennsylvania Press, 1932) and Per Seyersted's *Kate Chopin: A Critical Biography* (Baton Rouge: Louisiana State University Press, 1969). Toth provides much needed information on the class and, to a lesser extent, race relations that shaped Chopin's life.

2. Daniel S. Rankin did publish his *Kate Chopin and Her Creole Stories* prior to Seyersted, but his framing of Chopin's work simply reinforced her earlier dismissal as a Local Color writer. He describes her collection *Bayou Folk*, for instance, as depicting "a little world, it is true, but full of fresh life and interest," as chronicling "the quaint and picturesque life among the Creole and Acadian folk of the Louisiana bayou" (136; 136–37). He goes on to contend that Chopin "seems to have gone straight to the heart of the Nachitoches folk. She has heard their little confidences of joy and grief" in these " . . . simple stories simply told" (139). See *Kate Chopin and Her Creole Stories* (Philadelphia: University of Pennsylvania Press).

3. There was and still is some confusion over the distinction between Local Color and regionalism as literary categories. Chopin's contemporaries often used the two terms synonymously to describe fiction focused on a particular region and community within it. Twentieth-century critics, however, have differentiated the two categories on the basis of point of view. Judith Fetterley and Marjorie Pryse have been the driving forces behind this differentiation process, through their Norton Anthology, *American Women Regionalists 1850–1910* (New York: Norton, 1992). There they define local color as satirical or dismissive of the community it portrays, written by outsiders who make fun of the community for an audience of outsiders. Regionalism, in contrast, they see as emerging from within the community, written by insiders from a sympathetic point of view. They also argue that regionalism, defined in these terms, was a particularly female genre. Fetterley and Pryse explicitly note that they are establishing these categories, acknowl-

edging that the writers themselves probably did not draw these distinctions. I will use the term Local Color to refer to the literary category known variously as Local Color and regionalism, in part because most of the references to it by Chopin and her critics use this term. In addition I use Local Color to describe the specifically literary category, because by regionalism I want to suggest a broader usage of the term that carries the sense of cultural (rather than exclusively literary) categories loosely based on geographic regions.

4. Thus, even women writers writing of the privileged geographic area, New England, could be dismissed by twentieth-century critics as non-canonical. Sarah Orne Jewett, as I discuss in Chapter 1, despite writing of New England, became known as a Local Color nostalgic writer. For more on what Michael Davitt Bell calls the "heavily gendered assumptions at the heart of American realist thinking" (66), see his "Gender and American Realism in *The Country of the Pointed Firs*; see also Brodhead.

5. Helen Taylor provides a very helpful discussion of regionalism and Northern publishing practices. Cox also offers useful information but ultimately replicates a nineteenth-century hierarchy of value, locating America's "essence" in New England. My thinking here has also been shaped by Raymond Williams's *The Country and the City* (London: Chatto & Windus, 1973).

6. This description, it is important to note, is one that is relevant to the content of her stories rather than to her own geographic origins, as I will discuss below.

7. This figure was one that Chopin herself employed. See, for example, *Bayou Folk*'s "Ma'ame Pelagie," whose title character stands as a memorial not just to Southern womanhood but also to the antebellum South itself. Jones further argues that the ideal of Southern manhood—the planter gentleman—itself involved feminized values: the image invoked a man who was "gentle and genteel, leisurely and cultivated, a lover of beauty, goodness and grace" (41).

8. Or as Howells might have put it—and as critics did in objecting to *The Awakening* as showing French influences—Chopin was schooled in both a tradition of indecency and a tradition of decency.

9. Although much of Chopin's work is now available in a variety of editions, for consistency's sake I take all of my citations from Per Seyersted's two-volume edition of *The Complete Works of Kate Chopin*. Cited dates are the year the story was written, followed by the year of its first publication or, if the two are the same, the single year.

10. For a more in-depth reading of the reviews, see Toth. She points out that the *New York Times* review makes a number of factual mistakes in the long description of Acadian Louisiana, not the least of which is the misspelling of "Cajun."

11. Reviews of Chopin's second collection, *A Night in Acadie*, only confirmed both her categorization as a Local Color writer and the generic marginalization that it implied. *The Critic*'s review, for instance, described the volume as centered on "the simple childlike Southern people" (266).

12. My redaction of Cajun and Creole positioning in Louisiana is taken largely from Brasseaux and Domínguez, both of whom offer extremely clear and helpful discussions of these complicated categories.

13. While most of the New England writers (Sarah Orne Jewett, Rose Terry Cooke, and Mary Wilkins Freeman, for instance) considered regionalists were, in fact, generally born and raised in New England, other writers considered regionalists were outsiders to the regional community about which they wrote, either because of class (Mary Noailles Murfree, for instance), or because of some combination of geographic origins, ethnicity, or race (Chopin, Mary Austin, Alice Dunbar-Nelson, Sui Sin Far, Zitkala-Sä). The question of being an authentic voice of the community in geographic terms also dovetails for many of these writers with the question of authenticity in ethnic or racial terms, particularly for women of "mixed" racial or ethnic identity (Alice Callahan, Dunbar-Nelson, Sui Sin Far, or Zitkala-Sä, for example).

14. This shifting positioning of St. Louis testifies to the fact that it is not only the center that is able to collapse its "Others": here, the South collapses other regions into what is, essentially, the not-South.

15. Biographical information on Chopin is readily available; the most complete source, however, is Toth's biography.

16. Taylor makes a similar point in claiming that New South writers used Local Color "as a means of setting straight a record which, it was felt, had been left to the north to write" (18). She reads this revision as a nostalgic recreation of the "good old days" before the Civil War. While Chopin participates in such racist nostalgia, I am more interested here in her representations of her contemporary South and the ramifications of the intersection of racist discourse with more radical discourses of gender and region in these representations.

17. Given that critics insisted on viewing Chopin as a recorder of quaint, charming primitive people, it is not surprising that they were so offended by *The Awakening*, for not only does this novel fail to conform to Local Color standards, it also presents an upper-class white heroine whose identity is constituted at least in part by her various levels of desire.

In this overt representation *The Awakening* resembles its contemporary British New Woman fiction far more than Chopin's contemporary American women's fiction. Certainly, the rhetoric of *The Awakening*'s reviews bears out this identification: reviewers describe it in the same terms as critics used for New Woman fiction. The *Globe Democrat* describes *The Awakening* as "not a healthy book" (quoted in Toth 341); the *Chicago Times-Herald* states that with this novel Chopin "enter[s] the overworked field of sex fiction" (quoted in Toth 347); the *Providence Sunday Journal* calls Chopin "another clever woman writer" and claims that *The Awakening* "fairly out Zolas Zola" (quoted in Toth 347). It is the *Los Angeles Times*'s review, however, that most plainly signals *The Awakening*'s affinity to New Woman fiction, for the reviewer likens the novel to "one of Aubrey Beardsley's hideous but haunting pictures with their disfiguring leer of sensuality, but yet carrying a distinguishing strength and grace and individuality . . . it is unhealthily introspective and morbid in feeling, as the story of that sort of woman must inevitably be" (quoted in Toth 349). This is the language of British reviewers of New Woman fiction, from its invocation of Beardsley to its accusation of sensuality, morbidity, and illness. Thus, I would suggest, *The Awakening* fits far better into the New Woman novel genre than American Local Color fiction, and had it appeared in England, would not have caused such a stir, for critics would have been able to read it as part of a generic scandal. That is, rather than being an isolated and seemingly anomalous threat, it would have been labeled (and, at least partly, so contained) as a New Woman novel.

Taylor makes an analogous point in identifying Chopin with her French influences over her American ones, claiming that "St. Louis newspaper editors were happy to publish Maupassant and other European writers, but found Edna Pontellier too hot to handle; this heroine was, after all, an *American woman*" (151). While I would link *The Awakening* more closely to British New Woman fiction than French fiction, I would certainly agree with Taylor's point that Mrs. Pontellier's behavior was seen by American critics as appalling particularly *because* of her nationality.

18. For a particularly cutting depiction of the class privilege on which the model of proper "American" Womanhood rests, see Chopin's "Miss McEnders" (1892, 1897).

19. Although the story does not identify Mildred's origins explicitly, the fact that her family summers in Narragansett, Rhode Island, suggests that she is from New England or at least the (North) East Coast.

20. "At the 'Cadian Ball" (1892) offers a useful comparison here: the privileged Creole heroine of this story, Clarisse, responds as a proper lady to Alcée Laballière's declaration of love. Regardless of the fact that he is a Creole plantation owner, and so her social equal, when he "panted a volley of hot, blistering love-words into her face" (220), she responds with a disdainful dismissal.

21. Chopin generally codes her Cajun characters as white, usually by leaving them racially unmarked while marking other characters in the story. Thus, in "A Gentleman of the Bayou Têche," the Cajun Evariste and his daughter Martinette are left racially unmarked, while Aunt Dicey is identified as black; similarly, in "A Night in Acadie," Zaïda is unmarked while Douté, the cook, is marked as black.

22. Interestingly, in this case, in the face of Northern editorial opposition, even the marginalized shelter of Local Color could not provide a space for Chopin's original representation.

23. Almost completely ignored by early Chopin criticism, the issue of race in Chopin's work has recently come under scrutiny in a number of important studies. These works assess her representations of race and sometimes subsequently evaluate her character accordingly. Toth, for instance, reads Chopin's representations of race as "liberal in her day" compared to those of her contemporaries, whom Toth claims were "far more committed to the 'happy darky' stereotype" (269). Helen Taylor, on the other hand, argues that "Chopin's racism is a central element in her

writing and cannot be ignored or simply excused . . . her inability or refusal to confront it created critical problems and severely limited her achievement" (156). As should be evident, I concur with Taylor and am indebted to her work.

Chopin's racial politics are hardly surprising, given her background. As Taylor usefully points out, Chopin was in New Orleans for the last seven years of Reconstruction, and there and in Natchitoches she witnessed racial tensions and the rise of white supremacy groups. Indeed, both her husband and her brother-in-law Phanor Breazeale were members of such a group—the White League—and at least briefly supported a rebellion against the government in 1877. Whether or not Chopin herself supported the White League is unknown: unfortunately, she left almost no documentation in her papers or her work of her explicit position on political and, more specifically, racial issues. She did, however, produce a number of "loyal slave" stories that articulate a romanticized version of conventionally racist attitudes, among which "For Marse Chouchoutte" (1891), "The Bênitous' Slave" (1892), and "Tante Cat'rinette" (1894) stand out as perhaps the most obvious examples. She also offered slightly more complicated, though ultimately equally conciliatory, versions of interracial relations in stories such as "Ozème's Holiday" (1894, 1896), "A Dresden Lady in Dixie" (1894, 1895), and "Odalie Misses Mass" (1895). Toth's biography provides important background information on race relations in Chopin's New Orleans and Nachitoches. For contextualized information combined with literary analysis, two recent books are particularly nuanced in their readings: Taylor's *Gender, Race and Region in the Writing of Grace King, Ruth McEnery Stuart and Kate Chopin* and Anna Shannon Elfenbein's *Women on the Color Line: Evolving Stereotypes and the Writings of George Washington Cable, Grace King, and Kate Chopin*. Elfenbein traces with exceptional clarity the complicated history of New Orleans's racial mixture. See also Birnbaum's excellent article and Sandra Gunning, *Race, Rape and Lynching: The Red Record of American Literature* (New York: Oxford University Press, 1996).

24. I have enclosed *owner* in quotation marks in this section to underscore not only the story's discussion of the impossibility of owning someone else's desire, but also the more fundamental paradox on which it is based: the idea of one human being's "owning" another.

25. Moreover, Madame's coercive actions, especially over Zoraïde's marriage partner, also mirror aristocratic actions conventionally attacked by the middle classes.

26. Chapter 4 of Elfenbein's book focuses on Chopin and provides what may well be the definitive reading of "Désirée's Baby" as well as an extremely nuanced reading of "La Belle Zoraïde."

27. Elfenbein's reading here becomes more convincing when "La Belle Zoraïde" is read against Chopin's "A Lady of Bayou St. John," where Madame Delisle is shown renouncing the present and its promise of love and passion to focus upon her past and her dead husband.

28. Paradoxically, in this story Chopin both exploits the stereotype of the "exotic," "erotic" mulatta—naming her heroine Désirée, for instance—and undermines both the "purity" of categories of racial identity and the stability of the racist alignment of "erotic" and "African American."

29. Further, the story suggests that even the woman whose racial purity has not been called into question—Madame Valmondé—is powerless to save Désirée in the face of the white man's power.

30. The painful and vexed relation of slave women to maternity, as well as the legacy of that relation, remains at issue for many contemporary African-American women writers. See, for instance, Gayl Jones's *Corregidora*, Toni Morrison's *Beloved*, or Sherley Anne Williams's *Dessa Rose*.

31. And significantly, maternity here calls into question the racial "purity" of the "white" lady but not that of the "black" slave: if "La Blanche," the mulatto slave, is expected to have "little quadroon boys" (242) following Aubigny's visits to her cabin, Désirée is not.

32. Toth claims that Chopin was drawing on her father-in-law, Jean Baptiste Chopin, in this portrait (122). In more general terms one might see this characterization as the St. Louis outsider Chopin's sarcastic depiction of the New Orleans Creole culture for which she could never quite qualify.

CHAPTER 6: TRANSNATIONAL GEOGRAPHIES OF RACE

1. Unless otherwise indicated, all references to Sui Sin Far's work are taken from Ling and White-Parks's recent edition, *Mrs. Spring Fragrance and Other Writings*.

2. Because my argument in this chapter works to establish Sui Sin Far as a writer who moved between cultures and nations, persistently linking Canadian and American contexts, I will be focusing less on Sui Sin Far's representations of political and cultural events specific to either Canada or America and more on the analogies she draws between the two countries and their political climates.

3. See, in particular, Almaguer, Chan, Lowe, Motomura, Peffer, and Takaki for discussions of the legal status of Chinese immigrants in America. See also Blauner, Ling, and Lyman. For both a chronology of anti-Chinese legislation and a series of profiles, see Ruthanne Lum McCunn, *Chinese American Portraits* (San Francisco: Chronicle Books, 1988).

4. A more detailed account of Sui Sin Far's life is now available in Annette White-Parks's groundbreaking biography, from which this redaction comes.

5. A note on the terminology of this chapter: although born Edith Eaton, Sui Sin Far adopted Sui Sin Far as her pen name: my decision to refer to her as such reflects this choice; my use of her full name follows standard critical practice. Again following the author's usage, I will use the term "Eurasian" throughout to indicate peoples of mixed European and Asian parentage. While today one might call Sui Sin Far Chinese American or Chinese Canadian (the "or" here indicating another issue—that of her national affiliation), Eurasian was the standard term in

NOTES TO CHAPTER 6

her day. As I will discuss below, *Chinese American*, then and now, has several connotations, from Chinese immigrant now living in America to a person of mixed Chinese and American national background and/or parentage to second, third, or later generation person of Chinese ancestry born and raised in America. As this set of connotations implies, the argument I will make about the merged and overlapping definitions of ethnicity, race, and national identity which were salient in Sui Sin Far's day are no less at issue now.

6. I use the term *border* here specifically to underscore the degree to which the limits of racial and national categories intersect in Sui Sin Far's work.

7. Her representation might be read as a specifically Chinese-American version of Lisa Lowe's definition of the "Asian American constituency," which she reminds us "is composed of men and women of exclusively Asian parents and of mixed race, of refugees and nonrefugees, of the English speaking and the non-English speaking, of people of urban, rural, and different class backgrounds, and of heterosexuals as well as gays and lesbians" (43).

8. Anti-Chinese racism was also extremely rampant in Canada at this time. Sui Sin Far responds to this in "A Plea for the Chinaman" and elsewhere.

9. The Naturalization Law of 1790 limited naturalized citizenship to "free white" persons. The McCarran-Walter Act of 1952 finally reversed the racial restrictions of this act, although it continued a tradition of legal discrimination by limiting immigration from the "Asian-Pacific Triangle" on the basis of race rather than national origin (as was true of European immigration). See Takaki, *Strangers from a Different Shore*, Chapter 11, for a more extensive discussion of this legislation.

Comparisons between Chinese and African Americans were common in this period as well, drawing on discourses of evolution to argue for racial hierarchy, so that, as Lyman notes, "in the end both Negroes and Chinese were declared inimical and inferior to white society in general and to white labor in particular" (173). See Almaguer, Lyman, and Takaki, *Iron Cages* for more on this.

These sorts of comparisons between Chinese and Indians or African-Americans should not, of course, be taken to mean that oppression took exactly the same forms and degrees in various communities. Amy Ling provides a useful example of this in reminding us that African-American men got the vote in 1870; African-American and white women in 1920; American Indians in 1924; and Asian Americans in 1954 ("Reading" 70). And even this legal right, of course, did not guarantee these populations' right to vote in practice.

10. Lyman notes that "so few Chinese women came to America that it was not until the middle of the twentieth century that there occurred even a proximity in balancing the sex ratio. During the entire period of unrestricted immigration (1850–1882) a total of only 8,848 Chinese women journeyed to American shores. In the same period over 100,000 men arrived in the United States. . . . By 1890 only 3,868 Chinese women were reported to be in the country. . . . " (169).

This notion of the Chinese as a bachelor society is furthered by their regional alignment with the West, since the West was already seen in the eyes of Anglo-America as the "masculine" region of the frontier as opposed to the "feminized" and cultured East.

11. This widespread racism, coupled with a more positive image of the Japanese, resulted, as Ling and others point out, in some Chinese and part-Chinese people passing as Japanese. Sui Sin Far's own sister, Winnifred Eaton, published under the name Onoto Watanna and represented herself as Japanese, a situation Sui Sin Far acknowledges obliquely in "Leaves from the Mental Portfolio of an Eurasian," commenting:

> The Americans, having for many years manifested a much higher regard for the Japanese than for the Chinese, several half Chinese young men and women, thinking to advance themselves, both in a social and business sense, pass as Japanese. They continue to be known as Eurasians; but a Japanese Eurasian does not appear in the same light as a Chinese Eurasian. The unfortunate Chinese Eurasians! Are not those who compel them to thus cringe more to be blamed than they? (228)

This phenomenon points to the fact that while the Others internal to America could be and often were conflated in the eyes of the dominant culture, they also occupied varying and shifting positions in relation to each other and to the dominant culture such that while all Others were/are subject to oppression, the forms of this oppression were/are flexible and diverse.

12. This notion of Sui Sin Far as trickster is taken from Annette White-Parks, who elaborates upon it at length in her biography of Sui Sin Far.

13. This concept of Orientalism is taken from Edward W. Said, *Orientalism* (New York: Pantheon Books, 1978).

14. Drawing on the dominant nineteenth-century "one drop" model that assigned people of mixed heritage to the category of nonwhite, Sui Sin Far's contemporaries had no problem viewing her as a part of and hence spokesperson for these communities. In terms of the racial codes of the nineteenth century, the "one drop" model applied specifically to African-American, mixed-race people, on whom it was used in the antebellum period to increase the slave population. In popular usage, however, mixed-race peoples of various heritages have always been assigned to the category of Other, a move that worked to defend the privilege of whites by insisting upon the existence of "pure" white blood. The questions of how to define racial categories, how to assign people to them, and, perhaps most importantly, who gets to do that defining, have always been and continue to be central to American culture in both popular and juridical contexts. Lawrence Wright, for instance, points out, "how unsettled this country has always been about its racial categories is evident in the fact that nearly every census since [the original one in 1790] has measured race differently" (47). For a discussion of the legal and economic impact of racial categories' definitions in contemporary America, see his "One Drop of Blood," *The New Yorker* (July 25, 1994): 46–55.

For more on the issues that identity politics has raised in contemporary feminist theory and practice, see Linda Alcoff's extremely nuanced and thoughtful "The Problem of Speaking for Others," *Cultural Critique* 20 (Winter 1991-2): 5-32; for a general overview, see Diana Fuss's *Essentially Speaking: Feminism, Nature and Difference* (New York: Routledge, 1989).

15. White-Parks characterizes this comment as "positioning Sui Sin Far on an ambiguous borderland between race and country" (48), an image that might be interpreted in various ways but that does at least clearly raise the issue of national identity. Perhaps not surprisingly, Canadian reviews identify Sui Sin Far as Canadian, while American reviews claim her work, and implicitly her, as American. The *New York Times* calls *Mrs. Spring Fragrance* as "a new note in American fiction" (405); note also *The Independent*'s claim that the book focuses on "*American* immigration laws" (388, emphasis added).

16. This constellation of associations was fostered by a group of magazines of the period focused on the West, most notably *Overland Monthly, Land of Sunshine* (renamed in 1901 as *Out West*), and *The Westerner*. Charles Lummis, editor of *Land of Sunshine/Out West* from 1896 to 1906 and one of Sui Sin Far's publishers, was typical in producing an image of the West and California that emphasized a romantic past and a cultured present. As his biographer Edwin Bingham notes, "Such fare was highly palatable to the winter tourist or to the recently arrived local resident who had left behind his historical heritage but who carried with him his essentially middle-class cultural predilections and who was looking for reassurance that not all of the West was wild" (189), a comment that might remind us of the overlap of audience of many of the writers under consideration here. The armchair tourist/reader of Sui Sin Far's work might have put down a copy of *Out West* in order to pick up a copy of *Atlantic Monthly* or a number of other East Coast magazines containing stories by Jewett and Chopin, among others.

17. This conflation is aided, of course, by the association (whether accurate or not) in the mind of the general public between certain ethnic communities and specific geographical regions: Latino/as with the Southwest, Asian Americans with the West Coast, or Creoles and Cajuns with Louisiana.

18. This reassessment has been made possible on a widespread level largely through the ongoing work of Amy Ling and Annette White-Parks, who are responsible for getting Sui Sin Far's work back in print, as well as providing biographical information on her. *Reassessment* itself may not be a wholly accurate term, because *Mrs. Spring Fragrance* apparently has only one edition and received no serious critical attention until the 1970s. The text was out of print until Ling and White-Parks's edition appeared (in 1995), although a few of its stories appeared in Fetterley and Pryse's Norton Anthology *American Women Regionalists 1850-1910*.

19. The biographical does continue to be read as authorization or explanation of Sui Sin Far's work's content and even, at times, its form. Of course, biography can and does often inflect an author's work; my point here is not to attack the use of biographical and/or historical context. Rather, I would start with the fact that

even the critics most invested in fostering Sui Sin Far's reputation often take recourse in biography in order to "authorize" her voice. This suggests to me both the ongoing dismissal of marginalized voices (and hence critics' need to refute that dismissal) and the degree to which debates over identity politics have been played out on women of all races/ethnicities and people of color of both sexes. The corollary to this, of course, is the fact that the criticism published on dominant white male novelists of Sui Sin Far's (or any other) day does not focus to this extent on justifying those authors' knowledge of their subject and personal identification with the communities they represent.

20. That Sui was not wholly a product of Chinese, Chinese-American, or Chinese-Canadian communities is not under debate: the details of her biography establish this as does her own admission that upon arrival in San Francisco's Chinatown (in 1898) she knew only a "few phrase[s]" of what she calls "my mother tongue" (227).

21. An important distinction here, of course, is that the nineteenth-century theory was used to enforce racial boundaries and social hierarchies, insisting on a model of racial identity in which a person was either all "white" or not "white" at all. In contrast, this use of ancestry values both the ancestry and the community to which it provides entrée.

22. In her biography of Sui Sin Far, White-Parks more specifically argues that by 1898 Sui Sin Far was claiming her Chinese heritage publicly and that by the early 1900s she "was coding herself" as part of the Chinese-American community (37; 136).

23. This raises the complicated and much debated question of how one defines a category such as *Chinese American*, a question whose answers often seem to lead back into the quagmire of fictions of blood. For some the answers involve delineation of parentage, so that *Chinese American* (like the term *Eurasian* in Sui Sin Far's day) would indicate of mixed Chinese and American parentage. For others the answers involve cultural lines as well as blood lines, so that *Chinese American* might suggest either the Chinese immigrant to America or the original sense of Creole; that is, the first American-born generation of the foreign (here Chinese) immigrant or, more loosely, any American-born people of Chinese ancestry. In her own day the one-drop model made it easy for dominant culture to count Sui Sin Far as Chinese. In the eyes of the Chinese-American and Chinese-Canadian communities of her day, however, this affiliation was by no means naturalized; but while she was not automatically read by these communities as Chinese, neither was she simply read as white, suggesting that these marginalized communities had more than two conceptual categories of race available to them. As a disenfranchised group, Chinese-American and Chinese-Canadian communities would, of course, have had more incentive to question and complicate the dominant culture's versions of a reality structured by clear binary oppositions, and they would have had more need to make a space for a third term. This notion of a third term has been developed at length in terms of gender/sexuality by Mar-

jorie Garber. See her *Vested Interests: Cross-Dressing and Cultural Anxiety* (New York: Routledge, 1992).

24. Here critical treatments of Sui Sin Far parallel those of Pauline Hopkins: this use of content as determining of genre is analogous to the way that much of the fiction written by African Americans at the end of the century was defined exclusively in terms of "the race question."

25. For more discussion of the generic form employed by women attempting to represent community, see Sandra Zagarell's "Narrative of Community: The Identification of a Genre," *SIGNS* 13:3 (Spring 1988):498–527.

26. While we are imbricated in a cultural system structured partly by race, biographical questions of race will clearly continue to arise; that is, the racial positioning of authors will continue to inflect their work. At the same time, either reducing the work of a writer of color to the subject of race only or insisting that only non-white writers be "allowed" to write on race reinscribes racial hierarchies. These hierarchies guarantee that "white" remains the naturalized unmarked category (i.e., "not a race") and that race remains the "problem" of writers of color only.

27. There are two main autobiographical accounts: "Leaves From the Mental Portfolio of an Eurasian" (1909) and "Sui Sin Far, the Half Chinese Writer, Tells of her Career" (1912). While, of course, Sui Sin Far's autobiographical accounts stand as one source of biographical information on a writer who left few traces of her life, I have been struck by the unproblematic assumption of critics that Sui Sin Far is, in these accounts, simply offering "the facts." Or, to put it another way, I have been surprised that critics as astute as Ammons and White-Parks have not brought to bear on these essays the same critical reading skills they have used to illuminate her fiction.

28. This information is taken largely from White-Parks's cataloguing of Sui Sin Far's pseudonyms. See *Sui Sin Far/Edith Eaton* (61, 157 and passim) for details.

29. This story has not been republished; all my references are taken from its original publication. See "A Chinese Ishmael," *Overland Monthly* 34 (July 1899): 43–49.

30. The national border is irrelevant here in that it arbitrarily divides in two what Sui Sin Far sees as one larger North American system of racism and exploitation of the Chinese. As a whole in her work, of course, the border is not irrelevant at all, but rather formative, as I discuss below.

31. Interestingly, Sui Sin Far does replicate dominant cultural binary oppositions insofar as her discussion of "the Chinese" operates almost entirely in relation to the category of white American. Her work contains few representations of other Others: African Americans, Native Americans, and Mexican Americans in particular.

32. See Omi and Winant for an assessment of the strengths and limits of the model of internal colonialism.

33. In a related point Blauner argues that "In order to control a racially defined people systemically, and so maintain special privilege for the dominant group, limits must be placed on the mobility of the oppressed minority . . . both . . . the mobility of individuals in physical space and . . . collective mobility in socioeconomic status" (36).

34. The notion of interpellation is taken from Louis Althusser's "Ideology and Ideological State Apparatuses (Notes Towards and Investigation)," in *Lenin and Philosophy and Other Essays*, trans. Ben Brewster (New York: Monthly Review, 1971).

35. Interestingly, Sui Sin Far published four of her seven earliest pieces on Chinese subjects in Charles Lummis's *Land of Sunshine*, a magazine that represented not simply California but along with the *Overland Monthly* virtually embodied Western publishing in this period and consequently was largely responsible for forming Eastern ideas of the "the West." See White-Parks (89–96) for a detailed discussion of this fiction.

This transnational locating of America by means of viewing it from two perspectives recurs when one compares Sui Sin Far's "Chinese Workmen in America," first published in *The Independent* July 3, 1913, with "The Chinese in America," a series of sketches appearing in *The Westerner* in May 1909. The two pieces begin with almost exactly the same sentences, explaining both articles' intention to focus on ordinary (i.e., not "high rank" (231)) working Chinese in America. The 1913 piece goes on to describe the effects of these Chinese on "the old country" (231) both in terms of money sent back to build schools and churches and on the attitudes and "conduct of their countrymen toward people of the United States" (231). The 1909 article, in contrast, focuses on the contributions these same Chinese have made to American culture, contributions so numerous, the narrator asserts, that "every true Westerner will admit that the enlarged life in which he is participating today could not have been possible without the Chinese" (233).

36. There are, of course, other important differences between Ruiz de Burton's and Sui Sin Far's position and the positions of the Californios and the Chinese in America, not the least of which were, on the level of these two women, class privilege, and on the level of the two groups of peoples, length of time on the North American continent.

37. The fact that Sui Sin Far represents many of her female protagonists as having some measure of choice and mobility reflects, I would argue, her own position of (relative) choice and mobility as a result of her ability to "pass" as white.

38. The 1906 earthquake and fire destroyed all of San Francisco's municipal records and so allowed Chinese men to claim they had been born in the U.S. without having to produce the documentation to prove it. This in turn enabled them to bring over family still in China.

39. Sui Sin Far represents women's role in reworking both Chinese-American communities and those communities' gender norms in part simply through foregrounding women characters and women's speech. As Annette White-Parks ob-

serves, "it is through the voices of the stereotypically silenced Chinese-American females that most viewpoints emerge" (22). For more on this point, see her "A Reversal of American Concepts of 'Other-ness' in the Fiction of Sui Sin Far," *MELUS* 20:1 (Spring 195): 17–34.

40. Clothing functions not just as a marker of Americanization but also as an indicator of economic status and as the qualification for Americanization in "Chinatown Needs a School," where the narrator notes, "there is crying need for such a school, as there is a large number of families with children who ought not to be playing on the streets during the greater part of the day. These children will be admitted into the American schools if they were dressed in American fashion, but not otherwise, and this is a great hardship and inconvenience to Chinese mothers who in many cases are unable to make their children's clothes in American style and occasionally are too poor to afford the change" (203).

41. Both Ling and White-Parks here reflect critics' tendency to read "Leaves" as transparently true; neither considers that Sui Sin Far's use of "spinster" may have been a specific rhetorical choice; neither allows for any possibility of irony in her use of the term.

42. Sui Sin Far is not the first to use tears and the sentiment they represent as an indicator of whiteness or a mark of the process of whitening. For a compelling reading of this phenomenon in Antebellum literature, see Karen Sánchez-Eppler's "Bodily Bonds: The Intersecting Rhetorics of Feminism and Abolition," in *The Culture of Sentiment: Race, Gender, and Sentimentality in Nineteenth-Century America*, ed. Shirley Samuels (New York: Oxford University Press, 1992): 92–114.

43. Pan's narrative choice places this story in a tradition of fiction of "passing," since at least implicitly her choice is the choice of passing for white. That having choice as an option is dependent on one's connection to centers of power is illustrated here by the fact that "passing" means hiding one's "nonwhite blood" in order to claim the position of "white," whereas someone like Sui Sin Far, socially positioned largely by her father's Englishness and name and her "white" looks, claims her connection to the Chinese-American community without either being able to or needing to disclaim her "white blood."

44. Sui Sin Far aligns the maternal with the Chinese woman elsewhere as well, although in slightly different configurations. Described as a "little native of Asia" (260), for instance, the eponymous baby of "The Sugar Cane Baby" (reprinted in *Mrs. Spring Fragrance and Other Writings*) is depicted as a baby happily provided for by an essentialized maternal love, a care contrasted with the misinterpretation and miscare given him by the white Sisters of Mercy. Sui Sin Far repeatedly figures white women as a threat to Chinese mothers, in stories such as "The Wisdom of the New" and "In the Land of the Free." As Ammons points out, Sui Sin Far had historical precedent for this representation in the women missionaries who made Chinatowns a "cause" (109).

The other significant narrative alignment of the maternal and Chinese womanhood in Sui Sin Far's work appears in her autobiographical essay "Leaves," where as illustration of her claim of extreme sensitivity, the following curious passage occurs: "My mother's screams of agony when a baby is born almost drive me wild, and long after her pangs have subsided I feel them in my own body. Sometimes it is a week before I can get to sleep after such an experience" (221). That Sui Sin Far would perhaps feel this way as the second of thirteen children (and as the first girl, upon whom much of the care of her younger siblings fell) is understandable. That she would choose to add this representation to her autobiographical account as simply an illustrative aside gives it ambiguous weight. One might, I would suggest, read this as both a narrative alignment of maternity and Chinese womanhood and as a specific alignment of Sui Sin Far with both her mother and maternity, a strategic move that functions, among other things, to counter stereotypes of the single woman and the artist woman as unnatural/ unwomanly/unmaternal.

45. Although there was increasing Socialist activity in the U.S. in the early decades of the century (peaking in the twenties and thirties), Socialism was figured by the dominant culture as "un-American," a foreign threat.

46. Sui Sin Far repeats this image of the Chinese man as good father elsewhere, as, for instance, in "Half-Chinese Children," where she contends that the children of "American," i.e., white, mothers and Chinese fathers are "Taken Entirely in Charge by the Fathers" (187), whom she describes as being "as a rule, very kind and good to their offspring" (187). Pan's father in "Its Wavering Image" provides another example of this representation.

47. I would also read Sui Sin Far's representation of herself as not saying "No" to the possibility of marrying a Chinese man as a rhetorical gesture toward the issue of marriage as a whole, a rhetorical act that allows for the possibility that this persona rejects the institution of marriage generally or even, more specifically, the institution of heterosexuality on which it is based. I will return to this issue later in the chapter.

48. Contrast this with Frank Chin's reference to Sui Sin Far in "Come All Ye Asian American Writers of the Real and the Fake" in *The Big Aiiieeeee!: An Anthology of Chinese American and Japanese American Literature*, ed. Jeffrey Paul Chan, Frank Chin, Lawson Fusao Inada, and Shawn Wong (New York: Meridan, 1991, 1–92), where he characterizes Sui Sin Far as one of what he apparently considers to be only three tolerable Asian-American women writers on the grounds that "the only Chinese men who are not emasculated and sexually repellent in Chinese American writing are found in the books and essays of Sui Sin Far, Diana Chang, and Dr. Han Suyin" (12).

49. Since the entire poem appears on page 447 of the *Overland Monthly*, page citations have been omitted.

50. Sui Sin Far offers an example of this intersection's effect on masculinity in "The Chinese in America, Part IV" where she comments, "it seems that women who would sooner jump into the fire than ask a white man for money or presents will boldly demand such things of a Chinaman" (251). This comment reveals the

extent to which constructs of femininity are formed in relation to constructs of masculinity, as well as how these constructs are racially marked. Here, because of his race, the "Chinaman" does not count as a man, and hence does not elicit a performance of femininity from the white woman.

51. Recall Sui Sin Far's reference to her parents: "He is English, she is Chinese. I am different to both of them—a stranger, tho their own child" (222).

52. This treatment of the issue of difference as made manifest in racial "mixing" offers a useful reference point for a comparison of the authors under consideration in this book. While Sui Sin Far celebrates both difference and a complexity of interrelations, Hopkins treats racial mixing solely as "miscegenation," as the product of white rape. Ruiz de Burton erases racial difference in the Californios by displacing it onto the Indians, while Converse opts to celebrate sameness displaced onto same-sex unions. Chopin represents only the results of racial mixing, Creoles and Cajuns long established as "safe" ethnics, while Sarah Orne Jewett elides this issue altogether.

53. Figured as a friend and a double for Mermei, Sin Far can obviously also be read as a double for Sui Sin Far herself.

54. I follow the story's usage in referring to the princess as O'Yam.

55. Curiously, Ling goes on to assert that Sui Sin Far "would not have approved and would have striven to repress" this lesbian sensibility (48). It is by no means clear to me, given the evidence of Sui Sin Far's writing, that she would have felt this way, although certainly the homophobic culture in which she lived (and in which we continue to live today) would have encouraged her to do so.

56. By this reference to "both sides of her heritage" White-Parks means the Chinese custom of *laotongs*, or "sames," a notion of best friends forever, and the American context of what Carroll Smith-Rosenberg has labeled the "female world of love and ritual." For more on *laotongs* see Cathy Silber, "A 1,000-Year-Old-Secret," *MS.* 3 (Sept. 1992): 58–60.

57. One might also read the multiple connotations of the passage's use of "ejaculate" as undermining that recontainment.

58. Of course, these hierarchies are contextual and ever-shifting, inflected by class positioning as well as geographical locale, among other determinants. In the context of the story, to be Mexican might be preferable for the girl, since Mexicans were perceived as more "assimilable" than Chinese.

59. As the anecdote makes clear, both Sui Sin Far's use of "fearless" (for the girl whose racial privilege could not be lost) and her use of "friend" (for the girl who forces the other's disclosure) should be read as ironic.

Works Cited

Almaguer, Tomás. *Racial Fault Lines: The Historical Origins of White Supremacy in California*. Berkeley: University of California Press, 1994.

Ammons, Elizabeth. *Conflicting Stories: American Women Writers at the Turn Into the Twentieth Century*. New York: Oxford University Press, 1991.

———. "Material Culture, Empire, and Jewett's *Country of the Pointed Firs*." In June Howard, ed., *New Essays on The Country of the Pointed Firs*, pp. 81–99. Cambridge: Cambridge University Press, 1994.

Anderson, Benedict. *Imagined Communities: Reflections on the Origin and Spread of Nationalism*. Rev. ed. New York: Verso, 1991.

Andrews, William L. "Miscegenation in the Late Nineteenth-Century Novel." *Southern Humanities Review* 13.1 (Winter 1979): 13–23.

Baker, Houston A., Jr. *Workings of the Spirit: The Poetics of Afro-American Women's Writing*. Chicago: University of Chicago Press, 1991.

"Bayou Folk." *The Critic* 24 (May 5, 1894): 299–300.

Bell, Michael Davitt. "Gender and American Realism in *The Country of the Pointed Firs*." In June Howard, ed., *New Essays on The Country of the Pointed Firs*, pp. 61–80. Cambridge: Cambridge University Press, 1994.

Bennington, Geoffrey. "Postal Politics and the Institution of the Nation." In Homi K. Bhabha, ed., *Nation and Narration*, pp. 121–37. New York: Routledge, 1990.

Berlant, Lauren. "The Theory of Infantile Citizenship." *Popular Culture* 5 (1993): 395–410.

Berthoff, Warner. *The Ferment of Realism: American Literature, 1884–1919*. New York: The Free Press, 1965.

Bhabha, Homi K. "DissemiNation: Time, Narrative, and the Margins of the Modern Nation." In Homi K. Bhabha, ed., *Nation and Narration*, pp. 291–322. New York: Routledge, 1990.

Birnbaum, Michele A. "'Alien Hands': Kate Chopin and the Colonization of Race." In Michael Moon and Cathy Davidson, eds., *Subjects and Citizens: Nation, Race, and Gender from Oroonoko to Anita Hill*, pp. 319–41. Durham: Duke University Press, 1995.

Bishop, Ferman. "Sarah Orne Jewett's Ideas of Race." *New England Quarterly* 30 (1957): 243–49.

Blanchard, Paula. *Sarah Orne Jewett: Her World and Her Work*. New York: Addison-Wesley Publishing, 1994.

Blauner, Robert. *Racial Oppression in America.* New York: Harper and Row, 1972.

"Book Reaches the Heart." *Boston Globe* (June 29, 1912).

Boone, Joseph A. *Tradition Counter Tradition.* Chicago: University of Chicago Press, 1987.

Brasseaux, Carl A. *Acadian to Cajun: Transformation of a People, 1803–1877.* Jackson: University Press of Mississippi, 1992.

Brennan, Timothy. "The National Longing for Form." In Homi K. Bhabha, ed., *Nation and Narration*, pp. 44–70. New York: Routledge, 1990.

Brodhead, Richard H. *Cultures of Letters: Scenes of Reading and Writing in Nineteenth-Century America.* Chicago: University of Chicago Press, 1993.

Brown, Alice. Review of *The Country of the Pointed Firs* [from *Book Buyer* (New York) (15 Oct. 1897) 249–500]. In Gwen L. Nagel, ed., *Critical Essays on Sarah Orne Jewett*, pp. 37–39. Boston: G.K. Hall, 1984.

Brown, Lois Lamphere. "'To Allow No Tragic End': Defensive Postures in Pauline Hopkins's *Contending Forces.*" In John Cullen Gruesser, ed., *The Unruly Voice: Rediscovering Pauline Elizabeth Hopkins*, pp. 50–70. Urbana: University of Illinois Press, 1996.

Carby, Hazel V. Introduction. *The Magazine Novels of Pauline Hopkins.* New York: Oxford University Press, 1988. xxix–l.

———. *Reconstructing Womanhood: The Emergence of the Afro-American Woman Novelist.* New York: Oxford University Press, 1987.

Case, Sue-Ellen. "Toward a Butch-Femme Aesthetic." In Henry Abelove, Michèle Aina Barale, and David M. Halperin, eds., *The Lesbian and Gay Studies Reader*, pp. 294–304. New York: Routledge, 1993.

Castañeda, Antonia. "Gender, Race, and Culture: Spanish-Mexican Women in the Historiography of Frontier California." *Frontiers* XI:1 (1990): 8–20.

Cather, Willa. "Preface." *The Best Stories of Sarah Orne Jewett.* The Mayflower Edition. Gloucester, Mass.: Peter Smith, 1965.

Chan, Sucheng. *This Bittersweet Soil: The Chinese in California Agriculture, 1860–1910.* Berkeley: University of California Press, 1986.

Chauncey, George, Jr. "From Sexual Inversion to Homosexuality: The Changing Medical Conceptualization of Female 'Deviance.'" In Kathy Peiss and Christina Simmons, eds., *Passion and Power: Sexuality in History*, pp. 87–117. Philadelphia: Temple University Press, 1989.

Chopin, Kate. *The Complete Works of Kate Chopin, Vol. I and II.* Ed. Per Seyersted. Baton Rouge: Louisiana State University Press, 1969.

Christian, Barbara. *Black Women Novelists: The Development of a Tradition, 1892–1976.* Westport, Conn.: Greenwood Press, 1980.

Converse, Florence. *Diana Victrix.* Boston: Houghton Mifflin, & Co., 1897.

Country Doctor, A. Reviewed in *Continent* 6 (4 Nov. 1884): 127. In Gwen L. Nagel, ed., *Critical Essays on Sarah Orne Jewett*, pp. 32–33. Boston: G.K. Hall, 1984.

Country of the Pointed Firs, The. Reviewed in *The Bookman* 5:1 (Mar. 1897): 80–81.

Cox, James M. "Regionalism: A Diminished Thing." In Emory Elliott et al., eds., *Columbia Literary History of the United States*, pp. 761–84. New York: Columbia University Press, 1988.

Crawford, Kathleen. "María Amparo Ruiz Burton: The General's Lady." *Journal of San Diego History* 30 (Summer 1984): 198–211.

Cutter, Martha J. "Losing the Battle but Winning the War: Resistance to Patriarchal Discourse in Kate Chopin's Short Fiction." *LEGACY* 11.1 (1994): 17–36.

De Lauretis, Teresa. *The Practice of Love: Lesbian Sexuality and Perverse Desire.* Bloomington: Indiana University Press, 1994.

Dearborn, Mary V. *Pocahontas's Daughters: Gender and Ethnicity in American Culture.* New York: Oxford University Press, 1986.

Domínguez, Virginia R. *White by Definition: Social Classification in Creole Louisiana.* New Brunswick: Rutgers University Press, 1986.

Donovan, Josephine. "A Woman's Vision of Transcendence: A New Interpretation of the Works of Sarah Orne Jewett." *Massachusetts Review* 21 (1980): 365–80.

———. "Nan Prince and the Golden Apples." *Colby Library Quarterly* 22:1 (Mar. 1986): 17–27.

———. *New England Local Color Literature: A Woman's Tradition.* New York: Frederick Ungar Publishing Co., 1983.

———. "The Unpublished Love Poems of Sarah Orne Jewett." *Frontiers* IV.3 (1979): 26–31.

Doyle, James. "Sui Sin Far and Ooto Watanna: Two Early Chinese-Canadian Authors." *Canadian Literature* 140 (Spring 1994): 50–58.

duCille, Ann. *The Coupling Convention: Sex, Text, and Tradition in Black Women's Fiction.* New York: Oxford University Press, 1993.

Duggan, Lisa. "The Trials of Alice Mitchell: Sensationalism, Sexology, and the Lesbian Subject in Turn-of-the-Century America." *SIGNS* 18.4 (1993): 791–814.

"Editorial and Publishers' Announcements." *Colored American Magazine* 1 (Sept. 1900): 60–64.

Elfenbein, Anna Shannon. "Kate Chopin's *The Awakening*: An Assault on American Racial and Sexual Mythology." *Southern Studies: An Interdisciplinary Journal of the South* 26 (4) (Winter 1987): 304–12.

———. *Women on the Color Line: Evolving Stereotypes and the Writings of George Washington Cable, Grace King, and Kate Chopin.* Charlottesville: University Press of Virginia, 1989.

Ellis, Havelock. *Studies in the Psychology of Sex: Sexual Inversion.* Philadelphia: F.A. Davis Co., 1902.

Faderman, Lillian. *Surpassing the Love of Men: Romantic Friendship and Love Between Women From the Renaissance to the Present.* New York: William Morrow, 1981.

Fernández Retamar, Roberto. *Caliban and Other Essays.* Trans. Edward Baker. Minneapolis: University of Minnesota Press, 1989.

Fetterley, Judith. "Commentary: Nineteenth-Century American Women Writers and the Politics of Recovery." *ALH* 6:3 (Fall 1994): 600–611.

———. "Reading *Deephaven* as a Lesbian Text." In Susan J. Wolfe and Julia Penelope, eds., *Sexual Practice, Textual Theory: Lesbian Cultural Criticism.* pp. 164–83. Cambridge: Blackwell, 1993.

Fetterley, Judith, and Marjorie Pryse. Introduction. *American Women Regionalists 1850–1910: A Norton Anthology.* New York: W.W. Norton, 1992.

Fields, Barbara. "Ideology and Race in American History." In J. Morgan Kousser and James M. McPherson, eds., *Region, Race and Reconstruction.* pp. 143–77. New York: Oxford University Press, 1982.

Fox-Genovese, Elizabeth. "Between Individualism and Fragmentation: American Culture and the New Literary Studies of Race and Gender." *American Quarterly* 42.1 (Mar. 1990): 7–34.

Franchot, Jenny. *Roads to Rome: The Antebellum Protestant Encounter with Catholicism.* Berkeley: University of California Press, 1994.

Frankenberg, Ruth. Introduction. *White Women, Race Matters: The Social Construction of Whiteness.* Minneapolis: University of Minnesota Press, 1993. 1–22.

Fryer, Judith. "What Goes on in the Ladies Room? Sarah Orne Jewett, Annie Fields, and Their Community of Women." *Massachusetts Review* 30:4 (Winter 1989): 610–28.

Gaudet, Marcia. "Kate Chopin and the Lore of Cane River's Creoles of Color." *Xavier Review* 6.1 (1986): 45–52.

Gillman, Susan. "Regionalism and Nationalism in Jewett's *Country of the Pointed Firs.*" In June Howard, ed., *New Essays on The Country of the Pointed Firs,* pp. 101–17. Cambridge: Cambridge University Press, 1994.

———. "The Mulatto, Tragic or Triumphant? The Nineteenth-Century American Race Melodrama." In Shirley Samuels, ed., *The Culture of Sentiment: Race, Gender and Sentimentality in Nineteenth-Century America,* pp. 221–243. New York: Oxford University Press, 1992.

Goldman, Anne E. "'Who ever heard of a blue-eyed Mexican?': Satire and Sentimentality in María Amparo Ruiz de Burton's *Who Would Have Thought It?*" In Erlinda Gonzales-Berry and Chuck Tatum, eds., *Recovering the U.S. Hispanic Literary Heritage, Vol. II,* pp. 59–78. Houston: Arte Público Press, 1996.

González, John M. "Romancing Hegemony: Constructing Racialized Citizenship in María Amparo Ruiz de Burton's *The Squatter and the Don.*" In Erlinda Gonzales-Berry and Chuck Tatum, eds., *Recovering the U.S. Hispanic Literary Heritage, Vol. II.* pp. 23–39. Houston: Arte Público Press, 1996.

Greenslade, William. *Degeneration, Culture and the Novel 1880–1940.* Cambridge: Cambridge University Press, 1994.

Gutiérrez, Ramón and Genaro Padilla, eds. Introduction. *Recovering the U.S. Hispanic Literary Heritage*. Houston: Arte Público Press, 1993. 17–25.

Hall, Jacquelyn Dowd. "'The Mind That Burns in Each Body': Women, Rape, and Racial Violence." In Ann Snitow, Christine Stansell, and Sharon Thompson, eds., *Powers of Desire*. pp. 328–49. New York: Monthly Review Press, 1983.

Hall, Stuart. "Cultural Identity and Diaspora." In Jonathan Rutherford, ed., *Identity: Community, Culture, Difference*, pp. 222–37. London: Lawrence & Wihart, 1990.

Hathaway, Jo. "Ah Foy Yam." *Overland Monthly* 34:203 (Nov 1899): 447.

Higham, John. *Strangers in the Land: Patterns of American Nativism 1860–1925*. Westport, Conn.: Greenwood Press, 1981.

Hirata, Lucie Cheng. "Chinese Immigrant Women in Nineteenth-Century California." In Carol R. Berkin and Mary B. Norton, eds., *Women of America: A History*, pp. 223–44. Boston: Houghton Mifflin, 1979.

Hobbs, Glenda. "Pure and Passionate: Female Friendship in Sarah Orne Jewett's 'Martha's Lady.'" *Studies in Short Fiction* 17 (1980): 21–29.

Hopkins, Pauline E. "Club Life Among Colored Women." *Colored American Magazine* 5 (Aug. 1902): 273–77.

———. *Contending Forces: A Romance Illustrative of Negro Life North and South*. New York: Oxford University Press, 1988; repr. of 1900.

Horowitz, Helen Lefkowitz. *Alma Mater: Design and Experience in the Women's Colleges from Their Nineteenth-Century Beginnings to the 1930s*. Boston: Beacon Press, 1984.

Horsman, Reginald. *Race and Manifest Destiny: The Origins of American Racial Anglo-Saxonism*. Cambridge: Harvard University Press, 1981.

Howard, June. "Introduction: Sarah Orne Jewett and the Traffic in Words." In June Howard, ed., *New Essays on The Country of the Pointed Firs*, pp. 1–37. Cambridge: Cambridge University Press, 1994.

———. "Unraveling Regions, Unsettling Periods: Sarah Orne Jewett and American Literary History." *American Literature* 68:2 (June 1996): 365–84.

Howe, Helen. *The Gentle Americans, 1864–1960: Biography of a Breed*. New York: Harper and Row, 1965.

Howells, William Dean. *Criticism and Fiction and Other Essays*. Ed. Clara M. Kirk and Rudolf Kirk. New York: New York University Press, 1959.

———. Review of *Deephaven* [from *Atlantic Monthly* 39 (June 1877), 759]. In Gwen L. Nagel, ed., *Critical Essays on Sarah Orne Jewett*, pp. 25–26. Boston: G.K. Hall, 1984.

James, Henry. "Mr. and Mrs. James T. Fields." *The Atlantic Monthly* 116 (July 1915): 21–31.

———. *The Complete Notebooks of Henry James*. Eds. Leon Edel and Lyall H. Powers. New York: Oxford University Press, 1987.

Jewett, Sarah Orne. *A Country Doctor*. New York: Penguin, 1986; repr. of 1884.

———. *The Country of the Pointed Firs*. Ed. Mary Ellen Chase. New York: W.W. Norton & Co, 1981.

Johns, Barbara A. "'Mateless and Appealing': Growing into Spinsterhood in Sarah Orne Jewett." In Gwen L. Nagel, ed., *Critical Essays on Sarah Orne Jewett*, pp. 147–65. Boston: G.K. Hall, 1984.

Jones, Anne Goodwyn. *Tomorrow Is Another Day: The Woman Writer in the South: 1859–1930*. Baton Rouge: Louisiana State University Press, 1981.

Kaplan, Amy. "Left Alone with America: The Absence of Empire in the Study of American Culture." In Amy Kaplan and Donald E. Pease, eds., *Cultures of United States Imperialism*, pp. 3–21. Durham: Duke University Press, 1993.

———. "Nation, Region, Empire." In Emery Elliott, ed., *Columbia History of the American Novel*, pp. 240–66. New York: Columbia University Press, 1991.

Krafft-Ebing, Richard von. *Psychopathia Sexualis*. Trans. Franklin S. Klaf. New York: Stein and Day, 1978; repr. of 1882.

Ling, Amy. *Between Worlds: Women Writers of Chinese Ancestry*. New York: Pergamon Press, 1990.

———. "Reading Her/stories Against His/stories in Early Chinese American Literature." In Tom Quirk and Gary Scharnhorst, eds., *American Realism and the Canon*, pp. 69–86. Newark: University of Delaware Press, 1994.

———. "Writers with a Cause: Sui Sin Far and Han Suyin." *Women's Studies International Forum* 9.4 (1986): 411–19.

"Literary Notes." *The Independent* 72: 324 (Aug. 15, 1912): 338.

"Living Tales from Acadian Life." *New York Times* (Apr. 1, 1894): 23.

Lott, Eric. *Love And Theft: Blackface Minstrelsy and the American Working Class*. New York: Oxford University Press, 1993.

Lowe, Lisa. *Immigrant Acts: On Asian American Cultural Politics*. Durham: Duke University Press, 1997.

Lyman, Stanford. "Strangers in the City: the Chinese in the Urban Frontier." In Amy Tachiki, Eddie Wong, Franklin Odo, and Buck Wong, eds., *Roots: An Asian American Reader*, pp. 159–87. Los Angeles: University of California Press, 1971.

McCunn, Ruthanne Lum. *Chinese American Portraits*. San Francisco: Chronicle Books, 1988.

McDowell, Deborah E. "'The Changing Same': Generational Connections and Black Women Novelists." *New Literary History* 18 (Winter 1987): 281–302.

McWilliams, Carey. *Southern California Country: An Island on the Land*. New York: Duell, Sloan & Pearce, 1946.

Michaels, Walter Benn. "The Souls of White Folk." In Elaine Scarry, ed., *Literature and the Body: Essays on Populations and Persons*, pp. 185–209. Baltimore: The Johns Hopkins University Press, 1988.

Monroy, Douglas. *Thrown Among Strangers: The Making of Mexican Culture in Frontier California*. Berkeley: University of California Press, 1990.

Morrison, Toni. *Playing in the Dark: Whiteness and the Literary Imagination.* New York: Random House, 1993.

Motomura, Hiroshi. "The Curious Evolution of Immigration Law: Procedural Surrogates for Substantive Constitutional Rights." *Columbia Law Review* 92:7 (Nov. 1992): 1625–1704.

———. "Immigration Law After a Century of Plenary Power: Phantom Constitutional Norms and Statutory Interpretation." *The Yale Law Journal* 100:545 (1990): 545–613.

"Mrs. Chopin's 'Night in Acadie'." *The Critic* 32 (Apr. 16, 1898): 266.

Nee, Victor G., and Brett De Bary Nee. *Longtime Californ': A Documentary Study of an American Chinatown.* New York: Pantheon Books, 1972.

"New Art at the Old Bailey." *The Speaker* 11 (Apr. 1895): 403–4.

"New Note in Fiction, A." *New York Times* (July 7, 1912): 405.

Newton, Esther. "The Mythic Mannish Lesbian: Radclyffe Hall and the New Woman." *SIGNS* 9:4 (1984): 557–75.

Oakes, Karen. "'All that lay deepest in her heart': Reflections on Jewett, Gender, and Genre." *Colby Quarterly* 26:3 (Sept. 1990): 152–60.

Omi, Michael, and Howard Winant. *Racial Formation in the United States.* 2d ed. New York: Routledge, 1994.

Padilla, Genaro M. "Rediscovering Nineteenth-Century Mexican-American Autobiography." In Amritjit Singh, Joseph T. Skerrett, Jr., Robert E. Hogan, eds., *Memory, Narrative and Identity: New Essays in Ethnic American Literatures,* pp. 305–31. Boston: Northeastern University Press, 1994.

Pascoe, Peggy. *Relations of Rescue: The Search for Female Moral Authority in the American West, 1874–1939.* New York: Oxford University Press, 1990.

"Pauline Hopkins." *Colored American Magazine* 2 (Jan. 1901): 218–19.

Peel, Ellen. "Semiotic Subversion in 'Désirée's Baby.'" In Dorothy H. Brown and Barbara C. Ewell, eds., *Louisiana Women Writers: New Essays and a Comprehensive Bibliography,* pp. 57–73. Baton Rouge: Louisiana State University Press, 1992.

Peffer, George Anthony. "Forbidden Families: Emigration Experiences of Chinese Women Under the Page Law, 1875–1882." *Journal of American Ethnic History* 6:1 (Fall 1986): 28–46.

Persons, Stow. "The Americanization of the Immigrant." In David F. Bowers, ed., *Foreign Influences in American Life,* pp. 39–56. Princeton: Princeton University Press, 1944.

Peterson, Carla L. "Unsettled Frontiers: Race, History, and Romance in Pauline Hopkins's *Contending Forces.*" In Alison Booth, ed., *Famous Last Words: Changes in Gender and Narrative Closure,*" pp. 177–96. Charlottesville: University Press of Virginia, 1993.

Pitt, Leonard. *The Decline of the Californios: A Social History of the Spanish Speaking Californians, 1846–1890.* Berkeley: University of California Press, 1966.

Pomeroy, Sarah B. *Goddesses, Whores, Wives and Slaves: Women in Classical Antiquity*. New York: Schocken Books, 1975.

Porter, Carolyn. "What We Know That We Don't Know: Remapping American Literary Studies." *American Literary History* 6:4 (Winter 1994): 467–526.

Pryse, Marjorie. "Archives of Female Friendship and the 'Way' Jewett Wrote." *The New England Quarterly* 66 (1993): 47–66.

————. "Women 'at Sea': Feminist Realism in Sarah Orne Jewett's 'The Foreigner.'" In Gwen L. Hagel, ed., *Critical Essays on Sarah Orne Jewett*, pp. 89–98. Boston: G.K. Hall, 1984.

Renan, Ernest. "What Is a Nation?" Trans. Martin Thom. In Homi K. Bhabha, ed., *Nation and Narration*, pp. 8–22. New York: Routledge, 1990.

Rhodes, Albert. "The Louisiana Creoles." *The Galaxy* 16 (July 1873): 252–60.

Rich, Adrienne. "Compulsory Heterosexuality and Lesbian Existence." In Elizabeth Abel and Emily K. Abel, eds., *The Signs Reader: Women, Gender, and Scholarship*, pp. 139–68. Chicago: University of Chicago Press, 1983.

Robinson, Roxana. Introduction. *A Matter of Prejudice and Other Stories by Kate Chopin*. New York: Bantam Books, 1992. vii–xxi.

Rodríguez, Manuel M. Martín. "Textual and Land Reclamations: The Critical Reception of Early Chicana/o Literature." In Erlinda Gonzales-Berry and Chuck Tatum, eds., *Recovering the U.S. Hispanic Literary Heritage, Vol. II*, pp. 40–58. Houston: Arte Público Press, 1996.

Roman, Judith. "A Closer Look at the Jewett-Fields Relationship." In Gwen L. Nagel, ed., *Critical Essays on Sarah Orne Jewett*, pp. 119–134. Boston: G.K. Hall, 1984.

————. *Annie Adams Fields: The Spirit of Charles Street*. Bloomington: Indiana University Press, 1990.

Ruiz de Burton, María Amparo. Letter to George Davidson (June 9, 1884). George Davidson Correspondence (Bancroft Library, University of California, Berkeley, MSS C-B 490:4).

————. *The Squatter and the Don: A Novel Descriptive of Contemporary Occurrences in California*. Eds. Rosaura Sanchez and Beatrice Pita. Houston: Arte Público Press, 1992; repr. of 1885.

————. *Who Would Have Thought It?* Eds. Rosaura Sánchez and Beatrice Pita. Houston: Arte Público Press, 1995; repr. of 1872.

Sahli, Nancy. "Smashing: Women's Relationships Before the Fall." *Chrysalis* 8 (1979): 17–27.

Saks, Eva. "Representing Miscegenation Law." *Raritan* 8.2 (1988): 39–69.

Saldívar, José David. *Border Matters: Remapping American Cultural Studies*. Berkeley: University of California Press, 1997.

Samuels, Shirley. Introduction. In Shirley Samuels, ed., *The Culture of Sentiment: Race, Gender, and Sentimentality in Nineteenth-Century America*, pp. 3–8. New York: Oxford University Press, 1992.

Sánchez, Rosaura. *Telling Identities: The Californio Testimonios*. Minneapolis: University of Minnesota Press, 1995.

Sánchez, Rosaura, and Beatrice Pita. Introduction. Ruiz de Burton, *The Squatter and the Don*, 5–51.

Scudder, Vida Dutton. *On Journey*. New York: E.P. Dutton, 1937.

Sedgwick, Eve Kosofsky. "Nationalisms and Sexualities: As Opposed to What?" *Tendencies*, pp. 143–53. Durham: Duke University Press, 1993.

Sennett, Richard. "The Rhetoric of Ethnic Identity." In John Bender and David E. Wellbery, eds., *The Ends of Rhetoric: History, Theory, Practice*, pp. 191–231. Stanford: Stanford University Press, 1990.

Sherman, Sarah Way. *Sarah Orne Jewett: An American Persephone*. Hanover: University Press of New England, 1989.

Smith-Rosenberg, Carroll. *Disorderly Conduct: Visions of Gender in Victorian America*. New York: Alfred A. Knopf, 1985.

———. "The Female World of Love and Ritual: Relations Between Women in Nineteenth-Century America." *Disorderly Conduct: Visions of Gender in Victorian America*, pp. 53–76. New York: Alfred A. Knopf, 1985.

Solberg, S. E. "Sui Sin Far/Edith Eaton: First Chinese-American Fictionist." *MELUS* 8 (Spring 1981): 27–39.

Sollors Werner. *Beyond Ethnicity: Consent and Descent in American Culture*. New York: Oxford University Press, 1986.

Somerville, Siobhan. "Passing through the Closet in Pauline E. Hopkins's Contending Forces." *American Literature* 69:1 (Mar. 1997): 138–66.

Sommer, Doris. *Foundational Fictions: The National Romances of Latin America*. Berkeley: University of California Press, 1991.

Spillers, Hortense J. "Who Cuts the Border? Some Readings on 'America.'" In Hortense J. Spillers, ed., *Comparative American Identities: Race Sex, and Nationality in the Modern Text*, pp. 1–25. New York: Routledge, 1991.

———. "Mama's Baby, Papa's Maybe: An American Grammar Book." *diacritics* (Summer 1987): 65–81.

Sui Sin Far. "Letter to the Editor." *The Westerner* (Nov. 1909).

———. "A Chinese Ishmael." *Overland Monthly* 34:199 (July 1899): 43–49.

———. *Mrs. Spring Fragrance and Other Writings*. Eds. Amy Ling and Annette White-Parks. Urbana: University of Illinois Press, 1995.

Sundquist, Eric J. "Realism and Regionalism." In Emory Elliott, ed., *Columbia Literary History of the United States*, pp. 501–24. New York: Columbia University Press, 1988.

———. *To Wake the Nations: Race in the Making of American Literature*. Cambridge: Harvard University Press, 1993.

Takaki, Ronald. *Iron Cages: Race and Culture in 19th-Century America*. New York: Oxford University Press, 1990.

———. *Strangers from a Different Shore: A History of Asian Americans*. New York: Penguin Books, 1989.

Tate, Claudia. "Allegories of Black Female Desire; or Rereading Nineteenth Century Sentimental Narratives of Black Female Authority." In Cheryl Wall, ed., *Changing Our Own Words: Essays on Criticism, Theory, and Writing by Black Women*, pp. 98–126. New Brunswick: Rutgers University Press, 1989.

———. *Domestic Allegories of Political Desire: The Black Heroine's Text at the Turn of the Century*. New York: Oxford University Press, 1992.

———. "Pauline Hopkins: Our Literary Foremother." In Marjorie Pryse and Hortense J. Spillers, eds., *Conjuring: Black Women, Fiction and Literary Tradition*, pp. 53–66. Bloomington: Indiana University Press, 1985.

Taylor, Helen. *Gender, Race and Region in the Writings of Grace King, Ruth McEnery Stuart and Kate Chopin*. Baton Rouge: Louisiana State University Press, 1989.

Tichi, Cecilia. "Women Writers and the New Woman." In Emory Elliot et al., eds., *Columbia Literary History of the United States*. New York: Columbia University Press, 1988.

Tompkins, Jane P. "Sentimental Power: *Uncle Tom's Cabin* and the Politics of Literary History." In Elaine Showalter, ed., *The New Feminist Criticism: Essays on Women, Literature and Theory*, pp. 81–104. New York: Pantheon, 1985.

Toth, Emily. *Kate Chopin: A Life of the Author of 'The Awakening.'* New York: William Morrow & Co, 1990.

Vicinus, Martha. "'They Wonder to Which Sex I Belong': The Historical Roots of the Modern Lesbian Identity." In Henry Abelove, Michèle Aina Barale, and David M. Halperin, eds., *The Lesbian and Gay Studies Reader*, pp. 432–52. New York: Routledge, 1993.

———. "Distance and Desire: English Boarding-School Friendships." *Signs* 9:4 (Summer, 1984): 600–22.

Wald, Priscilla. *Constituting Americans: Cultural Anxiety and Narrative Form*. Durham: Duke University Press, 1995.

———. "Terms of Assimilation: Legislating Subjectivity in the Emerging Nation." In Amy Kaplan and Donald E. Pease, eds., *Cultures of United States Imperialism*. pp. 59–84. Durham: Duke University Press, 1993.

Washington, Mary Helen. *Invented Lives: Narratives of Black Women 1860–1960*. Garden City, N.Y.: Anchor Press, 1987.

Weber, David J., ed. *Foreigners in Their Native Land: Historical Roots of the Mexican Americans*. Albuquerque: University of New Mexico Press, 1973.

White-Parks, Annette. *Sui Sin Far/Edith Maude Eaton: A Literary Biography*. Urbana: University of Illinois Press, 1995.

Willard, William. "Toward an Anthropology of Anthropology: Cultural Heroes, Origin Myths, and Mythological Places of Southwestern Anthropology." In Arnold Krupat, ed., *New Voices in Native American Literary Criticism*, pp. 253–73. Washington: Smithsonian Institution Press, 1993.

Williams, Patricia J. *The Alchemy of Race and Rights*. Cambridge: Harvard University Press, 1991.

Wood, Ann Douglas. "The Literature of Impoverishment: The Women Local Colorists in America, 1865–1914." *Women's Studies* 1 (1972): 3–45.

Xiao-Huang Yin. "Between the East and West: Sui Sin Far—the First Chinese-American Woman Writer." *Arizona Quarterly* 47:4 (Winter 1991): 49–84.

Yarborough, Richard. Introduction. Hopkins, *Contending Forces,* xxvii–xlviii.

Zagarell, Sandra A. "*Country's* Portrayal of Community and the Exclusion of Difference." In June Howard, ed., *New Essays on The Country of the Pointed Firs*, pp. 39–60. Cambridge: Cambridge University Press, 1994.

Index

In this index an "f" after a number indicates a separate reference on the next page, and an "ff" indicates separate references on the next two pages. A continuous discussion over two or more pages is indicated by a span of page numbers, e.g., "57–59." *Passim* is used for a cluster of references in close but not consecutive sequence.

Abelove, Henry, 295n31
Abolition, 140, 144–45, 150, 156
African Americans, 146, 189; Chopin and, 197–19 *passim*, 318n21, 319n23; color and, 142–46, 305n15; Converse and, 75f; erotic desire and, 94f, 100, 105–6, 115, 117–20, 121, 129, 206f, 209–19, 320n28; freedom of, 14, 108, 110, 113; lynching of, 75f, 100, 110, 123, 189; mestizos and, 303n6; *Moynihan Report* and, 301–2n30; Ruiz de Burton and, 137, 143–46, 150, 307n26, 315n70; True Womanhood and, 94, 99–100, 104, 113, 115–16, 117, 124, 129–30, 201, 209, 211, 297n1. *See also* Abolition; *Contending Forces*; Hopkins, Pauline E.; miscegenation; mulattos; national identity, African-American women and; slavery
Aldrich, Thomas Bailey, 16, 281n1b
Almaguer, Tomás, 137, 242, 265
Amazons, 296n35
"America": author's use of term, 281
"American" identity. *See* national identity
American Indians, 197, 231, 310n45, 313n66; land of, 165, 168, 310n42, 311nn46,47. *See also* Californios, American Indians and
American New Women: Boston marriage and, 57, 77–78, 80–92, 286n24; Chopin and, 317–18n17; Converse and, 64f, 71, 77–78, 79–92; Cosslett and, 293n13; Hopkins and, 121
American True Womanhood: African-

American women and, 94, 99–100, 104, 113, 115–16, 117, 124, 129–30, 201, 209, 211, 297n1; Cajun women and, 201, 205–9; Californio women and, 11, 174–80, 182; Chinese women and, 265–66; Chopin and, 187, 190–91, 201, 202–26; class and, 174, 202–5, 208–9, 265, 318n18; color and, 148; Creole women and, 201, 211–12, 216–17, 219–25; ethnicity and, 208–9; maternity and, 99, 129, 130, 148–55, 174–80, 209–26, 265, 307n25; Mexican women and, 140, 148–55; New England as America and, 5, 140, 148–55, 174, 190–91, 202–5; passion and, 95, 100, 104, 116–18, 129–30, 151–55, 202–9, 211f, 265; race and, 174, 208–9, 265, 312n58; region and, 11f, 174, 209; religion and, 150–51, 174f; Ruiz de Burton and, 140, 148–55, 174–80, 182; Southern Ladies and, 189–90, 209f, 316n7. *See also* femininity
Ammons, Elizabeth, 15, 21, 29–30, 31, 36, 56, 239f, 259, 264, 282nn4,7, 325n27, 327n44
Anderson, Benedict, 313n65
Andrews, William L., 100
animality: otherness and, 171, 199, 311–12n52
Artemis, 86–87, 296n35
Asian Americans, 230, 321n7. *See also* Chinese Americans; Chinese Canadians; Eurasians; Far, Sui Sin
At Fault (Chopin), 186, 194, 197
Atlantic Monthly, 16f, 292n12

can Americans and, 75f, 76; author's
orientation to, 5f, 8ff, 13, 59; Baird,
Curtis, 65, 79f, 293n17, 293n18;
Bennett, Sylvia, 59, 64–92 *passim*,
118–19, 296n34; Boston marriage
and, 10, 30, 59, 64–92 *passim*; business and, 67f, 75, 88–89; Campion,
Roma, 65–83 *passim*, 91, 294n20;
Castaigne, Jocelin, 65–92 *passim*,
294n22, 295n30, 296n33; class and,
59, 73, 82; *Contending Forces* and,
118–19; conventional marriage and,
64–65, 78–91 *passim*; Creoles and,
10, 69–80, 92, 294n25; degeneration
theory and, 10, 63, 68, 69–75, 92;
determinism and, 71–72; Dumarais,
Jacques, 64–89 *passim*, 293n17,
294nn22f, 297n40; Dumarais, Jeanne,
78f, 81, 297n39; erotic desire and,
83–92 *passim*; ethnicity and, 69–80,
294n25; evolution and, 10, 63, 90,
294n24; family and, 67, 79, 89f;
friendship and, 64–65, 83–85, 91–92;
hereditary theory and, 69–90; heterosexuality and, 64, 67, 75, 79, 83, 87ff,
90; homosociality and, 30, 87, 90;
inversion and, 10, 58f, 63, 69–70,
73, 80, 85–88, 91–92; Italian immigrants and, 75–77, 295n28; love and
romance and, 64–65, 66f, 83–92 *passim*, 296n34; miscegenation and, 71,
74f, 77; New England and, 9, 58, 63,
65, 66–68, 71, 80–81, 293n18; New
Orleans and, 65–80, 89, 295n29;
New Women and, 64f, 71, 77–78,
79–92; North/South divide and, 10,
59, 65–82 *passim*, 89f, 92, 293n18;
overview of, 10, 58, 59, 63–65, 67,
91–92; "Prelude," 65–66, 73; public
sphere and, 68–69, 88–89, 91; Puritanism and, 71f, 81; race and, 59, 63,
69, 71, 74–78, 82, 92; regional and
national identity and, 10, 55, 59, 63,
65, 67–92, 295n29; sameness/differ-
ence and, 65, 71, 74f, 89, 92, 329n52;
sexuality and, 10, 59–60, 63, 71, 83–
85, 87–88, 91–92; social activism
and, 81f, 89f, 297n40; Spencer, Enid,
59–92 *passim*, 118–19, 246, 296n34,
297n40; transnational ties and, 65–

66, 67, 69, 71, 74–77, 89, 293n14;
"Two Old Maids," 84, 86; white
supremacists and, 75–77. *See also*
Converse, Florence
Dix, Gertrude, 291n7
Dixon, Thomas, 100, 299n11
domestic fiction. *See* sentimental fiction
domestic issues: imperialism and, 2–3,
8–9, 158
Domínguez, Virginia, 70, 196, 247,
317n12
Donovan, Josephine, 17–18, 20, 25–26,
31, 284n20, 285n22, 292n12
Doyle, James, 242
Du Bois, W.E.B., 121, 123
duCille, Ann, 98, 101, 120
Duggan, Lisa, 58
Dunbar-Nelson, Alice, 281n3,
317n13

East/West divide: Far and, 235, 245,
249, 253, 276; Ruiz de Burton and,
11, 136, 139–40, 160
Eaton, Edith. *See* Far, Sui Sin
education: New Women and, 81–82
Elfenbein, Anna Shannon, 213, 216,
218, 319n23
Ellis, Havelock, 60f, 85f
emotional repression, 140, 151–55,
307–8n27. *See also* New England
environment: heredity vs., 247
erotic desire, 208, 210f, 262f; African-
American women and, 94f, 100,
105–6, 115, 117–20, 121, 129, 206f,
209–19, 320n28; Boston marriage
and, 31–40, 45, 61–62, 83–85, 87;
Cajun women and, 205–9; Chinese
women and, 252–66 *passim*, 276;
Chopin and, 185, 201, 202–9, 210,
222–23, 317n17; class and, 222–23;
Converse and, 83–92 *passim*; Creole
women and, 208, 210, 222–23; Far
and, 252, 255–66 *passim*, 276;
heterosexual, 88, 210, 222–23,
296n38; Hopkins and, 94f, 100,
102, 105–6, 111–21 *passim*, 129;
Jewett and, 31–40, 45; maternity
and, 215, 217, 219–26, 257, 263–64,
265–66; Ruiz de Burton and, 151–55;
True Womanhood and, 151–55,

Library of Congress Cataloging-in-Publication Data

McCullough, Kate
  Regions of identity : the construction of America in women's
fiction, 1885–1914 / Kate McCullough.
     p. cm.
  Includes bibliographical references and index.
  ISBN 0-8047-3307-4 (cloth : alk. paper)
    1. American fiction—Women authors—History and criticism.
  2. American fiction—19th century—History and criticism.
  3. American fiction—20th century—History and criticism.
  4. National characteristics, American, in literature.   5. Women
and literature—United States—History.   6. Group identity
in literature.   7. Regionalism in literature.   8. Local color
in literature.   9. Race in literature.   I. Title.
  PS374.W6M29   1999
  813'.4099287—dc21   98-36884

Original printing 1999
Last figure below indicates year of this printing:
08   07   06   05   04   03   02   01   00   99